A
Ⱬistory
OF
TREASON

Chris Day is Head of Modern Domestic Records at The National Archives, where he has worked since 2013. An expert in the records of the Home Office, Chris is interested in popular politics, protest and resistance, and local government in Britain and the Caribbean in the eighteenth and nineteenth centuries.

Dr Daniel Gosling is Principal Legal Records Specialist at The National Archives, expert in the records created by the central law courts and the litigants bringing cases into these courts. His PhD (University of Leeds, 2016) examined statute interpretation in the late medieval and early modern periods.

Dr Neil Johnston is Head of Early Modern Records at The National Archives, specialising in the political, financial, and constitutional histories of Britain and Ireland in the seventeenth century. Awarded a PhD by University College Dublin in 2012, he is a co-investigator on the Virtual Record Treasury of Ireland project.

Dr Euan Roger is Principal Medieval Specialist at The National Archives, specialising in the records of medieval and Tudor government and the central law courts, with a particular interest in administrative, social, medical, and material history. His work has featured in *TIME* Magazine, the *Guardian*, and *The Times*, among other publications.

THE BLOODY HISTORY OF BRITAIN THROUGH THE
STORIES OF ITS MOST NOTORIOUS TRAITORS

A History

OF

TREASON

CHRIS DAY, DANIEL GOSLING, NEIL JOHNSTON
AND EUAN ROGER

jb

Published in the UK by John Blake Publishing,
An imprint of The Zaffre Publishing Group
A Bonnier Books UK company
4th Floor, Victoria House
Bloomsbury Square
London, WC1B 4DA

Owned by Bonnier Books
Sveavägen 56, Stockholm, Sweden

www.facebook.com/johnblakebooks
twitter.com/jblakebooks

Hardback: 978-1-78946-630-0
Paperback: 978-1-78946-629-4
Ebook: 978-1-78946-628-7
Audio: 978-1-78946-627-0

Design by www.envydesign.co.uk

Printed and bound in Great Britain by Clays Ltd, Elcograf S.p.A

1 3 5 7 9 10 8 6 4 2

Text copyright © The National Archives 2022

John Blake Publishing is an imprint of Bonnier Books UK
www.bonnierbooks.co.uk

To Dáithí, Síofra, Tom, Will, and Lisa for making it worth it; and to Alice, Emily, Sophie, and Úna-Frances for making it possible

CONTENTS

A NOTE ON THE DATING OF
THE TREASON ACT

The Treason Act is often described by legal commentators as the 1351 Treason Act as a consequence of the medieval method of reckoning the beginning of the year as 25 March. The act was passed in the twenty-fifth regnal year of Edward III, which ran from 25 January 1351 to 24 January 1352. The Treason Act was passed in the parliament that met at the end of this period and can therefore be dated historically as January 1352. To the medieval mind, however, it would have been considered to be the final months of the year 1351.

Lawyers and legally focused works use the old-style date of 1351, which is why the Treason Act appears as such on legislation.gov and in other legal works. Historians, however, normally use the new-style dating, silently 'correcting' dates to match modern understanding, and to ensure historical accuracy. Most modern historians therefore use 1352 as the historically accurate date of the Treason Act.

Dates have been silently modernised throughout this book.

FOREWORD

by Diarmaid MacCulloch

The words 'traitor' and 'treason' are emotive words, familiar to us. They came into English from Latin *traditor* via Norman French. This is what one might expect from legal concepts that are the special prerogative of the medieval monarchy created by the Norman conquerors of England; that was a normal linguistic route for many words that shape our understanding of English politics. It all looks quite straightforward, until you spot that the Classical Latin word *traditor* was not the word that an ancient Roman would have used for the sort of person who betrayed the Emperor or the Roman *Res Publica*; he or she was a *proditor*. A *traditor* is in origin simply someone who hands over something, and actually the allied noun *traditio* leads the inquisitive not towards 'treason' but 'tradition', which doesn't sound at all the same sort of animal.

How have we got to where we are, then, when we speak of traitors and treasons? The explanation is quite specific, pulling us back to a particular historic era. The Roman Empire suffered a general crisis of religion in the third century CE, when successive emperors sought to stem the growth of an alarming new faith in various parts of their Mediterranean dominions: Christianity. They came to fear Christian worship of a God who brooked no rivals, and who marshalled his claims in sacred texts which Christians called their Bible. Trajan Decius, an energetic senator and provincial governor who seized power as Emperor in 249, attributed the Empire's obvious troubles on the morrow of its thousandth year squarely to the anger of the old gods that their sacrifices were being neglected. Decius therefore enforced these traditional sacrifices on every head of a household in the name of all its members – a radical intensification of the custom that communities were ordered to offer sacrifices on an imperial accession. It was obvious that the group most systematically avoiding sacrifices in the Empire were the Christians, who now faced a crisis of morale amid unprecedented official pressure. Not only Decius but a successor, Valerian, and later in the century Diocletian pushed punishment for refusal as far as imprisonment or execution.

Some Christians did indeed die as martyrs for refusing to sacrifice; some who did not end up executed were nevertheless courageous enough to affirm their refusal in court. Hence in later Christian celebration of their heroism, they are known by the technical Roman legal term for those pleading guilty: 'confessors'. Nevertheless, the reality behind Christian martyr stories is that the overwhelming majority of Christians gave way. One compromise that would save them a martyr's death or a confessor's suffering was to surrender to the Roman authorities the holy scriptures and liturgical texts that governed their own Christian sacrifices in worship. These 'handers-over' were the original *traditores*: they were traitors, one notices, not to the government, but to their own Christian faith and Church. Of course, now the wheel has gone full circle in popular usage: we often speak of acts of personal 'treachery', or of traitors to a cause in our private lives, rather than their definition in English law.

It is a remarkable linguistic turn, then, to see the eight-century-long history of treason told in this book: the betrayal of an official regime, and not the violation of a set of private convictions. It testifies to that astonishing reversal of fortunes by which Christianity moved from its persecuted outsider status in the third-century Roman Empire to becoming the embodiment of a social system and monarchy claiming the sanction of the Christian God. Such was the case in Anglo-Saxon England, where in fact the institutions of the Christian Church re-imported from Rome by St Augustine in 597 predated the creation of a single unified kingdom that occupied roughly the geographical boundaries of modern England. The Church in England already modelled unity under Roman obedience before Anglo-Saxon kingdoms united. There were 'English' Christians before there was an English king.

By the tenth century, out of the diversity of various Christianised Anglo-Saxon kingdoms, there emerged one of the most coherent political units in Europe: a single monarchy of England. Its precociously centralised government eventually fell like a ripe plum into the grateful hands of Norman carpetbaggers in 1066. Small wonder that this Anglo-Norman monarchy created after 1066 a distinctively insular legal concept of treason, so basic to English law that the treason enactment of 1352 still remains at the centre of our criminal code. The authors point out that the Treason Act was put in place in Parliament as much to limit as to empower the Crown. They trace the ways in which monarchs sought to 'modernise' (for which read, expand to their own advantage) the concept of treason, notably in the Tudor age – they also note the successful pushback against several of those attempts by politicians worried about the implications for themselves and their successors.

The sixteenth-century Reformation marked a watershed in the history of treason, when the remarkable religious unity that had characterised Western Europe since the sixth century fractured into the Protestant Reformation. Sincere religious convictions that had been basic to a complex but enduring relationship between monarch and Pope suddenly became 'treasonous' when the English monarchy repudiated the Papacy in favour of Protestantism and an independent national Church. It is at this stage that 'treason' began broadening into an offence against an abstract political entity newly called 'the state', rather than betrayal of a person, the monarch. The effort of Guy Fawkes and his fellow-conspirators in 1605 to blow up the assembled Houses of Parliament together with the King and members of his family is the first clear instance of this new movement.

Treason became still further complicated when the three kingdoms of the Atlantic archipelago mutated into a 'United Kingdom' at the centre of a 'British Empire'. That phrase was first unselfconsciously used by Scots and English Protestant subjects of the Crown in seventeenth-century Ireland, where the effort to create a unified and unchallengeable Protestant and English-speaking society with a 'British' identity has had consequences long outlasting its failure. As much as the Reformation, the expansion of the British Empire worldwide created new treasons. The last execution for treason was within living memory. Where better but the incomparable collection of official records in the National Archives to seek understanding of treason, treachery and traitors? We are much in the debt of the authors who have so meticulously traced the complex story from the thirteenth century to the present day.

DIARMAID MacCULLOCH
Emeritus Professor of the History of the Church
University of Oxford

INTRODUCTION

Treason has a history that is all of its own.
FREDERIC MAITLAND *(1895)*

Treason. To become a traitor is to turn your back on those who trusted you. To betray, and to violate your allegiance to a person, institution, or group. Treason can have many forms, but it is always emotional. In English law, it is the highest crime for which an individual can be convicted, and one of the oldest pieces of legislation in force today.

It is also a complicated and multifaceted crime, a crime 'with a vague circumference and more than one centre' as Frederic Maitland, the modern father of English legal history, wrote in the nineteenth century. Treason is a feeling, a state of mind, but in England (and now Britain) it is also a specific crime, the ultimate crime against the Crown and the state. Defined for the first time in 1352, and still on the statute book today, treason marks the boundary between the state and its subjects, between the law and politics, drawing a line between what is acceptable and what is not. To kill, or attempt to kill the monarch, to violate the monarch's immediate family, or to wage war against the Crown or the state in England: these definitions of treason remain in law today but were set down in statute almost 700 years ago. The relationship between the Crown, the state, and its subjects may have radically altered from the days of Magna Carta, of Henry VIII and of Charles I, yet concepts of allegiance and betrayal are timeless. Why?

At its most basic, treason is a violation by a subject of their allegiance to the sovereign or the state, and in many ways the story of treason is also a story of power, and of the relationship between the state and its subjects. It is implicated in some of the biggest stories in the country's history, as well as lesser-known individuals and stories. Different generations would interpret, tweak and alter the definitions of treason in line with the concerns of their age, adding new legislation where required, but the core of the 1352 Act remains in force, relatively unchanged, today. Writing in the seventeenth century, Sir Edward Coke identified that the 1352 Act was the talisman of English treason law, the 'blessed act of 25 Edw III' that lawmakers returned to in times of state insecurity.

Treason is, by its nature, limited to those crimes considered to be of the utmost gravity, to the Crown and to Parliament, and has always been linked with the harshest punishments of the day. It is, and (since its definition in 1352) always has been, restricted, a show of force and a warning to others. If everything is treason, then nothing is. Sir William Blackstone identified the need for treason, the highest civil crime, to be precisely ascertained, 'for if the crime of high treason be indeterminate, this alone … is sufficient to make any government degenerate into arbitrary power'.

It is a crime defined initially by the Crown, and later by the state, which imposes concepts of allegiance, of control, of restriction. But while treason is defined, it places a limit on those that rule, and holds them accountable when rulers verge towards tyranny. At the Chartist John Frost's trial in 1839, the Attorney General argued that Edward III had codified the previously 'vague and unknown' law of treason to 'rescue the country from … miserable servitude'. In the pre-modern period, those who expanded the definitions of treason beyond reasonable boundaries were marked as tyrants, and their expansions were repealed at the earliest opportunity. Despite its terrible portent, the codified law of treason was seen as a bulwark against its tyrannical misuse.

All trials are theatrical, but perhaps none more so than that for treason.

JOHN FROST.

£100.

REWARD

The above Reward will be paid to any Person or Persons who shall APPREHEND and bring to Justice JOHN FROST, late of Newport, Draper, who stands charged with the Crime of HIGH TREASON.

BY ORDER OF

The Magistrates.

Borough of Newport, Nov. 4th, 1839.

JOHN O'DWYER, Printer, "Merlin" Office, Newport.

Poster offering a reward for the apprehension of John Frost, Chartist and leader of the Newport Rising, 1839. (TS 11/500)

It is more sensational, and the punishment more terrible, than any other. Judges and advocates deliver long soliloquys on the nature and history of the offence; the defendant waits, the protagonist, sometimes unable to reply or argue their case, to see if their fate would be death or redemption.

Frost's barrister called a charge of treason a 'stain ... of the blackest and the deepest dye', reflecting and refining the medieval concept that treason literally corrupted an individual's blood line, as the Crown pursued these convictions not just to deter others, but also to demean their ideas, their very conception of how Britain should be organised. The principal actors in these spectacles were usually of high office.

Stage management was key to trying to assure the correct outcome – acquittals were not just embarrassing but dangerous. But as the rule of law developed, and treason trials became more consistent with those for other crimes, the players on the stage frequently diverted from the script.

This book takes as its starting point the development and definition of treason, as established in 1352 and examines how treason has been adapted, framed and altered ever since, adapting to the shifting needs and concerns of each age. It examines what has, and has not, changed, the threads of history which have woven a complex tapestry of law, political thought, and ideas of 'statehood' through the history of England and its imperial possessions. It considers the connections between treason, nationalism and colonialism – from William Wallace to the American Revolution – as concepts of treason were defined, reflected and imposed upon conquered nations, and in times of war. It questions why, and how, as subjects we interact with the state, and provides lessons for the future from the warnings of the past.

In its 1977 review the Law Commission noted that law of treason 'is closely interwoven with the history of the United Kingdom'. By whom or what is considered treasonous we come to know what threatens the state. From 1352 until at least the mid-nineteenth century, every significant anti-government political movement was at least labelled and suspected of being treasonous, if it did not find itself in the dock. The history of treason is the history of who the state considered its enemy, and it was responsive, amending and expanding its definitions to meet new threats. Henry VIII, a prolific codifier of new treasons, added statutes to retrospectively meet the threat of poisoning, while in 1795 treason was re-codified to better prosecute those espousing the ideas of the French Revolution. It was reactive, retrospective, and emotional.

Treason trials were events of state importance and the documents and files that emerged from these trials were treated likewise. From the reign of Henry II, the legal business of the Curia Regis, or the King's Court, was split into cases heard nominally before the King at Westminster in what became known as King's Bench, and by justices on their itineraries across their shires. The Court of King's Bench was the highest court of common law and heard matters that directly affected the monarch, or those that impinged on the maintenance of the 'King's Peace'. Indictments were used to commence a trial by presenting a felony or offence to the court, and these make up the core of the King's Bench records. From the fifteenth century, the court's officials started to separate the records of treason and other state trials of particular concern to the Crown into a discrete closet for safekeeping. Known as the *Baga de Secretis* (The National Archives series reference KB 8), these records chart some of the key events in the history of England and are used heavily in this book. The closet had three keys, one held by the Lord Chief Justice, another by the Attorney General, and the third by the Master of the Crown Office.

Alongside the records within the *Baga de Secretis*, we use others that had not been specially separated, but these form a voluminous collection that run from the medieval period right up to the creation of the modern King's Bench Division of the High Court of Justice by the 1873 Supreme Court of Judicature Act. In taking such a wide approach in time as well as in topic, we came to realise that the Crown attached huge importance to precedent and took care to store the records. While not always maintained to a suitable standard, there now exists a remarkable collection to draw from.

Court documents are often procedural and formulaic, recording charges, witnesses called and other events of a case. They also briefly note outcomes of trials. They are, in effect, official documents that contain fact, but often little colour or detail. To supplement this, we used political correspondence and commentary, newspapers and public discussion, as well as unofficial (and often illegal) pamphlets. All of these types of sources need to be treated with caution and scepticism, but when used judiciously they allow us to reconstruct the motivations of the Crown and its legal apparatus as well as those who were charged and convicted of treason. To read popular accounts of treasons from different sides of the political spectrum is often to read two different stories. After the 1817 Pentrich Rising, which involved a government provocateur, supporters of parliamentary reform were at pains to mark the agent as the author of the treason, while the government and their supporters painted him as merely an informer. The truth, said the historian E. P. Thompson, 'is probably more complex' than either account. Treason is emotive, to successfully label someone as a traitor in the public consciousness is almost as valuable as a conviction in court. It is also dependent on the outcome. Those who succeed in treason can rewrite history – for which reason accounts of treason are deeply partisan. As historians, we have the benefit of seeing behind the curtain – the papers of the Crown as they detected or inflated treasons, and as they prepared the prosecution – but these are supplemented by popular accounts, which show us the emotional and political impact of treasons.

The functions of the Court of King's Bench evolved over the centuries, and it did not operate like modern courts. A Grand Jury was empanelled, but it was the role of the court officials, including the Lord Chief Justice, often working in tandem with the Crown's legal officials, the Attorneys and Solicitors General, to persuade the jury of the guilt of the prisoner. These officials wielded enormous power to dispense royal justice.

Treason stood above all other criminal law. All criminal prosecutions have the short title *Rex* (or *Regina*) v the defendant, but this was usually a half-truth – defendants were prosecuted by the court and their peers. But with treason, and perhaps treason alone, it was true: the state, the Crown, was arrayed in all its power, majesty and ceremony against those who stood accused. As will be seen, this was not always fair or just, but it remains part of the history of England and its possessions over the centuries.

Part I

DEFINING
TREASON

•

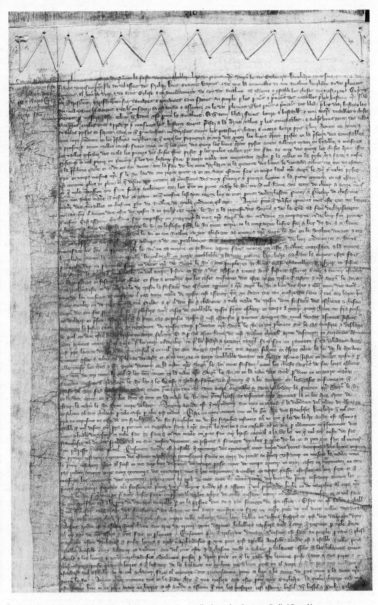

The Treason Act 1352 (25 Edward III, stat 5 c 2), enrolled on the Statute Roll. (C 74/1)

One

EARLY TREASONS AND THE
TREASON ACT, 1352

The 'Great Statute of Treasons' of 1352 was the first time that treason was defined in statute. The concept of treason, however, has long been part of the English legal system in one form or another. In England the earliest notions of treason were taken from the Germanic legal traditions, founded on ideas of betrayal and breaches of trust, and were later influenced by aspects of Roman law and European practice, particularly the concept of lèse-majesté – insults to those with public authority or those in power. Notions of betrayal (of both army and realm) are found throughout the earliest law codes. Breaking the bonds of fealty, which ordered society, was considered by the code of Alfred the Great to be the worst crime an individual could commit, the sense of betrayal harking back to no less a figure than Judas in his betrayal of Christ. Flight from battle features as a capital crime in the laws of both Cnut and, later, Henry I, with the deserter's lands forfeited to their lord or to the king. Over time, the concept of 'high treason' – that is acts against the king in particular, often threats against his life – began to become more prominent. It is in the laws of Alfred the Great that we find the first recognisable reference to a form of 'high' treason we might recognise today, where it was stated that plotting the death of the King was different from plotting the death of a lord. Such views were not entrenched, however – the law codes of Athelstan and Edgar made little distinction between the King and his lords, although those of Ethelred and Cnut were explicit in the processes to be followed in cases of 'high' treason against the King.

Throughout the twelfth century the notion of differentiating between the king and his lords developed slowly, but by the start of the thirteenth century the sovereign status of English kings within England was established (if carefully and regularly disputed). At the same time, ideas of what constituted treason slowly expanded too, even if they remained undefined and variable. Obvious breaches of allegiance, such as the violation by a vassal of their lord's daughter, or the forgery of the king's seal, came to be seen as treasonous, but others were slower to develop. Rebellion, or 'levying war' as it would be referred to in 1352, in particular was slow to become treasonous. To a modern mind, for barons to rise against their king, such as those who forced Magna Carta on King John in 1215, would seem an obvious example of treasonous behaviour. Prior to the mid-thirteenth century, however, it was acknowledged by both the king and his lords that the oaths of fealty and homage which bound English society together went both ways. The lords owed the king their loyalty, but in return the king owed them justice. A lord who was consistently refused justice by the king could therefore retract his fealty in an act of formal defiance, and indeed was honour-bound to do so. God would decide the just in pitched battle, and while those on the losing side would be punished, the consequences were often measured and limited. This was particularly important in an Anglo-French context, as the early English kings after the Conquest were not only kings of England but also lords in France, and as such owed the French kings homage. For an English king to deny his nobles the opportunity to resolve their concerns on the battlefield would have meant abandoning his own licence to wage war in France as King of England, without abandoning his own fealty as a French lord at the same time.

TREASON UNDER EDWARD I

Edward I (1239–1307) was the first English monarch to add levying war against the king in his realm to the concepts of treason, even though they remained undefined. This was companion to the idea that adhering to the king's enemies (the Scots in particular) was also treasonous – a notion that would develop at the same time – and clearly demonstrates Edward's obsession with the border warfare on his northern and Welsh boundaries. It is perhaps in this context that both rebellion and levying war came to be associated with treason. By the time of the 1352 statute, the Anglo-French connection had become less important, with Edward III the first post-Conquest king to renounce his homage to the French king. Indeed, not only did Edward renounce his homage, he went much further, asserting a claim to the French throne (through his mother Isabella, daughter of the King of France), which a series of successful military campaigns against France had encouraged him to believe achievable. In doing so, he would formally exemplify and demonstrate the sovereignty that had developed over the previous two reigns, and that had allowed the Crown to recognise rebellions as treasonous from the end of the thirteenth century.

Over the course of his reign, Edward I would execute over twenty of his enemies for treason, often involving himself in proceedings at a deep personal level, and in processes of dubious legality. Those tried and executed were largely reflective of the King's border concerns in Wales and Scotland. The first to feel his personal wrath, in what amounts to the first state trial for treason under an English king, was the Prince of Wales, Dafydd ap Gruffydd, in 1283. While the borders and independence of the Welsh lordships had ebbed and flowed ever since the Norman Conquest, Edward's reign had seen reinvigorated attempts to conquer Wales, and a concerted effort in 1277–83 in particular, which would end in the complete annexation of the Welsh principalities. Dafydd had succeeded his brother Gruffudd ap Llywelyn as Prince of Wales in December 1282, following Llywelyn's death to the English forces, but would himself be captured by the invading English forces the following June. Edward had a problem, however, in deciding what to do with the captured Welshman. Dafydd had royal blood, and by custom had to be tried by men of noble rank, who might not provide the result and sentence that a clearly furious Edward wanted. At the same time, it was customary in medieval legal thought at this time that an individual should not act as both accuser and judge at the same time. As high treason was a crime against the King himself, Edward could not act as both accuser and sentence-giver without subverting the legal norms of the day. So he responded with what appears to have been a set of clever, if legally dubious, schemes to force through his preferred judgement and sentence, schemes which he would repeat throughout his reign, and which would later attract criticism. Edward summoned a parliament to meet at Shrewsbury the following Michaelmas, to decide what should be done with the rebel, and asked the assembled nobles whether Dafydd's alleged crimes (details of which were most likely provided by the Crown) amounted to treason. When they answered in the affirmative, Edward's royal justices provided the sentence. In doing so, he was able to avoid being seen as providing the accusation himself, making it appear that the accusation had come from his lords, while in reality the crimes had been placed in front of them by the Crown. They simply declared that together the crimes amounted to treason. This was the first step in what would become known as the 'King's Record', a process of conviction in which the Crown's statement that an individual was guilty acted as proof in and of itself, without the need for a trial, a jury, or even any evidence.

The severity of the punishment passed by Edward I and his justices was extreme – probably reflecting the King's own personal anger and animosity – and was novel enough to attract comment from contemporary chroniclers, while also specifically linking elements of the punishment to individual acts. For betraying the King, Dayfdd was to be drawn at a horse's tail (the hallmark punishment for treasonable acts), and for killing certain English noblemen, he was to be hanged alive. For other murders committed during Easter, he was to be disembowelled (while still alive) and his entrails burned, and for plotting the King's death in different parts of the realm, he was to be quartered and his limbs despatched around the realm to act as deterrents. The brutal punishment of Dayfdd ap Gruffydd, fully carried out on 3 October 1283, was intended as a warning to all those who might consider rebellion against the King. It was also in marked contrast to the ways previous rebels – such as the followers of Simon de Montfort in the aftermath of the Second Barons' War – had been punished, but with Edward having gained complete control over the Welsh region, there was little resolve left among the Welsh to stand against the processes and the punishment instigated by the Crown. A new precedent and policy were now in effect.

Edward may have annexed the Welsh lordships to England, and quelled the initial rebellion, but discontent would continue throughout his reign, both in Wales and further north on the Scottish border, with treason charges a potent weapon in the royal arsenal. In these charges we can see a slow but fundamental change in royal procedure, building upon the procedures and processes used against Dayfdd ap Gruffydd. In 1292 Rhys ap Maredudd was described in the commission of gaol delivery in which he was brought to trial as 'manifest rebel', with the Crown now seeking to pass judgement on rebels summarily on the basis of notoriety or 'ill fame', without the need to stage manage proceedings as it had done with Dayfdd. A few years later, in the Scottish revolt of 1295–6, the allegations against John Balliol and his supporters, as recounted in a royal letter of 1301 to the Pope, included a mix of traditional charges such as 'going against their homage and fealty'. The rebels' deeds, however – which included the newer crime of levying war – were also reported as being of 'common report', or 'notorious'. Edward was once again pursuing an approach of dubious legality, given that Balliol had in fact formally renounced his homage at Berwick in April 1296, and presumably felt himself justified in his cause against his feudal overlord, nationalistic sentiments aside. An awareness of Balliol's cause, if left unstated in the letter of 1301, may have been behind Edward's logic in not pursuing formal treason trials against this group after his conquest of Scotland. As J. G. Bellamy, one of the foremost experts on the early history of treason, has noted, while Edward I was willing to use unsavoury methods in the process of such trials, he also seems to have been careful only to pursue allegations of treason where the Crown and royal lawyers felt there was a reasonable chance of success. Where Edward felt such charges could be taken forward, however, the Crown now had a powerful tool at its disposal – the King's Record – that allowed him to prosecute treason charges vigorously and without the opportunity for defence, as would become clear to the Scots within a few years.

With the Crown now emboldened by this strategy, the Scottish wars of independence that followed the initial revolt of 1295–6 saw treason charges and the King's Record now put to regular use in Scotland. In sharp contrast to the treatment meted out to the die-hard rebels, those who submitted to the Crown were shown considerable generosity in a shrewd move by the King.

The first – and perhaps best known – of those caught in the Crown's campaign was William Wallace, a leading rebel figure who was captured by the English forces near Glasgow in August 1305. The previous years in Scotland had seen some English advances, and the submission of several leading Scottish lords, including John Comyn, who all received generous terms for their surrender. Wallace, however, remained a thorn in Edward's side, writing to the English King through an agent in 1304, offering to submit to Edward's 'honest peace' but only on the basis that he, Wallace, should not submit his liberty while simultaneously requesting a financial inducement to do so. Furious, Edward refused and immediately offered 300 marks to anyone who killed the Scottish rebel, later ensuring Wallace was specifically omitted from terms of future settlements and declaring him an outlaw. Any Scottish lord who aided in Wallace's capture would have their own punishment mitigated in consequence of their aid.

Wallace was eventually captured on 3 August 1305, and would be the first Scot to be tried for treason. Once again, it is likely that Edward's personal animosity affected the trial proceedings and process, to ensure that the rebel's sentence and punishment would send a warning to the north. After his capture, Wallace was first sent to the King, who refused to see him and instead ordered that he be sent to Westminster Hall for judgement. On 23 August the rebel was led on horseback into Westminster, where he was accused of betraying his king. From the outside, the process resembled a normal gaol delivery, but a few vital differences point to Edward once again using the King's Record to ensure the outcome was as he wanted. There was no indictment by a jury, no appeal or indeed any accusations from the royal prosecutors for Wallace to answer, simply a statement of his crimes, with the King's own record serving as the only proof required, and the royal justices then proceeding to sentencing.

Modern perceptions of Wallace may be warped through the lens of the 1995 movie *Braveheart*, in which the rebel Scot summons an act of defiance against Edward in his final moments. While this depiction remains firmly within the realms of fiction, the accounts of the real-life Wallace's trial, however, do record his response to the charges against him. No formal response from Wallace was permitted in proceedings, and yet the chronicle accounts record that he replied. While he was guilty of many of the crimes brought against him, Wallace stated, he had never been a traitor to the King of England. No further elaboration was recorded, but Wallace presumably meant that he had not (or at least felt he had not) sworn allegiance to the English king, or done homage to him. In this he may have felt justified by the formal renunciation of fealty by Balliol – Wallace's king – in 1296, even if Balliol had later returned to the said fealty. For Wallace, if he owed no allegiance or fealty to the English king, he could not commit treason against him, regardless of any crimes he had committed. But to Edward, the community of Scotland – including Balliol – had done homage, and by extension so had Wallace, even if not personally.

The trials of both Wallace and Dayfdd ap Gruyffdd raise interesting questions about the application of treason in conquered nations, but the use of the King's Record denied them (for the most part) an opportunity for nationalistic arguments. In Wallace's case, the Crown stated that Scotland had been conquered because Balliol had forfeited it through his rebellion, and the King had established peace, installed his ministers and taken homage and fealty from the community leaders. Wallace was accused of being 'unmindful' of his fealty, but not that he had broken it (as Dayfdd had been) or had formally withdrawn from it. His alleged crimes included various felonies and sedition, but crucially he was charged with compassing (contriving) Edward's death, and bearing banners against him in mortal war. These were clear and obvious charges of high treason, and were limited to acts around which there could be little argument. There could be no doubt that Wallace had been present at battles including those of Stirling Bridge and Falkirk in the 1290s, and if he owed fealty to Edward – as the King's Record stated – then he was a traitor. Questions of fealty aside, the bearing of banners in open warfare was becoming a key aspect of 'levying war' at this time, as a clear demonstration of an individual's opposition to the Crown, and one which multiple witnesses could attest to. Interestingly, the judicial proceedings against Wallace do not state a charge that was later recorded in the accounts of the royal Exchequer, among the payments made for his execution. In this short and concise entry, 'William le Waleys' is described as a rebel, a public traitor and an outlaw, but it also claims that throughout Scotland he 'falsely sought to call himself King of Scotland' – the only contemporary source recording that he actually wanted to be king himself. Perhaps this was a claim too far for Edward to consider among the official proceedings, but it may also reflect contemporary views of Wallace at Westminster.

Having stated his alleged crimes, the justices now moved to sentencing and execution for treason. Wallace was drawn from Westminster to the Tower of London, then to Aldgate and to the Elms at Smithfield, a common place of execution. Being drawn to the place of execution was the traditional sign of a traitor's death, and the rest of his execution was designed to be impressive and ruthless as a warning to others, with individual crimes once again linked to specific punishments. For the robberies, homicides and felonies he had been charged with, he was hanged and disembowelled. Because he had lived and died an outlaw, he was beheaded. For his injuries to the Church and holy matters, his entrails (the internal organs that were thought to give rise to blasphemous thoughts) were burned. For sedition he was dismembered, and his quarters were to be displayed across the north – at Berwick, Newcastle, Stirling and Perth – with his head placed on a pike on London Bridge to be seen by everyone.

It was brutal, and a warning designed to be clear to all, as Dayffdd's execution had been, but Wallace's trial also demonstrates a more clinical approach from Edward and his justices, as they developed a more consistent policy for dealing with rebels in countries where the English Crown claimed lordship. The King's Record, and the summary execution of 'traitors' captured in times of war, now became the precedent of choice for Edward and his successor Edward II, a new approach which was quick and convenient, but of dubious legality. Questions remained around its use, particularly whether it could be used in times of peace, and there were fears under Edward II that the use of the King's Record might extend into use for other forms of treason, but such a use never materialised. By the reign of Edward III, the King's Record was almost only ever used in cases where the crime was one of fighting the king in open war, where it was obvious to all involved through the use of banners. Where it was used in other (limited) cases, it was condemned as unjustified.

TREASON UNDER EDWARD II

What does it serve, to resist the king, save to throw away one's life and lose all one's goods as well? For an islander to rebel against an island king is as if a chained man were to strive with the warden of his prison.
VITA EDWARDI SECUNDI, ANON., 1325

Treason, throughout the reign of Edward I, had developed from the earliest ideas of betrayal and the relationship between Crown and nobility, with an increased focus around ideas of levying war and high treason against the person of the King. The development of the King's

Record had provided the Crown with a powerful tool to use against rebels, primarily those in Wales and Scotland, reflecting two of Edward's primary concerns. It was used to harsh effect against rebels, and in many respects was outward-looking. With the King's death in 1307, and the succession of Edward II (1284–1327), however, a new form of treason soon began to develop, one which was more focused on internal politics within the realm. Under Edward I, the balance between the King and his nobility had begun to shift in favour of the Crown, but this was by no means a permanent move. The barons of the realm, even if they agreed that the rights of the Crown should be retained, remained willing to stand up for their own rights as required. The relationship between the king and his nobles went both ways, and the leading magnates of the realm expected to be able to provide the king with guidance in council on the leading issues of the day, and retained the threat of formally withdrawing their fealty if they were denied their rights. The reign of Edward II would see this relationship tested, frayed and ultimately broken, with treason used as a powerful weapon on both sides.

In the early fourteenth century, concepts of treason began to reflect influences from Roman legal traditions, particularly the ideas of lèse-majesté and 'accroaching royal power'. In England, unlike in France, such concepts remained limited and largely undefined, even after the statute of 1352, primarily as a consequence of Magna Carta and the barons' success in preventing the kings of England becoming theocratic monarchs. The Crown of England was sovereign, and separate from the body of the king. As such, while the notion of treason protected the person of the king, and attempts against his life, there was also a need for protection against the diminishment of the Crown's power, by the community of the realm, or by the king himself. For an individual who was not king to arrogate the powers of the Crown, or to diminish those powers, was unacceptable, but also difficult to define, and could easily lead to factionalism.

Under Edward II, the balance between the King and his lords came into sharp focus as a consequence of Edward's reliance on royal favourites and close friends, combined with an increased political

opposition from those who found themselves isolated and unable to
offer the royal counsel that was their right. Such concerns had begun
to reveal themselves even when Edward II was still a prince, his close
friendship (and possible sexual relations) with Piers Gaveston causing
problems in 1302 and 1307 to his father's fury. This concern – which
had been brought out by Edward's attempts to grant Gaveston a series
of royal lands – had led to Gaveston's exile from England. On taking the
throne, however, one of Edward II's first acts was to bring his friend back
to England (allegedly despite his father's deathbed wishes) and create
him Earl of Cornwall. Gaveston soon became entrenched as the King's
royal favourite despite rising hostility among both the nobility and
Edward's wife, Isabella, who resented his influence with the King and
his overly powerful status in England, stating that there were 'two kings
in one realm'. Accusations of the mismanagement of royal finances, gifts
and revenues, some of which dated back to Edward I's reign, alongside
the consolidation of power among a small clique of individuals close to
the King, began to be made. Over the years to follow, the magnates
– most notably the King's first cousin, the Earl of Lancaster – would
regularly call for royal reform and for Gaveston's exile as the threat of
civil war grew larger, reaching a dramatic climax in February 1310.

In a parliament notionally summoned to discuss the question of
what to do about the Scottish king, Robert the Bruce, Edward was
presented with a petition from the assembled company of magnates,
led by Lancaster, requesting the appointment of a group of barons to
address concerns with royal government and put in place a detailed
programme to institute reform. The King was accused of impoverishing
and shaming the realm, and of losing Scotland, although in order to avoid
a direct attack on the Crown, the losses were blamed primarily on the
'unsuitable and evil counsel' that had advised him. Such language was not
new, but clearly serves to highlight the changes in political thought that
were beginning to take effect, and the potential for factions to emerge
around the King. Edward initially resisted the requests for reform, but
was accused of breaking his coronation oath – in which he had agreed

to uphold 'the rightful laws and customs which the community of the realm shall have chosen' – and threatened with deposition if he would not accept the programme of reform. Under intense pressure, Edward conceded and a group of 'Ordainers' were elected to produce a series of measures, which would become known as the Ordinances of 1311 when they were published the following year. In total forty-one ordinances were published, to regulate royal finances, examine records of royal government and manage the appointment of significant royal officials such as the Chancellor. It is, however, the complaints around Gaveston that are of particular interest in the history of treason. The royal favourite had 'acted badly towards and has badly advised our lord the king and has incited him to do wrong in diverse and decèptive ways', all the while 'drawing to himself royal power and royal dignity'. All of these deeds had been done 'traitorously', and while Gaveston was not explicitly named as a traitor in the final document (although he had been in an earlier draft), the concept of treason by encroaching on the royal power of the Crown was evident.

Edward reluctantly agreed to the conditions imposed upon him, including the exile of Gaveston once again – although while the official announcement declared he had done so freely, he had clearly done so under duress, and he almost immediately sought to have the Ordinances revoked. Gaveston left the country in November 1311, while Edward took refuge at Windsor and Langley, with a significant stock of royal jewels as financial security. By the following January he was ready to retaliate, recalling Gaveston, and declaring the Ordinances revoked on account of the fact they had been agreed under duress. A handful of the reforms were kept to show willing, but the scene was set for a showdown between the King and his lords. Edward and Gaveston prepared their forces at Scarborough Castle, with Edward ordering his friend not to surrender the castle to anyone except him, even if he, Edward, was brought to the gates as a prisoner under threat of death – a striking order to make and a sign of the closeness between the two men. Edward was willing to meet any fate, including death, rather than give Gaveston up. While Edward and Isabella headed for York, Scarborough (under Gaveston's control) soon came under siege from the magnates, and was eventually forced to surrender despite the promises that had been made. Gaveston's safety was initially guaranteed, and it appears Edward was even willing to agree to reform (reluctantly), but only on the basis that his friend would not be labelled a traitor. As little progress could be made in negotiations a parliament was summoned to discuss the matter. Gaveston, however, was not to see an official trial. He was captured by the Earl of Warwick – either through neglect or a contrived plot – while a prisoner in Oxfordshire in the care of the Earl of Pembroke, met with the words 'Arise, traitor, thou art taken', and transported to Warwick for what amounted to a summary trial on 18 June 1312. Two royal justices, who were present in Warwick at the time, may have provided some legal process in the matter, but the overwhelming accusations against Gaveston were based on the published Ordinances of the previous year, with Lancaster giving approval of his execution on the grounds that he had been adjudged a traitor by the same Ordinances. The next day he was executed by two men at Lancaster's command, run through with a sword and decapitated. The language of treason, and 'deeds done traitorously' was used to sentence the King's favourite for a legally undefined crime. Unlike the treason trials of Edward I's reign – highly symbolic and performative acts, if entirely brutal – Gaveston's 'trial' and execution were swift and summary in nature, and almost entirely political. Like Edward's processes, they were legally dubious, and set a new precedent for factional disputes to be settled – despite the Ordainers themselves stating that their work should not set a precedent for future monarchs – and provoked an ongoing enmity and a desire for revenge between the king and his nobles, which would continue for the rest of the reign, and beyond.

With the loss of his favourite, Edward now spent much of his time attempting to get around or refuse the Ordinances, and the influence of the Earl of Lancaster – as the leading magnate in the realm – continued to grow. If the lords had expected the King to change his ways, however, they would be disappointed. In the spring of 1317, it was clear that a new group of royal favourites had become firmly entrenched at court, including a father and son both named Hugh Despenser, whose power and influence saw a rapid rise over the next three years. By 1320 they had almost complete control and influence over the King, and numerous complaints about their conduct arose, particularly in the Welsh Marches where they were seeking to establish their lordship. It was alleged that no baron could approach Edward without their consent (often gained through a bribe), that they had the power to imprison people at their will, and that Edward would listen only to their counsel. In a letter of January 1321 which highlights the Despensers' power, the younger Despenser remarked to the sheriff of Glamorgan that the King treated him better than any other, and that he needed things to go smoothly so that he could make the most of his situation while he could.

The two Despensers were also unafraid to use accusations of treason against their enemies, particularly in Wales, and the situation soon became perilous for Edward as his royal favourites clashed time and time again with the magnates. In 1321 the barons once again threatened to withdraw their allegiance from the King unless the Despensers answered several charges against them, including that they had wrongly advised Edward, to the dishonour and damage of both the King and the kingdom. The main charges were the new quasi-treasonous charges of usurping royal power, the impairment of the Crown and the person of the king, although at this stage the magnates held back from declaring them as traitors (probably to encourage Edward to consider a new programme of reform). At the same time, Lancaster was developing the concept of the 'Steward of England' – a position that he held as a senior magnate – and attempting to mould a constitutional role with the responsibility to intervene against evil counsellors, and to protect the Crown of England. The differentiation between the authority of the Crown, and the person of the king was increasingly being utilised to challenge Edward and the royal favourites around him.

In a parallel with Gaveston's final exile a decade earlier, the Despensers were sent into exile, although not for long. The younger Despenser seems to have spent much of this short period at sea in the Channel, indulging in some light piracy, and soon returned to Edward's side. The prospect of civil war was now a firm possibility, as Edward attempted to provoke Lancaster and his allies into battle. Lancaster, as Steward of England, called a meeting of his supporters, who came to be called the Contrariants, in which a new petition was drafted, drawing on the developing concept of the steward, but also on Magna Carta, and the Ordinances of 1311. Edward was accused of maintaining the Younger Despenser, bringing him back from exile without licence, and encouraging acts of piracy, and a special prison was created to detain the King if he was captured. This was a civil war in all but name, but this time it was Edward who would prevail. On 1 March 1322, the first piece of Lancaster's downfall was put in place, with the discovery of treasonable correspondence between the earl and the Scots, in which Lancaster was referred to as 'King Arthur'.

Fleeing to Pontefract Castle, the Earls of Hereford and Lancaster were now confronted by the royal forces at the Battle of Boroughbridge on 16 March, and defeated. Hereford was killed by a Welsh infantryman hiding under a bridge. Lancaster was captured while trying to escape on foot, and taken to meet the newly arrived King and the younger Despenser, who 'contemptuously insulted him to his face with malicious and arrogant words'. The earl was placed in the prison that he had created for Edward, indicted for his crimes and declared guilty of treason, without a chance to defend himself. According to one chronicle account, Lancaster's final words condemned his lack of defence: 'This is a powerful court, and very great in authority, where no answer is heard nor any mitigation admitted.'

On account of Lancaster's royal blood, the traitor's death of drawing and hanging was remitted; instead, he was beheaded without delay on the King's Record, a process which shocked contemporaries, even if it could potentially be justified under the laws of arms covering acts of war. The processes of 1322 went against the traditional legal procedures that were supposed to apply to the trial of an earl, and set a dangerous precedent for future nobles caught up in the civil wars that so often engulfed Edward and his favourites. Edward had avenged the death of his friend Gaveston, but in so doing, he would seal a brutal death for his new favourites.

In the wake of Lancaster's execution and the royalist victory, Edward now moved to formally revoke the Ordinances for overly restraining his royal power; in a conciliatory move, however, he opted to keep six of the clauses he considered to be valid, and had these republished. He also rewarded the Despensers extensively with a steady flow of patronage and gifts, leading them to act like kings themselves, building a grand new mausoleum and other high status buildings. Once again they sought to consolidate and control access to the King, with the younger Despenser acting in the role of what would later be considered that of chief minister, issuing the King's royal letters with cover notes, and even sending his own letters on royal business. As the historian Seymour Phillips has noted, 'the regime established in England after the victory over the Contrariants in 1322 acted within a framework of legality but in reality was arbitrary and brutal.' According to contemporary chronicle accounts, 'The king's harshness has indeed increased so much today that no one, however great or wise, dares to cross the king's will … For whatever pleases the king, though lacking in reason, has the force of law.'

Treason charges were used by the Crown and particularly by the Despensers to attack their enemies in the Welsh Marches to brutal and bloody effect. The tyranny of Edward II may have been complete in the aftermath of 1322, but within two years it would begin to fall apart, as his wife and son turned against him. Travelling to France in 1325 to pursue peace negotiations with her brother the King of France, and soon joined by her son Edward – who had gone to do homage to the French king on behalf of Edward II – Queen Isabella now became involved with an exiled Marcher rebel, Roger Mortimer, against her husband. Distrustful of the younger Despenser, and amid rumours that he or Edward would kill her, she initially refused to travel back to Britain, and instead returned with Mortimer in August 1326, at the head of an armed force. On landing in England the force encountered no resistance – indeed, Isabella's supporters flocked to the rapidly growing army as it moved through the south-east of the country, claiming to be there legitimately in order to counter the crime of the 'tyrant', the younger Despenser (while carefully avoiding using such terms about Edward himself). In London, the city rose up in revolt against the Despenser allies and royalist supporters in violent scenes. The Bishop of Exeter, and former treasurer, was cruelly beheaded with a bread knife outside St Paul's Cathedral amid a spate of attacks; the Tower of London was seized, and the prisoners within released as Isabella and Mortimer arrived. Fleeing west, with the invading forces in pursuit, Edward and Despenser made it as far as the Bristol Channel, aiming first for Lundy Island, and then probably to Ireland, where they could regroup. The weather, however, made a crossing impossible, and they were forced to stop in Wales, heading first for the refuge of Caerphilly Castle, but then moving west once again, possibly with a last hope of making it to Ireland. It was, however, not to be. Edward and Despenser were betrayed by a group of Welshmen at a location which would later become known as 'Pant-y-Brad' – the 'Vale of Treason' – and captured by Isabella and Mortimer's forces on 16 November 1326. The younger Despenser and Edward himself now faced the consequences of the 'tyranny'.

In order to avoid pursuing the King directly, prior to his capture, Isabella had claimed that as Edward had left the kingdom, and had left it without a government in his absence, Prince Edward was now guardian of the kingdom in his place. She summoned a parliament to be held in December under his new authority. With Edward II's capture in Wales, however, his guardianship would technically be over as soon as the King returned to England, and after initial protest, he agreed to hand over the Great Seal and official rolls of Chancery before crossing the border. He remained king, but deprived of the instruments and mechanisms of government. His fate had not yet been decided, but he was powerless to resist. For the younger Despenser, his fate was clear. His father, who had been captured in Bristol during a brief siege of the city, had been tried and sentenced on 27 October, in a process explicitly modelled on that of Lancaster in 1322. He was informed that, as he had created a law which allowed for the condemnation of men without defence or the right to respond, he was to be tried in the same way. Intriguingly this appears to be a variant form of King's Record, except in the absence of the King himself, indicating that Prince Edward's guardianship and record were sufficient in and of themselves to act as proof against the former favourite. For treason, the elder Despenser was drawn to the gallows, for robbery, he was hanged, for acts against the Church, he was beheaded, for dishonouring the rank of earl, his head was sent to Winchester, while his coat of arms was also ritually subverted during his execution. Aware that such a fate was in store for him as well, the younger Despenser tried to starve himself to death during his capture, but was brought before a tribunal before he could succeed, and faced a summary trial in the same way as his father. He was to be drawn and quartered for treason, hanged as a robber and beheaded as an outlaw, in the usual way, but for the younger Despenser there was more to come. For procuring discord between the King, the Queen, and the kingdom, he was to be disembowelled and his entrails burned before him, and he was declared a traitor, tyrant, and renegade. He may also have been castrated – either to designate the death of his family line, or because of a rumoured homosexual relationship with the King – although accounts of this vary, and may represent later attempts by the chroniclers to smear Edward and his favourites, with Despenser labelled 'a heretic and a sodomite, even it was said, with the king'. The dramatic occasion of the execution was exaggerated by the theatrics which accompanied proceedings. On his way to the place of execution, a specially built gallows fifty feet high, Despenser was dressed in a tunic upon which his coat of arms had been reversed, and the text of Psalm 51 written across the front, as well as a 'chapalette of sharpe nettles' on his head for the crime of accroaching royal power.

The theatrics which accompanied the execution of the younger Despenser were in sharp contrast to Edward's own fate. Edward had been threatened with deposition on multiple occasions throughout his reign, but the actual act of deposing a king was more complicated than mere threats. There was no precedent which could be followed, as no king had been deposed in England since the Norman Conquest. Should

Illumination depicting the execution of the younger Despenser, 1326. © Bibliothèque nationale de France, Français 2643.

Edward be restored, deposed, or even executed? The council opted for the second option, deposition and life imprisonment, which was confirmed in a meeting at Westminster in January 1327, a meeting which was a parliament in all but name (as only the King could summon Parliament). Justification for the deposition began almost immediately, with the Bishop of Hereford preaching that Edward was a tyrant and sodomite (although official accounts were careful to apply such accusations to the younger Despenser alone), an attempt to smear his reputation through gossip and rumour. Six articles of deposition were composed, in which Edward was described as an incompetent ruler and man, who had failed in a number of instances, including neglecting to hold his father's gains in Scotland. The final articles were put before Edward at Kenilworth Castle, where the envoys went to great lengths to frame events as an abdication, rather than a deposition. They first tried to persuade the King to abdicate for the sake of the country, but when this failed they moved to a second plan, threatening that the magnates of the realm would withdraw their homage and fealty and place someone of non-royal blood on the throne. For Edward, with his son and heir Prince Edward in line to take the throne, this seems to have been the final straw and with great grief and tears, he finally accepted the terms offered. Within a year he was dead, now believed to have been secretly murdered in response to reports of a plot to free the deposed King from captivity.

Edward II's reign had seen treason used as a brutal means of speedily and summarily dispatching enemies on both sides of what was in effect a long and protracted conflict between the King and his nobles. Charges of accroaching and usurping royal power expanded and developed throughout the reign, often not in response to the King's demands or wishes, but to challenge and remove those who were perceived to be too close to the King. The Despensers, and to a lesser extent, Gaveston, were in many ways guilty of this charge, acting like kings themselves and taking upon themselves the royal authority, but there were limits to what they could achieve alone. Edward's inability to rein in his favourites, and his personal need to recall them when they had been exiled, laid much of the blame at his door, provoking his nobles when conciliation might have proved a better course of action. At the forefront of his tyranny, however, was the increased use of the King's Record to execute his enemies without due legal process in times of war, and a fear among the nobility that this might be expanded to other instances of treason. Fortunately, it did not, but the events of the 1320s – with highly dramatic and theatrical executions, open warfare in the country and the deposition of his father – must have affected the new King, Edward III. In November 1330 he turned on his mother and her lover Roger Mortimer for themselves usurping his royal authority and for his deep involvement with Edward II's murder, indicting Mortimer in Parliament for treason. Treason had torn the country, and the royal family, apart in the first decades of the fourteenth century, and was continuing to expand both in scope and the extra-judicial processes available to prosecutors. It was time to define treason.

DEFINING TREASON: THE TREASON ACT 1352

In the early years of Edward III (1312–77), treason was, as we have seen, by no means a new concept, yet it remained undefined. As such – and as the previous reign had demonstrated – dubious charges, processes, and factionalism could run rife in a realm when the boundaries of acceptable behaviour were unclear, and the punishments brutal and utterly destructive. Treason affected more than just the rebel or traitor, but might affect their entire lineage. To declare a noble to be a traitor was to disinherit their heirs indefinitely – entire noble bloodlines declared to be corrupt as a consequence of one individual's betrayal.

Riding high after a series of successful military victories in France, Edward now moved to consolidate the Crown's relationship with the magnates of the realm, a relationship his parents had so badly broken. The act of January 1352 defined the crime of high treason in statute law for the first time, within a specific and limited definition, providing the nobility with a clear line in the sand in their dealings with the Crown. The incentive here was not from the Crown alone. Indeed, the Parliament roll

– the official account of parliamentary proceedings – notes that the 1352 definitions of treason were given by the Crown specifically in response to a request from Parliament to do so. There was clearly an element of stage management in place here, the details of which are partially obscured by the official nature of the roll, but a conciliatory element to events seems to be genuine.

The 1352 Treason Act was part of a wider policy employed by Edward III to reset the Crown's relationship with the nobility, and to forge a new sense of kinship. Military victories in France and Scotland helped, but we can also see more proactive moves from Edward in the establishment of new chivalric orders such as the Order of the Garter in 1348 (originally conceived as a new Order of the Round Table – with Edward as King Arthur). Not only did such measures keep his nobles united in events such as grand banquets, but the associated tournaments kept them busy. Re-establishing the social codes which linked the Crown and the lords of the realm further underpinned these relationships, emphasising equality among the magnates and legal certainty in their dealings with the King. Under the reign of his father and predecessor, Edward II, charges of treason had been arbitrarily imposed on the nobility under the vague definition of 'accroaching the royal power'. While it was undefined, charges of treason could be brought with impunity, despite the fact (as was made clear in the request for a definition in Parliament) that such charges had not commonly been regarded as treasonous previously.

The definition of treason in 1352 was deliberately limited, and is suggestive of careful deliberation between the King and his justices. 'When a Man doth compass or imagine the Death of our Lord the King, or of our Lady his Queen or of their eldest Son and Heir': the first of the articles of treason, as recorded on both the Parliament roll and the statute roll, defined treason as the act of plotting the death of the king, his queen or their eldest son, or of 'compassing or imagining' the same. The use of the latter phrase would be stretched to breaking point in the centuries to come, as seditious thoughts, words and writings were pulled into this slightly loose classification, but at its definition, the statute was clearly intended to cover overt acts of violence against the immediate royal family.

'If a Man do violate the King's Companion, or the King's eldest Daughter unmarried, or the Wife of the King's eldest Son and Heir': the second article was further concerned with the royal family, declaring the sexual assault of the queen (or the king's 'companion' or spouse as given in the original French), the king's eldest daughter (but only while she was unmarried), or the spouse of his eldest son and heir. Here the focus was not, primarily at least, the act of violation itself, but the implications that such an act might have on the royal blood line and line of succession.

'If a Man do levy War against our Lord the King in his Realm, or be adherent to the King's Enemies in his Realm, giving to them Aid and Comfort in the Realm, or elsewhere, and thereof be probably attainted of open Deed by the People of their Condition': the third article of treason dealt with 'levying war' against the Crown within the realm, or aiding the king's enemies within the realm, or elsewhere. The specification that levying war 'in the realm' alone was treasonous acknowledged the fact that some members of the nobility retained lands in France, so that they technically owed allegiance to the French Crown as well. Edward himself was no longer bound by such allegiance, having renounced his homage to the French king and indeed, going further, asserting a claim to the French throne (claiming the kingship through his mother), which his military campaigns enabled him to conceive bringing to reality. Riding armed against other individuals of the realm other than the king, whether openly or covertly, alone or with accomplices, was deemed to be felony or trespass (as it had been previously) rather than treasonous.

Having laid out the charges of treason against the royal family personally, definitions of treasonous activities against the state more generally were laid out. Counterfeiting, in both general and specific terms, was defined as treasonable. Article four stated that it was treason to counterfeit either the Great Seal or the coinage of the realm, while article five aimed to combat the import of coins 'such as the money named Lushbournes' (counterfeit coins originating in Luxembourg) or other similar coins, and trying to pass them off as English. Finally, article six defined that the murder of the king's royal officials, including the Chancellor, Treasurer and certain royal justices, was to be deemed as treasonous, provided only that the officials were performing their royal duties at the time of the murder. In such circumstances, the offence was not solely against the officials themselves (which would still, of course, have been murder), but projected onto the Crown's authority and governance, and thus exacted a higher penalty. Offences of lèse-majesté, including usurping or accroaching royal power, were interestingly not included in the new definitions, probably in an attempt to guard against a repetition of some of the excesses of Edward II's reign, although as we will see, they would remain a concern to future monarchs.

While the Treason Act of 1352 defined treason for the first time, it made little provision for new regulations on the punishment for treasonous acts, beyond clarifying the process of forfeitures for high and petty treason. It makes no mention at all of the manner of execution to be employed, or even that execution was to take place at all. These remained the same as they had before 1352, the act serving only to clarify and define the boundaries of treason, rather than to create a new offence.

In addition to what would become known as 'high' treason, although it was not defined as such in 1352, a secondary form of treason was clarified, which mimicked threats against the king. 'Petty' treason, the murder of one to whom an individual owed their allegiance, whether a servant killing a master, a wife her husband, or a churchman his religious superior, was also detailed in the act, with such crimes judged to be against the natural order of society. Later, a class of treason known as 'misprision of treason' was introduced – the concealment of treason, or the failure to report knowledge of a treasonous plot – although this would only develop slowly in its definition throughout the medieval and Tudor period. With the new forms of high and petty treason, the crime of treason was now clearly defined by statute for the first time. It was limited in the terms of its definition (broadly speaking), and clear. But Edward and his council also looked to the future with the act, and included a clause that would be invoked time and time again over the following centuries. The act noted that, 'because many other similar cases of treason will occur in times to come' – cases which might appear to be treasonous but sat outside of the limits of 1352 – a provision needed to be made for future expansion of the definition of treason, and the process for deciding this. Such cases were not to be decided on by the individual justices before whom they were brought, but only by the king in Parliament, where it could be judged whether the actions were treasonous or merely a felony. In the context of 1352, such an addition was uncontroversial, and indeed displayed a sense of awareness among its legislators that they might not have all the answers. At the same time – as the following centuries would demonstrate – it also placed the definition (and therefore the potential for prosecution) of new forms of treason firmly within the remit of Parliament. Under a strong monarch such as Edward III this represented no real concern but under a weak monarch, as we shall see, this crucial clause would set the scene for dramatic future events in Parliament.

The 'confession' of Thomas of Woodstock, one of the Lords Appellant, 1397. (C 65/60)

Two

FACTIONALISM AND
TYRANNY, 1381–99

The authors of the 1352 Treason Act may have considered the question of treason's definition to have been put to bed for the last time. The decades which followed, however, would prove such hopes unfounded, as England experienced mass revolt and the expansion of treason's definition under a teenage king. Within fifty years of its definition, the language of treason would be used in unprecedented circumstances, to depose the very individuals it was supposed to protect.

In 1352, the Crown of England was in the possession of a strong, powerful, settled king, riding high in the wake of a series of overwhelming victories in the French wars. Edward III, in the prime of his life, was a popular figure among his nobility and kingdom alike, able to enthuse his nobles through lavish tournaments and the foundation of institutions such as the Order of the Garter. The final years of his reign, however, had seen the tides of war in France changing, along with the King's increasing ill health, regency government in all but name, and questions arising around those counselling the frail monarch. As they had in Edward II's reign, accusations of treason came to the fore as the court fractured between those with the King's ear, and those without, a problem which was only exacerbated by his death in 1377 and the coronation of his grandson, the ten-year-old Richard II (1367–1400).

The son of Edward III's eldest son, Edward of Woodstock, better known as the 'Black Prince', who had died the previous year, Richard was crowned amid rumours that his uncle, John of Gaunt, was considering a coup. Unfortunately, given Richard's tender age, factionalism at court meant that no suitable regent could be decided upon.

In the absence of an agreed figure who might guide the realm through the King's minority, an uneasy and dangerous façade was settled on, in which it was claimed that the new King was fully able to govern on his own, despite his age. In reality, this was not the case, and a series of 'continual councils' were assembled to guide the King until he was of an age to fully govern in his own right. This was not entirely successful and the councils soon became framed as scapegoats for all of the country's woes, from foreign policy issues and financial concerns to, even, the weather. They were dismissed by Parliament in January 1380, with a renewed declaration that Richard was now of age to rule without them; in reality, however, the King (now thirteen) was still reliant on his councillors, who continued to advise, but now conducting their business in semi-secrecy, in that way opening themselves and the Crown up to charges of favouritism.

The first gaps in the 1352 Act and the expansion of treason's definition would come to light, however, not through factionalism, or noble coups, but with the unexpected, and indeed unprecedented events of summer 1381: England's first mass protest, the 'Peasant's Revolt', or 'Great Revolt' as it is now often referred to. Sparked by the poll taxes which had been imposed on the general population since 1377, alongside other concerns, the revolt saw men and women from across the country march on London, burning buildings and documents as they went, and killing leading officials in what amounted to summary executions. While the revolt itself was eventually put down on 15 June with the death of its leader Wat Tyler at Smithfield, it was obvious that the Crown and chief justices had a problem.

The rebels, in the eyes of the authorities at least, were clearly traitors, and therefore deserved to suffer a traitor's death, setting an example to those who might consider such actions in future. Under the legislation of 1352, however, the vast majority of the rebels were not guilty of treason, even if many of them were guilty of murder and other offences that also brought the death penalty. While the rebels had arguably risen up against the Crown in armed revolt, to those writing the legislation of 1352 (and indeed those active in 1381) the possibility of a popular protest was unthinkable, and so no provisions were easily available to prosecute such actions as treason. The focus in 1352 had been on 'levying war', with connotations of nobles riding in battle with banners unfurled against royal forces who were arrayed in like fashion. Those involved in the 1381 uprising could hardly be said to have acted in such a way. The authorities, however, and the new Chief Justice Robert Tresilian in particular, actively sought to frame crimes as treasonable, in order to set an example, broadening the scope of treason after the fact. This would be confirmed in law later that year, when it was declared that it was high treason to 'make [or] begin any manner of riot and rumour'. It set a dangerous precedent for the young regime, in which treason might be expanded (after the fact) in response to events or framed in order to secure a prosecution.

If the revolt of 1381 had hinted at the Crown and government's unpopularity among the general populace, dissatisfaction within certain sections of the nobility and Parliament would explode in no less violent a fashion only a few years later in the parliaments of 1386 and 1388. Provoked, once again, by taxation and perceived ill governance, the language of treason was at the fore of a remarkable breakdown between Parliament and the Crown. Throughout the first decade of Richard's reign, a particular source of discontent had been the problem of royal finances and the need to reform the management of royal revenues, which (it was claimed) were overly generous to those in Crown service. In short, the King needed to live within his means, and avoid regular tax burdens on his people to fund the French wars. By 1385, Parliament had been able to force a commission to review the royal finances on the Crown and Chancellor, and limit certain appointments and grants that the King wanted to make. Richard had, however, from an early age been a firm believer in the principle of royal supremacy, and was unwilling to approve any legislation that might in any way limit his regality and royal dignity. A year later, in the 'Wonderful Parliament' of October 1386, with none of Parliament's reforms implemented, matters would come to a head between Parliament and the Crown in extraordinary fashion.

The 1386 Parliament had been summoned in order to face the threat of a French invasion force, which had been growing throughout the spring and summer of that year, and threatened to depart for the English coast at any moment. Opening Parliament on 1 October, Chancellor Michael de la Pole, a royal favourite, outlined the King's intention to lead an army to France himself, but then made a crucial error in letting slip the exceedingly high sum of taxation he was seeking. In the circumstances, such a request was inflammatory and both Houses of Parliament immediately called for the Chancellor to be dismissed and impeached, a request that Richard denied, storming off to his manor of Eltham in fury. Having reached a stalemate, with Parliament refusing to consider its normal business until the Chancellor had been removed, and Richard refusing to budge, the King requested a delegation of forty members of the Commons to discuss the matter at Eltham. Fearing that they might be arrested if they were to do so, the Commons refused and two members of the Lords, the King's uncle Thomas of Woodstock, Duke of Gloucester, and the Bishop of Ely Thomas Arundel, long-standing critics of Richard and those around him, were sent instead to face the King.

If Richard was expecting to find a compromise and way forward in the matter, he was sorely disappointed. Gloucester and Arundel instead faced the King with a series of statements and threats, reminding him of his duties as king, which they claimed were backed up by certain ancient statutes and laws. Among their demands, Parliament was to be summoned by the King every year to provide public oversight of any errors or mismanagement, particularly regarding public finances, and if the King absented himself from Parliament for more than forty days, Parliament could dissolve itself without royal command. These claims in themselves, which appear to have been based on the 'Ordinances' imposed upon Edward II in 1311 but repealed in 1322, represented a radical change in the power balance between Parliament and Crown, but were similar in nature to the reforms requested in the previous year (if now given a dubious historical precedent).

More damning for relations was what followed. Richard, reacting to the two lords, threatened that he might ask his cousin, the French king, for support, a threat which was met with shock – the two countries were at war, and the King's father and grandfather had both had extensive careers fighting the wars in France. To suggest working with an enemy monarch against his own nobles was outrageous. Gloucester and Arundel had one further historical precedent, however, which they now invoked: the deposition of Edward II. They claimed that under another 'ancient law', if any king alienated himself from his people and refused to be governed by his lords 'then it would be lawful with the common assent and agreement of the people of the realm to depose the king from his throne and raise another member of the royal dynasty in his place'. The threat was clear: if Richard didn't obey his lords, he would be replaced, just as his great-grandfather Edward had been.

Concerned for his throne, Richard now had no option but to proceed with his friend's impeachment, as Parliament had demanded. De la Pole was dismissed as Chancellor, while the treasurer and Bishop of Durham, John Fordham, was also dismissed. De la Pole was then prosecuted for some of the charges against him, but was released on payment of a fine and allowed to return to the King's side within a year. A new 'great and continual council', however, was imposed on the court to bring about reform and undertake a full enquiry into royal revenues, with full supervision of the royal administration – an unprecedented series of powers (if time limited). While the parliamentarians were unable fully to realise their wishes to extend the scope of the council, its role was wide-ranging and clearly evoked anger from Richard, who made a defiant statement 'with his own mouth' in defence of the royal prerogative and the liberties of the Crown before Parliament was dissolved on 28 November. Within a few months of Parliament's dissolution, it became clear that Richard had little intention of cooperating with the new council any more than he absolutely had to, and every intention of being difficult where he could. As one of the stipulations of the new council stated that its members should be present in London while its business was ongoing, Richard deliberately kept his household at arm's reach, moving around the Midlands where its finances, procedures and personnel were free from oversight and investigation.

Bruised, slighted, and on the move, Richard now plotted his reaction to the chastening events of 1386. Clearly he believed that the conditions imposed on his royal prerogative and dignity were of a treasonous nature, drawing on pre-1352 ideas of lèse-majesté, and in August 1387, alongside his core inner circle, he set out to prove this. Drawing together the senior justices of the realm and other key officials, Richard laid a series of ten questions before the justices to establish whether the actions of the 1386 Parliament had affected the liberties and privileges of the Crown, with two further questions about how any such actions should be punished. Consultation with senior justices was not uncommon, but never before had they been asked to judge on such an important matter, essentially defining the extent of the royal prerogative.

It may be that the driving force behind the 'Questions', as they became known, was Chief Justice Tresilian, the architect of the 1381 treason prosecutions and one of Richard's inner circle.

The justices' response to the Questions was that Parliament had indeed affected the liberties and privileges of the Crown, and that both the impeachment of De la Pole and the commission which had been forced on Richard were illegal. The King could dissolve Parliament as he desired, and Parliament could not pursue their own affairs before dealing with royal business. Furthermore, those who had threatened Richard with their veiled references were to be punished 'as traitors'. This was clearly a deliberate choice of words, as the justices were well aware that no breaches of the 1352 statute had taken place, and so the charges had to be framed as treasonous in a broader sense. Such responses (which the justices would later claim had been imposed on them by the Crown and Richard's inner circle) were explosive and initially every effort was made to keep the outcome of the two meetings secret, while Richard planned his next steps. By October or early November, however, the secret had got out and had reached the ears of the Duke of Gloucester. The scene was set for a violent showdown.

Entering London on 10 November 1387, shortly before the commission on his government was due to expire, Richard summoned Gloucester and the Earl of Arundel, two of the principal architects of the events of 1386, to appear before him and when they refused, ordered their arrest. Aware of the treason charges which could be brought against them as a consequence of the justices' consultation, the two men joined forces in Middlesex, where they were joined by the Earl of Warwick. They then moved to Waltham Cross, where they presented a royal delegation with an appeal of treason against five of Richard's inner circle: Robert de Vere, the Duke of Ireland; Michael de la Pole; the Archbishop of York Alexander Neville; Chief Justice Tresilian, and the former Mayor of London, Nicholas Brembre.

Having presented their appeal to the royal delegation, the 'Lords Appellant', as they would shortly become known on account of this appeal, now marched on London with a significant armed force, and presented Richard with their appeal personally. Their speed clearly threw the King's plan into chaos, he was forced to accept their appeal, assigning the hearing to take place in the next parliament, which would take place in the following February. On hearing the news, the subjects of the appeal, who had been caught off guard, reacted quickly. Neville and De la Pole fled overseas, Brembre set about trying to consolidate his support in London, while Tresilian went into hiding in London. De Vere moved to Cheshire, a royalist stronghold, to mobilise a royal army against the Appellants. On travelling south again, however, his forces were routed in a series of skirmishes with the Appellants, who had by this point recruited two further lords, the Earls of Derby and Nottingham. De Vere was able to escape through the fog with his life, but now lacking an army he fled overseas to join De la Pole and Neville.

With his closest supporters scattered, and no army to defend him, Richard retreated to the Tower with a handful of councillors, and a week later on 27 December accepted a meeting with the Appellants, who had arrived with around 500 armed men, closing the gates behind them as they entered the Tower. Accounts of what happened behind the closed doors of the royal stronghold vary, although it is likely that Richard was actually deposed for three days, and only restored because Gloucester and Derby could not decide which of them would assume the throne instead. They strongly reproached the King for his treachery, possibly reiterating their concerns that he was planning on calling on French aid, and generally began preparations for the state trials that would take place in February 1388, in what would become known as the 'Merciless Parliament'.

On 3 February Richard entered the White Hall at Westminster arm in arm with the Appellants, who were dressed in 'golden suits', in a contrived show of unity, and the proceedings of the Merciless Parliament began. One of the first orders of business was the statement that Gloucester wanted to clear his name of certain treasons, most likely the claim that he wanted the throne for himself (and connected with the temporary deposition of the King), a statement which was rebutted on the fact that the King found him blameless. Such a piece of performance, given that Richard was isolated and essentially a bystander in proceedings, was to be characteristic of the Parliament. Next in proceedings was the appeal of treason, which took almost two hours to read out in full, such were the charges contained within thirty-nine articles. The articles included charges that the favourites had exerted undue influence over Richard and abused their power, particularly given his tender age; accusations that they had encouraged the King in submitting his questions to the justices, and pressed for military action against the Appellants, and claims that they had defied the council and considered asking for French aid.

As with the favourites of Edward II's reign, the treason charges were based on the concept of accroaching royal power, rather than charges as defined in the 1352 Act, but as his threats of 1386 had demonstrated, Gloucester was not afraid to use historical precedents, particularly those of Edward II's reign, to force through charges. Indeed, the process of state trial by appeal to Parliament was dubious in itself, and newly appointed justices were soon brought forward to state that due to the importance of the offences, they were to be judged under the rather vaguely defined 'law of parliament' rather than by civil or common law. This was an unprecedented expression of Parliament's judicial supremacy, which would set the scene for many of the biggest treason trials which would follow, with Richard a mere bystander in events which were stage-managed by the Appellants throughout.

As three of the King's supporters had fled, and Tresilian remained in hiding, the first business of the trial was to secure convictions *in absentia*. Over several days at the start of the month, De Vere, De la Pole, Tresilian and Neville were summoned to appear, and when they did not they were found guilty and condemned as traitors on all counts (although after discussion only fourteen of the articles were considered to be treasonous). De Vere, De la Pole and Tresilian were sentenced to a traitor's death, and Neville (as a man of the church) was sentenced to confiscation of his temporalities. On Monday 17 February Nicholas Brembre, as the only one of the five present, was brought in to trial. According to chronicle accounts of the trial, he requested legal counsel, and a copy of the accusations against him, both of which were denied. He then tried to defend himself, but was only permitted to answer 'Guilty' or 'Not Guilty' and claimed the latter, offering to prove his innocence through battle. His request was met with over a hundred gauntlets thrown down on the floor in challenge by those wishing to substantiate the charges (the traditional means of settling a dispute or dishonour through trial by combat), a demonstration of the anger against the former mayor in both the Commons and the Lords. The request for battle was denied. Richard himself, who had been present at the start of the trial but had then left, now returned to defend his friend against the charges, but his defence was

List of goods forfeited by Richard II's favourites on being charged with treason, 1388. (*E 36/66*) also met with a flurry of gauntlets. No decision on Brembre, however, could be made, and the matter was referred to a jury of twelve lords, who initially stated that he had done nothing to merit the death penalty.

Frustration among the Appellants at Brembre's inconclusive proceedings may have been relieved somewhat on the following Wednesday, when Tresilian was located in the nearby sanctuary at Westminster Abbey, and dragged into court to face sentencing. As a former Chief Justice, who had himself framed treason charges in 1381 and possibly 1387, he may have expected to be able to argue his case, and indeed tried to do so, but was informed that as he had already been convicted the sentence was irrevocable. He was immediately taken to the Tower, dragged on a hurdle to Tyburn, stripped naked and hanged. Whether this encouraged the Appellants to redouble their efforts to secure a capital sentence for Brembre is uncertain, but he was brought back into the chamber the next day, where further evidence was presented against him. Representatives from the London guilds and City officials were brought forward to determine whether they thought he was guilty, and while no definite answer was forthcoming, the Appellants were finally able to secure a conviction on the basis that Brembre may have known about the alleged treasons and concealed them. Asked whether they believed he was aware, the Mayor of London, Nicholas Exton, and a selection of civic officials stated that they 'supposed he was aware rather than ignorant of them'. Brembre's fate was sealed, and he was executed the same day, drawing tears from onlookers according to one chronicle, on account of his pious and repentant final journey to Tyburn.

The Appellants' reach now extended to officials and members of the royal household, with various accusations and impeachments, including the justices and officials who had answered the King's questions of August 1387. Despite claiming that they had been coerced into replying as they did, all six were convicted of treason for having aided and supported the appellees, and for concealing the convicted 'traitors'. Likewise Thomas Blake, the lawyer involved in drafting the Questions, and Thomas Usk, the under-sheriff of Middlesex, found themselves impeached, charged with treason for their parts in the events of 1387 and convicted of the same. If the Appeal had threatened to encompass events outside the limits of the 1352 Treason Act, these latter impeachments clearly ignored Edward III's definition of treason entirely, as a vengeful Commons prosecuted its enemies with vigour. Blake and Usk, having been convicted, were executed, but the justices were spared after some deliberation, and various intercessions from the bishops, the Queen and other members of the Parliament.

Finally, four clerks and four knights of the King's Chamber were brought to trial. The clerks were quickly released without trial, but the knights, Simon Burley, John Beauchamp, John Salisbury and James Berners remained, and were charged with treason, being closely associated with the appellees throughout the articles of impeachment against them. Beauchamp, Salisbury and Berners were convicted, and sentenced with little difficulty. Beauchamp and Berners were spared the drawing and hanging and were instead beheaded, but Salisbury, being closely linked with the French element of the plot, was charged with treason inside and outside the realm, and subjected to the full traitor's death. Burley's trial, however, was more controversial, and the subject of much debate within the chamber, including a fierce argument between Gloucester and his brother the Duke of York. York claimed that Burley (who had been a member of their brother the Black Prince's retinue) had always been loyal and offered to prove his point in one-to-one combat, while Gloucester stated the opposite and offered to take up the challenge, as both men resorted to calling each other liars across the parliamentary chamber.

A timely intervention from the King spared his uncles coming to blows, but the incident highlights the heated debate that the case seemed to provoke in Parliament. More important for Richard, however, was the rift it sparked within the Appellants themselves, with the two junior members of the group (Derby and Nottingham) pleading for Burley's life to be spared, in conjunction with Richard and his remaining friends, against the senior Appellants of Gloucester, Arundel and Warwick and the

Commons, who continued to push for a prosecution. Unfortunately for Burley, even the King's and Queen's personal pleas were not enough to save him from a conviction of treason, although some of the worst aspects of the execution were mitigated – he was allowed to walk to Tower Hill, rather than being drawn on a hurdle, and was beheaded rather than being hanged. It was perhaps little consolation for Burley, and a moment that Richard would not forget that he would contemplate as he retired to lick his wounds and recover. He was once again a monarch in name only, with governance of the country now in the hands of the Appellants, who shored up their power with a ceremonial re-coronation of the King before the high altar of Westminster Abbey, and legislation to ensure that the work of the 1388 Parliament would not be undone in the future. The Archbishop of Canterbury pronounced a sentence of excommunication of anyone attempting to do so, while Parliament itself declared that any such individual would themselves be charged with treason. A series of pardons and indemnities were issued to those who had taken part in proceedings in order to secure themselves against future prosecution.

It is perhaps telling that a further declaration recognised the gross expansion of the definition of treason which had developed over a short period of time in the winter and spring of 1387–8, and stated that: ' ... even though various points were declared treason in this present parliament which had not previously been declared by statute, no justice shall have the power to pass judgement on another case of treason, nor in any fashion which has not been obtained before the beginning of this present parliament.' Such a statement was clearly intended to limit the definition of treason at common or civil law to that defined in 1352, yet the use of the 'law [or procedure] of parliament' utilised on an ad hoc basis by a small group of nobles, backed by a supportive Commons, offered a new way for treason to be expanded and shaped. In 1388 the Appellants proved that using the language of treason effectively – and the emotions of disloyalty that it provoked – alongside a tactic of wide-ranging charges, some of which might be legally dubious – meant that a faction with support across the Houses could utilise Parliament as a powerful weapon to their own ends. Such a precedent had long-term implications, as we shall see, but for the Lords Appellant, their actions of 1388 would seal their own fates within a decade.

In the aftermath of the Merciless Parliament, the Appellants initially took over the mechanics of government, with Richard taking little active role. The return of a stabilising presence in his uncle, John of Gaunt, a counterbalance to Gloucester and his influence, alongside a new sense of mediation on the King's part saw him take a new, more assertive stance, and in 1389 Richard was able to bring the period of Appellant rule to an end peacefully. Richard's sense of his own royal dignity and kingship was by no means reduced, however, and throughout the 1390s he was swift to react to criticism, particularly from the Commons, but a sense of moderation and control now eased the difficulties which might arise among a powerful noble class. Interestingly he once again looked back to Edward II's reign, and the precedents of royal majesty from previous reigns, including imagery of his great-grandfather in the margins of texts, and commissioning in 1389/90 a volume of statutes relating to the prior king's reign, among others, which Nigel Saul has described as 'a manifesto for the reassertion of royal power'. This included a copy of the 'Ordinances' of 1311, the restrictions placed on Richard's predecessor by his peerage and clergy, just as he himself had been restricted by Parliament. The 'Ordinances' had also been the focus of the specific question posed to the judges in 1387, and Richard's interrogation of the latter clearly demonstrates a fascination with the precedents of royal power, and the constraints that had unjustly been placed on the Crown and his predecessors. He also became increasingly paranoid, surrounding himself with a bodyguard of Cheshire archers at all times.

In a brief spell between July and September 1397, the balance of power would swing back once again towards the Crown, a period often described as the 'Tyranny of Richard II', as the King re-established his reign and took dramatic revenge on the Appellants in Parliament. Grievances between the royalists and Appellants had revived and increased during the previous years and months, and it is possible that a plot was building against the

King (or at least the suspicion of one), which caused Richard to take drastic action. On 10 July 1397 the senior Appellants were suddenly arrested at the Crown's orders. Unlike in 1387, however, Richard now moved quickly and efficiently, seizing the initiative throughout. Gloucester was spirited away to Calais to the custody of Thomas Mowbray, Earl of Nottingham and captain of Calais. Arundel was sent to the Isle of Wight, and Warwick to the Tower, so that the three men couldn't coordinate as they had done a decade before. For those who had been involved in the events of 1388 this was a clear warning, and Richard had to calm nerves a few days later, stating that the three men had been arrested for new crimes, not for the actions of the Merciless Parliament. This – as would become clear when the charges were brought – was a complete fallacy but served to temporarily calm matters. On 18 July writs were issued summoning a parliament to meet in September, where the senior Appellants would be tried: the 'Revenge Parliament' of 1397–8.

With Westminster Hall out of action on account of ongoing building works, a temporary but dramatic marquee structure was constructed in the yard outside. Richard sat on an elevated throne with hundreds (if not thousands) of the King's own Cheshire archers assembled alongside the armed forces of his supporters. This was a stage upon which royal revenge could be meted out in symbolic fashion. It was also a dramatic display of force. The King positioned his archers so that they surrounded proceedings, primed to shoot if trouble broke out. In the opening speech on Monday 17 September, Richard announced a general pardon to those present, although crucially with exceptions, fifty men 'whom it would please the king to name, and all those who will be impeached in the present parliament' were excluded. This was an absolute masterstroke by Richard: by holding back the names of these fifty men temporarily, he both encouraged those who harboured guilty thoughts to approach the King or his officials to work out whether they were included among the unnamed men, and to broker individual pardons. It allowed the King to root out further dissatisfaction among his subjects, while maintaining an element of calm among those present at Westminster.

With appointments made, the religious members of Parliament were sent away, a sure sign that capital punishment was on the cards, and as they retired a certain 'bustle' in the crowd almost led to Richard's Cheshire archers opening fire, and the three senior Appellants were soon indicted for treason. Warwick, however, was deemed a lesser party than Gloucester and Arundel, and was alleged to have been drawn into the plot by his associates. Despite Richard's earlier claims, all of the charges related back to the events of 1386–8. Charges were brought – of coercing the King into agreeing to a commission and accroaching the royal power through this act; of rising up in rebellion against him in 1387; and of forcing him to oversee the execution of men Richard believed to be innocent, namely Simon Burley. The Archbishop of Canterbury, Thomas Arundel, the Earl's brother – one of those who had reproached and threatened the King alongside Gloucester in 1386 – was also charged as a traitor and impeached for his role in the commission and the Merciless Parliament, as well as for procuring a pardon for the Appellants to cover their conduct in 1388. Richard and his supporters also railed against the commission of government, declaring that it had been illegal and was repealed, with any future attempt to produce such a policy deemed treasonous. Finally, the pardon of 1388 was repealed, leaving the Appellants open to Richard's justice.

On Friday 21 September, however, the main business of Richard's 'Revenge Parliament' got under way with the trial of the Earl of Arundel, one of the most dramatic incidents as recounted by the chroniclers. With John of Gaunt, acting as Steward of England, presiding over events, Arundel walked into the room clad in a robe with a scarlet hood, which he promptly removed, and claimed the pardons which he had been granted in 1388 and 1394, which had just been repealed. If the authors of the Tract (an account of proceedings which would later be circulated and formed the basis of multiple chronicle descriptions) are to be believed, the trial soon descended into a series of insults between the two men, Gaunt replied to Arundel's claims with 'That pardon is revoked, traitor', and questioned why, if he was not a traitor, he might need a pardon.

Arundel's response was cutting, 'To silence the tongues of my enemies, of whom you are one,' before rounding on the assembled Commons in fury. When Henry, Earl of Derby, one of the junior Appellants, stated that Arundel had plotted to seize Richard in 1387, he too was met with the fierce response: 'You, Henry, Earl of Derby, you lie in your teeth! I never said anything to you or to anyone else about my lord the king except what was to his welfare and honour.'

Returning to the events of 1388, Richard now reminded Arundel of the desperate pleas both he and the Queen had made to spare Burley's life back in 1388, which the earl had ignored. Arundel by this stage in proceedings, if not before, had realised the likely outcome, and moved from anger and insults to a stoic silence, refusing to answer any of the charges against him, or to confess, claiming only his royal pardon, despite being informed by the Chief Justice of his fate should he continue in this way: ' ... of which the Earl of Arundel, notwithstanding the repeal of the aforesaid pardon and charter, did not speak, nor did he wish to say anything else, unless it was to ask for allowance of the aforesaid charter and pardon.'

Arundel's silence and stubbornness sealed his fate, and he was sentenced to death as a traitor by beheading the same day at Tower Hill, where Burley had been executed a decade previously. The chronicle accounts, many of which sought to portray Arundel as a martyr standing up to an over-mighty king, present dramatic scenes at his execution. According to the St Albans' account, Arundel's body rose up after his head had been struck off with a single sword blow, remaining upright for as long as it took to recite the Lord's Prayer, before falling back down again, while other reports stressed the earl's calmness and fortitude as he proceeded to his death.

With the first Appellant out of the way, a writ was now sent to Calais requesting that the Duke of Gloucester, the King's uncle, be brought to Westminster for his trial. This was almost certainly an entirely disingenuous move from the King, as Gloucester was most probably already dead, reportedly smothered with a featherbed at the King's request in the Prince's Inn at Calais. It was too risky to bring him to trial, for fear that Gaunt – Gloucester's brother – might refuse to pass judgement on him, or that Gloucester might be able to win over supporters through his defence. Instead, the hearing was presented with a 'confession' from the duke acknowledging his crimes:

> I, Thomas of Woodstock [Duke of Gloucester], in the year of my lord the king one-and-twenty, in the castle of Calais by virtue of a commission of my lord the king, in the same year directed to William Rickhill justice … I, amongst others, restrained my lord in his freedom, and amongst others took royal power upon myself, truly not knowing or understanding at that time, as I did afterwards, and do now, that I acted against his estate or regality. And because I knew afterwards that I had done wrong, and had taken upon myself more than I ought to do, I submitted myself to my lord, and prayed for his mercy and grace, and this I do as lowly and humbly as any man can, and I place myself high and low in his mercy and in his grace, as he has always been full of mercy and grace to all others … Also, in that I took my lord's letters from his messengers, and opened them without his permission, I acknowledge that I did evil: wherefore I place myself lowly in his grace.

Gloucester's 'confession' had been taken by William Rickhill, one of the King's justices, who had been sent to Calais on 17 August, and was able to secure a (possibly forced) confession on 8 September. Rickhill would be exonerated in the later investigation and trial of those accused of the murder, and the sterile nature of the Parliament rolls that recorded his statement plays down the suggestion of coercion. It was, however, extremely convenient for Richard to be able to produce the evidence of a confession, without fear of his uncle's presence at Westminster. Gloucester was found guilty posthumously and his estates were forfeited, along with the right for his heirs to use the royal arms as a direct descendant of Edward III.

With two of the senior Appellants now dead, the Earl of Warwick, older than the other two men, was brought into proceedings on the penultimate day of the parliamentary sitting. Any defiance he may have felt was swept away when he was faced with his likely fate, and the earl broke down, confessing his guilt and 'sobbing and whining ... like a wretched old woman', bringing many of those present to tears as they witnessed proceedings. Taking pity on him despite his guilty sentence, and relishing the sole personal confession to come from the three trials, the King opted to commute Warwick's death sentence to a life of exile on the Isle of Man with an annual living of 500 marks for him and his wife. In public at least, the two junior Appellants were forgiven, and commended for their loyal work in having restrained their senior peers. The Earl of Derby, Henry Bolingbroke, who was first cousin to the King, was even promoted to the dukedom of Hereford and would later seek a royal pardon for his actions in 1387–8, although whether he was fully reconciled with the regime at this point remains uncertain.

Alongside the business of the trials themselves, treason was once again redefined in four points. Plotting and planning the death of the king remained treasonous, but new or tweaked definitions were also included. The second point of treason added deposition of the king (or a plot and plan to do so) into the definition; the third added withdrawing of a subject's liege homage; and the fourth stated that to raise the people and ride against the king to wage war within his kingdom was treasonous (a subtle shift in emphasis of the previous 1352 and 1381 legislation). As in the previous parliaments, which had operated outside the statutory boundaries of treason, the members of 1397 were made to take solemn oaths in Westminster Abbey, declaring that none of the decisions made would be annulled, although their oath was given additional bite by a ruling to declare any such attempt treasonous in and of itself. This was likely an attempt to consolidate Richard's victories while Parliament was prorogued between the end of September and the start of 1398, and may have been tempered slightly when the second session reconvened and began the business of undoing the work of the Merciless Parliament, breaking the oath sworn a decade previously. Such a precedent must have been clear to all present – parliamentary procedure could be undone, even that which had been sworn to under oath, but only from a position of absolute power. On the surface it may have seemed to many around Westminster in 1397 that Richard had finally secured his throne and taken a firm grip on Parliament and its procedures, to the extent that by the time the second session began in January 1398, he was confident enough to contemplate asking for money. The hard-won victories that he had achieved, however, may have given the King a hubristic surge of over-confidence. He had never flown as high as he did in 1397. But within two years Richard would lose his wealth, his throne, and his life through a series of disastrous missteps.

Exactly how Richard's plans fell apart between January 1398 and his deposition in October 1399 is at times difficult to comprehend, but revolved around Henry, the new Duke of Hereford, one of the junior Appellants of 1387–8. Having secured his own royal dignity and majesty in the wake of the first session of the 1397 Parliament, Richard now sought to mend the issues of the past. He gave pardons to Hereford and to Thomas Mowbray, the new Duke of Norfolk, both of whom had played minor parts in 1387–8, for restraining the worst instincts of the Appellants. Richard may have underestimated the level of discontent and rivalry that remained among his nobility, exacerbated by the fact that he had yet to father a son. While he remained without a suitable heir, the question of who from among the nobility would succeed him persisted, prompting rivalries, rumours and noble gossip to spread throughout the kingdom. Richard's failure to keep control of his nobles would finally bring him down.

Rumour and rivalry would spill into the open at the start of the following year. On Wednesday 30 January 1398 Hereford read a bill to the second sitting of the 'Revenge Parliament' at Shrewsbury, in which he made several allusions to a plot against the King, certain nobles (including Hereford himself), and key judgements of Parliament going back to Edward II's reign relating to the Lancastrian inheritance.

The plot, Henry claimed, had been told to him in confidence by the Duke of Norfolk, the man who (it would later be claimed) had arranged for Gloucester's murder in Calais the previous year, sparked by fears that the pardons of 1397 were to be revoked. Having already informed the King of the alleged plot (perhaps through his father, John of Gaunt), Henry's repetition of the details in Parliament was intended to give Norfolk the right of response, but he failed to show up at Westminster and Richard broke up the parliamentary sitting a few days later. Instead, the matter was referred to a parliamentary committee, established to deal with various petitions that had been received but not considered (and whose scope would later be extended by the King). It was decided that the dispute would be settled through trial by battle on 16 September, an occasion which promised to be a major social event. But at the final minute (and once everyone had arrived to see the spectacle), Richard stepped in, cancelling the battle and exiling the two noblemen instead. Norfolk was exiled for life, while Hereford was exiled for ten years under the authority of the new parliamentary committee, and both men were given royal letters promising to honour any inheritances which might accrue to them while abroad. It is unclear why Richard decided to intervene, unless his intentions were to rid himself of two troublesome nobles at the same time. If so, his rehabilitation of the junior Appellant Hereford in 1397–8 may have been disingenuous, but in any case it is clear that Richard fundamentally mismanaged the situation.

If Richard's intervention was a misstep, re-opening as it did the possibility of discontent among his leading nobles, he would miscalculate once more in February 1399, this time fatally. The Hereford v. Norfolk dispute had ultimately arisen over concerns that the King's word was no longer to be trusted, particularly with regard to pardons and other royal grants. From now, those doubting the King's trustworthiness were proved correct. Having guaranteed to honour any inheritance claims of the two exiled lords, Richard's promise was tested for the first time with the death of John of Gaunt, Henry's father, in the early months of 1399. Gaunt's estates, as the Duke of Lancaster, were extensive and extremely valuable, and would have established Henry as one of the most powerful lords in the realm, as his father had been before him. This was too big a prize for Richard to resist. By March he had gone back on his word, revoking his previous letters of confirmation by claiming the Lancaster estates for himself.

Seizing the opportunity while Richard was travelling to Ireland, Henry sailed for England to reclaim his inheritance, landing at Ravenspur on the Humber estuary early in July 1399 and marching across Yorkshire, claiming he was only seeking the return of his inheritance and ancestral estates. Supporters soon flocked to his side, while Richard was slow to return, haemorrhaging support in the process. As his troops and lords capitulated or deserted one by one, Richard's position soon became untenable and he was captured by Henry at Conway Castle in North Wales. Unlike in 1327, Henry and his noble supporters now had a precedent to fall back on – the deposition of Edward II; and as in the previous coup, they presented the usurpation as a willing abdication. The 'Record and Process' – the official Lancastrian account of events – stated that, 'with a cheerful countenance', Richard agreed to abdicate, naming Henry as his successor. This was – of course – pure propaganda. Other contemporary writers recorded that Henry offered a peaceful settlement provided three demands were met: that his inheritance would be restored; that five of the King's councillors would be tried for treason; and that a parliament would be called, in which Henry would act as Steward of England. The parallels between 1399 and the strategy of an earlier Lord of Lancaster during Edward II's reign are striking, as the position of Steward was once again brought to the fore. After consideration, Richard agreed to his demands, but by the time the 'parliament' met in September 1399 he was no longer on the throne. Here the precedent of Edward II became difficult. Henry seems to have followed a similar approach to 1327, declaring several charges against the King including that he was unduly influenced, had lost Scotland and was guilty of neglect and dilapidation, but while Edward II had clearly been deposed (rather than had abdicated), in a legal sense he had not been. Further precedents were sought for Richard, and eventually a papal deposition from 1245 was used to justify the process of Richard's deposition under Church law, in combination with the Edwardian precedent. This was once again a dubious approach, as was Henry's own emerging claim to the throne. Refraining from declaring his right to the throne by conquest – even though he essentially had – he instead made an argument based on his descent from Henry III in the male line (disregarding the fact that under this argument there was, in fact, another, better qualified candidate in terms of descent in the Earl of March, Edmund Mortimer). Henry and his advisers now proceeded with a shaky compromise of half-formed, legally dubious arguments and eventually succeeded in forcing Richard from his throne. On 1 October 1399 news of his formal deposition in 'parliament' was delivered to Richard in the Tower, and a new parliament was called in the name of Henry IV. The precedents of Edward II's reign continued. Richard was sentenced to life imprisonment, and it is possible that a trial of the former king was contemplated. At this point, however, Parliament was not so brazen as to openly place a king on trial. That would come centuries later. By the following February, however, Richard was dead, in all likelihood secretly murdered. His death was explained as a combination of grief and abstinence from food, and his body displayed in public in an attempt to quash rumours of his survival. The 'tyranny' of Richard II was finally at an end.

Indictment of Eleanor Cobham and her associates, accused of using magic and necromancy to predict the King's death. (1441. KB 9/72)

Three

TREASONOUS WORDS AND TREASONOUS WOMEN, 1402–42

For one thing I say: say you not another day that you
are not warned about the things that may befall ...
I commit myself to the Devil, ever to lie in hell, body
and soul without departing ... if that person that was
sometime King Richard be not alive in Scotland.

WORDS OF JOHN WYGHTLOK, C.1413

One of the first tasks for the new king, Henry IV (1367–1413), was to right the wrongs of Richard II's final years in power. Those who had supported him in the deposition were protected, and all those who had been charged with treason in the 1397–8 Parliament had their judgements reversed, with the acts of that Parliament overturned. Those who were alleged to have killed Gloucester in the Prince's Inn in Calais, or been implicated, were brought before Henry in Parliament and examined. Furthermore, on account of the new forms of treason which had been declared by Richard in his 'Revenge Parliament', a decision was made to return the definition of treason as it was codified in 1352:

Whereas in the said Parliament holden the said one and twentieth year of the said late King Richard, diverse pains of Treason were ordained by Statute, in as much that there was no Man which did know how he ought to behave himself, to do, speak, or say, for doubt of such pains ... That in no time to come any Treason be judged otherwise than it was ordained by the Statute in the time of his noble grandfather King Edward the third.

It soon became clear, however, that this reset of treason legislation was not as comprehensive as it seemed. A new form of construction – if not a new form of treason itself – was advanced for the first time by the royal justices in response to rumours of the deposed King's escape and plots to restore him in 1402. They now sought to prosecute treasonous words. At least five cases of treason by words were recorded in 1402 alone, four of which were related to sightings of a 'false Richard'. In one case, a group of Franciscan friars had been told that Richard was alive and well in Wales. In the same year, a Cardiff man, John Sperhauk, had overheard a woman casting aspersions on the new King's lineage and claim to the throne, while declaring support for the rebel Owen Glyn Dŵr. Sperhauk later repeated these claims himself, and found himself charged with treason. All parties received the full traitor's death. None of these spoken words could be easily argued under the 1352 Act, but the royal justices, and probably Henry himself, claimed that such words acted to excite the people against their king to the destruction of the realm and that those speaking such words were compassing and imagining the death of the king, his magnates, and subjects. Intriguingly a chronicle account of these incidents describes Henry as personally interrogating two of the suspects, and asking one of the friars whom he would support if Henry and Richard were fighting on the battlefield. When the man replied the latter (although stating he just wanted to return Henry to his previous title of Duke of Lancaster), the King had all the justification he needed to force through a charge of treason. The new crimes (of both written and spoken words deemed to be treasonous) had to be framed within the old limits of the 1352 Act, but now set a clear precedent for a monarch who wished to crack down on rumour and loose-lipped subjects. That the

Crown was willing to push for such instances to reach a firm conclusion was further highlighted by the jury who declared the Franciscans guilty, and later sought the compassion of their fellow friars, weeping and claiming that they had been intimidated into providing their verdict.

In some cases, the actual words used by those condemned as traitors were themselves recorded in the vernacular English in the official legal process, capturing the spoken or written word on parchment. In the 1402 trial of another Franciscan, Nicholas Louthe, it was recorded that he had told a barber in the village of Walkern of Richard's survival, information he himself had been told by a woman in Westminster, who claimed that she had seen the former king and recognised him by a mark on his face and a distinctive white gown he was wearing. A letter Louthe had been carrying, which was recorded in the original English within the official Latin and French record, further implicated him, although not enough to warrant a charge of treason in and of itself. Taken together, however, and with what appears to be a forced confession under torture, these two sources of evidence gave the King's justices enough material to construct a charge of treason.

Of course, many of those who spoke treasonous words were indeed plotting, or undertaking acts which did fall under the original clauses of 1352. In 1413 John Wyghtlok found himself before the King's Bench on treason charges, having posted a series of anti-Lancastrian bills around London and its hinterland, stating that Richard II was still alive, that the recently deceased Henry IV had suffered from leprosy as punishment for the late King's deposition, and attacking the legitimacy of the new King, Henry V. Wyghtlok, who had been one of Richard's servants, claimed he had been with the deposed monarch in Scotland, where he was in the care of the Duke of Albany. He stated in his bill – which was enclosed with his official indictment – that he would submit himself to be imprisoned while his claim was tested (provided he was not mistreated while in prison), and if his claim was found to be false, he would submit himself to whatever 'vile death' was chosen by the justices. Through his association with the Scots (and allegedly the Welsh), Wyghtlok was open to a clear charge of adhering to the King's enemies, and indeed the enrolled proceedings of the King's Bench stated that he and his associates had brought a group of Scottish spies to Westminster without licence to look around. It was also claimed that he had previously been indicted and sentenced to death for his bill-spreading activities and that he had remained in hiding in the years since.

Wyghtlok's case was complicated – not least because he appears to have been part of a group known as the 'Lollards', deemed by the Lancastrian dynasty to be dangerous heretics with a strong political (as well as religious) agenda – and came at a time when the connections between heresy and treason were developing and overlapping. The Lollards – a proto-Protestant group who followed the teachings of Oxford theologian John Wycliffe and believed in a process of Church reform, personal connections to God, and the translation of the Bible into English – had been the subject of new legislation in 1406 that aimed to punish those spreading their doctrines. They were also politically active, particularly when it came to distributing bills and texts and preaching their doctrine, which often focused on the deposed king and the legitimacy of the new Lancastrian regime, and it was these activities that were the particular focus of 1406, delivered in deliberately obscure legislation which linked concepts of heresy and treasonous acts. In the face of the Crown's religious and political concerns in 1413, which would soon break out into a major Lollard uprising, Wyghtlok's trial was clearly manipulated by the Crown to reinforce the new King's strength and legitimacy. Henry V even attended in person – but he was not to get the result he hoped for. When asked to respond to the charges of treason brought against him, Wyghtlok asserted that he was not guilty, and was sent to the Tower while a jury was assembled. His statement would never be tested as he escaped from the Tower, aided by two officials, a sub-janitor and a servant of the keeper of the royal wardrobe. While Wyghtlok escaped, the janitor, Richard Bache, would not be so lucky. Outlawed for his role in events, he was later captured and drawn, hanged and beheaded in Wyghtlok's place.

If Henry V had wished Wyghtlok's trial to draw a line under the threat of bill-casters, Lollards and political dissent, and demonstrate his political strength and legitimacy, he had failed. That same year, a major uprising under the Lollard knight Sir John Oldcastle, Lord Cobham, would begin, in which Oldcastle would first be convicted of heresy, and then indicted for treason for leading a revolt against the Crown. In response to the uprising, the Crown pursued a huge investigation into Lollards around the country, headed up by some of the leading English nobles, with nearly 200 surviving records for ten rural counties and Bristol, detailing a variety of treason and heresy charges brought against individuals in a complicated mix of treasonous words, thoughts and beliefs. At the same time, new legislation was brought forward in Parliament, which explicitly linked heresy with the language of treason (even if the word 'treason' itself was never used) and expanded the concept of treasonous speech that Henry IV, and now Henry V, pursued as a useful political tool. Heresy, the statute said, had as its aim 'destroying our most sovereign lord the king himself and all the various estates of the same kingdom ... and also all manner of governance, and ultimately the laws of the land' and the statute set in place new measures to investigate, and root out, all heresies.

Oldcastle was captured in 1417 (having previously escaped the Tower), tried in Parliament, and condemned to death as both a traitor and a heretic. He was drawn from the Tower to gallows in the parish of St Giles outside Old Temple Bar in London, where he was hanged. He was not, however, quartered or beheaded: a new punishment for his heretical treason was devised to link the two concepts of treason and heresy. A fire was lit under the gallows, from which Oldcastle was suspended as the fire consumed the gallows, at once hanged for treason and burnt for heresy. A new precedent had been set, in which an individual's thoughts and beliefs could be treasonous, as well as their words.

TREASONOUS WOMEN

Farewell, all wealth and the world so wide.
I am assigned where I shall be;
Under men's keeping I must abide.
All women may beware by me.
'THE LAMENT OF THE DUCHESS OF GLOUCESTER',
FIFTEENTH CENTURY

In the summer of 1441, a great unseasonal storm hit the city of London, with heavy rain, hail and lightning forcing the citizens to remain in their houses. According to one contemporary chronicle, this great tempest had been caused by 'wicked fiends and spirits', conjured out of hell by a collection of clerks and 'wicches', with the purpose of 'destroying certain men and women, or whom they list, unto death'. Whatever the causes of the storm, supernatural or otherwise, it was soon linked in the chronicler's mind with the *cause célèbre* of the day, the investigation and trial of Eleanor Cobham, Duchess of Gloucester, and her associates on charges of necromancy, sorcery and treason, a case which would capture the public imagination throughout the second half of 1441 and beyond.

Eleanor and her husband Humphrey, Duke of Gloucester had gained significant prominence at court during the minority of Henry VI, Humphrey's nephew, who had gained the throne at the age of just nine months. Ambitious, extravagant and intellectual in their tastes, the couple were also next in line to the throne should anything happen to the young King. Once Henry had come of age in 1436, and began to rule in his own right, however, their influence at court began to wane. By 1440, Gloucester was becoming increasingly isolated by his rivals within the Royal Council led by his uncle Cardinal Henry Beaufort, while his marriage to Eleanor had been controversial from the start. She was his second wife and had been his mistress during his first marriage to Jacqueline of Hainault, whom she served as a lady-in-waiting. The Pope had annulled Humphrey and Jacqueline's marriage in 1428, in response to international concerns, but for Humphrey to then immediately marry one of his former wife's ladies-in-waiting, alongside Eleanor's alleged flaunting of her new status, seems to have made her deeply unpopular in some circles.

The Gloucesters may have expected to weather the factional disputes and unpopularity at court – they did after all share many intellectual and humanist traits with a young king who was in the process of establishing grand new educational foundations at Eton College and King's College in Cambridge – except for Eleanor's clear interest in the occult. This in itself was not unusual, and seems to reflect a more general interest in occult matters among women at the time – Queen Joan of Navarre (the wife of Henry IV) had been accused of being a witch during the reign of her stepson Henry V, and many noblewomen at the time owned items such as horoscopes and astrological tables. On the evening of 28 or 29 June 1441, while out dining at the King's Head in Cheapside, Eleanor learned that three of her associates and servants had been accused of conspiring to bring about Henry VI's death by means of necromancy and sorcery. Roger Bolingbroke, a priest from Oxford and a member of Humphrey's household, Thomas Southwell, a physician and canon of St Stephen's Chapel at Westminster, and John Home, a canon of Hereford and St Asaph and Eleanor's personal chaplain, all faced charges, even if Eleanor was yet to be implicated. They were initially accused of limited crimes – Bolingbroke was charged with using necromancy against the King, Southwell with celebrating an unlawful mass at Hornsey Park using heretical items and Home with taking part in both acts – and the authorities stepped in quickly to investigate. Southwell was soon arrested, placed in the Tower of London and stripped of his position at St Stephen's as early as 10 July, while Bolingbroke was initially placed under strict supervision by the council (possibly to see if he implicated any other associates), and was eventually brought in for questioning two days after his accomplice. Treasonous necromancy in this context involved both the imagining of the King's death and the pursuit of potentially dangerous magical outcomes, but had a further component. If the people of the realm heard rumours or stories about the King's imminent demise (if that was what the horoscope predicted), it was thought – or so the Crown argued – that they might withdraw their love from him, which in itself would cause the King to sadden and thus hasten his demise. The argument involved a considerable amount of construction, but soon became commonplace in such charges throughout the fifteenth century and beyond.

It was at this point that Eleanor probably first became implicated in the investigation, almost certainly during Bolingbroke's interrogation and, under cover of darkness, fled to the sanctuary at Westminster Abbey. But as investigations continued, events started to snowball, and Eleanor found herself summoned to St Stephen's Chapel within the Palace of Westminster to answer the charges of felony and treason which had been made against her. She presented herself before a council of archbishops, cardinals and bishops, as well as doctors of divinity on 24 July and was formally examined on twenty-eight separate charges, to each of which she protested her innocence. She was allowed to return to sanctuary temporarily while her answers were considered, but she was not the only member of the alleged conspiracy to be examined that day.

Bolingbroke had also been brought in for examination by the spiritual council, probably so he could make a formal accusation of Eleanor's involvement. He had been made to stage a very public recanting of his heretical beliefs at St Paul's Cross the previous day, in which he had sat on a scaffold wearing a paper crown and, surrounded by the tools of his necromancy, was subjected to ridicule in the presence of the council and a large crowd, while a sermon was preached.

When she was summoned back to St Stephen's the following day, Eleanor was faced by her former associate, who now provided evidence against her. Under further examination, she had no option but to admit to five of the charges (although which charges specifically is not made clear in chronicle accounts), and the council ordered that she should be sent to Leeds Castle in Kent, until her punishment could be agreed. It is possible that she attempted to escape from the council's custody to avoid being taken to Kent, and furthermore she seems to have feigned sickness in order to postpone the journey to the fortified location, from which escape would have been considerably more difficult, but such tactics would not last long. On 9 August she was ordered by royal letters patent to appear before Archbishop Chichele on 21 October, with a warning that no one was to interfere with the process of her imprisonment at Leeds, possibly indicating that further escape plots may have been suspected.

With the heretical aspects of the case having been assessed by the leading spiritual authorities, the secular arm of the investigation moved into place. On Wednesday 26 July, the day after her first admission, a commission of enquiry was ordered to examine events in London, with a series of investigations looking for evidence of felonies or treasonable acts with which the conspiracy could be charged, which would also come with the possibility of the death penalty (a sentence which the religious authorities could not pose). For women, the penalty for high treason was to be drawn to the place of execution and then burned – rather than being hanged, drawn, and quartered – and for petty treason the penalty for women was restricted to being burned at the stake. There was a precedent for female traitors in place by the fifteenth century. In Eleanor's alleged crimes, however, the council were faced with an additional and significant problem. How should a duchess, a peeress, married to the King's uncle, be tried? The process for male nobles was well established: under clause 39 of Magna Carta free men should be tried in all such cases by a jury of their peers or by the law of the land. It did not, however, make any mention of how a woman should be tried. Neither was there any applicable precedent, despite the fact that a royal peeress had been accused of a similar offence, treason by necromancy and sorcery, within living memory. For, as recently as 1419, Queen Joan of Navarre – the Duke of Gloucester's stepmother and second wife of Henry IV – had been accused of plotting to kill her stepson, Henry V, by means of witchcraft, after her husband's death.

Joan – who had been accused by her confessor (also implicated in the alleged treasonable acts) – had been placed under a form of house arrest for almost three years, albeit in relative comfort. She had not, however, ever been tried for her alleged crimes, in either a secular or religious tribunal. Indeed, the accusation appears to have been a crude means of temporarily seizing her substantial dowry to boost English cash flow during a tricky financial period, playing on societal and royal fears of witchcraft in a period when the Crown felt compelled to ask the Church to pray for protection against potential attacks from necromancers. Rather than risking the difficulties of a full trial, which was without precedent in post-Conquest England, and which had the potential to shame and even to condemn his stepmother, Henry V had opted for caution. A similar sense of reluctance seems to have been felt towards Eleanor some twenty years later. While the council opted to proceed with the secular arm of the enquiry, its primary focus was the actions of Bolingbroke and Southwell, with Eleanor's role limited to that of an accessory, whether they were acting on her behalf or not. Even if Eleanor was not, however, the principal defendant, the investigation soon brought out further details about her role in the affairs which had taken place.

The King's Bench indictments (the only official part of trial proceedings known to survive) details charges of sorcery and treason against the accused, claiming that Bolingbroke, Southwell and Home had used magical figures, implements, vestments and other artefacts at various times between 1440 and 1441, and at three London churches, St Martin in the Vintry, St Benet Hith and St Sepulchre. While Southwell chanted protective masses, the other parties were alleged to have invoked various demons and spirits in order to predict when the King would die, an event they believed would take place in late May or early June 1441. The prophesied cause of death was given as 'melancholy'. Eleanor had allegedly encouraged the three men and promised them gifts for their actions, as she wanted to know when she would become queen, while simultaneously promoting the rumour of Henry's apparently imminent demise in order to weaken him further. Perhaps most damning for Eleanor, however, was the appearance of a further character in the accusation, one Margery Jourdemain, known as the 'Witch of Eye next Westminster'. Margery was seemingly a well-known witch at the time, and it was noted in the inquisition that she had been employed by Eleanor for some years as a sorceress, concocting potions and remedies in order to help Eleanor conceive a child, but allegedly also to make Humphrey, Duke of Gloucester fall in love with her in the first place. The latter accusation may have simply been the consequence of the apparent unpopularity of the couple's marriage – especially given Eleanor's earlier position as lady-in-waiting to Humphrey's previous duchess – but the former charge seems more likely, and indeed Eleanor admitted in her later examination that she had used sorcery to try to conceive a child with Humphrey. The length of Margery's employment within Eleanor's household cannot be determined with any accuracy, although she had seemingly been working as a sorceress for much of the previous decade, and had been temporarily imprisoned in Windsor as early as 1430 for an unspecified crime involving sorcery.

It was this charge that would be the final straw for Eleanor. She was already facing punishment for the charges she had admitted to on 25 July, and now the secular investigation provided further evidence against her. Appearing at St Stephens on the prescribed date of 21 October, Eleanor was re-examined by the panel of leading spiritual figures (with the exception of Chichele, who was absent on grounds of ill health) and, as previously, admitted to a limited number of the charges against her. Two days later, however, her associates were brought before her to provide their evidence. Bolingbroke was once again present, with some of the artefacts of his necromancy, as was Southwell, but this time there was a third witness, Margery Jourdemaine. In the face of their evidence, Eleanor denied all charges of treason as she had before, but now admitted that she had encouraged her three associates to perform certain magical rituals in order to try and conceive a child with Humphrey. Combined with the previous admissions, this seems to have satisfied the council and spiritual authorities. Crucially for Eleanor no secular prosecutions – including those for treason – were to be brought against her, the charges and punishments were all of a spiritual nature only. She was allowed to abjure herself of her heresies, and was sent away to prepare for her penance to be decreed.

Her associates, however, were not as lucky. Three of the four were charged, Bolingbroke and Southwell with sorcery, felony and treason, and Jourdemaine with heresy. Bolingbroke and Southwell were sent to the Tower to await their prosecution in the secular courts, although Southwell would never find himself before the court, dying in the Tower three days later, possibly having taken his own life in anticipation of the brutal execution that he faced. Margery recanted her heresy, although unfortunately for her, her prior offences now caught up with her. Having previously been imprisoned for heretical misdeeds, her release had been conditional on an oath to set aside such practices, and the present charge clearly broke those conditions. Margery was handed over to the sheriffs of London, taken to Smithfield and burned at the stake on the same day. Further investigations were commissioned two days later, in order to find out the extent of necromancy around the country, and 'diverse doctors, clerks and notaries' were sent out to assess this, a process which cost the Crown £20.

As Eleanor had admitted to the use of fertility and love potions in the past during her examination, the first stage in her punishment was the annulment of her marriage to Humphrey on 6 November, on the basis that it had never been legal due to the use of sorcery. Three days later, details of her penance were announced by Chichele and the rest of the ecclesiastical commission. Eleanor was sentenced to walk through London on foot in a penitential fashion, dressed in black and bare-headed, carrying a lit taper of wax in her hand, on three separate market days in the following week, when the crowds would be gathered to see her plight. The crowds were ordered not to molest the fallen duchess – and she was escorted by two knights to ensure this – but for her shame, they were also not to show her any respect. On Monday 13 November she was taken by boat from Westminster to the pier at Temple, and proceeded down Fleet Street to St Paul's, where she was to present the candle and pray at the high altar. Two days later, on the Wednesday, she was taken, again by boat, to Swan Pier off Thames Street, walking north through the streets of London, past the busy Leadenhall Market, and east to Aldgate, where she again presented a candle and prayed. On Friday she endured the last of her journeys, travelling by boat to Queenhithe before heading north to one of the busiest streets in London, Cheapside, along which she proceeded east to the church of St Michael's Cornhill, where she completed the now familiar process of offerings and prayer.

The public aspects of the case reached their final stages the following day, Saturday 18 November, when Bolingbroke was brought from custody to the Guildhall in London. Once again, threats of an escape were on the council's mind, with Bolingbroke's gaoler later claiming money for the costs associated with his imprisonment, which included the use of boats, carts and additional guards over a period of eight weeks. There he was condemned for necromancy and treason by the Chief Justice of the King's Bench and drawn to Tyburn, where he was executed in the traditional form for traitors. The four quarters of his body were sent to various centres of Lollardy and heresy (although the chronicles do not agree on which). He claimed innocence from the charges until his final breath. The final associate in the plot, John Home, had received a royal pardon the previous day.

Eleanor's fate had not yet been decided; despite having been duly punished by the ecclesiastic authorities, she had escaped secular punishment, and again the Crown and council seem to have been guided by the precedent of Queen Joan. On 19 January 1442 after half a year of investigations, accusations and discussion, the decision was made by Henry VI to commit Eleanor into the custody of Sir Thomas Stanley, controller of the household, who was warned to ignore any claims of illness made by his prisoner. Less than a week later she began a slow journey to Chester, where she was to be subject to life imprisonment. Fears and interest around her sorcery remained, among some individuals and chroniclers at least, despite the public humiliation she had suffered. The authors of the *Brut* Chronicle noted an unusual storm on the day of Eleanor's departure from Westminster, similar to that which had precluded her sorcerous activities, marvelling that 'there was such weather of thunder, lightning, hail and rain, that the people were sore adread and aghast of the great noise and hideous[ness] of the weather'. She would remain imprisoned for the rest of her days, despite various threats of attempts to break her out of custody, including an attempt by Humphrey's servants in 1447. In response to these attempts, she was moved on two occasions, first from Chester to Kenilworth Castle in October 1443, and then to the Isle of Man in July 1446, where she died in c.1457.

The public reaction to Eleanor's trial, penance and long-term imprisonment appears to have been highly polarised. Clearly much of the population saw the duchess as overambitious and prideful and were happy to see her brought low. Numerous copies of the 'Lament of the Duchess of Gloucester' appeared in the fifteenth and sixteenth centuries. The poem, typical of the 'mirror for magistrates' model, presents Eleanor as being on fate's wheel, brought low by her pride and her desire to become queen, held up as a warning to others – particularly women – who might consider acting this way:

> With wealth, weal, and worthiness, I was beset on every side;
> Of Gloucester I was duchesse, of all men I was magnified.
> As Lucifer fell down for pride, so fell I from felicity;
> I had no grace myself to gwyde – all women may beware by me ...

> Some time I was in rich array, there might no princes be my peer;
> In clothes of gold and garments gay, me thought there was
> nothing too dear.
> I purchased fast from year to year, of poor men I had no pity.
> Now are my wits all in wear – All women may beware by me.

Others had more sympathy for the fallen duchess, notably those from Humphrey's household (even after his death), and those living around Greenwich, the site of Eleanor and Humphrey's manor and court, some

Charges brought against Juliana Ridligo, a supporter of Eleanor Cobham, for harassing the King and calling him a fool. (*KB 27/728*) of whom had extremely strong support. On 27 May 1443 a servant from Greenwich named Juliana Ridligo went as far as accosting the King while he was riding across Blackheath, demanding that he release Eleanor from prison and send her back to Humphrey. Juliana, who was described in some accounts as being of unsound mind, and a contingent including William Quick, a tailor from Greenwich, were themselves charged with treasonously compassing the King's death, with Juliana shouting, 'Henry of Wyndesore, ride carefully! Thy horse may stumble and break thy neck,' as the King passed. When given a chance to ask who she was speaking to (presumably to give her a chance to consider her 'treasonous' intent), Juliana pointed directly at the King and shouted:

It would become thee better to ride to thine uncle than he to thee. Thou wilt kill him, just as thou hast killed thy mother [Joan of Kent]. Send that uncle of thine back his wife whom thou detainest ...

Thou art stupid, and art known to be stupid by the whole realm of England.

These words were considered to be treasonous on the (now well-established) premise that they would deprive the King of his royal majesty and cause further insurrection across the country, which would in turn destroy the King and his realm. They also ensured a horrific death for Juliana, who was arrested and brought before the King's Bench for trial. Refusing to speak or enter any plea, she was detained in the Tower and made to suffer *peine forte et dure*, a form of torture designed to make silent defendants enter a plea. Juliana was made to lie on her back on the ground, naked except for a shift, in a specific area designed for such purposes, where a hole had been made in the ground for her to place her head. Stones and iron were then placed on her body until she couldn't bear the weight, and she was to be left there, deprived of food and water, until she decided to enter a plea, or until she died. She chose the latter option.

Eleanor's own legacy was, and indeed remains, polarised. Was she the victim of political manoeuvres among those trying to influence the young King, brought down by her interests in the occult and her desire to conceive a child, or was she a calculating, ambitious upstart who sought the King's death through the dark arts and thus become queen? Or, as seems most likely, a combination of the two? Whatever the answer, her trial, or rather, the lack of a (secular) trial had a legacy of its own. In the immediate aftermath of Henry VI's decision to commit Eleanor to life imprisonment rather than the fate of her associates, the knotty question of how to place a peeress of the realm on trial was finally grasped. In the Parliament of January–March 1442, a common petition was presented, asking Parliament to provide confirmation of how the process should be managed in future. The royal council (or members of it, at least) had clearly been frustrated by the lack of options available to them, and the lack of a precedent with which they could proceed on the secular front, yet had been unwilling or unable to push through a solution while the case was ongoing. Forced to comprise, they were now confronted with an additional cost to royal finances for Eleanor's custody of £100 each year, and while she retained popularity among pockets of society, they were also faced with the threat of continued rescue efforts and unrest. They now moved to settle the issue once and for all, with Parliament declaring that such peeresses who were indicted of any treason or felony should be brought to trial before the same judges and peers of the realm as would be convened for the trial of a man. Leaving aside the obvious gender imbalance under this new legislation, in which fertility medicine and female medical practices could be misconstrued (willingly or otherwise) into occult sorcery by their male peers, the Act of 1442 now put in place a clear precedent. Peeresses accused of treason were not automatically subjected to a secular trial in this way – as we have seen, charges of treason could be used as an accusation, without a further attempt to put the matter on trial – but the option was now available to those prosecuting, where it had not been previously. As we shall see, this precedent would have unfortunate consequences for not one, but two, queens less than a century later.

The attainder of Richard III after his death at the Battle of Bosworth, 1485. (C 65/123)

Four

THE WARS OF THE ROSES, 1450–85

A conspiracy against him, the Queen, their son and heir and a great part of the nobility of the land has recently come to his knowledge, which treason is more heinous and unnatural than any previous one because it originates from the King's brother the Duke of Clarence, whom the King had always loved and generously rewarded.

ATTAINDER OF GEORGE, DUKE OF CLARENCE, 1478

Plots, insults such as Juliana Ridligo's, and treasonous words, directed at the young Henry VI would only increase in number throughout the 1450s, as the King suffered a sudden and unexpected breakdown in his mental health, from which he would never fully recover, and which would plunge the country into a violent civil war. At the same time, a new process for prosecuting treason was emerging from the mid fifteenth century, a process which could prosecute treason *en masse*, particularly as the tides of civil war ebbed and flowed. This was the policy of parliamentary attainder in which political rivals could be charged and found guilty in their absence, and which acted as both charge and judgement. To attaint an individual – or group of individuals – was to declare in Parliament that they had committed a serious offence, normally treason (although not exclusively). Provided that the bill of attainder was agreed by Parliament, the named individual would be declared 'attainted' – their bloodline judged to be corrupted or stained – and their lands, possessions and titles forfeited to the Crown. The individual became a fugitive and could potentially be executed if they refused to submit or were caught, while their heirs were unable to inherit as long as the attainder remained. They were – in effect – legally dead.

This was a quick, utterly destructive, and systematic political tool, and had the appearance of legality through the involvement of Parliament, even if it was (in effect) a blunt instrument used to run roughshod over the English legal system. Attainder was not new in the fifteenth century – the Despensers had been attainted in the early fourteenth century – but with the advent of civil war it took on and developed a new importance, as loyalties were tested. It provided the Crown with two primary tools which enabled royal officials to win and retain the support of rival nobles. The lands and possessions of defeated rival factions who were attainted could be re-granted to loyal retainers, while at the same time, the prospect that an individual's attainder might be reversed offered the potential for reconciliation for those who had opposed the King but returned to the loyal fold (often at a cost). Suspended or provisional attainders, where execution of those attainted was not pursued, but nor was the corruption reversed immediately or entirely, was one of the most powerful tools used in the late medieval period. It was used regularly in Parliament to try to balance the need to reward supporters and win over former enemies, especially as rival kings fought for the crown of England. This was strategic, calculated, and utterly dependent on which faction controlled Parliament, meaning that mass attainders and reversals in Parliament categorised much of the period known as the Wars of the Roses. The dynamics of civil war meant that many of the parliamentary attainders of the fifteenth century listed whole swathes of individuals who had taken to the battlefield against the opposing faction. Yet other attainders were deeply personal, and none more so than that of the King's brother George, Duke of Clarence, in 1478. While the attainders of the previous decades had demonstrated a new, strategic approach to treason, Clarence's attainder, trial and execution illustrate the continual opportunity at the Crown's disposal to target individuals.

The middle child of three brothers, two of whom would become king, Clarence's relationship with his elder brother, Edward IV, had been fraught for many years prior to his downfall in 1477/8. In 1468 their relationship had deteriorated to such an extent that Clarence – alongside Richard, Earl of Warwick known as 'the Kingmaker', who had worked with his father, the Duke of York, to secure the Yorkist claim, and now served as the power behind the throne – had actually staged a coup and would force Edward into exile in Burgundy a few years later. The two brothers had made their peace in 1471, but a simmering resentment seems to have continued in Clarence's mind, exacerbated by a protracted tussle with his younger brother Richard, over some of the Neville estates they had received through their respective marriages. At Christmas 1476 matters came to a head. In the space of just a few weeks, the duke suffered a series of devastating losses, with the death of his wife Isabel on Sunday 22 December 1476, and that of his youngest son, Richard Plantagenet, just a week later on 1 January 1477. If Clarence had been considered rash, impulsive and over-powerful prior to this point in his life, these events may have tipped him over the edge, coupled with a further slight (perceived or otherwise) from Edward during the first months of 1477. His first falling-out with his elder brother had been, in part, brought about through a controversial marriage to Isabel without the King's approval. He now followed a similar course, coveting (in the eyes of the *Crowland Chronicle* at least) the daughter of the wealthy Duke of Burgundy, who had died in battle on Epiphany that year, and pursuing a match in unison with his sister Margaret, the now-widowed Duchess of Burgundy. Edward, however, did not agree, and refused to consider the match, leading Clarence into a series of decisions that would lead to his own attainder and execution over the course of the following year.

The duke's first move in the tableau of violence, necromancy and treasonous behaviour that would unfold between April and May 1477 was to seek some sort of justice for the death of his wife and child. While most scholarly opinion today suggests that the pair died from natural causes, Clarence thought differently, and claimed that they had been poisoned by members of his household over a number of months. On Saturday 12 April a large contingent of the duke's retinue (later suggested to number about eighty armed men or more) appeared at the house of Ankerett Twinho, widow and late servant to Isabel, in Keyford, Somerset, around 2 p.m. Without any warrant for her arrest, they seized her and spirited her away to Bath without delay. From there she was taken to Cirencester a week later and then to Warwick, where she arrived on the evening of Monday 14 April, around 8 p.m. Her jewels, possessions and other goods were confiscated by Clarence's retainers, and the friends and family (including her daughter Edith and her husband Thomas Delalynde), who had followed her movements in order to try to help her were ordered to stay out of Warwick on pain of death.

The following day Ankarett, alongside two other servants from the Clarence household, Roger Tocotes and John Thuresby, was taken to the Guildhall in Warwick where the local justices of the peace were holding the regular quarter sessions, where she was accused of poisoning Isabel and Richard the previous year. It was claimed that Ankarett had given Isabel ale laced with poison on 10 October, which had caused her to sicken until she finally succumbed to the poison just before Christmas. Thuresby, described in the indictment as 'late of Warwick, yeoman and late servant of Richard Plantagenet', was charged with giving Clarence's young son a similar concoction of poisoned ale on 21 December from which he died on 1 January, while Tocotes was charged with aiding the two alleged poisoners. In what amounted to a show trial, Ankarett and Thuresby were found guilty of felony by the assembled jury and sentenced to death, after which they were taken to the King's Gaol, drawn through the town to the gallows at Myton and hanged. The whole process, from start to finish, took place in less than three hours.

Even by fifteenth-century standards, this represented a significant instance of lawlessness from Clarence and his retainers, from the defendants' unauthorised arrests, their immediate transfer across county borders to Warwick, to the speed with which proceedings unfolded. Furthermore, while the two alleged poisoners were tried in an official legal capacity, later reports suggest that the jury were heavily intimidated, and unable to give a fair response to the indictments, individually approaching Ankarett after her sentence had been passed to ask for her forgiveness. She would be pardoned posthumously the following January in the Parliament of 1478, after a petition from her grandson and heir, Roger Twinho, in which Clarence was named as the key figure behind proceedings, but the duke's actions, while rash and dangerous, were not yet treasonous. He had abused the legal system, and acted in a lawless and overmighty fashion, and may have now expected a severe rebuke from his brother, but Clarence's fate was not yet sealed. In just over a month, details of dangerous new digressions would come to light, which would force Edward's hand once and for all.

On 12 May 1477, less than a month after Ankarett Twinho's 'trial' and execution, a commission of 'oyer and terminer' (to hear and to determine) was directed to investigate certain treasonous activities taking place in Middlesex. The resulting indictments, which were returned a few days brought several treasonous charges against one Thomas Burdett, from Arowe in Warwickshire, one of Clarence's retainers, alongside two Oxford men, John Stacey and Thomas Blake. As in the case of Eleanor Cobham, thirty years previously, the charges brought against the trio were those of treasonable necromancy and the casting of nativities for the King (in this instance also including his son, Prince Edward). These acts were said to have taken place some years previously, on 20 April and 12 November 1474 and 20 May 1475, in which year they also declared news of the imminent death of the two Edwards to one Alexander Russheton and other royal servants. These details of previous offences, as laid out in the official trial records, differ from the *Crowland Chronicle*, which places the emphasis on Stacey, and states that the target of the necromancy was Richard, Lord Beauchamp, at the request of his adulterous wife, possibly indicating the difficulties of prosecuting what was inherently a very private form of treason (as it had been with Eleanor).

What appears to have brought these plots to the attention of the officials was not, however, accusations of necromancy, but the actions of Thomas Burdett on three instances in March and May 1477, when he was recorded as disseminating seditious bills, writings, rhymes and ballads at Holborn on 6 March, 4 May and 5 May. These seditious writings were, it was claimed, intended to stir up the people of England against their king, so that they would withdraw their love for him and rise up against him. While Clarence was not named as being involved in the alleged offences, the actions of his retainer in the first months of 1477 (at the same time Clarence was seen as taking the law into his own hands) were at the very least suspicious, and it is entirely possible that the duke was behind the spreading of rumours and other propaganda against his brother.

This was not a new approach for Clarence, who had previously spread rumours around England of Edward's illegitimacy – almost certainly to give himself a clear route to the throne in the event of a deposition (having secured an agreement with Henry VI during the Readeption of 1470–71 that he would succeed as king if Henry died). It is entirely plausible that rumours of Edward's illegitimacy were among those circulated by Burdett. This may have been alongside the infamous rumour that Edward had been pre-contracted in marriage at the time of his marriage to Elizabeth Woodville, making the said marriage (and the children which resulted from it) illegitimate, which would appear prominently during the circumstances of Richard III's seizure of the throne in 1483. While the trial records do not record the exact rumours being circulated in 1477, either possibility would certainly have served Clarence's interests as the man who stood most to gain from the illegitimacy of Edward or his sons and heirs. While the accusations that arose during the trial may have aroused suspicion at court, particularly as the three men were found guilty on 19 May and sentenced to be executed for treason the following day, Clarence had not yet been directly implicated. The outcome of the trial, however, seems to have been the final straw. Burdett and Stacey were drawn from the Tower to Tyburn, where they declared their innocence, with Burdett quoted as shouting from the scaffold, 'Behold, I must die, whereas I never did such things as these.' Whether Clarence believed in his former retainer's innocence, or whether he merely sought to exonerate Burdett and his own retinue is unclear, but the following day he made the rash move of storming into the council chamber at Westminster with one Dr William Goddard, a renowned cleric and expert in matters of heresy, and declaring Burdett's innocence before all present. Edward was at Windsor so was not present himself in the council meeting, but in the face of his brother's brazen approach he clearly now had no option but to confront him. Clarence was arrested a few weeks later for interfering in legal process (although whether this related to Ankarett's execution or his statements about Burdett's innocence is not recorded), and writs of summons were issued in November for a parliament in January 1478 in which he could be tried.

It is not clear what charges were being considered when Clarence was arrested after a troublesome few months, or the level of sentence being contemplated against him. If Edward had initially hoped to avoid the possibility of a capital punishment, by the time Parliament met at Westminster on 16 January attitudes had hardened, and the duke was attainted of high treason. While the text of Clarence's attainder was not copied onto the Parliament roll for this year, and indeed the official proceedings of the January Parliament only hint at the magnitude of proceedings, the original act survives and provides specific charges, which give a fascinating glimpse into how treason was perceived in the late fifteenth century. Prior to this point in proceedings, while Clarence had evidently run roughshod over the English justice system, supported his brother's rival Henry VI and his restoration to the throne, and backed a condemned traitor against the decision of the common law courts, he had not technically committed treason as defined in 1352. Rather the process of attainder sought to use the language of treason to frame the Crown's argument so that it would convince a court of the duke's peers in Parliament without the need to place it within strict statutory limitations.

The attainder opens by pointing to the 'many conspiracies against [Edward IV] which he has repressed in the past', and the King's policy of showing mercy where possible, stating that a new plot had been brought to the Crown's attention, which threatened not only the royal family, but a significant part of the nobility as well. This treasonous act being 'more heinous and unnatural than any previous one because it originates from the King's brother the Duke of Clarence, whom the King had always loved and generously rewarded'. George's previous conduct, which had been forgiven, is also noted as including 'procuring [Edward's] exile from the realm and labouring parliament to exclude him and his heirs from the crown'.

The latter of these two previous misdeeds is particularly telling in the context of the specific charges which would follow, as it refers to the Readeption Parliament of 1470/1, in which Clarence was able to secure an agreement that should Henry VI's line fail, the crown would pass to Clarence and his heirs instead. If Clarence's conduct during the crisis years of 1468–71 had been forgiven, if not forgotten, the claim in 1478 that he had kept and secured an exemplification of the parliamentary act confirming the agreement represented a sign of his continued ambition and danger. The seriousness of this charge is further demonstrated by the fact that among the rest of the parliamentary business of January 1478, as enrolled in the official proceedings was the complete annulment of the 'feigned [Readeption] parliament summoned and called unlawfully and by usurped authority by your rebel and enemy Henry VI, late in deed and not by right king of England', the 'discussions, dealings and explorations [of which] remain in writing and some have been exemplified'.

Further accusations specifically related to the trial of Thomas Burdett and its aftermath. Clarence was accused of trying to turn the King's subjects away from him through his claims that Burdett had been falsely executed and was innocent, and of making claims about the King, which may relate to some of Burdett's seditious writings. Clarence had allegedly accused the King of resorting to necromancy (an interesting twist on the accusations made against Stacey and Blake), and of saying that Edward was a bastard and not fit to reign. Finally a set of charges related to Clarence readying his supporters for a possible coup, making men take oaths of allegiance to himself directly without excepting their loyalty to the King and asking them to be ready at an hour's notice for an uprising. In order to gain further support overseas it was claimed that he had smuggled his son abroad, for the security of Clarence's line, with an unrelated child smuggled into Warwick to cover up the move. It is unclear whether such charges were in any way plausible, or whether they were added to the attainder in order to provide additional ammunition to the weight of proceedings against the King's brother, and to force through charges of treason.

In the absence of an official account of the trial, we have to rely on the *Crowland Chronicle*, which paints a compelling and highly personal picture of proceedings, in which only the two brothers spoke against one another. Edward alone accused his brother of the offences contained in his attainder, bringing before Parliament a succession of witnesses, some of whom (it was claimed) acted more like accusers than impartial observers. For his part, George spoke entirely on his own accord, denying all the charges against him and pleading for a trial by combat through which he would be able to defend himself and his honour by his own hand. Parliament's descent to the level of a fraternal spat in 1478 clearly demonstrates the limits of attainder as a means of prosecuting treason, evoking the violent debates and reactions of the 1380s and 90s rather than the clear boundaries of the 1352 Act. Perhaps Edward's reaction was understandable, given the fraternal bonds which George had broken alongside the feudal obligations he owed to Edward as his king, a deeply personal and ongoing disloyalty which could no longer be tolerated.

Clarence's request for trial by combat denied, he was found guilty of the charges, and guilty of high treason. On 7 February 1478 Henry Stafford, Duke of Buckingham, was appointed Steward of England and asked to pass sentence, which he duly did. Clarence was sentenced to death, although he appears to have been spared the ignominy of the traditional penalty of a public and violent death. Indeed, there are some indications that after his anger had dissipated, Edward may even have regretted his actions, with several days passing before the sentence was carried out. Did he perhaps hold out hope for one last reconciliation, after so many acts of mercy throughout the brothers' fractious adulthood, or was he simply unwilling to take the final and irreversible step that George's conduct had led to? In the end it fell to the Speaker of the Commons, William Allington, to approach the Lords and request that the matter be resolved in some way. A few days later, on 18 February, Clarence was executed, possibly being drowned in a butt of Malmsey wine, as the later tradition would recount, but certainly in private fashion, a small consolation to the duke who had seemingly never recovered from the death of his wife and child the year before.

RICHARD III AND HENRY VII

The unnatural, wicked and great perjuries, treasons, homicides and murders, in shedding infants' blood, with many other wrongs, odious offences and abominations against God and man, and in particular against our said sovereign lord, committed and done by Richard, late Duke of Gloucester, calling and naming himself, by usurpation, King Richard III.

ATTAINDER OF RICHARD III, 1485

If the Duke of Clarence's treason trial highlights a very personal form of treason, as brother accused brother, the bloody civil war that we know now as the Wars of the Roses brought a very different and impersonal approach to the fore. Characterised by pitched battles, in which the rival Lancastrian and Yorkist factions openly waged war on each other, and as the advantage passed back and forth, the prosecution of treason increasingly became a standardised process, applied to swathes of individuals at a time.

As the fortunes of war ebbed and flowed, an inherent problem with the issuing of mass attainders became clear. Kings could be made and unmade through victory or defeat in battle – as recent events such as Henry VI's Readeption had demonstrated – but so could a king's supporters, armies and soldiers. A pretender to the throne, if successful in battle, might no longer be a pretender but, rather, the 'rightful' claimant to the throne – potentially dangerous for those who had supported the *de facto* [by fact] king. Tensions between the language of *de jure* [by right] and *de facto* kings had long been an issue for those usurping the throne, justifying their actions after the fact, but had increased importance in moments of outright civil war. In the aftermath of Henry VI's 'Readeption' of 1470/1, Edward IV and his Yorkist supporters, for example, had described the (now dead) Henry's second reign as a period when he was king *de facto* but not *de jure* and it is clear that Edward appreciated the dangers of eliminating all those who had supported the Lancastrian cause. It may have been that such a policy was an unspoken rule on both sides of the conflict, but while it remained undefined in law, concerns remained.

Perhaps the best-known example of such concerns is Henry Tudor's seizure of the throne at Bosworth in 1485. Henry had himself been attainted in 1484 for his role during the events of the unsuccessful coup known as Buckingham's Rebellion in 1483 (having been in exile in France since 1471), but returned to defeat and kill the incumbent king, Richard III, in battle at Bosworth Field on 22 August 1485. Under both the 1352 Treason Act, and the 1484 Act of Attainder, Henry was categorically a traitor. He had been attainted in full Parliament for his part in an armed rebellion (regardless of his actual actions, or lack of them) in 1483, and he had levied war on the de facto king of England within the realm, a battle in which that king had been killed. With victory at Bosworth, and the defeat of his rival, however, he had become the king *de facto*, although parliamentary recognition of his title was required before he would become king *de jure*. But was he still a traitor? And what should be done with those who had supported Richard?

As Parliament prepared to meet in the month after Bosworth, it is clear that some legal wrangling was now required to resolve any lingering legal concerns around Henry's status. The precedent of reversing attainders was not the primary issue, having become commonplace throughout the back and forth of the wars; the difference here, however, was that royal authority was required for a formal reversal, which Henry could not invoke on himself. This was the subject of much discussion among the justices in the build-up to Parliament's opening and throughout the session, who deemed that Henry was released from his attainder *de facto* upon becoming king, an opinion reiterated when the Chancellor asked them for confirmation with *une grande question* on the matter in the early months of 1486. In order to avoid any ambiguity, the king's title was presented in Parliament as a common bill, in which it was claimed that the Crown had been vested in the new king, but which avoided justifying his claim. This measure was not entirely new, and indeed had been employed by Richard III in 1483 with *Titulus Regius*, and seems to have caused little concern or comment. More disruptive was the bill of attainder against the deceased King and his supporters, which turned the established narrative on its head.

The beginning of the attainder brought the usual attempts to malign the usurped King's character and acts, claiming in Richard's case the 'unnatural, wicked and great perjuries, treasons, homicides and murders, in shedding infants' blood, with many other wrongs, odious offences and abominations against God and man' and claiming that Richard was himself a usurper. The new King, however, then went further. In order to navigate the muddy waters of his own treachery, Henry essentially attempted to rewrite history, dating the start of his new reign from the day before Bosworth (21 August) rather than that of his victory the following day. In doing so, he was able to use the language and charges of treason against the defeated Yorkists. In this new narrative, Henry claimed to be the right and lawful king, and those following the *de facto* king (Richard) were therefore traitors:

... on 21 August in the first year of the reign of our said sovereign lord [1485], gathered a great host at Leicester in the county of Leicester, traitorously intending, plotting and conspiring the destruction of the royal person of the king, our sovereign liege lord ... And they kept the same host in being, with banners displayed, strongly armed and equipped with all kinds of weapons, such as guns, bows, arrows, spears, glaives, axes and all other weaponry suitable or necessary for giving and advancing a mighty battle against our said sovereign lord, from the said 21 August until the following 22 August, when they led them to a field within the said county of Leicester, and there by premeditated intent traitorously levied war against our said sovereign lord and his true subjects present in his service and assistance under the banner of our said sovereign lord, to the overthrow of this realm and its common weal.

This clearly set a very dangerous precedent, as it meant that anyone supporting the *de facto* king in good faith against a rival claimant or usurper could be liable to charges of treason if they ended up on the losing side. This was a new way of proceeding. Previously, (although never stated as such), the Yorkist acts of attainder were implicitly passed only against those who had acted or stood against them after their royal kingship had been acknowledged. As in previous conflicts, many of those who submitted to royal mercy immediately could expect to be pardoned and restored, and the numbers actually attainted were relatively low. The threat, however, was clear, and accounts of the parliamentary sessions reflect concerns over the re-writing of history. One individual who was present reported back to Robert Plumpton that 'there was many gentlemen against it, but it wold not be, for it was the kings pleasure', while the journal of the representatives of Colchester, who recorded some of the proceedings, stated that the attainder 'sore was questioned with', and the *Crowland Chronicle* noted that the decision 'was not taken without considerable discussion, or, indeed, to speak more truly, considerable censure, of the measures so adopted'. In the face of fervent discussion in the Commons, however, Henry's mind was clear, and the bill was passed, posthumously attainting Richard and his closest supporters of high treason, the final act before Parliament was prorogued.

The decision to backdate his reign, and to turn the narrative of treason on its head, may have been a temporarily necessary act by Henry VII. He had destroyed much of his opposition, and won others over with his marriage to Elizabeth of York, but he was not yet entirely secure on the throne. The backdating of the new King's reign, and the dangers of

The *de facto* act: 'An Acte that noe person going with the Kinge to the Warres shalbe attaynt of treason'. (1495. C 65/128)

supporting an unsuccessful *de facto* king provided the real potential for royal support to fall away in moments of civil war, as supporters might weigh up the options of switching allegiance to save their own lives and livelihoods. As the Crowland chronicler declaimed: 'Oh God! What assurance, from this time forth, are our kings to have, that, in the day of battle, they will not be deprived of the assistance of even their own subjects, when summoned at the dread mandate of their sovereign?'

If Henry didn't immediately appreciate the dangerous precedent he had set, by 1495 he certainly had. In the Parliament of October 1495, a decade after his attainder of Richard III, Henry passed what has become known as the *de facto* Act – more formally 'An act that no person going with the king to the wars shall be attainted of treason' – which reiterated and formalised the Yorkist status quo that those supporting the de facto king would not be attainted in the event that they were defeated:

It is not reasonable [stated the act], but against all laws, reason and good conscience, that the said subjects going with their sovereign lord to war and being in attendance on his person or elsewhere at his commandment within or outside this land, should lose or forfeit anything for doing their true duty and service of allegiance, whatever fortune should by chance fall against the intention and weal of the prince in the same battle, as has some time ago been seen in this land.

'An act that no person going with the king to the wars shall be attainted of treason', 1495

Furthermore, those who were the recipients of royal favour and grants were obliged to serve the King in war, unless they were specifically exempt (as some Chancery clerks were). A return to the previous status quo, probably undertaken in response to the Perkin Warbeck conspiracy, which had seen several leading pro-Yorkist figures executed for treason earlier in the year for supporting the young pretender, was perhaps a welcome relief to both the nobility and the Crown. As the Treason Act of 1352 had done, it clarified what was, and what was not acceptable, both in the moment and after the fact. It would not, however, be applied retrospectively: Richard III and those who had fought and died at Bosworth would remain traitors.

The King's Bench record for the trial of Queen Anne Boleyn, held on 15 May 1536. (*KB 8/9*)

Five

NEW TUDOR TREASONS, 1509–58

Some termed them Draco's Laws, which were written
in blood: some said they were more intolerable than any laws,
that Dionysius or any other tyrant made.
THROCKMORTON ON HENRY VIII'S TREASON LAWS, PRINTED IN
REGINA V THROCKMORTON (1554), 1 STATE TRIALS, P. 896

The final years of Henry VII's reign had represented a return to normal standard of medieval life, in the aftermath of a bloody civil war. The *de facto* Act had restored the status quo, but at the same time the expansion of systematic treason charges by attainder had presented the Crown and Parliament with a devastating new tool to be used against its enemies, both individually and *en masse*. In the hands of a new king, Henry VIII (1491–1547), it would prove to be a dangerous one, as his reign saw an overwhelming expansion of treason charges against all levels of society and the creation of new, brutal forms of treason. The King, and his advisers – who became increasingly entrenched in the mechanics of government – sought precedents, created new treasons retrospectively and imposed violent new views on treason.

EVIL MAY DAY

Nothing is to be seen at the city gate but gibbets and quarters.
NICHOLAS SAGUDINO, SECRETARY TO THE VENETIAN
AMBASSADOR, LONDON, 1517

The final decades of Henry's reign in particular would see new treasons introduced, as the King became increasingly tyrannical, and lashed out at those who opposed the Crown. The first signs of his 'tyranny' however, could be seen much earlier in the reign, as the Crown and royal justices initially sought to frame crimes within existing treason legislation, even if it was in legally dubious ways. One early example was in the prosecution of a London riot in 1517, in which the Crown's use of force, fear, and theatre – which would be used to great effect in later years – became clear.

The riot had been provoked by a series of xenophobic rumours, grumbles and speeches which had spread through the city's apprentices, artificers and servants in the previous months. Hall's chronicle, one of the main sources for the events of the 'Evil May Day' (as it became known) picks up some of these complaints which were largely directed at the French, Dutch, Genoese and other Italian communities of strangers who lived and worked in London. A Lombard, Fraunces de Bard, had allegedly approached the wife of an Englishman on Lombard Street, enticing her to not only go into his chamber, but to bring her husband's plate with her. The Londoner, first requesting the return of his wife, and when that failed, the return of his goods, unsuccessfully attempted to sue the stranger in the London courts, and had once again been unsuccessful. His 'mock', as the chronicle frames this story, was furthermore compounded when the Lombard then succeeded in having him arrested on account of his wife's board and rent, all while she was being kept from him in the Italian's chamber. Elsewhere, a Frenchman who had killed an Englishman was walking through the street carrying a cross, as he prepared to abjure the realm as a consequence of his crime (having presumably sought sanctuary and confessed), when he was suddenly surrounded by his kinsmen. One of the Frenchmen, turning to the constable who had approached them, then asked if the cross was the price for killing an Englishman, while another said 'spitefully' that if that were the price, the French of London would be banished in their masses.

While the veracity of these allegations is uncertain, there does appear to have been widespread unhappiness surrounding the status and number of foreign merchants and artificers in the city, fears which were stoked further in Easter 1517 by two rabble-raising speeches. John Lincoln, a wool broker, had been attempting to rouse the London clergy into denouncing the foreigners during their regular Easter preachings, and after some initial failures he had been able to recruit one Dr Bele, a London-born canon of St Mary Spital. Bele's sermon – much of which had been written by Lincoln, and was read out as a bill – was inflammatory, provocative and xenophobic, and was noted by the chroniclers of the time. 'This land was given to Englishmen,' he stated, 'and as birds would defend their nest, so ought Englishmen to cherish and defend themselves, and to hurt and grieve aliens for the common weal.' The aliens, he claimed, 'eat the bread from the poor fatherless children,' and deprive artificers and merchants of their livings. According to God's law, he said, the English should fight for their country. While the initial response to Bele's sermon was perhaps more muted than Lincoln had wished – the gathered crowd did not rise up immediately – it is clear that discontent was growing.

A few days later, Fraunces de Bard and his friends were once again the focus of the Londoners' frustration, openly laughing about his amorous affairs on the street. They allegedly claimed that even if Fraunces had the mayor of London's wife in his chamber, he would not let her go, prompting one London mercer, William Bolt, to respond, 'Well, you whoreson Lombards, you rejoice and laugh, by the Mass we will one day have a day at you, come when it will.' Rumours swirled around the city that such an uprising was being planned for the upcoming May Day celebrations, a day usually marked with festivities, drinking and merriment. Standalone attacks on foreigners became more common and pronounced during the days leading up to the annual festival – strangers were struck and thrown in canals by the young men of the city – and things finally came to a head on the last day of April, as the King's councillors heard of the city's unrest.

Thomas Wolsey, the Chancellor, immediately moved to action upon hearing of the discontent, and sent for the mayor, John Rest, to raise his concerns, but was met with an official civic belief that the King's peace would hold. Leaving Wolsey's presence at 4 p.m. on 30 April, Rest consulted with his officials about the rumours, which had been spreading for days around the capital, and a meeting was announced to take place at the Guildhall that evening at 7 p.m. The civic response was limited, the spread of rumours was acknowledged but the primary response was to set a watch of responsible Londoners (although within an hour this decision would be reversed), and to declare a curfew in the city, with young male servants to be kept inside. They wanted, however, to avoid the sight of mounted men on the streets. Where possible the response was to be deliberately low key. Negotiations between civic and royal officials continued over the following hour, but at 8.30 p.m. the final decision was made and communicated to the mayor and aldermen at the Guildhall. A full curfew – with all men to shut their doors and keep servants inside – was to run from 9 p.m. through to 7 a.m. the following morning, and the aldermen were sent back to their respective wards to communicate this. The city was a tinderbox, ready to ignite into a fire of violence at the slightest provocation.

The spark for violence came in Cheapside, one of the city's main thoroughfares. John Monday, one of the city's aldermen, was passing through the street on his way back to his ward to announce the curfew when he encountered two young men playing a game known as 'Bucklers', who had attracted a large audience of their fellows. Wary of the impending curfew (which had yet to be announced in Cheapside), Monday initially attempted to disperse the group, but the crowd were understandably reluctant to leave, and questioned the reason for doing so. Frustrated by how events were unfolding, the alderman seized one of the men by the arm and attempted to take him to the nearby compter (a small gaol used to imprison minor transgressors) for punishment, which sparked resistance and violence from those assembled, resisting and seizing their fellow away from Monday. A cry of '[ap]prentices and clubs' went up around Cheapside and soon spread across the city, as apprentices and servants suddenly appeared at their doors, armed with clubs and other weapons. By nine, a crowd stated by the chroniclers as numbering 600 or 700 in Cheapside alone, 300 of whom had appeared out of the churchyard at St Paul's armed and primed for violence, had gathered, breaking prisoners out of the city compters, and prioritising those who had been locked up for assaulting foreigners in the previous days and weeks.

Further to the west, the first glimpses of a civic response to the uprising took place at Newgate prison, with an attempt from the mayor and sheriffs to calm matters down. They made an announcement to try to halt the breaking-out of prisoners, which failed, and before long, the rioters were running through St Nicholas Shambles towards the precinct of St Martin-le-Grand. They were met by a further delegation at St Martin's Gate, including the future chancellor Thomas More and others, who came close to stopping the rioters until the stones started falling. The residents of St Martin-le-Grand – many of whom were foreign craft merchants who used the precinct's historic privileges and liberties to ply their trades outside of city and guild control – fearing that they were about to come under attack, began throwing stones, bricks and even hot water at the rioters. One of those present who was hit on the arm and injured was Nicholas Dounes, who cried out 'Down with them!', bringing out a violent attack on the doors and windows of the precinct's buildings and riling up the mob.

Leaving a wake of destruction behind them at St Martin's, the rioters now moved east along Cheapside and into Cornhill, seeking the house of one John Mewtis, the King's 'secretary of the French tongue'. Mewtis was a Frenchman and was especially hated by the mob for his perceived influence with the King, and his protection of foreign artisans and workers in the capital. His house, called 'Greengate', was located to the east of Leadenhall market, and soon came under attack when Mewtis himself could not be found. Writing a few days after the 'Evil May Day', the Venetian ambassador reported home that Mewtis had escaped into the belfry of a nearby church upon hearing of the rioters' approach, and claimed that he would have been killed had he been caught. As it was, he was not caught, and, indeed, all the foreign residents caught up in Evil May Day managed to stay safe – no deaths were recorded throughout the city.

After sacking Mewtis's house, some of the rioters continued southeast, to the manor of Blanche Appleton, where several Italian merchants lived, but did little real damage, and already it seemed that the initial anger of the Rising was slowly abating. The mob continued rioting and causing damage, destroying the stock of foreign artisans – including throwing the boots and shoes they found along their way into the street – and causing property damage, but while the geographical spread of the riot may have increased, the mob itself had largely broken up by the early hours of the morning. When the Earls of Shrewsbury and Surrey arrived in London around five in the morning, along with their retinues and other lesser nobles, the riot had largely blown itself out. The consequences of the events of 30 April, however, were not over for those involved, as the King, his nobles and advisers reacted to the events of Evil May Day. If the civic response to the riot had been largely superficial and ineffective (at least initially), the royal reaction was hard line. Wolsey, the King's chief minister, had been kept up to speed with regular updates throughout the evening (some of which were reported by the chroniclers as being somewhat exaggerated), the lieutenant of the Tower of London had fired shots into the city to warn the mob. Hundreds of prisoners had been taken as they disbanded. Around 300 rioters may have been able to flee – notably watermen, priests and serving men – but hundreds, including the poorest among them and apprentices, were not. Those who had been captured now faced the question of what should be done with them.

Almost immediately the inquest and prosecution of the rioters came into sharp focus, with Wolsey himself said to be displeased with how events had unfolded. Armed men continued to flood into the capital, including the Duke of Norfolk with around 800 'men in harness', and while relations between the soldiers and citizens threatened to ignite, peace prevailed. Proclamations were made – several of which were focused on women, who were to be kept at home and banned from coming together to 'babble and talk' – commissions of oyer and terminer were summoned, investigations begun, and prisoners examined. The big question, however, was what to charge the rioters with. On the face of things, the only crimes they had committed were those of property damage and freeing prisoners from the civic prisons. No murders had been committed (although whether this would have been the case if foreigners such as Mewtis had been found is uncertain), no royal officials or institutions had been assaulted and, unlike the events of the Great Revolt of 1381, the riot could hardly be said to be a popular uprising. At the same time, the events of May Day could hardly be allowed to go unpunished by royal officials, or even subjected to the regular processes of the common law. A meeting of the King's Council was summoned at the house of the Chief Justice of King's Bench, Sir John Fyneux, at St Bride's by Fleet Street to consider the royal response. Dr Bele and John Lincoln were both questioned and sent to the Tower, and initial examinations found that – with the exception of Lincoln – no evidence of the Rising being pre-planned could be found (or at least proven). Those assembled – of whom Fyneux must be seen as the primary instigator – came to a remarkable, and indeed entirely questionable conclusion. Those who had participated in the events of Evil May Day, regardless of whether they had actively taken part in the acts of violence which had flooded across the city, or had just been present, were to be charged with high treason.

The framing of treason charges against all those who had taken part in the riot was clearly intended as a show of force, and a warning to Londoners, but at the same time they were of dubious legality. Richard II had responded to the uprising of 1381 with new statutory legislation, declaring that it was treasonous to 'make nor [begin any manner] Riot and Rumour, nor other like', but to indict hundreds of individuals *en masse* was problematic to say the least. Furthermore, the mob's sole focus on foreigners made it difficult to claim that the riot had been against the Crown or even royal officials (with the exception of Mewtis). Among the lawyers, however, Fyneux had a double strategy to ensure that the treason charges would stick. Holinshed's chronicle sheds light on the arguments put forward by the Chief Justice, stating that Fyneux claimed that 'the insurrection in itself was high treason', regardless of whether the individuals were 'principal dooers' or 'those that did not commit any robbery', as a 'thing practised against the regal honour of our sovereign lord the king'. Fyneux now produced evidence that there was a precedent for such charges, a minor Kentish Rising against the statute of labourers, which had taken place in Patrixbourne in October 1496, which he had been involved with early in his King's Bench career.

The Patrixbourne Rising numbered fewer than twenty malcontents, but crucially (as Fyneux pointed out), 'certain persons within the county of Kent began an insurrection … and were attainted therefore of high treason, and had judgement to be drawn, hanged, and quartered'. He did not, as it appears from Holinshed, seem to have taken note of the fact that only two of the Patrixbourne rebels actually suffered this fate. Of the five men who were attainted of treason, three were pardoned in February 1497, and the rest of the rebels were pardoned without treason charges having been brought against them. Fyneux produced his precedent to the assembled group of legal advisers and 'showed where and when this chanced', but this was not the only legal argument he had in mind. As is evident within the surviving indictment and accounts of Evil May Day, the primary legal charges were brought under a slightly obscure statute from 1414 (2 Henry V, stat. 1 c. 6), which stated that it was treasonous to attack the subjects of a country with whom the king had a peace treaty. Originally designed to curb acts of piracy in the English Channel, and to aid Henry V's ongoing negotiations with his European counterparts, the old statute was now put to a new use. Almost immediately, on 1 May, the royal serjeants-at-law and attorneys were sent to Wolsey to check for evidence of treaties that could be used to push forward a charge of treason.

Only one of the original indictments is known to have survived – largely because the indicted individual, Richard Marten, was pardoned two years later – which demonstrates how Fyneux now manipulated the statute to cover the events of May 1517. The charge brought against those indicted named five Dutch artisans living within St Martin-le-

Grand, Isbrond of [de] Roe, Andrew Gaynes, Deryk Andrew, John Blowe and Henry Pylgym, who had been born under the obedience of Charles, Prince of Spain, Archduke of Austria, and Duke of Burgundy and Brabant. As Henry VIII had signed a trade treaty with Charles in the previous year (1516), guaranteeing the safe passage of goods, Marten (and his fellow rioters) were thus – Fyneux argued – guilty of high treason on account of breaking that peace. As Shannon McSheffrey has noted, in the absence of all the indictments apart from Marten's, it is not clear whether the same five names were repeated in the charges brought against each rioter, but it seems likely that they were, as Fyneux framed the indictments to maximum effect.

With indictments and precedents prepared, the King's officials now proceeded to bring the prisoners before the justices and to hear their fate, in what were a series of remarkably stage-managed and performative acts, the details of which were recorded by a royal or civic official, and which are preserved in a precedent book of the royal Chancery. On 4 and 5 May, the prisoners, 278 of them according to Hall's chronicle, were led through the city streets tied together amid mourning and tears around them. They were a mix of ages and professions, 'some men, some lads, some children of thirteen year', as the chroniclers noted. They were arraigned and thirteen of their number were found guilty of high treason, sentenced to the full traitor's death, and executed immediately, although nine men had their sentences partially commuted as a mark of royal mercy.

William Alday, James Anderson, Henry Darby and Richard Borrell, however, all suffered a full traitor's death, drawn to Cheap, St Martin's, Cornhill and Blanche Appleton, where they were hanged and quartered. A fifth man, Thomas Gibson, was drawn to Cheap and hanged, although given his occupation in the precedent book was noted as 'the clipper of money', it is possible that his punishment may have been linked to more than just the riot. A further eight men were led from the Tower to their places of execution, but only hanged. The gallows – eleven pairs in total – which had been set up around the city, were placed at sites where the violence of 30 April had played out, particularly for the most severe executions, as a clear warning to anyone contemplating similar riots in the future.

Two days later, on Thursday 7 May, John Lincoln himself was brought forward for sentencing, as the principal individual who had provoked tensions with his xenophobic bill, alongside three other named men 'and diverse others', who were sentenced to a full traitor's death. Lincoln was unrepentant to the last, giving a short gallows speech in which he repeated his complaints about foreigners in the kingdom, but prayed for mercy: 'My lords I meant well, for you and I know the mischief that is ensued in this realm by strangers, you would remedy it, and many times I have complained, and then I was called a busy fellow: now our lord have mercy on me.'

The four men were then put on hurdles and drawn to the standard at Cheapside, where Lincoln and a man named William Shyrwyn were executed. The Crown's stage management, however, now came into play, with a last-minute royal reprieve arriving at the gallows even as the rest of the men had ropes around their necks. With this news – which brought a cry of 'God save the King' from the assembled crowd – the investigation of oyer and terminer was put on hold, and the remaining prisoners sent back to their cells to stew, while the thousands of armed men who had been brought into the city departed once again. The threat of execution still hung over the heads of the condemned, with the possibility of hundreds more deaths, a threat which the King and his ministers now leveraged in a grandiose show of royal mercy. First, on 11 May, the King met with city officials at his palace of Greenwich. Dressed all in black, the civic dignitaries grovelled before Henry and asked for mercy for their negligence in letting affairs get out of hand, as well as compassion for the condemned. Henry initially refused, claiming that they had not done enough to stop the riot, and refusing all offers of favour, goodwill and mercy, telling them to take up their concerns with Wolsey instead. Humbled, the civic officials retreated, and the prisoners remained in their cells until Thursday 22 May, three weeks after the events of Evil May Day, when a grand meeting was called at Westminster Hall, in which matters would finally be brought to an end.

Arriving at 9 a.m., the King, Wolsey, and the kingdom's leading nobles were seated on a 'lofty platform' at the upper end of the hall, with the city officials dressed in their best livery, and the hall dressed with fine fabrics and cloth of estate, before the prisoners were brought in to face their fate. Dressed only in shirts and with halters around their necks, the chronicles state that some 400 men and eleven women were brought into the hall, the 'poor younglings and old false knaves', as Hall's chronicle records. Wolsey once again castigated the civic officials for their negligence in letting the riot develop, and told the assembled prisoners that they deserved to die for their crimes, but pleaded with the King to spare them, which he initially declined. Upon hearing the King's decision, a cry of 'Mercy, gracious lord, mercy!' arose from the condemned and Wolsey, along with the assembled lords and officials alike, once more petitioned the King to be merciful in what appears to have been a staged opportunity for the King to demonstrate his compassion for those whom his officials had cast as traitors. This time he agreed, and Wolsey announced this to the crowd, with (as the Venetian ambassador's accounts state) 'tears in his eyes', urging them to lead good lives, and comply with Henry's desire and to treat foreigners in the kingdom well.

As Henry announced his official pardoning of all those present, 'all the prisoners shouted at once and altogether cast up their halters in to the roof top, so the king might perceive they were none of the discreetest sort'. On hearing of the general pardon, Hall recounts that some Londoners – who had evaded arrest and imprisonment – went immediately to Westminster (or were already there), stripped down to their shirts (with halters) and joined in the press of prisoners so as to receive the benefits of the general pardon as well. The contrast between the initial brutality and later displays of mercy was not lost on those contemporaries writing about the events of May 1517, including the Venetian ambassador, who wrote: 'It was a very fine spectacle, and well arranged, and the crowd of people present was innumerable ... Nothing is to be seen at the city gate but gibbets and quarters.'

The gallows were taken down, but several of the proceedings were recorded by a Crown or civic official, including lists of those indicted, the locations of their executions, and the writs and proclamations issued, marking a precedent for any future actions. Fyneux's legal manipulations however, set their own precedent, which would play out throughout Henry VIII's reign. Actions could be framed as treason for maximum effect, with brutal executions and staged acts of royal justice and mercy creating a powerful and dramatic display of the King's power. The London mob were xenophobic, caused significant damage to property, physically assaulted foreigners in the build-up to the riot, and might have committed murder had they not been thwarted in their search for Mewtis and others. They were riled up by hate-filled speeches, gossip, and slander from Lincoln and Bele, and had gone against the orders of Crown and city officials. But they had not set out to commit high treason. The rules had been changed, despite Fyneux's dubious precedents, and the actions of the mob had been framed as treason after the fact. If those individuals present in 1517 felt a sense of foreboding for the rest of Henry's reign, it was not recorded, but the King and his ministers had given an early sign of what would recur time and time again over the next thirty years.

Some eighty years after the Evil May Day riots, treason would again be utilised against a minor uprising of apprentices. On 29 June 1595, towards the end of Elizabeth I's reign, a group of London and Southwark apprentices were arrested for throwing stones at the warders of the Tower Street ward, and were whipped as punishment following judgement in Star Chamber. In retaliation, some of their colleagues conspired to set the apprentices free, kill the mayor, and seize weapons from the Tower ward, and drew a crowd of 300 people to assemble near the Tower to achieve these goals. As in the May Day case, the chief justices of the realm, along with the master of the rolls and two barons of the Exchequer, judged these acts treasonous, even though the Queen's life and title weren't directly at stake. The rioters had incited war, rebellion and insurrection against the Queen by attacking the sheriffs of London and attempting to kill the mayor, considered treasonable by a 1571 Treason Act.

RICHARD ROOSE

The king of his blessed disposition inwardly abhorring all
such abominable offences because that in manner no person can
live in surety out of danger of death by that mean if practise
thereof should not be eschewed, hath ordained and enacted by
authority of this present Parliament that the said poisoning be
adjudged and deemed as high treason ... It is ordained
and enacted by authority of this present Parliament that the said
Richard Roose shall be therefore boiled to death.
ATTAINDER OF RICHARD ROOSE, 1531

While under Henry VIII, the Crown might have used historical precedent as a means of framing treason, this was not the only tool at its disposal. Falling back on the loophole of 1352, in which 'any other similar cases of treason' might be brought before Parliament for judgement, treason legislation could be expanded by statute as the King and Parliament decided. One such example – the first of three parliamentary attainders which created new forms of treason – was the attainder of Richard Roose, a cook in the household of John Fisher, Bishop of Rochester, in February 1531. Roose's crime was unusual on several fronts. He was not a political target as the attainders of the fifteenth century had been, nor was he in any way charged with crimes against the King or the government. Instead, the accusations against him were that he had placed poison – certain powders as one foreign ambassador recounted – in the bishop's porridge. Fisher, for some reason, did not eat the porridge that day, but other members of the household did, leaving seventeen people seriously ill and causing the death of one Bennett Curwen. Furthermore, leftovers of the contaminated porridge had been given to the poor and needy at the palace gates, which had led to several more illnesses, and the death of a poor widow named Alice Tryppytt.

Roose was immediately arrested and placed on the rack, where he was severely tortured, and eventually confessed that he had placed purgatives in the bishop's food, but only 'as a jest', and 'which he had been given to understand would only hocus [stupefy or drug] the servants without doing them any harm'. He claimed he had not meant to kill anyone by his actions. In some accounts it was stated that he was given the powder by another unnamed individual, or that he had been out of the room when the powder was added, while rumour would also circulate of the King's complicity in the poisoning, and of the possible involvement of his future wife Anne Boleyn (or her family). Fisher – the alleged target of the poisoning – was a strong opponent of Henry's planned divorce in order to marry Anne, and as a firm supporter of Katherine of Aragon was deeply unpopular with both parties. Regardless of the motives, and Roose's own complicity, however, it was the cook alone who faced punishment for his crime. But what should he be charged with? Murder (a felony) was the obvious charge, as two individuals had died as a consequence of his actions, but for Henry – who was personally fearful of poisonous plots against his life (a regular occurrence at the papal curia in Rome, but uncommon in England) – such a charge did not go far enough. Had Roose been successful in his alleged attack on Fisher, he could have been charged with petty treason – for killing his superior within the household – but the bishop's failure to consume his porridge meant that this was a difficult course to pursue. It might, however, have given the King and his legal advisers inspiration for a new charge, as Roose became the subject of parliamentary attainder for high treason, despite the fact that his actions did not fall under any of the statutory definitions of treason. In the circumstances, attainder was an interesting choice for the King to pursue and seems entirely intended to deny Roose his rights under the common law. At the same time, Parliament passed a new act that declared poisoning to be a new treason.

Unlike many who had been attainted in the fifteenth century, Roose was alive and already in royal custody, so it could not have been used as

'An act for poisoning', the attainder of Richard Roose for high treason, and his sentence to be boiled to death. (C 65/139)

a means of summoning him to answer charges. Neither was it a means of claiming his lands and titles – as a cook he was unlikely to have owned much in any case – as the new legislation declared that forfeitures were to go to the individual's superior, not the Crown (as was the case in petty treason). It can only have been used to deny Roose the benefits of a common law trial, which might have found him innocent. The parliamentary proceedings themselves give an insight into the concerns, conversations, and legal wranglings which clearly went on behind the scenes. A draft copy of the new legislation – containing amendments and notations – survives and provides an interesting comparison with the final enrolled 'Act for Poisoning'. In the initial draft, the bill read: ' … the said

Richard Roose for the said murder and poisoning by him committed and done as is aforesaid shall stand and be attainted of voluntary murder of the said two persons by him poisoned and thereof being deceased.'

Roose was to be attainted of voluntary murder, not for treason, and the word treason, neither high nor petty, does not appear in the text that survives. By the time the final act was enrolled, however, this had been altered so that: 'the said Richard Rose [Roose] for the said murder and poisoning of the said two persons as is aforesaid by authority of this present parliament shall stand and be attainted of high treason.'

Roose's charges had been upgraded following an extended parliamentary discussion, in which Henry VIII himself gave a long speech on the subject of poisoning. It is clear that the King felt deeply about the subject, and feared the dangers of potential plots against him, opting not just to punish Roose, but to ensure all future poisoning charges would meet the full force of the state. It may be that he, or his advisers, used ideas of petty treason (as demonstrated in the particulars of forfeiture) to force through charges of high treason in Parliament, while sidestepping the political and legal inconvenience of a common law trial.

The punishment for poisoning, as newly defined by the act, was that the accused individual was to be boiled to death. As in previous punishments for high treason, the punishment was theoretically linked to the crime. For Roose the cauldron in which he was publicly boiled at Smithfield on 5 April 1531 represented the cauldron in which he had prepared the bishop's porridge. The Greyfriars' chronicle's record of the actual process of boiling was brutally visual: Roose 'was locked in a chain and pulled up and down with a gibbet at divers times until he was dead'. As a warning to other would-be poisoners, it was effective. Eyewitness accounts reported that Roose 'roared mighty loud, and divers women who were big with child did feel sick at the sight of what they saw, and were carried away half dead; and other men and women did not seem frightened by the boiling alive, but would prefer to see the headsman at his work.'

Roose's guilt or innocence remains difficult to untangle. Was he an innocent servant caught up in the high politics of the realm, or a murderer? Shortly after the execution, it was noted that Fisher had left London for his diocese in Rochester, despite suffering from an unrelated illness, which may indicate that he feared further attacks on his life by the King, the Boleyns or other agents. As the ambassador Chapuys claimed, 'He fears there is some more powder [poison] in reserve for him.' What is clear is that Roose never set out to commit treason, nor could he have anticipated that he would be charged with high treason. He was accused, sentenced, and executed in a violent and brutal fashion, for a crime that had not existed at the time, with the legal process manipulated by Henry and his advisers to secure the outcome they desired.

The events of 1531 would set a precedent in more than one way. One other individual – a servant, Margaret Davies, in 1542 – is known to have been boiled alive for poisoning her mistress, although the act seems to have been little used, and would be abolished at the end of Henry's reign. A more dangerous precedent, however, was in the King's mind. Henry and his ministers had established and tested the potential use of attainder and treason charges to sidestep the normal processes of the law, in a time of peace, and against a servant who posed little political threat (even if his master did). This would not be the last time they would utilise the tactic.

ANNE BOLEYN AND THE ACTS OF SUCCESSION

In terms of expanding the scope of treason, the years 1530 to 1536 were the most crucial for Henry VIII. The King's anti-papal policy, attempts to subjugate the English Church, and his matrimonial affairs all attracted criticism; new acts were designed to protect the King from this unrest, and furnish him with the legislative tools necessary to punish those that opposed him. The 1352 Treason Act – still the dominant treason legislation in England – had been designed to protect the Crown from insurrection. It was, however, insufficient at enforcing the obedience that Henry and his ministers required to see through the revolution begun by Henry's break with Rome and marriage to Anne Boleyn.

The deficiencies of the 1352 Treason Act in dealing with opponents of the king are highlighted in the case of Elizabeth Barton, the so-called Holy Maid, or Nun, of Kent. Barton was a Benedictine nun and visionary who, by 1530, was a minor celebrity in the southeast of England, known for her visions and pronouncements on matters of religion. Barton's revelations had reached the ears of the highest in the realm, including Henry himself, and while the King was defending the Catholic faith, Barton's visions proved complimentary to him. However, Henry's marriage to Anne Boleyn and renunciation of the authority of the papacy were anathema to Barton, who remained staunchly Catholic. Her visions turned critical of Henry VIII, prophesying that if he married Anne Boleyn, he would be struck down by God within a month. To Henry and his chief adviser, Thomas Cromwell, this constituted treason, and the King pressed for a treason trial, ordering Cromwell to draw up indictments for Barton and her followers. However, when the judges, lawyers, bishops, and nobles of the realm assembled in November 1533 to discuss the matter, the judges took the opinion that Barton's actions did not constitute treason. The King's argument that Barton had withheld traitorous dreams and plans from him, which put his life in peril, was countered by the fact that Barton had presented her visions to the King in person a year earlier. Though Barton had publicly declaimed against the King's marriage and warned that God would punish him for his actions, there was no treason in the 1352 Act for those that prophesied the King's harm through words alone (although as we have seen, there were ways and means to crack down on treasonous thoughts and words if the Crown decided to do so).

With Henry and his ministers unable to prosecute Barton through the common law, in 1534 they moved to attaint her by statute through Parliament, in lieu of a trial. The subsequent act of attainder against Barton not only allowed Henry to convict the Nun of Kent and her most prominent followers of treason, but also to discredit Barton's claims and publicise her offences. Barton was subsequently executed, and her head was placed on London Bridge as a warning to others (the only woman in history to have suffered this fate).

To ensure that critics of the King's marriage and religious policy could be punished with the full force of the law in future, a new act was passed in the spring session of 1534, the first Act of Succession, which included an expansion of the 1352 Treason Act. The 1534 Act made it a treason not only to compass the king's death, but also to attempt to endanger the king's person or attack the security of the Crown. Any activities deemed to slander or to be to the prejudice of the King's marriage with Anne Boleyn, or to interfere with the order of succession as defined in the act, were also treasonous. These treasons could be committed by writing, or by any 'exterior act or deed', so that anyone publishing hostile propaganda could be accused of treason. The 1534 Act did not, however, yet make purely verbal attacks on the King's marriage a treason: at this stage such verbal attacks were only defined as misprision of treason. Through the 1534 Act of Succession, Henry VIII had made a public statement in law of the legitimacy of his marriage to Anne Boleyn. It was unfortunate, then, that fewer than two years later the act would have to be amended in response to Anne Boleyn's alleged treasons.

The downfall of Anne Boleyn has been well rehearsed by historians for decades, with every aspect of her decline debated and analysed at length. Even with documentary evidence the full story is impossible to ascertain, as it rests on the private thoughts and feelings of the major parties involved, not least the King himself. What we do know for sure from the trial records of Anne and her alleged lovers is what charges were laid against them – adultery and treason for all parties, with an added charge of incest for Anne and her brother Lord Rochford – that the court judged them guilty on all counts, and they were all executed for treason.

The first court documents relating to these accusations are dated 24 April 1536. These were commissions of oyer and terminer – commissions to investigate and determine the validity of a wide array of treasons and other offences – set up in Middlesex and Kent, to look into the possible wrongdoing of the Queen and her alleged lovers. Three days later writs to summon a new parliament were sent out, only two weeks after the previous parliament – which had passed several acts in favour of Anne – was dissolved. This strongly suggests that there were those in government, chiefly Thomas Cromwell, who anticipated Anne's fall and the need to amend the new legislation as quickly as possible. By the time Parliament assembled in June, Anne was dead and it was confirmed that the reason for the summons was to amend the statutes of succession that favoured Anne in light of her treason. On 9 May, writs were sent out to the sheriff of London to assemble a grand jury on the next day to decide whether there was sufficient evidence to proceed with a trial; the jury concluded that such serious accusations warranted a full trial. On 11 May, John Baldwin, chief justice of the Common Pleas, travelled to Deptford, where the Kent grand jury reported that the oyer and terminer set up there on 24 April had found positive evidence of Anne's misdeeds. Similar conclusions were drawn from the Middlesex oyer and terminer.

The charges laid against Anne and her alleged lovers were as follows. First, that Anne had made several of the King's servants her adulterers and concubines, so that they became inclined to the said Queen. Second, that she had committed a number of illicit acts with Henry Noreys, Gentleman of the King's Privy Chamber, George Boleyn Lord Rochford, her own brother (which carried the added charge of incest), William Brereton and Francis Weston, two other gentlemen of the King's Privy Chamber, and Mark Smeton, musician and groom of the Privy Chamber. The indictments also give times and places of these alleged liaisons. These men, thus inflamed by carnal love for the Queen, had allegedly become very jealous of each other and continued to satisfy the Queen's desires to secure her affections. Anne further inflamed their lust by giving gifts to them, in November 1535 and at other times. The charges continue, stating that Anne used her influence over these men to imagine the King's death, with the Queen promising to marry the traitors when the King died. Finally, the accused had apparently imperilled the King's life because when he learnt of these infidelities and treasons, he became so upset that his health deteriorated.

Much has been made of the adulterous accusations for their scandalous nature, and the largest part of the indictments of April and May 1536 concerned the times and places of these liaisons. It is interesting to consider whether consensual relations with the Queen would have amounted to treason according to the 1352 Treason Act, both on the part of her alleged lovers and that of the Queen herself. If the accused men had forced themselves upon the Queen then they could have been charged under the 1352 Treason Act for 'violating' the King's consort, but the indictments all hinged on the trysts being consensual. The charges against Anne Boleyn described her as having 'frail and carnal sexual appetites', not the sort of language used to describe an unwilling participant in these liaisons. There was little in the 1352 Act, however, that could easily be used to charge Anne with treason, outside of the Church courts, which normally dealt with matrimonial matters. The fallout from the Boleyn affair resulted in moves to make adultery treasonous in the 1536 Act of Succession, but it wasn't until Katherine Howard's adultery in 1542 that legislation was enacted to make any 'unchaste woman marrying the king' guilty of high treason. The most salacious accusations were reserved for Anne and her brother, George Boleyn Lord Rochford. Anne was accused of 'alluring him with her tongue in the said George's mouth, and the said George's tongue in hers, with their eyes wide open'. That only left the claim that Anne had committed all these adulterous acts to gain the influence of these men in order to usurp the King and plot his death, and that these actions had caused the King harm when he learnt of them. The former, if true, was undoubtedly treasonous, though there was no direct evidence of such plots. The treason case against Anne – generally assumed to have been masterminded by Thomas Cromwell – therefore rested on proving her infidelities, which in turn would imply that Anne was guilty of the more treasonous charges in the indictment. If the prosecution could get one of the accused lovers to admit to having illicit liaisons with Anne, then this would discredit any defence Anne or the others had relating to the other charges.

Four of Anne's supposed lovers – Henry Noreys, William Brereton, Francis Weston, and Mark Smeton – were tried on Friday 12 May, the day after the oyer and terminer returns, in Westminster Hall.

Defendants in a Tudor treason trial were at an enormous disadvantage. They were not allowed defence counsel, and were only informed of the specific charges laid against them on the day of trial, so they were little match for the well-prepared Crown prosecutors seeking to prove their guilt. Of the four, only Smeton pleaded guilty to adultery with the Queen; he refuted the remaining charges. The others pleaded not guilty on all counts. However, Smeton's admission of guilt cast enough doubt on the others that the jury found the men guilty, not just of the adultery that Smeton had admitted to, but on all other counts, including those charges deemed treasonous. It was therefore judged that they be executed in the manner customary for cases of high treason, to be hanged, drawn, and quartered at Tyburn.

Anne and her brother, Lord Rochford, were tried in the Great Hall of the Tower of London on 15 May, three days after the Westminster Hall trial. Contemporary accounts suggest that Anne gave a quietly dignified and assured rebuttal of all the accusations made against her, but it was to no avail. The jury of peers all found her guilty, and the lord Steward of the court, the Duke of Norfolk – Anne's uncle – proclaimed sentence:

> Because thou has offended our sovereign the king's grace in committing treason against his person and here attainted of the same, the law of the realm is this, that thou hast deserved death, and thy judgement is this: that thou shall be burned here within the Tower of London, on the Green, else to have thy head smitten off, as the king's pleasure shall be further known of the same.
> WRIOTHESLEY, *CHRONICLE*, I, P. 38

The choice of execution was unusual. In cases of high treason, women found guilty were to be burned (as opposed to men, who were hanged, drawn, and quartered). However, because she was Queen, the lord steward also gave the King the option for Anne to be beheaded instead. This judgement prompted a bemused murmur among the judges, not because of the forms of punishment proposed, but because the lord steward offered the King a choice, which was most improper and irregular in court judgements. In the end, the King opted for death by the sword for Anne, in the French style (the English favoured the axe), and an executioner was summoned from Calais to perform the act. The warrant for Anne's execution claims that Henry chose death by beheading to spare his queen the indignity of burning and to grant her a swift death.

The success of the 1534 Act of Succession was reliant on the legitimacy of Anne Boleyn – and her marriage to Henry VIII – remaining untarnished. Her execution for treason therefore necessitated a new act, one that kept all the amendments to the 1352 Treason Act but removed any allusions to Boleyn's legitimacy as queen. This was not a simple process. The new 1536 Act of Succession opens with a recital of the 1534 Act, stating that it needs repealing in light of Anne's treason. However, the English government needed to ensure that those committing treason between the enactment of the 1534 Act and the new 1536 Act could still be tried, so the new Act of Succession has a clause stating that the 1534 Act should remain in force until its repeal in the current Parliament. But this meant that technically all those who had accused Anne Boleyn of adultery and treason as part of her trial – and even those drawing up the new legislation – were guilty of treason themselves under the terms of the 1534 Act of Succession. This meant that the 1536 Act needed a retroactive pardon for all those who could be accused of treason through remarks about Queen Anne and her daughter Elizabeth. The 1536 Act of Succession therefore preserved the treasons outlined in the 1534 Act, while also fully denouncing Queen Anne and confirming her treasons. It also furnished the King with a more comprehensive treason act. Refusal to take the oath of succession and words against the monarch were now full treasons, any mention of misprision of treason having been removed.

The case of Anne Boleyn and the Acts of Succession show how Henry VIII's government were willing to stretch the limits of the 1352 Treason Act in order to realise their revolutionary policies. When these limits were met, Henry and his advisers amended the law to suit their needs.

THOMAS MORE AND THE BREAK
WITH ROME

When Henry VIII declared himself Supreme Head of the Church in England and broke with Rome, treason laws took on a new responsibility: to enforce the King's controversial religious policies. Treason in England was forever changed after the break with Rome, as plotters and dissenters now had religious cause to oppose their sovereign. The 1534 Treason Act (26 Hen VIII, c 13), which primarily dealt with treasonous words, including in the definition of such words claims that the King was a heretic or infidel for rejecting the authority of the Pope. The Crown needed to ensure that people such as Elizabeth Barton could, in future, be prosecuted with the full force of the law. One of the earliest victims of this new act was Sir Thomas More. Initially a silent critic of Henry's decision to marry Anne Boleyn – he had made his excuses to not attend their wedding – and the religious policies Henry pursued, the increased need for Henry to receive sworn oaths of allegiance from his ministers forced More's hand.

As a man with former political power, who was held in high esteem by many, More's continued refusal to acknowledge Henry as Supreme Head of the Church in England was problematic, and prompted action from Henry's other chief ministers to ensure the King's new religious policies were accepted by the populace. In early 1534, before the Act of Supremacy was passed, Thomas Cromwell accused More of previously giving counsel to Elizabeth Barton, the Holy Maid of Kent. In April the same year, More had been asked to appear to swear his allegiance to the Act of Succession. He had acquiesced, but only in so far as to accept Parliament's right to declare Anne Boleyn as the legitimate Queen of England; he would not accept the spiritual validity of the marriage. He also refused to sign the Oath of Succession, for which he was arrested and transferred to the Tower of London.

In November 1534, the Act of Supremacy declared Henry VIII to be Supreme Head of the Church of England. More's gaolers visited him to ask his opinions of the new act, and pressed for him to accept Henry as head of the Church. More refused. Under the new acts, this was a treasonous offence, and preparations for More's trial began in earnest.

More had made his choice. When asked to choose between the King and God, he chose the latter. To disobey one's sovereign could only lead to death; to disavow your God would lead to eternal damnation. Of the recent Act of Supremacy, More said that this law was like a two-edged sword; for in consenting to it, a person would endanger his soul, and in rejecting it would lose his life.

In answering the charges laid against him, More challenged how far – if at all – his actions constituted treason. He had, he proclaimed, also been upfront with Henry about his second marriage, 'according to the dictates of my conscience'. To his mind, this was not high treason, the opposite in fact. If More had answered Henry falsely, when expressly asked for his opinion on the King's marriage, then that would be a more traitorous act:

> If I have offended the King herein; if it can be an offence to tell one's mind freely, when his sovereign puts the question to him; I suppose I have been sufficiently punish'd already for the fault, by the great afflictions I have endured, by the loss of my estate, and my tedious imprisonment, which has continued already near fifteen months.

Regardless of whether More believed his acts treasonous, all the jury were asked to consider was whether More had committed these acts. As he had denied the King's supremacy and refused to swear the oath, he was guilty of treason according to the 1534 Treason Act. The jury took less than fifteen minutes to reach this guilty verdict.

The Lord Chancellor then proceeded to sentencing, but was interrupted by More, who requested the opportunity to argue why judgement should not be pronounced against him. The Lord Chancellor granted More this request, and More was relentless in his criticism:

> This indictment is grounded upon an Act of Parliament, directly repugnant to the Laws of God and his Holy Church, the Supreme

Government of which, or of any part thereof, no Temporal Person may by any Law presume to take upon him, being what right belongs to the See of *Rome*, which by special Prerogative was granted by the Mouth of our Savior Christ himself to St. Peter and the Bishops of Rome … it is therefore, amongst Catholic Christians, insufficient in Law, to charge any Christian to obey it.

These laws, he continued, went against the first clause of Magna Carta – that the English Church shall always be free – and against the King's own coronation oath, in which he promised to uphold the rights and liberties of the Church.

His piece done, judgement was finally made against him. More was sentenced to death by hanging, drawing, and quartering, as was customary in cases of high treason. Later, this sentence was reduced to merely beheading. Sir Thomas More was executed at the Tower on 6 July 1535.

HENRY VIII'S LEGACY

For his many faults, Henry VIII at least ensured a smooth succession to his son Edward VI. In an attempt to appease his new subjects, Edward and his council, led by the Lord Protector Edward Seymour, First Duke of Somerset, sought to scale back some of Henry's more severe treason laws. One of the most unpopular laws was the Act of 1534 (26 Hen VIII, c 13) that made it treasonable to speak words against the King, such as referring to Henry VIII as a heretic or infidel. To Catholics, this was exactly what Henry had become when he rejected the authority of the Pope (and, by extension, God), so this legislation ensured that the government had the means to punish anyone condemning the King for breaking with Rome. However, the act was unpopular as it meant that dissenters were at a greater risk of being prosecuted for treason just for speaking out of turn. In the first year of Edward VI's reign, the new king therefore passed a new act, the Act for the Repeal of Certain Statutes concerning Treasons, Felonies, etc (1 Edw VI, c 12). The preamble to the act justified these repeals, saying that subjects 'should obey rather for love ... of a king and prince, than for fear of his straight and severe laws'; his father's laws had been too harsh, this was Edward attempting a fresh start. The act itself made the printing of treasonable words a tiered offence: on the first conviction you would be imprisoned and have your goods and chattels seized; on the second, you could be imprisoned in perpetuity and suffer permanent loss of all goods, chattels, and offices; finally, on the third, you were subject to the penalties of high treason. The statute also stipulated that a complaint of such treasonable acts should be made within a span of thirty days and that there should be two witnesses, that is, a single person could not accuse someone of treason.

Mary I's reign began with a treason trial of the men who had supported Lady Jane Grey, the 'nine days queen', whom they had been instrumental in placing upon the throne. Edward VI had not wanted his Catholic half-sister to undo his Protestant reforms, and so nominated Jane Grey, granddaughter of his aunt Mary, in his will. His half-sister Mary, next in line to the throne according to their father Henry VIII's will, was quick to act; she rallied her supporters and had overpowered the Queen's followers within days to take her place on the throne.

The new Queen, Mary I, did not need to enact any new treason legislation in the trial of those implicated in placing Lady Jane Grey on the throne. In declaring Jane queen, and in levying war against Mary – the true queen – John Dudley, the Duke of Northumberland, and his co-conspirators (including his eldest son, the Earl of Warwick) were guilty of treason under the acts of Edward VI and – most important – under the Treason Act of 1352. Jane herself was charged with treason because she had signed several documents 'Jane the Queen'. Initially, though, Mary spared Jane's life. The Duke of Northumberland was blamed for the coup, and was executed for orchestrating it, on 22 August 1553. However, Wyatt's Rebellion in February 1554, which included among its supporters the Duke of Suffolk, Jane's father, sealed her fate. Mary could not allow a Protestant figurehead to remain alive.

Mary I was more emphatic in resetting the clock to 1352. Her first act

(1 Mary, Stat 1, c 1) stated that only acts of treason as defined in the 1352 Statute of Treasons were treasonable offences, essentially clearing away all of Henry VIII's treason statutes. All this amending and repealing of treason laws unsurprisingly caused some confusion. In 1554, Sir Nicholas Throckmorton was charged with treason for supporting Thomas Wyatt's Rebellion, instigated in response to Mary's plans to marry King Philip of Spain. At his trial, Throckmorton showed considerable legal knowledge, enough to know that the charges laid against him did not constitute treason as defined by the 1352 statute. When the judges insisted he was guilty of treason, Throckmorton asked:

> To what purpose serves the Statute of Repeal the last parliament, where I heard some of you here present, and diverse others of the Queen's learned council grievously inveigh against the cruel and bloody laws of King Henry VIII, and against some laws made in my late sovereign lord and master's time, King Edward VI? Some termed them Draco's Laws, which were written in blood.
> TRIAL OF THROCKMORTON, STATE TRIALS I, 896

He accepted the accusation that he was not in favour of the Queen's marriage to Philip, but argued – successfully – that this was not a treasonous act, saying, 'It was no treason, nor no procurement of treason, to talk against the coming hither of the Spaniards.' The jury acquitted Throckmorton, much to the judges' displeasure. The jurors were fined in the Court of Star Chamber for their verdict shortly afterwards.

Henry VIII's eldest legitimate son and daughter, Edward and Mary, had both shunned the treason laws of their father, in favour of the 1352 Treason Act, which by this point was steeped in centuries of legitimacy. However, their brief reigns meant that the longer-term implications of Henry VIII's break with Rome would not be felt until Henry's younger daughter, Elizabeth, came to the throne in 1558. Her forty-five-year reign would witness the rise of religious and overseas treasons, a direct consequence of her father's actions.

Part II

FROM CROWN TO STATE

•

THE
HISTORIE
OF
THE LIFE AND
Reigne of the moſt Renow-
med and Victorious Princeſſe
ELIZABETH,
Late Queene of England.

Contayning the moſt Important and Remarkeable
Paſſages of State, during Her Happy, Long and
Proſperous Raigne.

Compoſed by Way of ANNALS, *by the moſt*
Learned Mr. WILLIAM CAMDEN.

And faithfully Tranſlated into Engliſh.

LONDON:

Printed for *Benjamin Fiſher* and are to be ſold at his ſhop
in *Alderſgate* ſtreete, at the ſigne of the
Talbot. MDCXXX.

Title page of William Camden's *Annales rerum Anglicarum et Hibernicarum regnante Elizabetha.*

Six

THE CATHOLIC TREASONS AGAINST ELIZABETH I, 1558–1603

*As for me, I see no such great cause why I should either be
fond to live or fear to die. I have had good experience of this world,
and I know what it is to be a subject and what to be a sovereign.
Good neighbours I have had, and I have met with
bad: and in trust I have found treason.*

ELIZABETH I, SPEECH TO PARLIAMENT, 1586, IN WILLIAM
CAMDEN *ANNALES RERUM ANGLICARUM* (1615), BK. 3

During her forty-five-year reign, Elizabeth I faced various attempted treasons of a kind which her father, Henry VIII, had not. The break with Rome had long-lasting implications not just for the English Church, but also for anyone planning to usurp or kill the monarch: religious beliefs could now be a motive for treason. The Protestantism of England and Wales under Elizabeth put the Queen and her realm at odds with the great Catholic powers of Spain and France, not to mention the Pope himself. Consequently, treason in the reign of Elizabeth I was marked by religiously motivated plots and attempts by foreign powers to undermine the Queen's authority.

Religion was high on the agenda at the start of Elizabeth's reign, with the young Queen and her government seeking to pursue a 'middle way'; the reigns of her half-siblings Edward and Mary had shown Elizabeth the dangers of committing to one faith at the expense of another. It was prudent, too, for Elizabeth to appease the many Catholic nobles who still resided in England. The Elizabethan Religious Settlement, formed from the 1559 Acts of Supremacy and Uniformity, sought to allow the Queen's subjects to practise whatever faith they preferred in private, so long as it was not detrimental to the Queen. The Act of Supremacy required all clergy and government officers to take an oath of supremacy, including an acknowledgement of Elizabeth as supreme governor of the Church. The wording was intended to appease Catholics by allowing them to both acknowledge Elizabeth as governor of the Church while still considering the Pope head of the Church. Refusal to take the oath carried harsh punishments: those who refused three times were judged as treasonous, and punished as in cases of high treason. The Act of Uniformity authorised a new Book of Common Prayer, similar to the protestant prayer book introduced in Edward VI's reign but with some Catholic elements retained, in the hope that all parties would be appeased.

Broadly speaking, the Elizabethan Religious Settlement was accepted by most parties. And yet not everyone was happy with the compromise: extreme Protestants – Puritans – did not wish to concede anything to the Catholic faith. Conversely, some Catholics, who in Mary I's reign had enjoyed religious freedom, did not like that they were now asked to hide or deny their beliefs. Some of these disaffected Catholics moved to the European continent; others begrudgingly accepted the new status quo in England and Wales.

Yet, disaffection with Elizabeth's religious policies was not enough on its own to incite Catholic subjects to treason; there needed to be a viable Catholic alternative to Elizabeth. The harsh punishments dealt out to traitors in the reigns of Henry VIII, Edward VI, and Mary I were still fresh in the memory. Removing the head without a guarantee that the Catholic faith would be restored was not worth the risk. Unfortunately for Elizabeth, such a person not only existed, but from 1568 was resident in England. For the first two-thirds of her reign, Elizabeth had to deal with attempted treasons citing her cousin, Mary Stuart – Queen of Scots – as the rightful Catholic heir to the English throne.

Mary was destined to be a rival to Elizabeth. She was a Catholic. She was a direct descendant of Henry VII, the father of the Tudor dynasty, through the line of Henry's eldest daughter, Margaret Tudor, who married James IV of Scotland. And, as long as Elizabeth remained unmarried and childless, there was an unspoken assumption that Mary was her most likely heir. Indeed, Mary Stuart's line would eventually inherit the English crown with the accession of her son, James VI of Scotland (James I of England). Additionally, there was among Catholic dissidents the question of Elizabeth's legitimacy. Though Henry VIII's Act of Succession had legitimised his daughter, the fact that Elizabeth's mother was Anne Boleyn, who had been so thoroughly besmirched and disinherited in her treason trial, subsequent execution, and legislation after her death, gave Catholics plenty of (treasonous) ammunition to question her legitimacy.

Elizabeth would have been well aware of the threat that Mary's existence had to her position as Queen. After all, she herself had been in that position: when she was Princess Elizabeth during the reign of her sister Mary I, Thomas Wyatt's Rebellion had listed among its aims the desire to replace Mary with her Protestant half-sister and to reinforce the Protestant throne by marrying Elizabeth to Edward Stafford.

One of the earliest plots to invoke Mary Stuart's name in vain was the plot of Arthur Poole, who was tried and executed for treason in February 1563. Poole's plot was complex, involving his travelling to Europe, declaring himself 'Duke of Clarence' (a defunct title since the execution for treason of Edward IV's brother George, Duke of Clarence, in 1478), securing the support of the European powers and of the Pope, and having his co-conspirator Edmund Poole marry Mary, Queen of Scots. At this time, Mary had returned to Scotland following the death of her first husband, Francis the Dauphin of France. Two of Poole's conspirators, John Prestall and Edward Cosyn, were also accused of performing various incantations and conjurations of evil spirits to carry out their treasons.

Poole's attempted treason aside, Mary's threat to Elizabeth did not become pronounced until the exiled Scottish Queen was forced to seek refuge in England in 1568. The year before, Mary was implicated in the murder of her second husband (and father to James VI), Lord Darnley. That Mary married James Hepburn, Fourth Earl of Bothwell, the man many believed to have orchestrated Darnley's death, just three months later, was viewed at the very least as being in bad taste. In July 1567, Mary was forced to abdicate in favour of her one-year-old son James. She fled to England a year later, after failing to regain the Scottish throne in an attempted coup.

With Mary in England, Elizabeth's disaffected Catholic subjects and rival foreign powers had someone to rally behind. Whether Mary was complicit in any of the plots against the Queen was irrelevant – what mattered was her existence as a viable Catholic alternative. It is no coincidence that the number of attempted treasons against Elizabeth I picked up after 1568 once there was a Catholic figurehead on English soil.

Just a year after Mary's arrival in England, the first serious rebellion against the Elizabethan regime was raised in the name of the 'true' Catholic faith. This rebellion, dubbed the Northern Rebellion, saw Charles Neville and Thomas Percy, the Earls of Westmorland and Northumberland, storm Durham with over 4,500 men. Percy was the son of Sir Thomas Percy, executed in 1537 for his part in the Pilgrimage of Grace, the popular uprising against Henry VIII's Dissolution of the Monasteries. The Northern Rebellion was similarly a religiously motivated uprising. The first thing the rebel earls did after storming Durham was to hold a Catholic mass in Durham Cathedral, an illegal act. They ripped apart Protestant books and overturned the communion table. Their aim, to remove those surrounding the Queen who subverted the true Catholic faith.

The rebels lacked a coherent plan, however. From Durham Cathedral, some followers besieged Barnard Castle, while others went to Hartlepool, where they took the port. But one thing was clear from the uprising: there were large pockets of people throughout England and Wales who wished a return to Catholicism, and did not oppose the earls' actions. When news of the uprising reached the Queen and her Council, they were uncertain just how large in scale the uprising was – in this respect the rebellion's disorganisation worked to its advantage. Fearing the worst, Elizabeth mustered an army of some 14,000 men to quell the uprising.

Most of the rebels dispersed when they learned of this army, led by the Earl of Sussex, heading north, and after the uprising many rebels appeared in court to apologise for their actions, while people in the north celebrated the defeat of the Rising with bonfires. Those who had disbanded early were offered a pardon; if they persisted in their uprising after the pardon was issued, however, they could face the full force of the law. Hundreds of rebels were executed for their part in the rebellion. The main instigators, the Earls of Westmorland and Northumberland, initially escaped justice by fleeing north to Scotland. Westmorland evaded capture by escaping to Flanders. However, Northumberland was captured and handed back to the English three years later, in 1572, when he was executed for treason. He was stripped of his titles, including that of Knight of the Garter.

All those punished as part of the Northern Rebellion were regarded as treasonous and punished as traitors. In cases of treason, the Crown received the goods and chattels of all those found guilty. But most of the lands of these traitors were located in Durham, which posed an interesting legal problem regarding the interpretation of the 1352 Statute of Treason. Durham was a palatinate, presided over by the Bishop of Durham. This meant that in most criminal and legal matters, any goods forfeited should go to the bishop, rather than the Crown. Keen to reap the financial rewards of the uprising, the Queen's Attorney General, Gilbert Gerard, argued that treason was so severe an offence that it superseded any claims of lesser lords. Additionally, Gerard argued that as treason was a sin against the sovereign, Elizabeth had the right to any of the goods or lands received by forfeiture. The bishop's counsel unsurprisingly disagreed, and in this instance the rest of the Queen's justices agreed with them; the bishop retained the right to most of the lands forfeited within his palatinate.

News of the Northern Rebellion buoyed those on the continent who wished to see England and Wales return to Catholicism. The rebellion had shown that supporters of the 'true' faith were willing to rise up with the right motivation. On 25 February 1570, the Catholic cause in England and Wales was granted the ultimate seal of spiritual approval when Pope Pius V excommunicated Elizabeth I. The papal bull which detailed this excommunication, *Regnans in Excelsis*, was published in part to support the Catholic aims of the 1569 Northern Rebellion (though released too late to do the rebels any good):

> But the number of the ungodly has grown so strong in power, that no place is left in the world which they have not tried to corrupt with their abominable doctrines; among others assisting in this work is the servant of vice, Elizabeth, pretended Queen of England, with whom, as in a place of sanctuary, the most nefarious wretches have found refuge. This same woman, having acquired the kingdom and outrageously usurped for herself the place of Supreme Head of the Church in all England and its chief authority and jurisdiction, has again plunged that same kingdom back into a wretchedly unhappy condition, after it had so recently been reclaimed for the Catholic Faith and prosperity.
> POPE PIUS V, REGNANS IN EXCELSIS

This was merely the introduction to a document which wholly rejected the authority of Elizabeth I. She was accused of heresy, of ejecting bishops of the true faith from her realm, and of deciding legal cases which should rightly have been heard within the Church. For these reasons the Pope declared Elizabeth to be deprived of her 'pretended claim' to England and absolved all those who had sworn fealty to her from their oaths.

Circulating such an inflammatory text, which denied Elizabeth's sovereignty and endangered her life by releasing Catholics from fealty to her, was a treasonable act, and the English government were quick to punish anyone publishing such literature in the realm. John Felton and Cornelius Irishman were among the first of these casualties. At about 11 p.m. on 24 May – three months after the papal bull was issued – Felton and Irishman nailed a copy of *Regnans in Excelsis* to the Bishop of London's palace adjacent to St Paul's Cathedral.

Elizabeth I and her Parliament responded to this excommunication in kind, by enacting statutes more strongly denying the authority of the Pope within Elizabeth's realms and dominions. These acts emphasised that to deprive Elizabeth of the office of monarch in any way, be that by plotting her death or by usurping her power, was treason. The second of these acts made it treason not only to bring papal bulls into the realm, but also merely to possess them or circulate them within the realm. This statute was significant because the language suggested that treason was not only a crime of regicide – of even just trying to kill the king or queen – but also one of usurping the Crown, to deprive the monarch of their title.

The first person convicted under this new act was the seminary priest Cuthbert Mayne, executed at Launceston on 29 November 1577. His crime was receiving letters of absolution from outside the realm and publishing them in Golden, Cornwall. Others tried in the 1570s for treason because of their faith were John Nelson, a Jesuit, tried in 1578, and Thomas Sherwood, a Catholic layman tried two days after Nelson.

A new sermon – the *Homily Against Disobedience and Wilful Rebellion* – was also published, to dissuade would-be traitors. This was to be delivered in churches throughout the realm. The sermon stressed that disobedience to the monarch was disobedience to God. It also reminded people that those that attempted to rebel rarely met happy ends.

By the 1580s, further legislation against the Pope – and those that followed him – was passed in Parliament. The papacy was framed not only as a challenge to the Queen's spiritual authority within her realm, but also to her authority or sovereignty in general, because the Pope encouraged her subjects to withdraw their allegiance to her. The Jesuit

Act' of 1585 extended the punishment of treason to any Jesuits or seminary priests who entered the realm, and commanded that any such persons depart the realm within forty days of the act. All Englishmen currently studying abroad in such colleges were to return home. As Jesuits had sworn allegiance to the Pope, they were enemies of the Queen, and therefore treasonous.

After 1570, Elizabeth I now had three main causes for concern with regard to Catholic threats. The 1569 Northern Rebellion had shown that there was still support for Catholicism across the realm, from both the nobility and the wider populace. An outright censure of Catholic practices would surely result in popular uprising. Secondly, Elizabeth's excommunication put a target on her back, not only from Catholic sympathisers in her realm, but also from foreign powers on the continent. Catholic leaders such as King Philip of Spain (Mary I's former husband) could now openly support attempts to usurp Elizabeth, in defence of the 'true' faith. Finally, Mary, Queen of Scots, the favoured Catholic alternative to Elizabeth, was now in England.

The Ridolfi Plot, instigated a year after Elizabeth's excommunication, involved all three of these. The plot was named after Roberto de Ridolfi, a Florentine merchant who had settled in London in the 1560s. Although he was a Catholic, he was employed by William Cecil Lord Burghley, Elizabeth's chief adviser, and others as a financial agent, and consequently held great influence and credibility at the English court. Yet Ridolfi was one of many who wished to see England return to Catholicism, and by the late 1560s he was working as an agent of the French and Spanish, supplying them with information that could help the Catholic cause. From 1566, he was a secret envoy – *nunzio segreto* – of Pope Pius V, sowing the seeds of discontent in England. During the Northern Rebellion of 1569, the Pope had given Ridolfi 12,000 crowns to aid the rebels in their cause. After Elizabeth's excommunication the following year, he helped to smuggle copies of the papal bull into England and disseminate copies throughout the realm.

The plot to which Ridolfi gave his name had the ultimate aim of

Left: Marginalia drawing of Edward I, 1296–7.

© *The National Archives*

Right: Depiction of Edward II by George Vertue, 1684–1756. The lower part (unseen) shows him being murdered horribly, according to rumour.

© *Classic Image / Alamy Stock Photo*

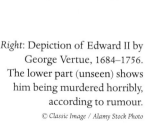

Payments made for the execution of 'William de Waleys', 1305. © *The National Archives*

Above: Illumination from Froissart's
Chronicles depicting the events of the
'Great Revolt' of 1381.

© *Art Collection 2 / Alamy Stock Photo*

Right: Richard II, as depicted in a
contemporary portrait from
Westminster Abbey.

© *GRANGER – Historical Picture Archive / Alamy Stock Photo*

Left: Posthumous portrait (around 1520) of Edward IV. Unknown artist of the Anglo-Flemish school.

© *Art Collection 3 / Alamy Stock Photo*

Right: Portrait of Richard III, late sixteenth century, by an unknown artist.

© *Chronicle / Alamy Stock Photo*

Act of Attainder against George, Duke of Clarence, the King's brother, 1478.

© *The National Archives*

Left: Portrait c. 1527 by Hans Holbein the Younger of Thomas More, who was executed for treason in 1535 for refusing to acknowledge Henry VIII as Supreme Head of the English Church.

Right: 1572 commission appointing George, Earl of Shrewsbury, as Lord High Steward for the trial of Thomas, fourth Duke of Norfolk. With the sign manual and great seal of Elizabeth I.

Left: Printed copy of *Regnans in Excelsis*, the 1570 papal bull that excommunicated Elizabeth I for heresy.

Above: The Gunpowder Plot conspirators. Based on the 1605 engraving by Crispijn de Passe the Elder. © *The National Archives*

Right: Portrait of Henry Garnet, created as part of the hunt for Garnet who was wanted for his association with the Gunpowder Plotters. He was executed for treason in March 1606.

© *The National Archives (SP 14/216/2 fo 165a)*

Si quid patimini propter iustitiam, beati i petri: Henricus Garnetus anglus e sociclate IESV passus · 3 · May · 1606 ·

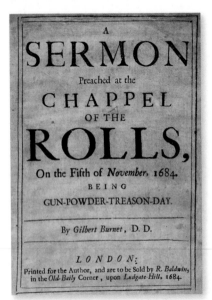

A
SERMON
Preached at the
CHAPPEL
OF THE
ROLLS,
On the Fifth of *November*, 1684.
BEING
GUN-POWDER-TREASON-DAY.

By *Gilbert Burnet*, D.D.

LONDON:
Printed for the Author, and are to be Sold by *R. Baldwin*, in the *Old-Baily* Corner, upon *Ladgate-Hill*, 1684.

Left: Title page of a 1684 sermon preached at the chapel of the rolls on 5 November, commemorating Gunpowder Treason Day. An act passed in March 1606 had made 5 November a day of thanksgiving. ©
The National Archives (PRO 30/26/66)

A. *Seine Kön : May : an dem Block .* B. *Doctor Juxon .* C. *Colonell Tomlinson .* D. *Colonell Hacker .* E. F. *die* 2. *Executorn* . C.R.V.N 1649

Top left: Portrait of Charles I, which can be found at the front of a 1643 King's Bench Plea Roll. © *The National Archives* (KB 27/1681/2)

Top right: Portrait by Sir Anthony van Dyck, 1527, of Thomas Wentworth, first Earl of Strafford, who was executed for treason in 1641. © *IanDagnall Computing / Alamy Stock Photo*

Below: Contemporary German print of the execution of Charles I outside the Banqueting House at the Palace of Whitehall in January 1649. © *history_docu_photo / Alamy Stock Photo*

Orlandus Bridgeman Miles et Baronettus Custos Magni Sigilli Angliæ.

Top left: Portrait of Charles II circa 1660–5, by John Michael Wright.

© *Stocktrek Images, Inc. / Alamy Stock Photo*

Top right: Sir Orlando Bridgeman, Lord Chief Baron of the Court of Exchequer and Lord Chief Justice of the Court of Common Pleas, 1682, by Robert White after William Faithorne.

© *Danvis Collection / Alamy Stock Photo*

Right: Skull of Oliver Cromwell, who was posthumously executed for treason for his involvement in the beheading of Charles I.

© *Look and Learn / Bridgeman Images*

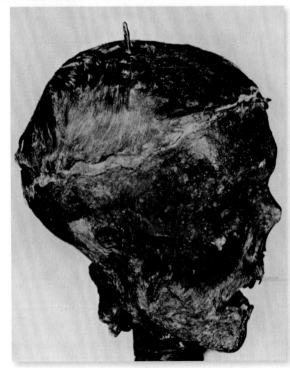

returning England to the Catholic faith by replacing Elizabeth I with Mary Stuart. The plot had many high-profile conspirators: Pope Pius V, King Philip II of Spain, Mary, Queen of Scots, her trusted adviser the Bishop of Ross, and the highest peer in England, Thomas Howard the Fourth Duke of Norfolk. Like Mary, Norfolk was a cousin of Elizabeth I; Elizabeth's great-grandfather through her mother, Anne Boleyn, was Thomas Howard, Second Duke of Norfolk.

Unlike the Northern Rebellion, the Ridolfi Plot carried clear aims. First, Mary Stuart would be freed by a Catholic uprising. This was initially the plan for the Northern Rebellion, but Mary was moved to a more secure location when rumours of an uprising began to occur. The second part of the Ridolfi Plot would see Mary march on London with an army of Catholic and Spanish forces to supplant Elizabeth. Finally, to ensure a Catholic succession and to solidify her claim to Elizabeth's throne, Mary was to marry the Duke of Norfolk. In planning this uprising, Ridolfi persuaded Thomas Howard to sign a declaration stating that he was Catholic.

To secure overseas support, Ridolfi left for Europe in March 1571. He met with Pius V, King Philip II of Spain, and the Duke of Alva, Governor-General of the Low Countries. The Pope was particularly enthusiastic about the plot, and wrote letters to both Mary, Queen of Scots and Philip supporting the uprising. Ridolfi then wrote letters – in cipher – to the Bishop of Ross and Mary to relay this success. While Ridolfi was on the continent, however, the English government had uncovered his plot, not least because Ridolfi had been extremely vocal about the plan while in Europe. When staying in Florence, he told Grand Duke Cosimo (I) de' Medici of his plans, who immediately warned Elizabeth. The government had also found out details of the plot through the seizure of the goods of Charles Bailly, a papal agent and servant of Mary, Queen of Scots and the Bishop of Ross. Bailly was arrested upon his arrival at Dover; in his baggage were a number of banned books and some ciphered correspondence about the plot between the Duke of Norfolk and his brother-in-law, Lord Lumley.

Many of the details of the Ridolfi Plot are listed in the treason trial for Thomas Howard, who was executed for the part he played. The indictment against Howard, made in December 1571, found him to be involved in many treasonous acts: to deprive the Queen of her crown; to incite sedition; to levy war and rebellion against the Queen; to subvert the government; to convert England to Catholicism; and to bring in strangers and aliens to invade the realm. These accusations became three treason charges at his trial: that he sought to deprive the Queen of her crown and life; that he sheltered and assisted the English rebels who fled following the failed Northern Rebellion of 1569; and that he assisted the Queen's Scottish enemies.

One of the key charges levelled against Norfolk was that he had planned to marry Mary, Queen of Scots in order to usurp Elizabeth. Though a marriage between Norfolk and Mary had been mooted by Elizabeth in the early 1560s, discussions about a possible match after 1568 – once Mary was a captive in England – were made behind Elizabeth's back. Norfolk, through either naivety or arrogance, worsened matters by lying outright to Elizabeth when asked whether he had any part in clandestine marriage discussions. In November 1568 (by which point Norfolk had met with Mary's contacts in earnest regarding a match), Elizabeth asked him what he thought about the rumours concerning a proposed marriage between him and Mary. Norfolk replied that he did not like such rumours, nor was he keen for such a marriage.

By June 1569, Mary, Queen of Scots had agreed to a marriage match between Norfolk and herself. Crucially though, she was keen to do so with Elizabeth's knowledge and consent. The longer discussions went on behind Elizabeth's back, the more dangerous it was for all involved, considering the strong claims to the English throne both Mary and Norfolk had. When told of the marriage match, Elizabeth was furious, no doubt in part because Norfolk had denied any such plans only a few months before. She immediately chided Norfolk, commanding him to free himself of any such match, and not to pursue it further. To do so would show disloyalty to her.

When reports of a potential uprising in the north started coming in later in 1569, Norfolk was ordered to the court, and placed in the Tower. While en route to London he sent a message to Northumberland and Westmorland, urging them not to rebel, fearing for his life if they did so. Norfolk was in the Tower during the failed Northern Rebellion, which may have contributed to his being spared punishment at this time for any suspected involvement in the uprising. In August 1570, Norfolk was released after promising never to deal in any cause of marriage between Mary, Queen of Scots and himself again. Especially damning for Norfolk was that as part of the investigation into his treasonable actions, which were revealed during his treason trial, it transpired that throughout 1570 Norfolk had continued to court Mary from the Tower. He sent her gifts at Christmas 1569 and midsummer 1570, and she sent him letters affirming her love and devotion to him. Worse still for Norfolk was that in 1571 he gave verbal agreement to Ridolfi to support Spanish military assistance in a planned removal of Elizabeth I, and in plans to legitimise Mary's claim to the throne by marrying her. Ridolfi's letters to the Pope, Philip II, and the Duke of Alva, were all subscribed by Norfolk.

Further proof of Norfolk's involvement in these matters was found in August 1571. Two of Norfolk's secretaries, William Barker and Robert Higford, gave Thomas Browne, a Shrewsbury draper, a bag of silver coins to deliver to Laurence Bannister, one of the duke's officials in the north of England. However, Browne was suspicious of this delivery, as the bag felt too heavy to only hold silver. Upon opening the bag, Browne discovered £600 in gold from the French ambassador, destined for Scotland on Mary's behalf. He also found several ciphered letters. This discovery was shared with William Cecil, the Queen's principal secretary, who ordered a search of Howard's property for the cipher key, where they found another ciphered letter from Mary hidden under a doormat.

Norfolk was not aware of the discovery of the letters or of the confessions of his secretaries – who had been arrested following the discovery of the gold – and so continued to deny any charges laid against him. The evidence was produced at his treason trial in January 1572.

He requested legal counsel, which was refused because in cases of high treason there could be no counsel for the defence. He pleaded not guilty, to no avail. The judges unanimously declared him guilty. He was to be executed at Tyburn, as was customary for cases of high treason. However, the execution didn't take place until June 1572, when he was beheaded on Tower Hill, following parliamentary pressure to punish the man who had attempted to marry Mary, Queen of Scots and remove Elizabeth; even after all his crimes had been revealed, it seemed that Elizabeth was still reluctant to execute Norfolk until she was forced to.

As for Ridolfi, he wisely did not return to England, and all the failed plot cost him was the value of his goods in England – nearly £3,000 – seized by the English government when his involvement in the plot was discovered. He died in Florence in 1612, after a lengthy career as envoy to the Grand Dukes of Tuscany, the Medici.

Mary Stuart in this instance escaped punishment. There was nothing in writing pinning her to the plans to overthrow Elizabeth, and her pursuit of a marriage match did not overtly connect her to the part of the plot that was treasonous. Yet, attempts to dethrone Elizabeth in favour of her Roman Catholic cousin continued to use Mary's name. In 1572, the year that Thomas Norfolk was tried for his part in the Ridolfi Plot, John Hall and Francis Rolston were accused of, and executed for, attempting to change the 'pure religion of the realm' by freeing Mary, Queen of Scots from the custody of George, Earl of Shrewsbury, and declaring her queen instead of Elizabeth.

Attempts to remove Elizabeth in favour of Mary continued into the 1580s. In 1583, two plots against the Queen were uncovered and swiftly dealt with. On 22 October of that year John Somerville, from an old Warwickshire Roman Catholic family, along with his wife Margaret, parents-in-law Edward and Mary Arden (another old Catholic family) and Hugh Hall, a priest, allegedly conspired to bring about the death of Elizabeth, motivated by a desire to change the religion established in the kingdom. Two days later, on 24 October, Somerville publicly declared that he would 'go up to the Court and shoot the Queen through with a pistol'. This foolhardy announcement was picked up by the Queen's 'spymaster' and his men, who were ready for him when, the following day, he took a pistol, gunpowder and bullets, and journeyed to London to carry out his intention. Somerville and the Ardens were arrested, and at their trial, he pleaded guilty while the others pleaded not guilty. All were found guilty, to be executed for high treason. The women and Hugh Hall were pardoned, however, and Somerville reportedly hanged himself before he could be executed. Edward Arden, Somerville's father-in-law – who had served as sheriff of Warwickshire, and was a distant cousin of William Shakespeare – took the brunt of the blame and was hanged, drawn, and quartered at Smithfield on 20 December 1583.

The Throckmorton Plot, also thwarted in 1583, planned to set free Mary, Queen of Scots with the aid of a foreign invasion force led by Henry, Duke of Guise, and remove Elizabeth as queen. This information was gained through the torture of Francis Throckmorton, the person after whom the plot is named. Investigations found that the foreign forces were already amassed, and the King of Spain had agreed to bear half the cost. Francis Throckmorton and his brother were to form the welcoming party at Arundel in Sussex. Throckmorton felt that in his failure to liberate Mary, he had betrayed her, and at his trial in November 1583, when asked to name all his co-conspirators, he lamented, 'Nowe I have disclosed the secrets of her who was the deerest thing to me in the worlde ... I see no cause why I should spare anyone.' Yet, despite the discovery of letters written to and from Mary as part of this plot, there still wasn't enough for Elizabeth's government to convict her. They would need an airtight case to justify regicide. Throckmorton himself, however, was not spared – found guilty of treason, he was executed at Tyburn in July 1584.

The breakthrough for Mary Stuart's enemies came with the Babington Plot. Like many of the plots before it, the main aims were to remove Elizabeth from the throne, release Mary, and utilise foreign forces to restore Catholicism to the realm. But the Babington Plot went further. In order to ensure that Elizabeth would not be a threat to the Catholic coup, six noblemen were tasked with assassinating her. On 6 July 1586, Anthony

Babington wrote a letter to Mary outlining the aims of the plot and asking for her approval and advice to ensure that the plan was a success.

The so-called Gallows Letter, Mary's response to Babington on 17 July 1586, was the smoking gun that would condemn her. In the letter, she authorised the plot and advised them to act swiftly, for Catholic support in England was diminishing with the growing persecution by the Protestant English government. Mary ended the letter by urging Babington to burn it after reading it. Unfortunately for Mary, the letter was intercepted by agents working for Francis Walsingham, Elizabeth I's spymaster. The letter was then passed to his cryptographer, Thomas Phelippes. Once he realised that the content of the letter was enough to clinch Mary's fate, Phelippes drew a gallows on the deciphered letter. The original letter was then resealed and completed its journey to Anthony Babington.

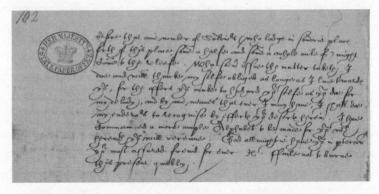

Copy of the 'Gallows Letter' from Mary, Queen of Scots to Anthony Babington, in which she declares her support for the planned assassination of Elizabeth I. The letter ends 'fail not to burn this present [letter] quickly'. (*SP 53/18, fo 112v*)

A month later, the plot started to unravel. One of Babington's co-conspirators, John Ballard, was arrested. Unaware that Walsingham was one step ahead of him, Babington tried to expedite the assassination of Elizabeth. He ordered John Savage to go at once to court to kill the Queen, and gave him money for clothes so that he could blend in at court and get close enough to Elizabeth to carry out the act. Babington happened to be at dinner at an inn when he chanced to discover that one of his dining companions, a man called Scudamore (who turned out to be one of Walsingham's undercover agents), was under orders to arrest him; he left the table without giving rise to suspicion and then fled, to hide with some companions in St John's Wood. From there they made their way to Harrow, where they were sheltered by a sympathiser, but some ten days later they were captured, arrested and, in due course, were tried for treason.

John Savage was the first to be tried. He pleaded guilty to conspiracy, but not guilty to assenting to kill the Queen. However, his confession – and those of his co-conspirators – stated clearly that he had sworn an oath to kill Elizabeth. He was found guilty on all counts. The other conspirators, when tried, also all admitted to trying to free Mary and alter the religion of England, but denied planning to kill Elizabeth. Eventually, however, they too pleaded guilty to that charge. They were all found guilty and condemned to be executed as traitors to the Crown. Babington was executed, along with six of his co-conspirators, on 20 September 1586, near St Giles-in-the-Fields. Their execution was particularly harsh. They were hanged, drawn, and quartered, as was typical of those found guilty of high treason. However, they were only hanged for a short time, meaning that their subsequent castration and disembowelling were particularly cruel. The remaining seven conspirators, executed the next day, were spared this cruel fate by the Queen, who ordered that they be hanged until they were dead, after which their bodies should be castrated and disembowelled.

Francis Walsingham had allowed the Babington Plot to progress in order to give Babington the rope needed to hang not only himself and his co-conspirators, but also Mary, Queen of Scots. When Mary's response to Babington showed her complicity in the attempted assassination of Elizabeth, Walsingham had all the evidence he needed to bring her to trial.

Mary was tried by a special judicial commission under the terms of the 1585 Act for the Surety of the Queen. This empowered the Privy Council and leading members of the Elizabeth's court to create special commissions in cases where the Queen's person was endangered. What this meant for Mary's trial was that all the arrangements could be laid out in advance, and Lord Burghley did precisely that, preparing everything ahead of time, from the timetable for the trial to the seating arrangements for those who attended.

Mary's trial began on 14 October 1586. The former Queen of Scotland made an impassioned defence. She questioned the jurisdiction of the commission to try a queen. Sixty years later, Mary's grandson Charles I would put a similar question to the High Court of Justice that tried – and executed – him. What right did they have to try a king, who has no equal? The commission had a firm response to Mary: in the realm of England, they only served one queen, Elizabeth, and it was for her that this trial was going ahead.

Mary initially denied even knowing Babington, let alone writing letters to him supporting the assassination of Elizabeth I. She was not aware just how thoroughly Walsingham and his spies had unravelled the plot. As far as she knew, Babington had burnt her letters as soon as he had read them, so she believed there to be no paper trail connecting her to him. She did not know that Babington and his conspirators had all confessed, and that the letters she had sent and received to and from him had been intercepted and deciphered by those now putting her on trial. During the final stages of the interrogation of Mary's secretaries, the knowledge of these letters was revealed to them and, in the face of overwhelming evidence against their mistress, they confessed everything. Their confessions could then be used to tie Mary to the Babington correspondences.

Mary was not immediately judged, guilty or otherwise. Elizabeth had sent a letter to Burghley ordering him to delay Mary's sentence: this wasn't a judgement to be made lightly, and shouldn't be rushed. The commission convened in the Star Chamber at Westminster on 25 October. There, the commissioners were again presented with all the evidence laid against Mary, and Mary's secretaries were brought before the court to give written statements under oath. Mary was found guilty.

Still, though, Elizabeth was hesitant about signing an execution warrant for Mary. She did not want to justify executing a queen, albeit one that had abdicated their throne, as a legal precedent, particularly not one based upon a parliamentary act, the Act for the Queen's Safety. Doing so would theoretically allow Parliament to dictate the royal succession in future. She was not to know that less than a century later, Parliament would be dictating the execution of their own king, Charles I. Parliament, in no small part driven by Elizabeth's chief secretary, William Cecil Lord Burghley, had been pushing for the execution of Mary ever since her implication in the Ridolfi Plot in 1572. Then, only the execution of Norfolk saved Mary. In 1586, after the discovery of Mary's involvement in the Babington Plot, Parliament persisted in pushing Elizabeth to execute Mary. The MP Sir Ralph Sadler echoed the views of his fellow parliamentarians when he remarked that while Mary lived, Elizabeth could not truly be safe. It was at the opening of this parliament that Elizabeth gave an impassioned speech about the close ties between her and Mary, emphasising her reluctance to authorise the death of her cousin. During her long reign she had many difficult decisions to make regarding the execution of those close to her.

It wasn't that Elizabeth didn't want Mary removed, she just didn't want to create, or Parliament to create, any legal precedent to do so. Elizabeth preferred to have the basis for Mary's execution come from the 1584 Bond of Association. This was a document, conceived in the fallout of the Throckmorton Plot in 1583, in which the signatories agreed to hunt down and kill any person that imperilled the life of Elizabeth, or attempted to usurp her throne. Under the terms of the Bond of Association an execution warrant was not needed; Elizabeth preferred this so she could avoid direct involvement in the execution of her cousin.

Elizabeth could not, however, put off the inevitable indefinitely. She finally signed Mary's death warrant on 1 February 1587, following rumours of another threat to her life. Even after signing the death warrant, Elizabeth did not wish for it to be used. She hoped that it would prompt those that signed the Bond of Association to do away with Mary without using the warrant. But Burghley, wishing to put the matter of Mary, Queen of Scots to bed, convened a secret meeting of the Privy Council to dispatch the signed death warrant to Fotheringhay, where Mary still awaited her fate. She was beheaded on 8 February. Elizabeth was not told of Mary's execution until after the act.

The death of Mary, Queen of Scots did not solve Elizabeth's Catholic problems. If anything, and for all her protestations that she did not truly wish her cousin dead, her involvement in Mary's execution only galvanised those foreign powers that wished the Protestant monarch removed. Treason trials of the 1570s and 1580s regularly cited the Pope as complicit in plots to kill or remove Elizabeth, while, in the early 1580s, King Philip of Spain – Elizabeth's former brother-in-law – had been planning an invasion of England, following English raids on Spanish ports in the Caribbean and the military intervention of Elizabeth in the Netherlands. After Mary Stuart's death, Philip felt bolstered in his resolve to remove Elizabeth by any means necessary, and pursue his great 'Enterprise of England'. The subsequent Spanish Armada of 1588 was seen as one of Elizabeth's greatest victories against an invading foreign force. She couldn't, however, charge Philip or the Pope with treason; they were not her subjects.

After the Armada, though, negotiating with foreign powers became a common theme in treason trials. In 1592, Sir John Perrott, the former Lord Deputy of Ireland, was tried and convicted of treason for his actions leading up to the attempted Spanish invasion in 1588. Perrott was accused of receiving letters from the King of Spain and encouraging a Spanish invasion of Ireland – to free it from the dominion of the Queen – and was also charged with encouraging and writing letters to support the Spanish Armada in 1588. He was found guilty of all charges.

Two years later, in 1594, Patrick O'Collun of London was found guilty of treason for meeting and conspiring with known traitors to the English Crown in Brussels. He agreed to bring enemies of the Queen to England with the express purpose of killing her. Equally damning, in the eyes of the law at least, was that O'Collun had accepted a monthly pension of 15 crowns from Philip, King of Spain, despite O'Collun knowing Philip was an enemy of the English Crown.

A more serious attempt on the life of Elizabeth I was one made by Dr Roger Lopez (Rodrigo Lopez/Roderigo Lopes), one of the Queen's physicians, and therefore close to her. Of Jewish descent and a refugee from his native Portugal, Lopez had formerly served the Queen's favourite, the Earl of Essex, though the earl had turned against him when he revealed in conversation what diseases he had treated Essex for. It was Essex who found letters implicating Lopez in a plot to kill Elizabeth. Lopez was found to have sent King Philip secret messages and intelligence to the detriment of the Queen as far back as 1591 (his trial for treason wasn't until 1594). Additionally, like O'Collun, Lopez had accepted a gift from the King of Spain, in his case jewellery set with gold and gems worth £100 (worth nearly £20,000 in today's money). In January 1593, Lopez allegedly met with Emanuel de Andrada, acting on behalf of King Philip, when they purportedly planned for Lopez to poison the Queen. Lopez continued to write letters to the Queen's enemies throughout 1593, keeping them updated on his plans to poison her. Alongside two supposed co-conspirators, also Portuguese, Lopez was hanged, drawn and quartered at Tyburn, on 7 June 1594.

In 1598 another attempted poisoning on behalf of Philip of Spain was thwarted. Edward Squyer, or Squire, a sailor who, while imprisoned in Seville, Spain, had a meeting with agents of King Philip during which they discussed how a Spanish invasion of England could be successful, and hatched up a plot to kill Elizabeth. Squyer – who prior to becoming a sailor, had worked in the Queen's stables – was given a poison, contained in a double bladder wrapped in parchment and paper, and sent back to England with instructions to smear the pommel of the Queen's saddle with the poison so that when she next went for a ride and put her hand on the pommel she would poison herself. This scheme had no effect, but some days later, Squyer, now on board the Earl of Essex's fleet, wiped the rest of the poison onto the arms of the chair in which the earl was accustomed to sit, in the hope that this would weaken the English fleet in advance of a Spanish invasion. This attempt was also unsuccessful; unfortunately for him, his erstwhile accomplices informed the English government of his actions, and Squyer met the same fate as the hapless Dr Lopez.

The treason trial of one Valentine Thomas in 1598 once again saw the accused conspiring with a foreign power to depose Elizabeth, in this case Scotland, implicating James VI, who was subsequently at pains to deny any involvement in the plot. Thomas's plan was to deliver a petition to the Queen, so that he could get close enough to her to kill her. He was, however, arrested before he could commit the act, and held in Marshalsea Prison. While incarcerated, he wrote these words on the wall of his cell with a piece of coal:

> I shot at a very fair wight, and in the loosing of my arrow my elbow was wrested, but I melt for grief to lose such a game having so fair a mark; but if I had won that game, to the great comfort of England and profit of himself.
> TAKEN FROM THE INDICTMENT AGAINST VALENTINE THOMAS, KB 8/54

This was almost a confession on the part of Valentine Thomas. He had attempted to kill Elizabeth, but had been captured – had he succeeded, he declared, it would have been to the great benefit of England.

In 1586, when addressing Parliament on the topic of Mary, Queen of Scots, Elizabeth remarked, 'in trust I have found treason'. Little could she have known then that one of the final treasons she would face in her life would come from someone she had trusted very dearly, her former favourite Robert Devereux, Second Earl of Essex. In the 1590s, Devereux disgraced himself during Elizabeth's (attempted) conquest of Ireland. He was unable to secure victory, returning to England with an unpopular peace treaty instead. In an effort to regain the favour of Elizabeth, he rushed to her court in September 1599, but made an error in rushing into the Queen's chamber without announcing his arrival; she was only half-dressed and her hair was in disarray. They met (fully dressed) later that day, but this was the last time they met in person. In November that year the council met in Star Chamber and agreed that Essex's actions in

Ireland warranted imprisonment. Although he survived the Star Chamber investigations, he was left heavily in debt, and was barred from the Queen's court. When Elizabeth, as punishment, refused to renew Essex's profitable customs licence on sweet wines, his only source of income was wiped out. He knew that he was ruined, and would remain so as long as Elizabeth was on the throne. His thoughts turned treasonous; the only answer to his predicament as he saw it was to depose the Queen, and accordingly he began to amass followers (of which he had many), and appeal to foreign rulers, such as James VI of Scotland (at this time not confirmed as Elizabeth's successor), to join him in plotting a rebellion.

When Essex received a summons to appear before the council on 7 February 1601, he and his followers feared the worst and brought forward their plans to rebel. Essex refused the summons, and locked up the privy councillors who arrived at Essex House to demand why he had failed to appear. He then led 300 armed men into the City of London, expecting support from there, but the Lord Mayor ordered the gates shut, and by mid-afternoon Essex's troops were surrounded by those loyal to the Queen. At his trial, it was revealed that Essex and another conspirator, the Earl of Southampton, had been plotting this insurrection for months. They were both, with a number of others, found guilty of treason. Essex was beheaded at the Tower on 25 February, just three weeks after his failed rebellion. The Earl of Southampton had his death sentence commuted to life imprisonment (and was freed barely two years later with the accession of a new monarch), but four other co-conspirators were executed.

Despite the many attempts on her life, Elizabeth I lived until 24 March 1603, six months shy of her seventieth birthday. Her reign was one marked by religious treasons of a kind that her predecessors had not endured. Yet, her death did not resolve these tensions. Although the newly crowned James I (VI of Scotland) was the son of Mary, Queen of Scots, the Catholic thorn in Elizabeth's side for so much of her reign, he still had to be wary of religious dissidents and threats from abroad. Catholic plots aided by foreign powers did not die with Elizabeth, as James was to find out in 1605, when an audacious attempt was made to blow up Parliament.

gehan vpon it shoulde seeme that he hath bene recomendit by
some personne to his maisters service only for this use, quhairin only he
hath servid him, & thairfore he wolde not be askit in publice companye, & quhy
he went oue of englande, & the force he shypped in, & the lyke questiounis
wolde be askit anent the forme of his returne, as for these crimpo[...]
wair[...] founde vpon him the significatioun & use of euerie one of
thaime wolde be knowin, & quhat I have obseruit in thaim the bearar
will showe you, now that ye remember of the crewallie villanouse pasquill
that rayled vpon me for the name of britranie; if I remember rite
it spoke some thing of haruest & prophecied my destructioun aboue that
tyme, ye maye thinke of this for it is lyke to be the laboure of suche a
desperate fellow is this is, if he will not other wayes confesse, the gentler
torturis are to be first vsid vnto him & sic per gradus ad ima tenditur,
& so god spede your e goode worke.

                                                James R

Seven

THE GUNPOWDER TREASON, 1605

The matter that is now to be offer'd to you, my lords the commissioners, and to the trial of you the knights and gentlemen of the jury, is matter of Treason; but of such horror, and monstrous nature, that before now, the tongue of man never deliver'd; the ear of man never heard; the heart of man never conceited; nor the malice of hellish or earthly devil ever practised.

SPEECH OF SIR EDWARD PHILIPS AT THE OPENING OF THE TRIAL OF THE GUNPOWDER CONSPIRATORS, FROM *STATE TRIALS*, II, P. 164

The Gunpowder Plot, foiled in the early hours of 5 November 1605, is perhaps the most famous incidence of treason in Britain. It has persisted so long in the public memory in part because of the unprecedented way in which the plot was commemorated. A 1606 act of Parliament made 5 November a public day of thanksgiving, when prayers would be performed in all churches throughout the land, to remind the populace how the King and his government had survived such an audacious attack and how the conspirators had been punished. For hundreds of years after the plot itself, stories were told – and continue to be told – of the men who tried to blow up Parliament. Even after the 1606 Act was repealed in 1859, much of the ritual persisted, with bonfires and 'pennies for the Guy' keeping the story of the Gunpowder Plot alive.

The plot itself was also noteworthy for its sheer scale; this was treason on another level to what had come before. Had it succeeded, the gunpowder explosion would have blown up not only the King and his closest relatives, but also the members of the Privy Council and other senior officers of the realm, plus all those who would have attended the State Opening as Members of Parliament; it would not have been possible to avoid innocent blood being spilled. Westminster Palace, where Parliament sat, would have been utterly destroyed, and many of the surrounding structures would have been damaged. Removing the head was not enough for the Gunpowder conspirators. To be sure of their aims, they planned to destroy every person involved in running the country. The Gunpowder Plot was therefore not only a treason against the person of the King, but also a treason against the state.

In many ways, the Gunpowder Plot was the culmination of the Catholic unrest that had been building up in the final decades of Elizabeth I's reign. It became increasingly difficult for Catholics to practise their religion as, with every plot instigated in the name of the Roman Catholic faith, harsher laws, in the form of the Recusancy Acts of 1587 and 1593, against Catholics were enacted to protect the Queen and the state religion. This, in turn, only increased Catholic frustrations, leading to attempts at more audacious treasons to see Elizabeth (and the Protestant faith) removed.

These tensions did not immediately dissipate after Elizabeth's death in 1603, though there was an awakening of hope from Catholics that they would be granted more rights under James I. The new king was, after all, the son of Mary Stuart, late Queen of Scots, who had been a figurehead for the 'true' religion and an alternative to Elizabeth I for as long as she had lived, and after her death seen as a Catholic martyr.

The new King's religious policy wasn't dissimilar from that of Elizabeth's early reign, before decades of plotting had necessitated harsher measures. Like Elizabeth, James favoured a policy that allowed people to follow their own beliefs in private, so long as they conformed to the state religion in public. But, for some Catholic extremists, this wasn't good enough. Early in James's reign, the Bye Plot was uncovered, whereby the priests William

Watson and William Clark planned to hold the King in the Tower of London until he agreed to be more tolerant towards Catholics. A more serious plot, the Main Plot, was uncovered at the same time. This plot involved removing James and replacing him with his cousin Arbella Stuart, also a direct descendant of Henry VII. Although the priests Watson and Clark were executed for their part in the Bye Plot, James did not wish his reign to begin too bloodily, and granted several of the Main conspirators, one of them allegedly Sir Walter Raleigh, a reprieve on the scaffold.

In 1604, James renewed Elizabeth's Recusancy Acts, and, though he still wished to avoid religious persecution, he made it clear that he did not wish to see Catholics within his realms increase in number; English and Welsh Catholics would therefore not be able to thrive while James remained on the throne. When the Treaty of London was signed in August 1604, bringing an end to the Anglo-Spanish War that had been raging since the 1580s, the great Catholic hope of foreign intervention from Spain was dashed; if English Catholics wished to usurp James, they would have to act alone.

One such man driven to extremism was Robert Catesby, from a wealthy Catholic family from Warwickshire. Catesby had been implicated in plots against the Crown before, and was known to English authorities as a possible troublemaker. In 1596, he and several other future gunpowder plotters were imprisoned in the Tower of London on suspicion of poisoning Elizabeth I; they were released when the Queen recovered from what was likely no more than a stomach bug. Catesby was arrested again during Essex's rebellion of 1601. He was wounded and arrested while fighting in support of the earl at Essex House. This time, he was released only after agreeing to pay a significant fine of £3,000 (over £400,000 in today's money).

Catesby was the ringleader of the Gunpowder Plot, and early in 1604 began to recruit men to assist him in his plan. In February 1604 he recruited Thomas Wintour, who then travelled abroad to gauge Spanish interest in supporting the plot; while in Flanders, Wintour met an English – and Roman Catholic – soldier, Guy Fawkes, who joined him.

A meeting of the first five plotters – Catesby, Wintour, Fawkes, Thomas Percy, and John Wright – took place in May that year. The initial plan, according to the later confessions of Fawkes and Wintour and their treason trials, involved tunnelling through to the foundations of Parliament House from a nearby residence leased by Thomas Percy. Once complete, the tunnel would be filled with gunpowder and blown up. However, the plotters underestimated the thickness of the foundations, and work was slow; so slow that there was doubt that the tunnel could be dug in time for the next parliament planned for February 1605. Even when that parliament was postponed, there was still doubt that the plan could succeed. Their luck appeared to change early in 1605 when a vault beneath the House of Lords became vacant. Thomas Percy leased the room and had Guy Fawkes pose as his servant. They amended their plan and instead filled this vault with gunpowder, concealed beneath firewood. In March 1605, a further three members were added to Catesby's conspirators: Robert Wintour (Thomas's brother), Christopher Wright (John's brother) and John Grant (the Wintours' brother-in-law). To bankroll the plot, Catesby recruited Ambrose Rookwood, Sir Everard Digby and Francis Tresham in the summer of 1605.

The second part of the plot involved having someone to replace James as monarch. As the attempted usurpations of Elizabeth had shown, removing the monarch without a valid replacement would result in anarchy and confusion; in such a climate, any would-be assassins were unlike to achieve their longer-term aims. The Gunpowder Plotters therefore planned to kidnap James's eldest daughter, nine-year-old Princess Elizabeth, and set her up as a monarch through whom they could restore the Catholic faith.

With the gunpowder primed and everyone in place, the plot seemed set to succeed. Some days before Parliament was due to assemble, however, Lord Monteagle, a Catholic peer, received an anonymous letter warning him not to attend. A prominent Catholic in England at a time when persecution was all too fresh in the memory, Monteagle immediately became suspicious and took the letter to the King and his ministers. James then ordered an investigation. Guy Fawkes was actually spotted in the Westminster vaults twice on 4 November as part of this investigation. The first time, it was Lord Chamberlain Suffolk that encountered Fawkes in the Westminster vaults. He took Fawkes to be a servant, and though he noted the firewood in the vault (concealing the gunpowder), he did not look too thoroughly upon learning that its owner was Thomas Percy, a respected (and trusted) gentleman pensioner to the King. It was only when Suffolk returned to court that Lord Monteagle commented how odd it was that Percy should have a vault in Westminster, as he already had a London house. The King then ordered a second search of the cellars at Westminster, undertaken by Sir Thomas Knyvett, keeper of Whitehall Palace. Knyvett discovered Fawkes, who gave the alias John Johnson, still in the vaults at around midnight on 4 November. Fawkes was arrested, and Knyvett's men subsequently discovered the thirty-six barrels of gunpowder hidden under the firewood.

Fawkes was immediately taken for interrogation, though initially he gave little information away, other than that which was obvious from the nature of his arrest. There was no point trying to argue away the huge amount of gunpowder hidden under the House of Lords, and Thomas Percy was implicated as 'John Johnson's' master, and as the leaseholder of the Westminster vault. A proclamation ordering the search and arrest of Percy was immediately drawn up, printed, and distributed across the country.

News of Fawkes's arrest spread through London rapidly, and Catesby, Percy, and John Wright fled north as soon as they heard. They travelled quickly, arriving at Dunchurch, where they hoped to meet with some of their fellow conspirators; however, all but the ringleaders refused to involve themselves further in the conspiracy. Disappointed, but not disheartened, Catesby and company raided the stables of Warwick Castle for fresh horses at around 3 a.m. on 6 November – less than 36 hours after Fawkes had been captured. During the theft, John Grant was recognised, and a second proclamation against Thomas Percy issued on 7 November, denouncing him and his compatriots as traitors, specifically

A HISTORY OF TREASON

mentioned the theft. The plotters spent the next couple of days trying to drum up Catholic support for an uprising, to little avail. Worse still, on the evening of 7 November, Catesby, Rookwood, and John Grant were all injured when some damp gunpowder was placed too close to their fire and exploded. Grant was blinded; the others burnt. The irony wasn't lost on the conspirators, who thought that God had now abandoned them as well. However, they still would not surrender. On 8 November, a further proclamation against Thomas Percy was issued, offering a reward to anyone that could apprehend him. The plotters made their final stand at Holbeach the same day, as the sheriff of Worcestershire arrived with around 200 men to try and capture the rebels. A shootout occurred, killing John and Christopher Wright. Thomas Percy and Robert Catesby were also killed, brought down by a single shot which passed through the two of them. Thomas Wintour, Ambrose Rookwood, and John Grant were all captured, and taken back to London to await trial with the other surviving conspirators.

The confessions of Thomas Wintour and Fawkes – two of the original conspirators – would prove invaluable to completing the full picture of the plot, at least as full as possible considering that probably the only person who knew the true extent of everything, Robert Catesby, was dead. Attorney General Edward Coke remarked at the trial of the plotters in January 1606 that there had been twenty-three full days of examinations; the prosecutors had been thorough in their investigation. Guy Fawkes, as the first captured and one of the last executed, was interrogated multiple times. Such was the nature of the alleged offence, torture was permitted.

Between November 1605 and January 1606, nine remaining conspirators were captured, examined and tried for their roles in the Gunpowder Plot. One of their number, Francis Tresham, died in the Tower (allegedly of natural causes) on 23 December 1605. The remainder were tried in the Court of King's Bench in January 1606. Seven of the plotters were tried together: Thomas Wintour, Guy Fawkes, Robert Keyes, Thomas Bates, Robert Wintour, John Grant, and Ambrose Rookwood.

During their trial, Sir Edward Coke echoed the comments of Sir Edward

Philips, the prosecuting serjeant, that these were 'the greatest treasons that ever were plotted in England'. Coke went further, saying that as this treason was without precedent, it needed an apt name, for it tended 'not only to the hurt, but to the death of the king, and not the death of the king only, but of his whole kingdom'. In targeting the King in Parliament with the majority of his government in residence, the plotters were (perhaps unwittingly) supporting the idea that treason was not only a crime against the person of the monarch, but of the state, against those in government (including the king) that held sovereignty in the realm.

The remaining surviving plotter, Sir Everard Digby, was tried immediately afterwards. He gave a lengthy confession, pleading guilty to his crimes and begging forgiveness (if not mercy). The jury found all eight men guilty. Digby, Robert Wintour, John Grant, and Thomas Bates were executed on 30 January, hanged, drawn and quartered in St Paul's Churchyard; the same fate awaited Thomas Wintour, Ambrose Rookwood, Robert Keyes, and Guy Fawkes on the following day, 31 January, in the Old Palace Yard, Westminster.

The death of the key players did not mean the end of the state response to the Gunpowder Plot. James and his government were doggedly determined to find and punish anyone involved with or supporting the plot, and to ensure that no one attempted the like again. For James, the method of the Gunpowder Plotters was a personal one. His father, Lord Darnley, had been murdered when he was only eight months old. Two barrels of gunpowder had been placed under Darnley's sleeping quarters and, while the ensuing explosion didn't kill Darnley, he was killed while attempting to escape the aftermath.

At the same time that the Gunpowder Plotters were being prepared for trial, two acts were introduced in Parliament that would ensure that the failure of the plot – and the fates of the plotters – lived long in the memory. The first act, introduced by Edward Montagu, was brought on 23 January 1606. It proposed a day of thanksgiving annually on 5 November to commemorate the King's (and state's) survival of these 'damnable treasons'.

This act – 'An Act for a public thanksgiving to almighty God every year on the fifth day of November' – was legislation as propaganda, designed to impress upon the populace the inhumanity of the Catholic plotters versus the King, whose piety had granted him the wisdom to discover the plot. As with so many of the plots against Elizabeth, it was framed as the creation of 'devilish papists, Jesuits, and seminary priests'. The preamble described how these Catholic dissidents had planned to blow up the Houses of Parliament, an unprecedented act 'the like was never before heard of'. But the plot was thwarted thanks to Almighty God, who 'inspired the King's most excellent majesty with a divine spirit, to interpret some dark phrases of a letter shown to his majesty'. This was predominantly a religious act, to ensure prayers of thanksgiving annually, as can be seen from the enacting part of the statute:

> Be it therefore enacted by the King's most excellent majesty, the Lords Spiritual and Temporal, and the Commons in this present Parliament assembled and by the authority of the same, that all and singular ministers in every cathedral and parish church or other usual place for common prayer within this realm of England and the dominions of the same, shall always upon the fifth day of November say morning prayer and give unto almighty God thanks for this most happy deliverance.
>
> AN ACT FOR A PUBLIC THANKSGIVING TO ALMIGHTY GOD EVERY YEAR ON THE FIFTH DAY OF NOVEMBER. C 65/182

Despite this act, and the trial and execution of the lead plotters, James did not want to start an all-out war with the Catholic faith. In his letters to foreign powers, he was keen to stress that this was the work of a select few extremists, and that it did not colour his opinion of – nor did he blame – the Catholic faith as a whole. But the act did incite anti-Catholic sentiment for centuries. 'Gunpowder Treason Day' became a public holiday, which some workers were entitled to take off. Every year on 5 November, after the prayers of thanksgiving, the act – with its descriptions of 'devilish papists' – was to be read out in full (another stipulation of the act itself), further reinforcing anti-Catholic feeling.

With the future commemoration of the thwarting of the Gunpowder Plot secured by the first act of this 1606 Parliament, the second act dealt with the plotters themselves – 'An Act for the Attainders of diverse offenders in the late most barbarous, monstrous, detestable, and damnable treasons'. This act lists all those the state deemed responsible for the Gunpowder Plot, and their respective fates: Robert Wintour, Thomas

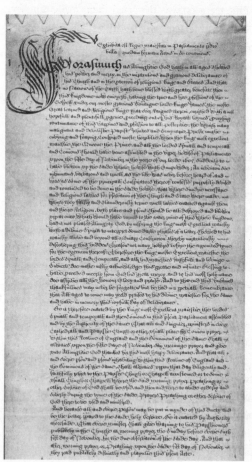

'An act for a publick thanksgiving to Almighty God every year on the fifth day of November', which declared that thereafter 5th November would be a day of thanksgiving. (C 65/182)

Wintour, Guy Fawkes, Robert Keyes, Ambrose Rookwood, John Grant, Thomas Bates, and Everard Digby, who were all tried and indicted in King's Bench, found guilty, and subsequently executed; Robert Catesby, Thomas Percy, John Wright, and Christopher Wright, who were slain in open rebellion; and Francis Tresham, who died in the Tower after confessing himself guilty of the treasons of his fellow plotters. This act ensured that even if the conspirators had not been brought to trial, there was nevertheless a legal record of their guilt (which could be used in seizing forfeited lands of the traitors).

Finally, another act of the same Parliament – the Popish Recusants Act – tightened the restrictions (imposed by the Popish Recusants Act of 1592) on practising Catholics in England and Wales. This act prohibited Catholics from practising law or medicine. They could not hoard arms or anything that could be used to incite rebellion against the state, and magistrates were granted increased powers to search Catholic houses for suspected arms. A new oath of allegiance, which had to be taken by all subjects in the realm, more firmly denied the power of the Pope to depose monarchs and carried harsh punishments for those that refused to sign.

The main conspirators being punished, the government moved onto those that knew about the Gunpowder Plot but chose not to reveal it; misprision of treason – the deliberate concealment of a treasonous act – was also a crime. The nature of the plot itself meant that it was unlikely that many people knew of the plot in advance, and the pool of likely people with foreknowledge boiled down to Catholic priests who may have heard the confessions of Catesby and his compatriots, and peers of the realm who did not attend Parliament for the planned State Opening on 5 November (suggesting prior knowledge of the plot).

Two Jesuit priests became implicated in the plot from these investigations. The first, Oswald Tesimond, heard confession from Robert Catesby, who asked the priest for advice about the morality of the collateral death of innocents. It's unlikely Catesby revealed the exact nature of the plot, and there were plenty of Catholic causes on the continent which imperilled the lives of innocents, but Tesimond was disquieted enough to ask the advice of the premier Jesuit in England, Henry Garnet. Garnet, who had seen how the state reacted to Catholic plots, even those instigated by individuals, urged Tesimond to dissuade Catesby. He later told Tesimond that the Pope also urged caution: Catholic disturbances in England and Wales only brought harsher treatment.

Neither Tesimond nor Garnet revealed what they knew of the plot, as they had received that information under the seal of the confessional. As such, their names were both included in the act of attainder against the Gunpowder Plotters. A proclamation to capture both men was made on 15 January 1606. Tesimond managed to escape capture and move to the continent. Garnet wasn't so lucky. On 6 November he had learnt the full details of the failed Gunpowder Plot from the fleeing conspirators led by Catesby, hoping to drum up Catholic support across the country. Garnet was horrified, urging them to stop any further uprisings. Knowing that he would be under suspicion for his (small) part in the plot, Garnet went into hiding. He was captured on 27 January 1606, after the main conspirators had been tried and found guilty.

Garnet was first questioned by the Privy Council in early February 1606, and kept in the Tower for the next two months while information and evidence was gathered. His trial for treason began on 28 March 1606, held at the Guildhall in London. Garnet was tried as a Gunpowder conspirator in his own right, accused of hearing the details of the plot during a meeting with Catesby and Tesimond on 9 June 1605 and failing to reveal those details. Garnet's direct involvement in the Gunpowder Plot was minor, and so the Attorney General Edward Coke sought to pile on the historic charges against him. As he was the superior Jesuit in England, Coke proceeded to list all the treasons attempted for the Jesuit cause since Garnet's arrival in England in 1586. Coke was keen to comment that Garnet's arrival in England was itself a treasonable act, as all priests created by the authority of the Pope were not to enter England by this point. In Coke's long speech, all the treasons of Elizabeth's reign linked in any way to the Catholic cause, from Elizabeth I's excommunication, were listed; Garnet was directly involved in very few of them.

It was with Catesby's asking of advice concerning the loss of innocents – and Garnet's response – that Coke attempted to seal Garnet's fate to that of the chief Gunpowder conspirator. Allegedly, Catesby came to Garnet and asked,

> … whether for the good and promotion of the Catholic cause against heretics, (the necessity of time and occasion so requiring) it be lawful or not amongst many nocents [guilty parties] to take away some innocents also.
>
> THE TRIAL OF HENRY GARNET, STATE TRIALS, II, 218

Garnet's response was measured but – in Coke's eyes at least – damning – 'If the advantage were greater to the Catholic part, by taking away some innocents together with many nocents, then doubtless it should be lawful to kill and destroy them all.'

Garnet apparently then gave the comparison of a town or city that was taken by an enemy. In order to liberate the city, some innocents may indeed lose their lives, but to the common destruction of the enemy. It's likely that Garnet used this comparison because he believed that Catesby was enquiring about conflict in the Dutch wars; it's unlikely that anyone except Catesby could have known his true intent.

Though Garnet admitted to having had these conversations with Catesby, he continued to deny any involvement in the treason itself. Before receiving the letter on 6 November telling him that the plot had failed, he believed that his advice to Catesby had been listened to. He was nevertheless found guilty under the terms of the 1352 Treason Act and executed for high treason in May 1606.

Finally, James's government had to ascertain whether there were any nobles bankrolling the plotters or assisting them in some other way. The most serious threats to Elizabeth I during her reign had come from Catholic peers in England, egging on conspirators behind the scenes. So any peer who did not attend Parliament that fateful day was immediately under suspicion.

One of the peers immediately implicated was Lord Montagu. He had connections to the plotters. He'd previously employed Guy Fawkes as a servant (though only for about four months) and Robert Catesby allegedly warned him to stay away from the opening of the 1605 Parliament. But his father-in-law was the Earl of Dorset who, as Lord High Treasurer, was a trusted servant to James I, and Montagu escaped with a fine.

Lords Stourton and Mordaunt were brought to trial in the Court of Star Chamber for contempt for not attending Parliament. Their excuses for non-attendance were unconvincing. Lord Stourton rattled off a list of reasons: he owed £130 in rent; he was concerned about the increase in plague; his wife had recently given birth; his father-in-law, Sir Thomas Tresham, had recently died. Finally, he weakly claimed that he would have come to London on the Friday afterwards. Lord Mordaunt, on the other hand, claimed that he had needed to go down to his estates to check on his farmlands. Sir Edward Coke, the prosecutor, was quick to remind the court that Mordaunt had had all summer to settle these affairs. Stourton and Mordaunt were each fined several thousand marks and imprisoned.

Lord Monteagle, who had passed on to the government the letter warning him of a 'terrible blow' to be suffered by Parliament, was not punished for any potential involvement he might have had with the plotters; he was instead rewarded for his service, receiving lands worth £200 a year and a sizeable yearly pension.

Punishment of the plotters was necessarily harsh, but it also had to be fair. There was no knee-jerk reaction against all Catholics (though many were kept on a short leash after 1605). The King and his government could not afford to have public opinion turn even a little towards the plotters. As such, those speaking in support of the plotters, or even against the manner in which they were punished, were also prosecuted against in the King's Court. In the Court of Star Chamber in June 1606, Sir Edward Coke, the Attorney General, brought just such a case against James Fitzjames and Edward Prater, recusant Catholics. The case concerned the imprisonment, and death, of Henry Oven, who was a servant to Henry Garnet. Oven had been committed to the

Tower of London 'upon suspicion of the late most horrible treasons of blowing up the parliament house with powder'.

Coke accused Fitzjames of spreading malicious gossip to the detriment of the King and his state because Fitzjames had told Prater that he had heard that Henry Oven was tortured to death in the Tower. In his information, Coke explained that though Henry Oven was indeed dead, it was suicide: Oven, Coke determined, knew that he was guilty of the said 'most horrible treasons' and feared execution.

After 1606, with the main conspirators dead or no longer a threat to the realm, there were no further government sanctions or legislation concerning the Gunpowder Plot. However, the episode – and government response – formed public opinion against Catholics for centuries afterwards. During the remainder of James's reign, being associated with a Gunpowder Plotter still presented a very real danger, and parties had to be sure to refute any such accusations. In the 1610s, many years after the plot had been thwarted, Sir Stephen Proctor – who had been employed to collect evidence against the Gunpowder Plotters – was brought into the Court of Star Chamber accused of imagining plotters where there were none, slandering those he accused as Gunpowder Plotters. Also, though there was no question that the government had acted soundly in punishing those involved with the Gunpowder Plot, some resentment remained in the families of those men lost as part of the plot. In 1612, relatives of uncle and nephew Humphrey and Stephen Littleton – who were executed for supporting Catesby at his final stand at Holbeach – were brought into court by a local ironmonger because they had been preventing his workmen from making charcoal, in revenge for his prosecution of the Littletons following the Gunpowder Plot.

In many ways the Gunpowder Plot marked a continuation of the treasons attempted during Elizabeth's reign. In the ensuing legislation, much was made of the fact that it was a Catholic plot. In the initial interrogation of Guy Fawkes (then going by the alias John Johnson), one of the first things the interrogators tried to ascertain was what countries on the continent Fawkes had recently visited – foreign support for

Catholic attempts against the King was still fresh in the memory. Fawkes was also asked for the names of any Catholic peers involved in the plot, again as a response to the patterns that had emerged during Elizabeth's reign. However, the Gunpowder Plot was ultimately different from any attempted treason that had come before. There was no overt foreign state support. Though it was driven by Catholic ideology, it was the work of a few extremists: most Catholics preferred or advised caution, having seen how the monarch and their government responded to plots against their person, preferring instead to worship privately. When Catesby and his motley crew had attempted an uprising akin to the Northern Rebellion of 1569 (which did have a modicum of popular support) immediately after the failed plot, they had died alone and hounded by an outraged mob.

The scope of the attempted treason of 1605 clearly shocked and horrified contemporaries at the time. On multiple occasions – during the trial, subsequent acts, correspondence after the event – the sheer scale of what had been attempted was remarked upon. The 1606 Act that made 5 November a public holiday may have been anti-Catholic propaganda, but the shock as to what was planned was palpable, describing the attempt to blow up the Houses of Parliament as 'an invention so inhumane, barbarous, and cruel, as the like was never before heard of'.

It was this shift in scale that is probably the Gunpowder Plot's most lasting legacy in terms of the development of treason. In attempting to remove not only the head but the entire governing body of the state, the plot introduced into the public consciousness the idea that treason was bigger than just an attempt on the monarch's life. Attempts to destroy or subvert the kingdom, the state, or the commonwealth were equally valid. During James's reign, this acknowledgement that there was a distinction between the king and his kingdom – and that both could be the targets of treasonous acts – did not cause any constitutional crises; so long as the king and his government were in accord, then treason legislation could be used to protect both of them. However, when the king and his kingdom were not in agreement, who then did the Treason Act protect? This was the question James's son, Charles I, would have to face.

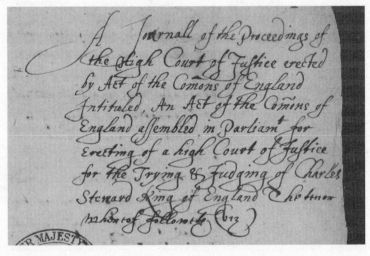

First page of the 'Journal of the Proceedings of the High Court of Justice', detailing the trial of King Charles I. (*SP 16/517*)

Eight

KILLING THE KING,
1625–49

I shall mind you, that by the Common Law of the realm, the
statute of 25 Edward III, and all others acts concerning Treason,
it is no less than High Treason, by overt act, to compass or
imagine the deposition or death of the King.
WILLIAM PRYNNE, *BRIEFE MEMENTO...*, PP. 3–4

On 30 January 1649, the Commons of England and Wales achieved something that had never been done before. They executed their king, Charles I, for treason against his people. They turned legislation that had historically protected the monarch against him. They were able to do this for a number of reasons. Treason had, since its codification in the fourteenth century, always protected both the person of the monarch and their ability to maintain a peaceful and orderly realm. Levying war against the king or queen, deemed a treasonable act for centuries, was as much an act against the kingdom as it was against the person of the king.

During the sixteenth century, particularly after the break with Rome, treason legislation expanded to protect the realm from new religious and overseas threats, protecting not just the person of the king or queen but also the society they created. The Gunpowder Plot was an early indication that treason had become greater than just the monarch; as treason legislation protected both the king and their kingdom, a successful coup needed to target both.

When the king and his kingdom were acting in harmony, treason laws could protect both. However, during his twenty-five-year reign Charles I and his Parliament were rarely in agreement. This discord tested the limits and definition of treason. When the executioner's axe fell on 30 January 1649, treason – and the state – were changed for ever.

When Charles I came to the throne in 1625, there is no way he could have foreseen how his reign would have ended. Though treason had expanded to include crimes against the state, the 1352 Treason Act was still the core treason legislation, and still protected the person of the monarch above all. Those treason trials that occurred during Charles's reign still tended to adhere to the 1352 statute to define treasonable acts as:

1. Attempting to kill – or imagining the death of – the king, queen, or eldest male heir to the throne
2. Violating the king's 'companion', his eldest unmarried daughter or the eldest male heir's wife
3. Levying war against the Crown in his realm
4. Adhering to the king's enemies in his own realm or elsewhere
5. Counterfeiting the great or privy seal, the king's coin, or bringing counterfeit coin into the realm
6. Killing the king's officers and justices in the execution of their offices

For treasonable acts which fell outside of these distinctions, lawyers utilised the idea of 'common law treasons', that judges could define what was and wasn't a treasonable act. The 1352 Statute did not – could not – cover all treasonable acts; there were acts relating to religious treasons in particular that could not have been imagined in 1352. At the trial of Sir Nicholas Throckmorton in 1554, the prosecuting lawyer, Serjeant Stamford, warned Throckmorton that though the 1352 statute outlined some treasons specifically, there were other treasonous acts which could be defined by judges. This was important during the reign of Charles I because in many of the most high-profile cases the prosecutors were interpreting treason, and the treasonable acts as defined in the 1352 statute, to suit their own aims.

Despite the evolving interpretation of treason during the seventeenth century, however, it would still have been unthinkable at the outset of his reign that Charles I could be tried and executed for treason just twenty-five years later.

One of Charles's fatal mistakes was to underestimate how much power and authority Parliament had over the running of the kingdom. If a person, or a corporate body such as Parliament, held a degree of sovereignty in the realm, then treason legislation could be used in defence of them. When Elizabeth I had to make the difficult decision to execute her cousin Mary, Queen of Scots, she had tried to limit how much of this legal decision was made through Parliament, for fear of setting a dangerous legal precedent about the power of Parliament to decide the fates of monarchs. Similarly, when the Gunpowder Plotters targeted both the royal family and the leading parliamentarians during the state opening of Parliament in 1605, they were acknowledging that they had an important part to play in the running of the kingdom.

In dealing with Parliament, monarchs therefore had to be careful. Parliament had some important powers, not least the ability to grant money to the king or queen. This gave Parliament some leverage over their monarch, in being able to withhold or grant subsidies based on their own needs. As we have seen, historically, Parliament had been able to depose, invalidate and degrade individual monarchs at times of constitutional crisis, yet it had never been able to take the final, irrevocable, step of publicly executing a king or queen. The mechanics of the depositions (and murders) of Edward II and Richard II had taken place in the shadows, not on a public stage.

Relations between Charles and his Parliament started poorly. The first session of his reign, in 1625, dubbed the Useless Parliament, set the stage for the fatal disagreements to come. Charles asked that he be granted the duties of tonnage and poundage for life, as had been customary at the beginning of each monarch's reign since Henry V in 1414. However, the House of Commons voted instead to grant the King those duties for only a year. The Commons may merely have been trying to review a system that had remained unchanged for centuries, but the manner in which they tested the new monarch set the relationship between them on bad terms from the off. Charles instructed the House of Lords to reject the bill, hoping that he would eventually be granted the lifelong duties his predecessors had enjoyed.

However, Charles still needed money, and so was forced to recall Parliament on 1 August. Now, the Commons had a new demand in return for the money; the impeachment of Charles's favourite, the Duke of Buckingham, who had become notorious during the later reign of James I for his extravagance. Charles, not wishing to submit to Parliament's demands, dissolved the session, with nothing granted.

In 1626, Charles assembled another Parliament, in the hope that they would finally agree to grant him money. Again, they demanded the impeachment of the Duke of Buckingham. Again, Charles refused and the stalemate continued. Thereafter, Charles looked at other ways in which he could bolster the royal coffers without needing to turn to Parliament for a subsidy. He imposed forced loans on people, then imprisoned those who refused to pay. This was ruled unlawful by Sir Randolph Crewe, Chief Justice of the King's Bench, who was dismissed for failing to support the King's (illegal) initiative. Dozens were imprisoned without trial for refusing to pay these forced loans, and in 1627 five of these individuals – the Five Knights – submitted a joint petition to secure their freedom by issuing a writ of habeas corpus. This was a right enshrined in Magna Carta that granted subjects freedom from unlawful arrest. In the Five Knights case (also known as Darnell's Case), the Crown argued that it had the power to commit people to prison at its own discretion; this went against the freedoms contained in Magna Carta. Charles also resorted to martial law to furnish his army with the food and clothes that they needed for his foreign wars. This could also be viewed as a contravention of an individual's personal liberty.

Seeing that these initiatives were deeply unpopular, and illegal to boot,

Charles resorted to calling another parliament, to attempt once again to get money – but Parliament required confirmation that Charles would not again attempt to subvert the law for his own financial gain. The result was the 1628 Petition of Right. This petition made explicit mention to the Five Knights case being contrary to the 'Great Charter of the Liberties of England', and required the King to reaffirm these basic liberties.

Under pressure from both Houses, Charles accepted the Petition. This included a reaffirmation that Englishmen had various rights and liberties, including the freedom from unlawful arrest. The King had to accept that no person should be forced to provide a gift or loan without an Act of Parliament, and that no one could be forced to feed, house, or clothe soldiers.

Yet, by the time Parliament reassembled in January 1629, Charles had already begun to renege on his promise to uphold the Petition of Right, continuing to collect tonnage and poundage despite it never being granted him by Parliament. The King's opponents in the Commons issued a protestation known as the Three Resolutions, which encouraged merchants to refuse to pay tonnage and poundage – to do so was to be 'reputed a capital enemy to this kingdom and commonwealth, and a betrayer of the liberty of England'.

Charles angrily tried to have Parliament adjourned for what he viewed as insubordination, but a group of MPs held down the Speaker of the Commons, Sir John Finch, preventing Parliament from being adjourned until the Three Resolutions had passed. The Commons then voted their own adjournment. The message was clear: Parliament decided what it could and could not grant, and when to adjourn; not the king.

A royal proclamation was drawn up and Charles announced the dissolution of Parliament on 10 March 1629. In a long declaration, the King defended his domestic and religious policies and asserted the Crown's right to collect tonnage and poundage without Parliament's consent. He denounced his opponents in Parliament and resolved to govern without them, beginning his eleven-year 'Personal Rule'.

So far, neither side had invoked charges of treason as a political weapon.

At this stage, it was unlikely that any but the most extreme republicans truly believed the King could be tried for treason anyway. However, Parliament had begun to assert their power of sovereignty, their ability to run the kingdom and the commonwealth. Although Charles complained that they overstepped their responsibilities, and at times impeded his ability to rule, they had not yet committed treason against the King.

The decade of Personal Rule did little to resolve the issues between the King and his Parliament. Charles continued to look to long-forgotten taxes and customs to raise money, and still collected tonnage and poundage. The most unpopular of these taxes was ship-money, a custom that required coastal towns to pay for the upkeep of naval defences. In 1635, Charles extended the tax to include inland counties, on the pretence that new warships needed to be built to repel pirates and corsairs in the Channel. In 1637, John Hampden was prosecuted for challenging the legality of these taxes – and though the judges found in the King's favour, the judgement was far from unanimous and Hampden gained a moral victory against the King's tyranny.

Religion was also a rising concern during the years of personal rule. Charles's queen, Henrietta Maria, was a Catholic, and practised her religion openly. Many of Charles's advisers during this period of personal rule were also Catholic, or sympathised with the Catholic faith. This caused resentment among Puritans. Seemingly confirming their fears that the King was sympathetic to the Catholic cause was the fact that in December 1634, Charles I became the first English monarch since the break with Rome to receive an emissary from the Pope.

In 1633, Charles appointed William Laud Archbishop of Canterbury. Laud was a strong supporter of the king as head of the Church, which tied in with Charles's sympathies concerning his God-given right to rule. However, Laud was unpopular among Puritans, who believed that he wished to return the Church of England to Roman Catholicism. This was untrue, though it is true that Laud did not see Catholicism as a threat to the Church of England; he viewed the more extreme Puritan ideology as the main threat to the Anglican Church. Laud's campaign to impose religious uniformity throughout Charles's kingdom was deeply unpopular, and more so because of his use of the conciliar courts such as Star Chamber to punish his critics.

It was Laud's attempts to reform the English and Scottish churches that led to the end of Charles's Personal Rule. In 1637, Laud and Charles introduced a new Book of Common Prayer in Scotland, without first consulting the Scottish Parliament or the Kirk (the Presbyterian Scottish Church). By February 1638, a large number of Scottish noblemen, gentry, and clergy had drawn up and signed a National Covenant, which outlined their aims and desires for a national Scottish Church. The Covenant rejected so-called 'innovations' in religion, though it did emphasise Scotland's loyalty to the King (so long as he did not move towards Roman Catholicism).

As with his negotiations with the English Parliament in the 1620s, Charles did not accept being told what he could and could not do. While his representatives met with Covenanters in the summer of 1638, he made military preparations to subdue the Scots. However, the Covenanters had made preparations of their own and it became clear that there was no immediate military advantage for the King. At the end of 1638, a General Assembly of the Scottish Kirk met in Glasgow to discuss the King's proposals. None of the King's representatives were present at the assembly, and a sweeping rejection of Laud's reforms was declared.

With the rejection of Charles's religious authority came the need for the King to respond militarily. The two Bishops' Wars of 1639 and 1640 – so-called because the Glasgow Assembly had thrown out the King's bishops – meant that Charles once again had to turn to the English Parliament to secure much-needed revenue.

The opening speech of the Short Parliament, which ran from April to May 1640, stressed the need for Parliament to grant subsidies to fight the rebellious Scots. King Charles hoped to rally support against the Scots by revealing to the House of Commons a letter from the Covenanters to King Louis XIII of France apparently requesting his help against England.

But Parliament had an eleven-year axe to grind, and demanded that the nation's grievances, exacerbated over a decade of personal rule, be addressed before any subsidy was granted. More alarming to Charles was the establishing of special committees by the Commons to collect and investigate complaints against royal policy during the Personal Rule. Fearing that his opponents in Parliament were in communication with the Covenanters, he dissolved Parliament just three weeks after it had assembled, without the much-needed money to fund the Bishops' Wars against Scotland. Lacking the necessary funding, the English were defeated in the Bishops' Wars and Charles was advised to assemble another parliament in November 1640.

The Petition of Right, submitted by Parliament to Charles I in 1628, asking the King to confirm the individual rights and liberties of his subjects. (C 65/190)

The November 1640 Parliament – later dubbed the Long Parliament – marked a turning point in the relationship between the King and his MPs. Parliamentarians seized the opportunity to condemn and punish the non-parliamentary policies of the Personal Rule. Officially, this Parliament wasn't dissolved until 1660, long after the civil wars, execution of Charles I, and English period of interregnum. One of the acts passed early on in this Parliament ensured that it could not be dissolved without its members' consent.

The first target of the Long Parliament was Thomas Wentworth, Lord Strafford. During the Personal Rule, Strafford had acted as Charles's Lord Deputy of Ireland, and became a leading adviser to the King in his disagreements with Parliament. On his arrival in Parliament, a committee of the Commons accused Strafford of high treason and impeached him before the Lords. The treason trial of Thomas Lord Strafford is one of the most controversial in the long history of treason. It was a statement by Parliament that they had the power to impeach a man who had the support of the King. In essence, Strafford was tried for his role in Charles's Personal Rule. It was also the first major trial to have a printed transcript of the proceedings made.

But, to try Strafford for high treason was difficult to justify. He was one of the King's favoured ministers, and he hadn't acted against the person of the King in any way. There was, however, precedent for removing royal favourites deemed to be detrimental to just rule. The reigns of Richard II and Edward II, in particular, had seen royal favourites targeted as bad influences on the Crown.

As they didn't have the strongest case that Strafford had committed treason, Parliament initially favoured an 'accumulative treason' approach. They hoped that the sum of a number of lesser offences, of which they could accuse him, would constitute treason. The articles of impeachment against the Earl of Strafford consisted of seven general articles and twenty-eight specific articles. The general articles were drawn up quickly and read to him in the Tower, where he was detained, before the end of November 1640. The prosecution then spent the winter months preparing the specific articles against Strafford, produced in January 1641.

The first of the general articles laid out the case for treason, alleging that:

Thomas, Earl of Strafford hath traitorously endeavoured to subvert the fundamental laws and government of the realms of England and Ireland, and, instead thereof to introduce an Arbitrary and Tyrannical Government against Law, which he hath declared by traitorous words, Counsels, and Actions, and by giving

His Majesty Advice, by force of Arms, to compel his Loyal Subjects to submit thereunto.

Also included in these articles was the idea that Strafford's actions had weakened the kingdom; he had abused his privileged position during the Personal Rule of the King by subverting the fundamental law in both England and Ireland. The destruction of the kingdom as a treasonable act was not new, and had been raised during the prosecution of those involved in the Gunpowder Plot.

The two key articles against Strafford in terms of getting the treason charge to stick were the fifteenth and twenty-third. Article 15 accused Strafford of forcibly billeting troops in Ireland to levy great sums of money from the inhabitants there and to enforce the orders of the Lord Deputy. This was – according to the prosecution – a levying of war against the King under the 1352 Treason Act. They also cited the Irish statute of 18 Henry VI, c 1, which made the billeting of troops on the king's subjects without their consent a treasonable offence. The prosecution argued that as Ireland was in a state of peace when the billeting occurred, Strafford's actions amounted to the raising of troops against the King's loyal subjects.

Article 23 accused Strafford – together with Archbishop Laud – of persuading Charles to dissolve the Short Parliament, then counselling the employment of the Irish army in England (i.e. bringing a foreign army onto English soil). The single testimony for this charge was the Secretary of State, Henry Vane the Elder, who alleged that Strafford had reminded the King that 'he had an Army in Ireland … which he might employ to reduce this kingdom'. The case was a weak one. Even if Strafford did say these words, it is most likely that the 'kingdom' referred to was Scotland, as it was at a meeting discussing Scottish affairs. Indeed, Vane was challenged whether 'this kingdom' meant Scotland or England when he gave his statements.

On 10 April, Strafford gave an impassioned rebuttal of the charges laid against him. He had identified that his prosecutors were attempting a two-pronged attack: accusing Strafford of treason as defined in the 1352 statute, and accusing him of 'common law treason', the accumulation of several lesser offences to equal treason. Strafford saw right through the legal fiction of the 'accumulated treason', and made short work of denouncing the idea:

> As to the other kind, viz., constructive treason, or treason by way of accumulation; to make this out, many articles have been brought against me, as if in a heap of mere felonies or misdemeanors (for they reach no higher) there could lurk some prolific seed to produce what is treasonable! But, my Lords, when a thousand misdemeanors will not make one felony, shall twenty-eight misdemeanors be heightened into treason?
>
> JOHN RUSHWORTH, THE TRYAL OF THOMAS, EARL OF STRAFFORD

Still, he responded to each of the charges against him, whether he considered them treasonous offences or not. The House of Lords deliberated on Strafford's defence, and voted that the main facts alleged by the prosecution (the Commons) had been proved. They therefore referred the question of whether these acts constituted the crime of treason to the judges of the Court of King's Bench.

Before they could receive a response, however, the Commons changed tack. They introduced a bill of attainder in the House, charging Strafford with treason. He was accused of levying war against the King, intending to levy war, constructively compassing the King's death, and subverting the law and introducing an arbitrary government. By going through Parliament, the Commons removed the question of whether the individual acts amounted to treason according to the common law; if the attainder passed both Houses, then Strafford was deemed guilty, regardless of any trial outcome.

There were some in Parliament, nevertheless, who were uneasy about this course of action. Lord Digby, though no friend of Strafford's, urged caution on introducing a bill of attainder if the case for treason was not strong enough. He believed that Strafford ought to die for his crimes against the state, but he was unconvinced that the argument against him was strong enough to justify a death sentence under the treason laws:

Let every man lay his hand upon his own heart, and seriously consider what we are going to do with a breath: either justice or murder – justice on the one side, or murder, heightened and aggravated to its supremest extent, on the other! For, as the casuists say, He who lies with his sister commits incest; but he that marries his sister, sins higher, by applying God's ordinance to his crime; so, doubtless, he that commits murder with the sword of justice, heightens that crime to the utmost.

THE LORD DIGBY HIS LAST SPEECH AGAINST THE EARLE OF STRAFFORD

Unfortunately for Strafford, Digby's speech against his attainder did not deter the Commons, nor did the House of Lords save him. On 7 May, the Chief Justice of the King's Bench informed them that the judges of that court believed Strafford's crimes constituted high treason. The bill of attainder against him passed the upper House on 8 May 1641. A plot to liberate Strafford by force and pressure Parliament militarily turned favour against the King, which gave the Lords further incentive to pass Strafford's bill of attainder. On 12 May, Strafford was beheaded on Tower Hill.

The trial of Strafford was an important precursor to the trial of Charles I less than a decade later. It showed the Commons acting independently of the King to try traitors. Strafford was executed for creating discord between the King and his kingdoms. His treason hadn't been the attempted destruction of the King, but the destruction of the state by providing bad counsel to Charles I.

Between Strafford's impeachment and his trial, another of Charles's close advisers was targeted. On 18 December 1640, William Laud, Archbishop of Canterbury and largely seen as the cause of much of the religious animosity in Scotland, was also impeached for high treason in the Commons. He was accused of altering the true religion in the realm – introduced as a treasonous act in the sixteenth century – subverting the fundamental laws of the realm, and alienating the King from his subjects. Laud, however, was less of a direct threat to Parliament, and they were in no rush to try him. He wasn't taken to the

Tower until March 1641, and his trial wouldn't commence until three years later, in March 1644.

By the time William Laud was tried for treason, England had erupted into civil war. Neither the King nor Parliament trusted the other, and so Parliament made several proposals that would give them greater powers within the realm. In March 1642, Parliament passed the Militia Ordinance, which claimed the right to appoint military commanders without the King's approval. In June, they approved the Nineteen Propositions, which would give them greater control over ministerial appointments and the royal household. On 22 August, Charles raised his standard at Nottingham, declaring war on the Parliamentarian rebels, and by September the two sides had fought each other on the battlefield.

Charles's declaration of war on the Parliamentarians in August 1642 was later included among his treason charges, as levying war against his own people. On the other hand, viewed through the earlier interpretation of treason law, of crimes against the King's person, it was Parliament that had committed many treasonous acts. By 1644, they had levied war against the King, they had denied and usurped his royal authority in passing ordinances empowering them to act without his permission, they had counterfeited the Great Seal, and they had adhered to the King's enemies by colluding with the rebellious Scots. All while Parliament was trying some of the King's favourites for treason.

While civil war was raging, Laud remained imprisoned, but in 1643 the archbishop's papers were seized to search for evidence against him. By the end of the year, a further ten articles against Laud were sent by the Commons to the Lords for consideration. Laud, perhaps wishing to avoid the 'cumulative treason' argument controversially applied in Strafford's trial, asked, in October 1643, that the articles of misdemeanour against him be made distinguishable from those of high treason.

Like Strafford, many of the charges against Laud did not alone constitute treason, and relied on being combined with other lesser offences. Laud's defence argued that none of the accusations against him constituted treason according to the statute of 25 Edward III. This defence necessitated a statement on the parliamentary interpretation of treason. They argued that there were treasons found in the common law that had not been included in the 1352 statute. They stressed that treason could be both against the king and against the realm. Most important, they asserted that Parliament was the only judge of treasons against the realm.

Again, Parliament opted to proceed by bill of attainder after gathering the evidence against Laud. His attainder was introduced in the Commons in November 1644, though wasn't passed in the Lords until January 1645. Laud was executed, by beheading, on 10 January, on Tower Hill.

The trials and executions of Strafford and Laud had been made on the basis that they had led the King astray. At this early stage, Parliament still maintained that they were defending the King from evil advisers. However, by the late 1640s, after years of civil wars across Charles's kingdoms, they were resolved to try the King for the crimes he had committed against his state.

To try to punish a king was a radical move, and there were some in Parliament who could still not be persuaded to pursue so drastic a course of action. To ensure, therefore, that only those who supported punishing the King were involved in the discussions, the New Model Army marched on Parliament and purged the House of Commons of those who were unlikely to favour putting the King on trial. This event became known as Pride's Purge, named after Colonel Thomas Pride, commander of the troops. The remaining MPs then moved towards bringing Charles I to justice.

The role of Parliament in deposing kings was not without precedent. The parliaments of Edward III, Henry IV, Edward IV, and Henry VII all played a part in denouncing the royal rights of their predecessors. However, in each case the deposed monarch had been replaced by a rival claimant to the throne.

The trial of Charles I in January 1649 would be the real test of where sovereignty lay in the realm and answer the question of whom treason laws protected. On 1 January the House of Commons declared that 'by the fundamental Laws of the Kingdom, it is treason in the King of England, for the Time being, to levy War against the Parliament and Kingdom of

England'. Four days later, they stressed that they – not the King or the House of Lords – were 'the supreme power in this nation'. They were establishing their parliamentary sovereignty, laying the foundations for their next grand claim, that they had the power and authority to try a king in his own realm.

In the eyes of the law, the actions of the would-be regicides were undoubtedly treasonous. There were even MPs who had supported the treason trials of Strafford and Laud in the early 1640s who thought that these actions went too far. William Prynne, who had pushed for Laud's trial and execution, published a lengthy tract in January 1649 warning those that remained in the Commons that their actions were illegal.

On 6 January, the Commons passed a bill establishing a High Court of Justice in order to try Charles I for high treason. The act laid out the general reasons that this trial was necessary, alleging:

> That Charles Stuart, the now King of England, not content with those many Encroachments which his Predecessors had made upon the People in their Rights and Freedoms, hath had a wicked Design totally to Subvert the Ancient and Fundamental Laws and Liberties of this Nation, and in their place to introduce an Arbitrary and Tyrannical Government, and that besides all other evil ways and means to bring this Design to pass, he hath prosecuted it with Fire and Sword, Levied and maintained a cruel War in the Land, against the Parliament and Kingdom, whereby the Country hath been miserably wasted...
> SP 16/517

As this was a newly established court, it did not need to adhere to the traditional format of a treason trial, i.e. a trial by jury at common law. Instead, the act named 135 men who could form a judicial body to sit in judgement of the King.

The main treasonable act allegedly committed by Charles was levying war against his kingdom. The depositions of witnesses during his trial focused on proving that Charles had been present at the skirmishes which had caused bloodshed. To levy war against the Crown was undeniably treason, and was enshrined in the 1352 Treason Act. However, to apply this to the King himself would require a broad interpretation of the statute. The King's prosecutors needed to ensure sovereignty was on their side, and would repeat this claim throughout Charles's trial.

While his prosecutors pressed on, hoping to ensure a veneer of legitimacy to the proceedings by treating it like a normal trial, Charles questioned what right they had to try him. John Bradshaw, the Lord President of the Court, responded that the King was summoned 'by the authority of the Commons of England assembled in parliament in the behalf of the people of England by which people you are elected Kinge, which authority requires you in the name of the people of England to answer them'.

In order to justify their claim to being Sovereign – and therefore their ability to try the King – the court had to argue that the office of king was an elective one, rather than a hereditary right. If the king was merely an official, then he was subject to the laws of the kingdom and could be charged with undermining the state through bad rule. Charles denied that this was ever the case in England, and repeated his demand to know by what authority he had been called. On 22 January, with no end to this stalemate in sight, the court met privately and resolved that it had gained its authority from the Commons, as they had passed the bill creating the court. You could not appeal a judgement made by the Commons, therefore the legitimacy of the court could not be challenged. Not the most convincing argument, but one which gave them reason to reject any further questions raised by Charles of their jurisdiction.

On the afternoon of 23 January, with Charles still refusing to recognise the authority of the court, the chief prosecutor John Cook opened proceedings. The King was accused of violating his coronation oath, which required him to maintain the law and to keep the peace in his kingdom. Cook warned the King that if he continued to refuse to answer the charges laid against him, then the court would proceed to sentencing. Charles remained resolute.

On 25 January, therefore, following the depositions, the court resolved to proceed to sentence of condemnation. They decided that this should be 'for a Tyrrant Traytor and Murtherer'. In his sentencing, Bradshaw remarked that Charles's doing away with Parliament during the Personal Rule was an illegal act, accusing the King of intending to subvert the fundamental law of the land by removing the ancient institution of Parliament. Ironically, this was exactly what the Commons was shortly to do to the monarchy and House of Lords. In looking for further precedents to their actions, Bradshaw cited the example of Charles's grandmother, Mary, Queen of Scots, who had been deposed by the state in Scotland in favour of her son James VI when she had failed to uphold her royal duties.

Charles was formally sentenced on 27 January 1649. Here, at this crucial juncture, it was of the utmost importance that the Commons assert their sovereignty and their authority over the King. The sentencing reiterated that the King had been entrusted with 'a limited power' to govern by his people, to use this power for the good of his subjects. As he had failed to do so, then that power could – and should – be taken away. He had overthrown 'the rights and liberties of the people', and 'traitorously and maliciously levied war against the present parliament and people therein represented', thereby causing 'many thousands of the free people of this nation to be slain'.

After this recital of the charges and the course of the trial proceedings, Charles's sentence was declared:

> Now, therefore, upon serious and mature deliberation of the premises, and consideration had of the notoriety of the matters of fact charged upon him as aforesaid, this Court is in judgement and conscience satisfied that he, the said Charles Stuart, is guilty of levying war against the said Parliament and people, and maintaining and continuing the same; for which in the said charge he stands accused, and by the general course of his government, counsels, and practices, before and since this Parliament began (which have been and are notorious and public, and the effects whereof remain abundantly upon record) this Court is fully satisfied in their

judgements and consciences, that he has been and is guilty of the wicked designs and endeavours in the said charge set forth; and that the said war hath been levied, maintained, and continued by him as aforesaid, in prosecution, and for accomplishment of the said designs; and that he hath been and is the occasioner, author, and continuer of the said unnatural, cruel, and bloody wars, and therein guilty of high treason, and of the murders, rapines, burnings, spoils, desolations, damage, and mischief to this nation acted and committed in the said war, and occasioned thereby.

For all which treasons and crimes this Court doth adjudge that he, the said Charles Stuart, as a tyrant, traitor, murderer, and public enemy to the good people of this nation, shall be put to death by the severing of his head from his body.
SP 16/517

Charles I was executed on 30 January 1649 outside Banqueting House at Whitehall. Yet, treason outlived its king. As there was still a sovereign authority to protect – Parliament – treason legislation remained relevant. The new republic immediately created their own treason laws to consolidate power. On the day of the King's execution Parliament passed 'An Act prohibiting the proclaiming any person to be King of England or Ireland, or the Dominions thereof'. This act prohibited the automatic declaration of the new King (as was customary when British monarchs died, to ensure an unbroken chain of succession), and made it treason to declare Charles's son – the future Charles II – the rightful king. Just a few months later, the first treason act of the Commonwealth was passed, which used language similar to the Elizabethan treason statutes. Though they served no king, in their treason legislation the Commonwealth followed the monarchical example:

Be it Enacted by this present Parliament, and by the authority of the same, That if any person shall maliciously or advisedly publish by Writing, Printing, or openly Declaring, That the said Government is Tyrannical, Usurped or Unlawful; or that the Commons in Parliament assembled are not the Supreme authority of this Nation; or shall, Plot, Contrive or Endeavor to stir up or raise Force against the present government, or for the subversion or alteration of the same, and shall declare the same by open deed, That then every such Offence shall be Taken, Deemed and Adjudged, by the authority of this Parliament, to be High Treason

An Act Declaring what Offences shall be adjudged Treason, in Acts and Ordinances of the Interregnum

Despite committing undeniably treasonable acts, by the mid-1650s it looked as if those Parliamentarians who had tried and executed Charles I for treason had gotten away with it. As with usurping kings of the medieval period, they had done so in part by consolidating their authority through refreshed treason legislation. The only difference being that now – there being no king – treason was overtly a crime against the state.

Over the first half of the seventeenth century, the king's status in relation to sovereignty had shifted. The person of the monarch – that treason laws had once protected exclusively – was now just a part of the broader sovereign authority of the state. The law of treason protected the sovereign. Charles's fatal error was underestimating how far that locus of sovereignty had shifted, and not realising – or refusing to acknowledge – that treason laws could be used in defence of anyone with sovereign authority within the state. The regicides' actions during the trial – and, indeed, for much of Charles's reign – had been designed to assert their right to sovereign authority within the realm. It is what their whole justification for trying the King relied upon.

During the 1650s, as the King's killers went about administering the realm they had taken from him, the law of treason protected them as it had monarchs in the past. However, when Charles II regained the throne in 1660, the question of who the treason laws protected would again be raised. The individuals who had not only compassed the King's death in 1649, but successfully executed him, had cause to be worried.

(13)

HIS

MAJESTIES

DECLARATION

CHARLES REX,

CHARLES, By the Grace of God, King of England, Scotland, France, and Ireland, Defender of the Faith, &c. To all our loving Subjects of what Degree or Quality soever, Greeting. If the General Distraction and Confusion, which is spread over the whole Kingdom, doth not awaken all men to a Desire, and Longing, that those wounds which have so many years together been kept bleeding, may be bound up, all we can say will be to no purpose: However, after this long silence, we have thought it our Duty to Declare how much we desire to contribute thereunto; and that, as we can never give over the hope in good time to obtain the Possession of that Right, which God and Nature hath made Our Due; So we do make it our daily Suit to the Divine Providence, that He will in Compassion to Us and Our Subjects, after so long Misery and Sufferings, remit, and put Us into a quiet and peaceable Possession of that Our Right, with as little Blood, and Damage

D   mage

Excerpt from His Majesty's Declaration of Breda, dated 4/14 April 1660. (SP 18/221)

Nine

RESTORATION AND REVENGE, 1660-7

How does a king respond to the execution of his father, the loss of his kingdoms and a decade in exile? Does he unleash reprisals on his political enemies to avenge his frustrations as well as those of his supporters who also suffered loss and exile? Or does he seek to limit the political damage by targeting only the most culpable? Charles II's unexpected restoration to his thrones – of England, Scotland and Ireland – gave him the chance to pursue those who murdered his father, but as one who was reluctant to refight the civil wars, having secured his restoration in 1660 not through force, but by promising to limit the punishment of his enemies to just those who were directly implicated in the sentencing of his father to death. The restored king, having spent a decade in exile, had no intention of compromising his position by wildly attacking his enemies, yet neither was he willing to absolve the leaders of the movement that executed his father. In a move that blindsided his opponents, he chose not to reopen the caustic debates that were fought between the government and Parliament in the 1640s, but instead the King used Parliament and the courts to settle scores, allowing him to remain removed from the process of enforcing royal justice.

Charles Stuart was forced into exile in 1651 as hope of securing support to reclaim his thrones dwindled and he reluctantly accepted the loss of his kingdoms. He escaped to France, where he took up residence at the Louvre with his mother, Queen Henrietta Maria, and then St Germain-en-Laye, but the meagre financial support the French promised was rarely forthcoming. As the English Commonwealth became a stable regime in the early 1650s, the French, led by Cardinal Mazarin, sought an alliance with Oliver Cromwell's government, and thereafter Charles's presence in France became a political inconvenience. While Charles and his supporters' penury remained constant, his residence was to change over the coming years: he first accepted the support of the Imperial Diet and the Archbishop of Cologne, but their overtures did little to enhance his dignity or that of his fellow exiles. He then moved his court to Brussels, which was under the control of the Spanish, from whom he sought to extract support for an invasion of England, but the jeopardy of retaking his thrones without popular support in England meant these overtures were never realised. Likewise, the shambolic nature of the domestic risings that emerged during the 1650s left him no closer to recovering his thrones. Oliver Cromwell's death in September 1658 failed to act as a catalyst for the downfall of the Republic, but it did begin the steady decline of the English Protectorate as Richard Cromwell, Oliver's son, lacked his father's political experience and failed to control the competing factions within Parliament and the army, who opposed the Cromwellian Protectorate. By late 1659, political confusion engulfed England as Parliament and the army's differences proved irreconcilable, and the Protectorate was overthrown by militant forces in the army.

The final blow to the Commonwealth came from an unlikely source, General George Monck, commander of the army in Scotland, who marched his troops into England in January 1660 in defence of Parliament, whereupon almost all military resistance melted away. Monck's arrival at London in February, and his demands that the Long Parliament, which had sat since 1640 and oversaw the trial and execution of Charles I, dissolve itself brought about the demise of the Commonwealth. Only now did a path to restoration become obvious to Charles. After elections to a new parliament in April saw many of the Republic's prominent proponents lose their seats in the Commons, Monck recommended that Charles move his court from Brussels to Breda in the United Provinces in expectation of a return home. The Convention Parliament, so-called as it was not elected under royal authority, proved amenable to a restoration, although there was an element within it that sought to impose some restrictions on the King's authority. When Monck refused to countenance any impediment on the King's remit, especially the revival of restrictions that had been pressed upon Charles I in 1640–42, Charles's messenger, Sir John Grenville, presented the King's proposals for a settlement to the Houses of Parliament, the fleet, and the city on 1 May 1660.

Drafted by Charles's closest advisers, the Declaration of Breda directly addressed several of the major challenges that the King would have to overcome if he were to secure his restoration without any political compromises or parliamentary restraints being imposed upon him. By offering a 'free and general pardon', the declaration mapped out a scenario for a settlement that was acceptable to both Houses of Parliament by confirming Charles's intention not to seek retribution on the majority of his political enemies but instead to restrict any vengeance to a limited number of men who had directly participated in the trial of his father. In what was a clever and unexpected move, he confirmed that he wanted to contribute to the peaceful healing of a fractious nation 'with as little Blood and Damage to our people as is possible'. The core of his proposal revolved around three promises: to restore the traditional system of government by 'King, Peers, and People to their just, ancient and fundamental rights'; to issue a 'free [full] and general pardon, which we are ready on demand to pass under the Great Seal of England; to all Our Subjects, of what Degree or Quality soever'; and to pass on to Parliament the thorny questions of exemptions from pardon, of land ownership, and of a religious settlement. Each of these were considerable issues in their own right (and were to cause significant political tensions after the Restoration) but none would have been possible without ensuring the widespread pardon of involvement in the wars. Without it, he was unlikely to secure parliamentary support for either his restoration or his political agenda. By presenting himself as a peacemaker to the political and financial grandees in London, Charles indicated that he would rule within the law, which calmed the fears of many who may have had doubts about this return.

Charles II had quite a different character from that of his father. A more malleable and less dogmatic man, he was also less easily offended. This is borne out in the declaration, which was a success, with both Houses of Parliament accepting it on 1 May and a week later publicly declaring their support for Charles, who now left the United Provinces and sailed for Dover, arriving back in London on 29 May 1660, his thirtieth birthday. The roads and streets leading to and around the capital city were lined with cheering revellers, seemingly overjoyed at the end of the Republic. Yet Charles understood the festivities that ensued were not as heartfelt or genuine as they appeared, and support for his regime was dependent on him delivering on his promises.

For a religious settlement, he had proposed a 'Liberty to tender Consciences: and that no man shall be disquieted or Called in Question for Differences of Opinion in Matter of Religion, which do not disturb the peace of the kingdom'. This was critical as it suggested that he was willing to place competing faiths on equal footing, thereby both undermining his enemies who sought to impose religious restrictions, and reassuring his less dogmatic supporters, who had tired of evangelicals and puritans. Unlike his father, Charles II had a detached attitude to religion, one that unnerved his supporters as well as his enemies.

Charles performed a similar trick on his political opponents when it came to retribution. His declaration made clear that once those who had been present at his father's sentencing were brought to justice through an act of Parliament, the rest of his 'Subjects, how faulty soever, [could] rely upon the Word of a King, solemnly given by this present Declaration, that no Crime whatsoever, committed against Us or Our Royal Father ... shall ever rise in Judgement, or be brought into Question against any of them, to the least Endamagement of them, either in their Lives, Liberties, or Estates.' He also bowed to pressure from Monck and promised not to unilaterally recover Crown properties, instead indicating that he would refer the matter to Parliament. For obvious reasons, those who had fought for the Crown in the 1640s and suffered financially at the hands of the English Parliament had an expectation that they would recover their losses, but many were to be left disappointed. The King, it was often said, forgot his friends as quickly as he forgave his enemies.

Through the Declaration of Breda Charles showed an astute under-standing of the concerns of those who might oppose his restoration and he largely, if temporarily, reconciled much of the political nation into accepting his return. But who was to suffer? His supporters expected some vengeance and it was necessary to satisfy their understandable frustrations. The King was consistent that those who had passed sentence on his father were to be excepted [excluded] by Parliament from any pardon and instead were put on notice that they would be pursued by the state and convicted of treason. These were the regicides – men who had been present at the High Court of Justice in Westminster Hall on 27 January 1649 when the death sentence was passed on Charles I. Accordingly, on 14 May 1660, the House of Commons ordered that 'all those persons who sat in judgement on the late King's Majesty when the sentence was pronounced for his Condemnation, be forthwith secured [arrested]'. A list containing sixty-seven names was passed to the serjeant-at-arms, with a request that civil and military forces seek to detain those on the list.

Immediately excepted from pardon for symbolic reasons were John Bradshaw, the president of the commission that tried King Charles I; Oliver Cromwell; Henry Ireton, a hated parliamentary army officer; and Thomas Pride, the commander who had led the purge of moderates from the Commons in 1648. All had died during the 1650s and their attainder was symbolic, but it began a process of negotiation between the two Houses of Parliament over who should be excluded from pardon and oblivion (for both past offences and to prevent future prosecution for past misdeeds). In effect, the act was expected to create a tabula rasa. This proved impossible, however, as Parliament was intent on seeking vengeance beyond the parameters that the King had laid down, and individual resentments and vendettas were pursued, which in turn slowed down the passage of the legislation. A royal proclamation was made on 15 June, reminding the populace that the government were working to ensure justice would be done, although its real purpose was to pressurise MPs and peers to resolve their differences and pass the bill. Crucially, it clarified the Declaration of Breda by condemning those who had failed to respond to the summons to surrender to Parliament. They were now automatically guilty and could expect to be pursued as traitors. Continued political delay meant that Charles II was forced to attend the House of Lords on 27 July to address the peers directly, requesting that they expedite the bill. He did not mince his words and reiterated that he 'had the same Intentions and Resolutions now I am here with you, which I had at Breda'. The King's intervention did little to advance the process as the delay was caused by their haggling over whom was to be excepted, with the Lords asking for the death warrant that condemned Charles I in order to compare the names of those who had signed it with those who had passed sentence, after which six more persons were added to the list of traitors.

Despite his involvement in drafting the Declaration of Breda, and his likely contribution to drafting the bill, especially the preamble, Edward Hyde (and from 1661 elevated to the earldom of Clarendon) was not impressed with the King's indirect approach to the issue of pardoning enemies, especially as it blocked the rest of Parliament's business. In the end, MPs largely failed to secure guarantees for the lives of those men who had rendered to Parliament. According to Clarendon's memoirs, the Lords then agreed 'that all the persons who were fled, and those who had not rendered themselves, should [upon arrest] be brought to trial and attainted according to law', while those who had surrendered may be shown some clemency. Around the same time as non-signatories were included, so were others who had had no direct involvement in either the trial or the execution of the King, but were heavily implicated in the civil wars, such as Sir Henry Vane the Younger and Major-General John Lambert, as we shall see.

The political process ground on and by the end of August the bill had been approved by both houses and was presented to the King for the royal assent. The Act of Free and General Pardon Indemnity and Oblivion (12 Ch. II, c. xi) announced itself 'out of a hearty and pious Desire to put an end to all Suites and Controversies' that had arisen, or might arise in the future between the King and his subjects in order to 'bury all Seeds of future Discords' so that 'noe crime whatsoever Committed against His Majesty or His Royal Father' will prove detrimental to any man's reputation. Except for those accused of direct involvement in the regicide itself, the act revoked 'All manners of Treasons, Misprisions of Treason, Furthers Felonies Offences Crimes …' committed between 1 January 1637 and 24 June 1660. The act was legally but not politically comprehensive, in that it acquitted and absolved 'all and every Subject' of England, Scotland and Ireland of any crimes committed previously against the King or his father (section 5) and then expunged the possibility of charges being brought against anyone by refusing officials who worked in the courts of law permission to hear cases against any subject (section 9), except for murder and rape (section 10). It also demanded that any cases of treason related to the period 1637–60 must be tried before 24 June 1662. In many ways, the act legislated for the promises Charles had made in his Declaration of Breda.

The King was now legally empowered to seek retribution on a select number of men who had passed sentence on his father, and it did so in a tiered series of punishments, ranging from execution to exclusion from holding office. While the King was publicly restrained, his ministers were adamant that the proclamation calling on men to surrender had not been a promise of pardon. Forty-nine named men then living, plus two unknown executioners, were designated as persons 'to be proceeded against as traitors' for their 'execrable treason in sentencing to death, or signing the instrument for the horrid murder, or being instrumental in taking away the pretious life of our late soveraigne Lord Charles the first of glorious memory'.

Alongside those named in the act as being exempted from pardon, nineteen were exempted from ever holding public office again. Posthumous exceptions were also made for Oliver Cromwell, John Bradshaw, president of the High Court of Justice that tried the King, Henry Ireton, Cromwell's son-in-law and deceased former parliamentarian army commander, and Colonel Thomas Pride, who led the purge of the Commons in December 1648 that left the rump of the Long Parliament to try the King the following month. On the orders of the House of Commons, their bodies were disinterred, ritually mutilated and put on public display in early 1661. The act also made special mention of others who had not been directly involved in the trial or execution of the King but were prominent opponents of the Crown and were to suffer for their political actions in the 1640s and 1650s. Nineteen others who had fled or remained at large were also listed as being excepted from the pardon and the act made clear that were they to be arrested, they would be subject to a future parliament's justice.

The men who were condemned by the act have been known as the regicides since the 1640s, but the Act of Indemnity did not use the word 'regicide'. Instead, those attainted by the act were brought to justice for the crime of high treason, which was described as compassing and imagining the death of the king in the 1352 Act, regicide being unrecognisable in law. While it was a sin, it was not a crime. So when the trials commenced, the indictment avoided using the term. The signatories of the death warrant might be damned loosely for regicide, but they were to be condemned legally for treason.

What the King didn't do in the Act of Indemnity was engage in the debates that Charles I had fought, or even reject the charges that were laid against his father, especially that he had acted treasonously by raising the royal standard at Nottingham and thereby instigating the civil wars on his own subjects. Nor did Charles explicitly attack the Rump Parliament's claims that it had authority to execute his father, which the deceased King had vehemently denied. In effect, he didn't relitigate the charges brought against his father but left it to his senior judges to argue these points of law (both *de jure* and *de facto*) at the regicides' trials. In effect, Charles II bypassed the issues that so occupied the House of Commons and Charles I in the 1640s.

The numbers of those liable for exception from pardon have been used by historians as a justification for arguing that Charles II demonstrated considerable clemency before moving on in their narrative analysis of the Restoration. But the trials of the regicides deserve more attention for not just the perceived restraint, but also for the particular acts of retribution.

The government wasted little time in pursuing those it had exempted from pardon and within weeks it indicated that a special commission of oyer and terminer would be established under the jurisdiction of the Court of King's Bench to hear the cases against the regicides. In September it laid out the commission's remit and terms of reference and appointed the legal officials to preside over it, led by Sir Orlando Bridgeman, the Lord Chief Baron of the Exchequer and Lord Chief Justice of the Common Pleas. Exemplified by Bridgeman, the Crown's legal representatives were all royalists, jurists and experienced legal professionals. Bridgeman already had a formidable reputation in legal circles by 1660, but he came to widespread prominence as the presiding judge at the trial of the regicides. He was seconded by Sir Heneage Finch, the Solicitor General for England. As an avowed royalist, Finch retreated from public life during the 1650s and instead had built up a successful legal practice before he was elected to the Convention Parliament in April 1660 as MP for Canterbury. He was appointed Solicitor General in June 1660 and began an intense period of work, managing government business in the Commons because the Attorney General for England, Sir Geoffrey Palmer, was not an MP.

The court, or commission of oyer and terminer 'in order to the Tryal of the pretended Judges of his late Sacred Majesty' convened on 9 October at Hick's Hall in Clerkenwell and the cases were heard between 10 and 19 October at the Old Bailey. Alongside Bridgeman were the senior judges and what Pepys described as 'such a bench of noblemen as had not been ever seen in England'. In his opening address to the jurors on 9 October, Bridgeman laid out the grounds on which the treason charges were made, arguing that unlike the pretended trial of Charles I, this

Indictments listing the charges against each regicide, October 1660. (*KB 8/64*)

court had the authority of the 1352 statute behind it. He also explained the charges to the jury: the treasonous act of which the defendants were charged was the compassing and imagining the King's death and proof of this was the defendant's presence at Charles I's trial on 27 January 1649. Any other actions, such as signing the death warrant, were 'overt-acts', or evidence, but the main charge was being present on the day the King was condemned. In an attempt to pre-empt the arguments of several defendants, Bridgeman made clear to the Grand Jury that 'no Authority, no single person, no community of persons, not the people collectively, or Representatively, have any coercive power over the King of England'. While the proceedings that followed were largely for show, and the outcome never in doubt, Bridgeman was careful to proceed according to law. In doing so, he developed his argument by stating that while the 1649 trial had no foundation in law, this trial was based solely on laws enacted by Parliament. Or as Pepys noted, Bridgeman 'did wholly rip up the unjustness of the war against the King from the beginning'.

On the 10 October, proceedings transferred to the Old Bailey and the indictments were read to the defendants, who were expected to enter a plea. Of the twenty-nine defendants, almost all disputed the charges as listed in the indictment, which read:

> That He, together with others, not having the fear of God before His eyes, and being instigated by the Devil, did Maliciously, Treasonably, and Feloniously, contrary to his due Allegiance, and bounden Duty, sit upon and condemn our late Soveraign Lord, King Charls the First of ever Blessed Memory: and also did upon the thirtieth of January, 1648: Sign and Seal a Warrant for the Execution of His Late Sacred and Serene Majesty, of Blessed Memory.

The charge was first addressed to Sir Hardress Waller by the Clerk of the Crown (Edward Shelton), who asked 'How Sayeth Thou, Sir Hardress Waller? Art thou guilty of that Treason whereof thou standeth Indicted?' Waller attempted to dispute the charge by arguing that he had no counsel, but Bridgeman immediately interrupted him and demanded that he enter a plea because there was 'no Medium: Guilty or Not Guilty? It is that which is the Law'. Waller tried to dodge the question several times, pleading that he had been in Ireland for several years and could not take a position through ignorance of the law; then asking for more time to consider the question. But the court was persistent, and not a little ruthless, and demanded a response. In the end, Waller conceded and accepted the charge, answering 'In as much as I have said, I dare not Say Not Guilty: I must say Guilty'. Much the same pattern followed for the other defendants: some challenged the authority of the court, while others pleaded ignorance. All, however, besides Waller, pleaded not guilty.

A jury was sworn on 11 October and Solicitor General Sir Heneage Finch addressed the court. Expanding on Bridgeman's remarks of 9 October, he demanded that the jury remember the events of 1648–9, when the Rump of the Long Parliament had 'taken it upon themselves to dissolve the House of Peers [which was opposed to the trial], they pass a Law, and Erect, Forsooth! an High Court of Justice, as they call it, a Shambles of Justice.' The jury then received their instructions, that 'twenty nine persons do now expect your Justice'.

The trials of the twenty-nine individuals took place over the next ten days. The first, of Thomas Harrison, was as much for spectacle as for justice. Harrison was a Puritan of the most zealous form and emerged as the leader of the Fifth Monarchists in the 1650s, but had been bent on destroying Charles I since 1642, when he joined the Earl of Essex's guards in order to wage war against the Crown. The Fifth Monarchists were millenarian Puritans who believed in the coming of God and took their name from a prophecy in the Book of Daniel that four ancient monarchies (Babylonian, Persian, Macedonian, and Roman) would precede the kingdom of Christ. Harrison saw considerable action during the first civil war, serving at the battles of Marston Moor, Naseby and at the siege of Oxford, before joining the New Model Army when it was created in 1645. By 1647, he publicly declared his wish to prosecute Charles I because 'the king was a man of blood'. After the capture of Charles in

1648, Harrison acted as one of his gaolers, personally escorting the King to London from the Isle of Wight. He then played a prominent role in the trial and signed the death warrant. Subsequent to the execution of the King, he continued to pursue Charles II and led the rout of the royalist forces at Worcester in 1651 that ended Charles II's attempts to overturn the Commonwealth.

At his own trial, Harrison showed little remorse and was adamant that his actions (and by extension those of Parliament) in executing the King had been just. The Solicitor General was required to prove that Harrison was guilty of the charges in the indictment that he had both compassed and imagined the death of the King. This was the treason. Everything else that Harrison may have done was the overt act. Therefore, witnesses were called to attest that he had undertaken the actions of which he was accused, as much to establish a protocol, for the outcome was never in doubt. The court then sought to solidify its case by producing documentary evidence of Harrison's involvement: the first was his signature on the instrument that convened the High Court of Justice. The second piece of evidence was the death warrant itself with Harrison's signature and seal. Despite this strong start, the court seemed to falter a little by giving Harrison ample opportunity to dispute each point of law, an error it tried to avoid with the other regicides.

In his own rebuttal, Harrison sought to assert that the High Court of Justice had been established by the House of Commons, which was a superior court to that trying him, 'and that being so, whatever was done by their Commands, or their authority, is not questionable by your Lordships, as being (as I humbly conceive) a Power Inferior to that of an High Court of Parliament'. This enraged many members of the court (especially those who were ejected from the Commons at Pride's Purge in December 1648) and the response was fulsome, especially about how the Rump had not been a full parliament, therefore it did not have authority over the King's life. When Harrison pressed his point, the court lost its composure and efforts were made to silence him, but Harrison continued: 'I would have abhorred to have brought him [Charles I] to account: had not the blood of Englishmen … been shed'. At this point, he was again cut off and Bridgeman reprimanded him for his behaviour and language, chastising him that the court had been lenient and given him opportunity to defend himself, but it would not tolerate his behaviour.

Given a final opportunity to speak, Harrison was unrepentant, announcing that he had publicly undertaken his actions in 1649 and he repeated his assertion that 'what I did was by the Supreme Authority. I have said it before, and appeal to your own consciences that this court cannot call me to question.' At this point, the court moved to seek a verdict and, unsurprisingly, the jury returned a unanimous decision of guilt. Thereafter, Bridgeman read the macabre death sentence:

> The judgement of this court is, and the Court doth award: that you be led back to the place from whence you came, and from thence to be drawn upon an Hurdle to the place of Execution, and there you shall be hanged by the Neck and being alive shall be cut down, and your Privy-Members to be cut off, your Entrails to be taken out of your Body, and (you living) the same to be burnt before your Eyes, and your Head to be cut off, your Body to be divided into four Quarters, and your Head, and Quarters to be disposed of at the pleasure of the King's Majesty: and the Lord have Mercy upon your Soul.

The following day, the court reconvened but proceeded more promptly by giving the defendants less opportunity to dispute the charges in the indictment. Cases progressed quickly, with several defendants throwing themselves on the mercy of the court and King. Others deserve some commentary as the Crown and government's motives emerge, especially its pursuit of those who created the apparatus to murder Charles I. One particular case worth noting is that of John Cook, who acted as solicitor for the High Court of Justice in 1649. Cook argued that he was not a regicide, merely counsel for the body that had tried and executed the King, therefore he could not be guilty. The King's legal officers, however, saw it differently. 'His part and portion', they argued, 'will be different in this matter ... as he stood as a wicked instrument of that matter at the Bar.' While detailed arguments followed, the case revolved around the fact that when Charles I was asked to enter a plea to the charges laid against him on 26 January 1649, Cook refused to let him respond except (as the present court was doing) that the King merely enter a plea of guilty or not guilty. Cook was also accused of having commented 'that the king must die and monarchy with him'. In response, Cook repeatedly claimed that he had had no personal authority to charge the King, but unsurprisingly this was deemed unacceptable, especially as it was clearly remembered that he had harangued the King during the 1649 trial. Cook was found guilty but had the sense of decorum to acknowledge that he had a 'fair trial' according to law.

Under the Act of Indemnity, some of the men who had surrendered themselves after the Restoration had been excepted from indemnity and were to be brought to trial, but if found guilty, were not to be executed. Instead their fate would be further considered by the King and Parliament. One such regicide was Sir Hardress Waller, the soldier and religious fanatic who had backed Pride's Purge of December 1648 and had personally prevented the Speaker of the House of Commons, William Lenthal, from entering the chamber to take his seat. Waller was also a commissioner at the King's trial, missing only one session before signing the death warrant. Like many who had risen to prominence during the 1640s, he subsequently had a complicated relationship with the Cromwells, being personally loyal to Oliver and his son Henry, who from 1657 ran the Irish administration, while he also opposed the offer of the crown to Cromwell, as well as his accommodation of religious pluralism. After Oliver's death in 1658, Waller's behaviour became erratic as political uncertainty engulfed Britain and Ireland. He arrested Henry Cromwell in Dublin before launching a coup against the Dublin administration, but this was quickly overturned and Waller was himself arrested. He fled to France at the Restoration but returned to England hoping to take advantage of the clemency offered to repentant republicans. This was not forthcoming and he was excepted from the pardon and brought to trial.

Waller was the first to acknowledge his guilt and with it he petitioned the Crown for mercy. This was an unwelcome move for some republicans and Waller was disparaged as 'one who would say anythinge to save his life'. There may be some justification to this scorn as Waller lied that he had done more than any other to preserve the life of Charles I but events took him over and he could not influence the eventual outcome. The court reminded Waller that it did not have authority to commute sentence and that he was not condemned to death but nonetheless was convicted of treason. The case encompasses the contradictions of the way royal justice was dispensed. Waller was undoubtedly guilty of compassing the death of the King. In pleading for his life, and seeking to avail himself of the King's clemency, however, Waller escaped a hideous death and saw out the remainder of his days in prison on the island of Jersey, dying in 1666.

The remaining trials were completed by 19 October and of those condemned to death, the executions were quickly performed. Sentenced to the gruesome end reserved for traitors, Thomas Harrison was executed on Saturday 13 October; John Carew on Monday 15 October; John Cook and Hugh Peters on 16 October; Thomas Scot, Gregory Clement, Adrian Scroop and John Jones on 17 October; and finally, Daniel Axtell and Francis Hacker on 19 October. With that, royal justice had been exercised for those guilty and unrepentant of their part in the trial and execution of Charles I. The reaction in London was initially one of relief that justice was being served, but this did not last. Pepys noted that he was glad to see those who had murdered the King brought to justice, but the population of London soon became weary of the public executions, to the point where sympathy for the traitors outweighed that for the King. The Crown may have also overestimated the public's appetite for such brutal displays: Axtell and Hacker were to die on 18 October but after four executions had been performed on 17 October, the authorities gave the two men a day's reprieve to give the public and the executioners a respite from the gore. Descriptions survive of the executioners themselves struggling to perform their duties, while the public were understandably repulsed by the spectacle of so much blood. There are also reports of a deeply unpleasant smell in the air at Charing Cross from the burning of human entrails. Nonetheless, justice was served in the most public way. As a final warning, Harrison and Jones's heads were put on spikes and displayed at Westminster Hall as a reminder to those who might step out of line.

Through the Act of Indemnity and General Pardon, Charles II had attempted to placate his supporters while publicly punishing a limited number of those who had personally brought about his father's death. With the trials over, it is worth pausing briefly to consider what Charles had promised in his declaration from Breda: that none but those who had direct involvement in the murder of his father would suffer retribution by the new regime. In general, and while in public, he lived up to his promise to the Lords on 27 July: 'I knew well there were some Men who could neither forgive themselves, or be forgiven by Us; and I thank you for your Justice towards those, the immediate Murderers of my Father.' While it is unsurprising that he was not satisfied, Charles was astute enough to accept that a limited number of deaths would have to suffice if his new government was to prosper.

The King was much more direct with Parliament after the passage of the Act of Indemnity, perhaps revealing more of his true opinion: 'I do very willingly pardon,' he told the Lords, 'all that is pardoned by this Act of Indemnity, to that Time which is mentioned in the Bill; nay, I will tell you, that from that Time to this Day, I will not use great Severity, except in such Cases where the Malice is notorious, and the public Peace exceedingly concerned.' In a marked change of tone, he informed the peers that 'the same Discretion and Conscience, which disposed Me to the Clemency ... will oblige Me to all Rigour and Severity, how contrary soever it be to My Nature, towards those who shall not now acquiesce, but continue to manifest their Sedition and Dislike of the Government, either in Action or Words.' Justifying his attitude, he reminded the Lords that they were to ensure that 'exemplary Justice ... be done upon those who are guilty of seditious Speeches or Writings, as well as those who break out into seditious Actions; and that you will believe those who delight in reproaching and traducing My Person, not to be well-affected to you and the Public Peace.' In a key line, he also noted that there was a deadline of 24 June 1662 in the act, but few seemingly paid much attention to this at the time. But the King was obviously aware of it. In the coming years he was to continue to pursue those whom he deemed to be a threat to his regime, as well as those who had previously harmed his father.

The initial response to the executions was likely to have been frustrating for the authorities as support for the Crown's policy ebbed away in favour of those who were brought to the scaffold. But this was temporary and largely limited to people who witnessed the executions or were never going to be reconciled to the restoration of the Stuarts. The passage and implementation of the act allowed the King to prove he would stick to his word while it created space for the government to progress its agenda, which was focused in the short term on raising sufficient money to pay off and reduce the size of the army, and on resolving the religious settlement. Within days of the final executions a conference was convened at Edward Hyde's residence to try to secure a deal that would reflect the 'liberty of conscience' promised in the Declaration of Breda. The King's more liberal inclinations, however, were not matched by those of his ministers and he had to compromise on his intentions as the bishops and proponents of an episcopal Church of England sought to put themselves to the forefront of any settlement. This in turn roused religious independents to action and there were several fruitless attempts to challenge the King in the coming years. The most immediate was Thomas Venner's efforts in early 1661. Venner had assumed leadership of the Fifth Monarchists after Thomas Harrison's execution and sought to continue resistance to the monarchy, leading a doomed foray of some forty or fifty fellow fanatics against the Crown. Despite the small numbers, Venner's Rising managed to remain active across London for several days before the authorities subdued it. The fact that it took several days to quash became a concern for the government. Venner was eventually captured and executed after a trial at the Old Bailey on 17 January 1661, and by 21 January, thirteen of his co-conspirators were also executed. If nothing else, Venner's efforts succeeded in unnerving an already anxious administration and the government was soon flooded with letters announcing rumours of plots. Repression quickly followed as the authorities imposed themselves on religious dissenters. The government took the threats seriously, and were probably right to do so, as many in power could not quite accept that most republicans had merely resigned themselves to the new regime.

A new parliament was also needed, as the current Convention Parliament contained remnants of the republic, which chaffed the Crown and its ministers. If nothing else, the tortuous negotiations around the Act of Indemnity demonstrated that it had to go. Once the Convention had agreed to raise the necessary sum to pay off the debts the King inherited from the army and navy, it was dissolved. Its successor, known as the Cavalier Parliament, was elected in April 1661 and was intended to sweep away the last vestiges of the English Revolution. Whereas men who had fought for the King and his father had deliberately been excluded from the Convention, the Commons was now avowedly royalist. It was also less indulgent to those who were deemed to be threats to the regime. This included John Lambert and Sir Henry Vane the Younger, both of whom were excepted from the Act of Indemnity despite not having had any direct involvement in the regicide. They were, however, guilty by association. The execution of royal justice, and by extension the King's approach to his subjects, is reflected in how both men fared. The Convention Parliament petitioned the King on 5 September 1660 to spare both Vane and Lambert should they be attainted, because the King was proceeding 'only against the immediate Murderers of Your Royal Father'. But this approach was not to last. Lambert had initially been listed in the bill for punishment not extending to life, but the Lords insisted he be wholly excepted. This was the eventual outcome, as Lambert and Vane's fates became entwined as non-regicides who were thought too dangerous to be pardoned.

Throughout the 1640s, and while still in his twenties, Lambert garnered a reputation as a superb military commander, having joined Parliament's forces in Yorkshire when the conflict broke out in 1642. He played a leading role in many of the major victories for Parliament and then served in the New Model Army from its creation in 1645, culminating in his command of Parliament's army in Scotland and in the eventual rout of the Royalists in 1650–51. It was here, with Thomas Harrison, that he ended any hopes Charles II had of immediately recovering his throne. Already a major-general at this point, he was barely thirty-two years old. While he had been named as a commissioner to try Charles I, he played no part in the trial as he was serving in the north of England, but he did nothing to oppose the execution of the King. He established himself as a politician of some cunning and authority in the 1650s, and for a time was considered a rival of Oliver Cromwell's, such was the breadth of his influence over Parliament. Lambert, however, was first and foremost a soldier and was unwilling to allow the civil authorities too much influence over the army. This stance ultimately led to his falling out with Cromwell by 1657, when Lambert was forced from public life. By 1659 and the implosion of the Protectorate, Lambert returned to Parliament as the remnants of the New Model Army were clashing with the Rump to ensure that it could not re-establish its authority over the army. Monck's intervention created an external threat for those who espoused the 'Good Old Cause' and Parliament ordered Lambert to march north to face Monck. He did so, but with undue haste as his army was not properly provisioned and winter took its toll on his men, while Monck's men were both better provisioned and paid. As a result, Lambert's men capitulated before the two armies met and much of it melted away as Lambert was forced into a retreat to London, harried by Monck's forces. He was arrested in February 1660 and placed in the Tower of London but managed to escape in April to lead a hopeless effort to resist the Restoration. He was rearrested in humiliating circumstances and so ended his military and political career.

Like Lambert, Sir Henry Vane the Younger was not a regicide, having not signed the death warrant, but was excepted from pardon. Vane, however, represented a different threat to the Stuarts. He had the benefit of an entry to court in the 1630s through his father. After a disastrous spell as Governor of Massachusetts he returned to England chastened from over-promotion at too young an age, but he was rehabilitated by

1639 with a revived administrative position in the navy and thereafter he was elected to the Commons as MP for Hull in 1640. Increasingly averse to Archbishop Laud's reforms of the Church of England, and in what he perceived as the arbitrary nature of Charles I, Vane supported Parliament in opposition to the Crown and emerged as one of the most formidable politicians of the period. He displayed a remarkable administrative ability in the 1640s through his management of the navy, and from there built a political career in Westminster.

Vane played no part in the King's trial or execution, having voluntarily retired from Parliament in 1648 after Pride's Purge, but within weeks of Charles I's execution he had reconciled himself to the Commonwealth and, in February 1649, was elected to the Council of State. He was to openly acknowledge Parliament's deficiencies, but he consistently opposed any revival of the monarchy, stating that 'Parliament caused justice to be done on the late King'. He, however, failed to reconcile himself wholly to the Protectorate, and like Lambert, but for different reasons, fell out with Cromwell, and he periodically retired from public life. In the 1650s he bestrode Westminster and Whitehall, commanding a leading, if often unwelcome position in the Commons while continuing to demonstrate his administrative worth to the government. But like Lambert, by the time of the Restoration he was a spent political force, yet both men remained notional threats to the Crown. Lambert's name was regularly mentioned as being an inspiration to unreconciled soldiers who sought to use him as a figurehead for their grievances, while Vane's publications and political legacy were similarly used by enemies of the Crown, especially as it was he who had coined the term 'the Good Old Cause'. As a result, both men were detained in the Tower in 1660.

Their responses to the Restoration thereafter determined their fates. Having escaped from the Tower but failing to rouse a force to resist the return of the King in April 1660, Lambert sought mercy, quickly petitioning in May 1660, maintaining that although he fought for Parliament, he did so in defence of 'the Lawes, and Libertyes of the Subject, the true reformed Protestant Religion, and the Privileges of the Parliament, which they declared to be in danger'. He attempted to justify his actions by telling the King that he had felt honour-bound to follow Parliament's commands and serve, but that he was not in favour of the murder of the King or the change in government. 'Yet,' he wrote, 'having complied with and beene active in some later transactions which have proved obstructive to the settlement of these Kingdomes and of that happinesse which they now enjoye under your Majesty whereby your Petitioner maye have justly incurr'd your Ma[jes]ties displeasure,' and not having any hope of forgiveness, Lambert promised that he had no intentions of resisting the new government. If granted the benefit of the indemnity and pardon, he promised he would live peacefully, 'being perfectly resolved to spend the remainder of his life in Loyalty and obedience to your Majesty'. As petitions for clemency go, it was perfect. There is no record of Vane having petitioned for clemency.

There may initially have been hope for both men as the King indicated that he would only seek to punish those directly involved in the trial, but the Lords had other ideas, insisting that both were excepted from pardon. A compromise was reached whereby the two Houses agreed to petition the King for clemency if Lambert and Vane were attainted by Parliament. This was granted but both men continued to be held in the Tower until October 1661, when for increased security and to prevent a potential escape attempt, Vane was moved to the Scilly Isles and Lambert to Guernsey. The clemency offered by the Convention Parliament was not extended by its successor and from July 1661 the Commons was seeking a bill to punish those excepted who had escaped with their life. The Commons also asked that the King reconsider opening proceedings against Vane and Lambert, and ordered the Attorney General to begin preparing evidence against them. The King didn't respond in any meaningful way when Commons repeated the request in November 1661, but in February 1662 (and at the Commons' third time of asking), Charles spoke to Clarendon about how to proceed. In a note passed between the two men in a Privy Council meeting, Charles informed Clarendon that the Commons had again asked him to proceed against Vane and Lambert, but Clarendon advised that there was by then not enough time in the legal session to initiate a case, instead advising the King to inform Parliament that a case would be brought later in the year. Time, however, was running out if the government wanted to proceed against them before the statute permitting it expired on 24 June 1662. The government followed through and the necessary orders were issued in April for Vane and Lambert to be brought back to the Tower of London, where they were to be kept under a strict watch.

Vane was brought to trial at the Court of King's Bench on 2 June 1662 but showed none of the contrition that would ultimately save Lambert. Unlike the other regicides, he was not charged with compassing and imagining the death of Charles I, but instead of obstructing the return of Charles II. Vane's actions, the King's counsel argued, fell under the charge of compassing and imagining treason, which Vane rejected and pleaded not guilty. It was now up to the counsel to prove to the jury Vane's guilt, and Vane's accusers knew where to look for evidence against him. On 6 June they presented papers that alleged Vane's guilt of treason through his membership of the Council of State that was established after Charles I's execution. The House of Commons journal was shown to the court, proving that on 7 February 1649 Vane had voted to create a Council of State, and on 14 February was elected as one of its members. Crucially, the first responsibility of the Council of State was to 'oppose and suppress whomsoever shall endeavour to go about to set up or maintain the pretended Title of Charles Stewart, eldest son to the late King ...'. Numerous further examples were then produced that showed Vane's role in both perpetuating the Commonwealth and seeking to ensure that no restoration took place. The government may have known it was on dubious legal ground as many others could have been charged for the same actions, and Vane had put up a robust defence, challenging the court on each point it presented, and even endeavouring to present his own witnesses who were willing to contradict the King's counsel.

Both Lambert and Vane were brought before the court on 11 June, where Vane's conduct was contrasted with Lambert's. Vane continued his unrepentant stance, while Lambert only queried whether the court had the correct John Lambert before offering no further resistance. While he did not deny what he had done, Lambert did try to downplay his involvement in the events of the 1640s and 1650s. It seems that the judges were won over by his tactics as he was told that as he had not 'spoken in justification of what he had done but onely in extenuation', the King had indicated that he was 'pleased to respite execution'. Lambert was returned to the Scilly Isles and he remained a prisoner until his death in 1684.

For Vane, there was no mercy and he was condemned to be hanged, drawn and quartered. Vane's defence, that he acted under the authority of Parliament and was therefore innocent, was rejected out of hand and his refusal to show any remorse for his actions guaranteed his fate. As the sentence was read out, Vane was told that 'had not the prisoner's high crimes been heightened by his very ill deportment, he might have had some hopes of mercy'. The nature of Vane's defence, as well as his comportment during the trial did worry the King and he insisted that Vane be executed after hearing reports of his conduct, especially his rejection of royal authority, promptly despatching a letter from Hampton Court to Clarendon insisting that Vane was 'too dangerous a man to be suffered to live, if we can honestly put him out of the way'.

Vane was executed by beheading on 14 June (conveniently the anniversary of the Battle of Naseby, a decisive Parliamentarian victory) at Tyburn. His execution was quite the spectacle as a multitude turned out to witness it, but the authorities made none of those mistakes they had done for the regicides. Vane is reported to have conducted himself with dignity and defiance, attempting to address the crowd, but the sheriff tried to snatch his papers while a troupe of trumpeters were placed at the foot of the scaffold to drown out his words. In the end, Charles extended some mercy. Vane's friends had petitioned the King that Vane not suffer and the King granted the wish, personally ordering the sheriffs of London to behead rather than prolong the suffering of the prisoner. The King also allowed his body to be quietly buried. Vane's murder established him as a martyr, and his name was repeatedly invoked by enemies of the King. None more so than those who championed his republican ideas, and his rejection of monarchical authority. In 1667, a 'eulogy' condemning Vane's death found its way to the government. Celebrating Vane as 'A Priest a Prophet and a King, Victime of a very worthii thing, Dying that Liberty might live, the English cause he doth retrieve', Vane's cause and spirit lived after he was killed.

As to how, once he had the chance, Charles II responded to the execution of his father – he was strategic in his use of vengeance. And he was restrained – but then he had little choice if he was to win over much of the populace and not revive the angst of the civil wars. In passing the decisions to the Houses of Parliament, Charles distanced himself from the trials, and in allowing his judges to bear the brunt of the work, he was able to demonstrate his strength to his foes as well as his friends. The Act of Indemnity was an important moment in the King's reign, establishing as it did Charles as a dominant ruler but also his willingness to extend a hand to his enemies. The trials were equally important events for the King as they allowed him to punish some of those who had procured the death of his father. The process also reveals one of the troublesome traits about the King's character. He was content to individualise rather than generalise guilt, which then allowed him to readily pardon many who had caused his father's suffering.

Charles was a complicated but intelligent man. Although he did not stand on ceremony to the same extent as his father, he was content to allow the likes of Lambert and Waller, who had shown due deference, to live out the rest of their lives in prison. Others, such as Vane, were seen as enemies to be disposed of. The King, despite his inexperience at governing, dealt ably with the challenge of securing his restoration and establishing himself as a monarch. While he had the goodwill of his ministers, government and the populace in the early 1660s, this was not to last as the realities of ruling three kingdoms increased the demands on him. The Act of Indemnity was one of the high points of the King's reign. Within a few years, the problems that emerged from his religious settlement, as well as those not of his making, would challenge his authority like none previous.

At the Court at Whitehall
September 28th 1678
Present

The Kings most Excellent maⁱᵉ

His Highnes Prince Rupert
Lord Archbⁱˢᵖ of Canterbury
Lord Chancelor
Lord Treasurer
Lord Privy Seale
Duke of Monmouth
Duke of Lauderdale
Earle of Ossory
Earle of Peterborow

Earle of Bathe
Earle of Craven
Earle of Carbery
Lᵈ Viscount Newport
Lord Berkeley
Mʳ Vice Chamberlain
Mʳ Secʳʸ Williamson
Mʳ Chancelor of the Exchequer
Mʳ Speaker.

Mʳ Oates &c
their Examinacōn
about the Plot

His maⁱᵉ hauing appointed an Extraordinary Councill to meet this morning there was presented by mʳ Secʳʸ Williamson a bundle of Papers received from one Dʳ Tonge, importing a Conspiracy of the Papistry againſt the Life of his maⁱᵉ. Whereupon his maⁱᵉ toke occasion to acquaint the Board, a little before his late going to Windsor wᶜʰ was on the 13th of August, He had information brought him by the said Dʳ Tonge about a Conspiracy, And that he had referred the matter to the Examination of the Lord Treasurer. That one mʳ Kirby an acquaintance of Dʳ Tonge, was to Conduct the Doctor to his Loᵖ as accordingly he did, And that his Loᵖ desiring to see some other proof by Letters or Papers from the Conspirators themselves, wᶜʰ might convince the truth of their information, and be a Concurrent Evidence with what was testifyed from one mʳ Oats, His Loᵖ by a Letter from Dʳ Tonge of the third of September he entreat, wᶜʰ was sent him to Rycaut being then in Oxfordshire, was advised, that there wᵒᵘld come Letters directed to mʳ Bedingfield at Windsor; wᶜʰ if intercepted might giue further Evidence of the matter. That upon receipt of this Letter, his Loᵖ returning immediately to Windsor, was there at his arrival, and waiting on his maⁱᵉ, told of one single Letter, that came directed to mʳ Bedingfield at his Lodging in Windsor to be left with the Postmaster there, and of another Packet to the same mʳ Bedingfield, recommended to the Postmaster till it should be called for. In wᶜʰ letters mʳ Bedingfield obſerving some mysterious Expressions, tending to a designe of something unlawfull did bring the said Letters to his Royall High̄ signifying that he knew not any of the hand writings, but feared there was some Contrivance of mischeif againſt him, That his Royall Highnes soon brought the said Letters to his maⁱᵉ, and by these steps, they came raw to be presented to the Board by mʳ Secʳʸ Williamson, Where being looked upon, and examined by seuerall of the Lords, the writing in moſt of them seemed to be forct and by the ill spelling of names, and other suspitious marks, thought to be a Counterfeit matter.

But Dʳ Tonge attending without was called in, Whereupon he presented his maⁱᵉ with a short writing, wherein Thomas White, and some others were named whom he desired might presently be seazed on as hostages for his maⁱᵉˢ life &c. And being demanded what he could inform in this matter, he desired to refer himself unto the Papers presented, wᶜʰ gaue the narratiue of all things, That of his owne knowledge, he knew little or nothing, but that he had his information from One mʳ Oats, and was thereupon willing to become Instrumentall in writing down the thing in some order for the better discoverye, of so dangerous a matter.

Hereupon the Paper was read, Intituled a generall brief account of the Conspirators and Conspiracy, Extracted for the moſt part out of the Papers of August the 13th 1678, and afterwards a long writing of many sheets said to Contain forty three Articles, but it Conteined seaventy one.

Deēt

Titus Oates's first appearance at the Privy Council on 28 September 1678. (PC 2/66, f. 392)

Ten

POPISH PLOT, 1678–81

There has now for divers Years, a Design been carried on,
to change the Lawful Government of England into an Absolute
Tyranny, and to Convert the Established Protestant Religion
into down-right Popery.

Andrew Marvell, *The Growth of Popery and Arbitrary*
Government in England (London, 1678)

On 20 November 1678, William Staley was brought before the Court of King's Bench accused of compassing and imagining the death of Charles II. Staley was a goldsmith from Covent Garden, but also a Catholic who had the misfortune to be caught up in the maelstrom of anti-Catholic hysteria that engulfed England known as the Popish Plot. His business had been badly affected by the turmoil that overcame London and he was angry that his creditors had called in his debts because he was a Catholic. At the trial, Sir William Scroggs, Lord Chief Justice, made clear to the jury that Staley was guilty of treason as he was overheard (despite speaking in French) calling the King a heretic and threatening that he would murder Charles if he got the chance. By definition, this was treasonous. Scroggs established Staley's guilt for the jury by having an act from 1661 read out that made it a treasonable offence to threaten the King's person or declare him a heretic. He then produced two witnesses who confirmed that Staley had loudly and publicly stated he would kill the King.

Despite his attempts to deny the charges, Staley's case proceeded quickly and he was convicted and executed as the first victim, but not the first suspect, of the Popish Plot. It did not seem to matter to the court that Staley was unknown to the authorities before his arrest, nor was it a concern that there were reasonable doubts about the character of the witnesses used to convict him. Scroggs's conduct during sentencing is also questionable, suggesting caustically, and without any evidence, that it was likely that Staley was also a priest and thus deserved his fate. Staley has all but been forgotten yet the circumstances of his death are symptomatic of the hysteria that gripped England in the late 1670s as fears of Catholicism, and a Catholic heir to the throne, overwhelmed the government between 1678 and 1681 and led to multiple treason trials.

The origins of the Popish Plot lie in the mind of Titus Oates, but the circumstances that allowed his ideas to proliferate with such lethal consequences stretch back beyond Charles II's reign. Primarily, and often in the imagination of many, was the threat of popery, or militant Catholicism espoused by the Society of Jesus (Jesuits), that intended to eradicate the Church of England and place a Catholic on the throne. There were of course clear examples in English history, no more so than the Gunpowder Plot of 1605 or the Irish Rebellion of 1641, but by 1678, these fears were largely illusory. There was only a tiny population of Catholics in England in the 1670s, no more than 100,000, and even fewer of these were Jesuits. Most Catholics did their best to worship privately and avoid recusancy fines. Certain of the King's policies, however, gave the more hysterical a breeding ground to imagine a much larger conspiracy against England and its Protestant faith, and many came to view religion as the primary danger to the status quo.

The first policy was Charles's willingness to support religious dissenters, including Catholics, and his ambiguity in religious matters exacerbated tensions. Having tried to introduce some sort of accommodation for religious pluralism in the 1660s, Charles tried again in 1673. Through his Declaration of Indulgence, he sought to extend religious pluralism to Protestant nonconformists and Roman Catholics by suspending the Penal Laws. The response was ferocious as the Commons demanded that the King rescind the declaration, which he had no choice but to do.

In its stead, the Commons introduced the first of the Test Acts, which demanded that all office holders must take communion in the Church of England as a stipulation to hold office. Failure to do so would lead to dismissal and significant fines.

The second policy grew out of Charles's eagerness to ally himself with Louis XIV, the autocratic king of France who was seen as the bogeyman of Europe, commanding as he did a massive and permanent army, which he ranged against his enemies. When their alliance, initially secret, codified by the Secret Treaty of Dover (1670) was revealed, it seemed to confirm the fears and prejudices of many that their monarch was not acting in the best interests of England. Protestantism was one of Louis XIV's main targets, so when England and France went to war against the Protestant United Provinces in 1672, there was little domestic appetite for the conflict. Despite the French king's overwhelming dominance, the Dutch held out and public opinion in England soured, with Charles being forced to withdraw his support.

The third issue that created such trouble for the Crown came from within the court itself and was centred on the King's brother, James, Duke of York. Authoritarian by nature, he was outed by the Test Act as a Catholic in 1673 when he refused to agree to take communion and was thus forced to resign his commission as Admiral of the Royal Navy. As Charles had no legitimate children, the potential for James to succeed to the throne was not an unwarranted fear. Alongside James at court was Charles's Catholic Queen Catherine, whose private chapels were known to be a haven for priests, as were the chapels within the residences of Catholic ambassadors.

These circumstances within themselves do not solely explain how the outlandish allegations Oates made gained such traction in England. The Popish Plot was a convenient cover for opposition politicians, known from this time onwards as Whigs, whose overriding aim was the exclusion of James from the succession. The Popish Plot was really the precursor, or catalyst for a period of extreme political tension in England, although Charles's own position was never really under threat.

The Exclusion Crisis, as it has become known, was a vessel for politicians who wished to limit the Crown's prerogative powers. Led by the spurned and cunning Anthony Ashley Cooper, first Earl of Shaftesbury, it was into this environment that Oates poured his poisonous allegations in 1678.

Titus Oates was a discredited and failed cleric who had just enough knowledge of Catholic practices, and a sufficient source of bravado, to impress upon the King's ministers, as well as a credulous House of Commons, that there was a legitimate threat against the King's life. Oates had a record of failure and exclusion and his rise to prominence can only be explained by his mendacity, as well as the perfidy of those who were willing to believe his claims with the sole purpose of embarrassing the King and his brother. That Oates himself ultimately evaded the gallows is hard to explain although he was severely punished in the 1680s.

Oates's early life was unhappy: a sickly child, his family do not appear to have cared for him. The same can be said of his tutors, first at school in London, where he was expelled, and then at Cambridge, which he left in 1669 without a degree. Oates then secured a preacher's licence from the Bishop of London after falsely claiming that he held a degree. In relatively quick succession he secured and lost several livings in the Church of England, having repeatedly unimpressed his parishioners through drunkenness, boorishness and coarse behaviour. He then made false claims, including of sodomy, against those in his orbit. His behaviour resulted in him being called to the assizes to answer charges of perjury, but he fled England, serving in the navy as a chaplain to the garrison at Tangier. It was here that he later claimed he had first heard whispers of a Jesuit-led plot to murder the King and place James on the throne. Returning to England, Oates was subsequently thrown out of the navy for homosexual practices. From this point he gravitated towards the company of London Catholics before securing a living in the household of Henry Howard, the Catholic Earl of Norwich, but he was dismissed from this too and was effectively destitute.

The year 1676 was a turning point in his life as he was introduced to the secret activities of Catholics in London, although their plotting

12 Jan — That in another packet bearing date the 1st of down[...] 16[...] in the which it was specified that the fathers [...] of the society of Jesus had written from Rome and [...] had removed Richard Strange from being provin[...] ciall and had conferred the provincialship [...] the [...] white alias Whitebread and the said Thomas Whitebread ordered that one father [...] Conyers [...] should preach on St Thomas [...] Canterbury day in the sodality Church in the English seminary against the oaths of supremacy and allegiance and that hee should exhort the fathers to stand As the new provinciall who would bee as zealous to promote [...] religion the bringing in of Catholique religion into England as ever his predecessour was and would not leave a stone unturned to promote the same which said letter was directed [...] and [...] by the said Richard Ashby and comunicated by him to the deponent and this was about decemr 24 that Ashby comunicated it to the said deponent

13 Jan — That in another packet bearing date decr 26 it was ordered by Thomas Whitebread Richard Strange John Keines Basil Langworth John Hensworke father Gray father Harcoat senr father Harcoat junr father [...] father Bonfield father Ireland father Blundell father Jennison and some others of the society that father Ashby should bee written unto by Richard Ashby and the fathers at St Omers and informed that the fathers before named had mett together to contrive the advancement of the intended designe of a happy dispossess of his maty of great Brittaine and of his R highness if hee should not appeare to our best their expectations but the former giving noe hopes at all they would endeavour his dispatch with all speed that might bee that hee might not hinder their designs in bringing in Catholique religion and that if they could not finde an opportunity to take him from his kingdom they would soone take his kingdome from him which letter the deponent saw in the hands of Richard Ashby and [...] to reade but the said Richard in compliment would read it to him in his chamber on the second day of January

14 Jan — That in the said letters of decr 26 it was specified that Richard Nicholas [...]dell was constituted by patent from the provinciale to our ordinary at newgate to goe and visit the condemned prisoners there

Excerpt from Titus Oates's allegations in his own hand, endorsed at the bottom of the page by Israel Tonge. (SP 29/409, f. 16v)

211

rarely amounted to much. Oates also undertook his supposed conversion to Catholicism at this time. By 1677 he had met the provincial of the Jesuits in England, Father Richard Strange, who arranged for Oates to travel to Valladolid in Spain to attend the English Jesuit College in the city. Why Strange did this is unclear, but Oates was a convincing liar and perhaps Strange was persuaded of his sincere desire to train as a priest. Nonetheless, the authorities at the English College in Valladolid were not fooled and within months Oates was expelled and returned to England claiming that he had received a doctorate from the University of Salamanca (and he used the title of Doctor for the rest of his days). While his journey to Spain ended in personal failure, it armed him with knowledge of the Jesuits. It also brought him into contact with a significant acquaintance: William Bedloe. For a further unexplained reason, Father Strange dispatched Oates again, this time to St Omer in France to attend the English college there, but Oates was quickly revealed as being unsuitable for training and was dismissed. He had very poor Latin and was deemed an unsuitable student. Rejected by the Catholic authorities who oversaw the mission to England, Oates returned to London in June 1678 and was forced again to beg for his bread. It was that summer that he fell in with one Dr Israel Tonge, a former acquaintance and academic Puritan who was convinced that the Jesuits were hatching a plan to overthrow the reformed religion in England. Tonge was also adamant that it was the Jesuits, not happenstance, that had led to the devastating Fire of London in 1666, an event which seems to have left him permanently unhinged. Their alliance, however, was to have terrible consequences for the lives of many people in England and left a legacy that is as shocking as surprising.

In Tonge, Oates found an audience that satisfied his craving for attention; in Oates, Tonge landed on a source for his prejudices and misplaced sense of danger. Encouraged by Tonge, Oates concocted an elaborate web of lies that alleged that he had uncovered a Jesuit-led plot to murder Charles and revealed these in forty-three allegations, later expanded to over eighty. These were elaborate creations that contained just enough truth to demand official attention but were all almost entirely fabrications. At the core of these was a meeting of Jesuits that took place in May 1678 at the White Horse Inn on the Strand. The meeting had taken place, which Oates knew, but he fabricated its subject matter. Oates and Tonge then connived to bring the allegations to the King's attention through William Bedloe, who approached Charles on the evening of 10 August. Aware that he could not simply ignore such a threat, but unconvinced by the veracity of the claims, the King passed the matter to his chief minister, the Earl of Danby, who despite his best efforts, failed to uncover or even corroborate Oates's claims. Nonetheless, Oates was brought before the Privy Council to attest to the plot in September 1678 and through sheer self-confidence, he managed to convince the King's Council of the truth behind his claims.

Oates's inventions had the veneer of truth, or certainly what appeared to the Privy Council to be sufficiently accurate to warrant taking them seriously. While he had sufficient tangential knowledge of the functions of scores of Jesuits in England to appear authoritative, he was also canny enough to know that he would have to produce evidence of a conspiracy, so soon after he had first used Bedloe to inform the King of the plot, Oates forged several letters that were supposedly written by Jesuits who were active in England, all of which discussed plans to kill the King. Oates then ensured that he left enough of a trail for the letters to be intercepted and presented to Danby. This appeared to give substance to his claims but when they were shown to Charles, he disregarded them. Danby's investigations continued and Oates was eventually called before the Privy Council on 28 September to account for himself. Armed with an expanded account of an imminent plot, as well as a newfound sense of self-importance, Oates still needed luck if he was to have his story believed, and he was fortunate to receive it from several impressionable members of the Privy Council. During his cross-examinations, he presented to the Council what he had supposedly uncovered and in doing so he inadvertently alighted on one half-truth that acted as a lubricant for all his others: he suggested that the Duchess of York's former secretary, Edward Coleman, should be arrested and his papers confiscated. When this duly happened, Coleman's papers from 1674 revealed correspondence between him and Louis XIV's confessor, François La Chaise, and laid bare proposals that Coleman had discussed with the French to overthrow Protestantism in England and replace parliamentary government. In effect, Coleman had conducted an alternative foreign policy to that of Charles, but there was little action behind his words. Nor had the French given them much credence. Coleman had approached this intrigue with all the zealousness of a convert, but he was quite tone deaf to the likelihood of his plans succeeding. Little of substance had emerged from Coleman's intriguing, but the letters were used as evidence of treason within York's entourage and Coleman was thereafter condemned. It is quite likely that several of the Council concluded that Oates was lying, but the Coleman evidence confirmed the generally held fear that England's Catholic enemies were actively conspiring for regime change. Immediate warrants were issued for the arrest of those Jesuits that Oates accused of having attended the White Horse Inn meeting in May 1678 and William Ireland, John Grove, John Fenwick and Thomas Pickering were detained. They were also the first in multiplicity of arrests in the coming weeks as the authorities were ordered to detain anyone whom Oates made allegations against or was believed to be associated with the plot.

From this point on, the response to the plot gathered momentum that was to last for a further three years. A committee of the Privy Council was established to investigate Oates's claims and to cross-examine those who were detained. During their interviews, the Council put Oates's allegations to the men and in each instance all flatly denied what had been said against them. This did them little good, however, and all were remanded into custody, mainly to Newgate prison. Doubts should have entered the councillors' minds when William Ireland was interviewed as he was accused of having attended the White Horse Inn on the Strand in London in May 1678; that he had subsequently formed cells to conspire the death of the King; and that he had written the letter that Oates had forged; and that he had been at St Omer in August receiving orders for the plot. To each of these he had an answer. He acknowledged that he had met with his fellow Jesuits in May, but it had not been to conspire. When he was asked to demonstrate his handwriting and signature, it was obvious they were not the same as the forged letters. He also took issue with factual and typographical errors in the letter, which he argued proved they were inadmissible. Yet, when this was put to Oates, he had a ready answer, assuring the Council 'that the letter aforementioned was of Ireland's handwriting, and that Ireland can write a Secretary hand with great Deal of art, and as to the ill spelling of names, or such like defects, that it is industriously practised by all, to vary there [sic] hands, and to write so, as they may disown the letter if needs be'.

When accused of having travelled to St Omer in August, Ireland had solid alibies for his whereabouts. Having left London on Saturday 3 August, he spent the night at St Albans before travelling to Staffordshire throughout the following week 'where he made a Pilgrimage to the Royale Oake' before holidaying until mid-September at Walter, Lord Ashton's home in the company of Sir John Southcote. Further letters that had been confiscated were then shown to Ireland that demonstrated he was the Treasurer of the Society of Jesus in England, which he did not deny but it hardly mattered. He was guilty in Oates's eyes, therefore he was similarly condemned by the Privy Councillors. What should have been obvious to the Council was unfortunately not: while there were fleeting truths in Oates's allegations against Ireland, the core of what he said was a lie. Ireland put up a strong defence of himself, to the point where Oates lost his composure and asked to retire from the interviews for several hours, claiming that he had been up for several nights and was suffering from exhaustion. While he was no doubt tired, this was merely a pretext for being unable to maintain his composure under sustained challenge.

By the time the interviews were finished that day, proceedings had descended into farce as Oates's allegations were refuted by Dr William Fogarty, who acknowledged that he was Oates's physician but denied he was actively conspiring to kill the King; and by Father Thomas Jenison, who verbally attacked Oates and demanded to know why his allegations against so many men were given substance by the Council. Oates made his first major blunder when he alleged that the Queen's physician, Sir George Wakeman, also a Catholic, was also involved in the plot against the King and that he had conspired to poison Charles in return for £15,000 and that £5,000 had already been paid to him by Edward Coleman. The Privy Council immediately acknowledged that 'altho there were no charg that could be particularly laid home by proof against him, yet, twas his misfortune to be named in a very unhappy Circumstance and twas wisht there might be no fire, where there appear smoke'. In response, Wakeman attested both his innocence and his service to the King, and that he expected some compensation for the false charges laid against him. To this, the Privy Council 'insinuated to him that he ought with more concern to express his innocence' but Wakeman was permitted to leave, having not been arrested.

The final man interviewed that day was Edward Coleman and the charges laid out to Wakeman were repeated to him, alleging that he was a courier for funds that were intended to finance the murder of the King. Unsurprisingly, Coleman rejected these 'with the highest protestations'. Nonetheless, he was imprisoned at Newgate on charges of Treason for 'holding Correspondence with forreiners for the destruction of the King and the Subversion of the government'. Two orders left the Privy Council after the interviews ended on 30 September: one instructed the authorities in Ireland to arrest Father Peter Talbot, Archbishop of Dublin, on allegations of conspiring to murder James Butler, Lord Lieutenant of Ireland as the first move in an attempt to reverse the Reformation in Ireland and restore the Catholic Church. The second order was to the Lords Lieutenant of multiple English counties, commanding them to search for weapons held by Catholics.

The second piece of luck that Oates had was the disappearance of a magistrate, Sir Edmund Godfrey, on Saturday 12 October. Oates and Tonge had approached Godfrey in September, asking that he depose them of their revelations about the plot so that they would have sworn oaths to the truth of their revelations. Godfrey had been hesitant to involve himself as his own background and ambiguous political leanings demonstrated some sympathy for Catholics. Nonetheless, he did depose Oates, but he sat on the evidence for over a week before bringing it to the attention of the Privy Council. What is clear is that he did not investigate the claims with any rigour and may even have left himself open to charges of misprision of treason for not disclosing what he had been told to the full extent. Then, and unexpectedly, he disappeared on 12 October, only to be found dead in Primrose Hill, on the outskirts of North London on Thursday, 17 October, having apparently been strangled and stabbed. No definitive conclusion has ever emerged as to the circumstances of his death and it remains an unsolved mystery to this day. But it was immediately politicised as further evidence of a Catholic plot. Godfrey was proclaimed a martyr for the Protestant cause and his disappearance politicised by both the authorities and his family. It also gave Oates further cover by exposing the supposed threat to the public and in turn created a hysteria in and beyond London that did not reflect reality. Godfrey's death also served as a rallying cause for several opposition groups, from republicans who had never been reconciled to the Restoration to senior courtiers who opposed the succession, and they began to emerge as an organised opposition that was at first guided, and then outright led, by the Earl of Shaftesbury.

Godfrey's unfortunate death also further increased Oates's value and he was invited to address the House of Commons, which was eager to take over the investigations into both the magistrate's death and the alleged plot. Appearing under oath on 23 and 24 October, he regaled the MPs with his inventions and in return received the thanks of a credulous House that expressed its appreciation for exposing the plot and acting in the vanguard for the Protestant nation. Unsurprisingly, the immediate outcome of his appearance was a flurry of orders to make more arrests. The following week, he was examined by the Lords. Over the coming days, Israel Tonge was also summoned by Parliament and he recounted what he believed about the plot, before providing information on his favourite subject: the Great Fire of 1666, which he continued to assert was the work of Jesuits, a conspiracy theory that quickly caught on with the public. In a sign that the Commons was completely invested in the plot, a delegation of MPs was dispatched to search the rooms below the Commons' chamber as a rumour had emerged that there was a design to emulate Guy Fawkes and blow up Parliament. What was becoming clearer at this point, however, was Oates's inability to stand up to scrutiny. As both Houses continued to question him, and spot inconsistencies in his testimony, his behaviour changed and was initially defensive, then more aloof as it became evident that his story did not hold water.

Later that week, the Lords sought to expand the investigation, and turned its attention to Edward Coleman, who was interviewed while in Newgate Prison. His attitude had changed over the course of the month, for now his papers had been fully searched and evidence had emerged of him acting beyond his remit, which he acknowledged. He refused, however, to admit to any involvement in a plot to kill the King. Coleman's main aim, at this point, seems to have been to distance, as much as he could, the Duke of York from the affair.

Despite all this activity, however, the Crown's law officers moved very slowly. Sir William Jones, the Attorney General, had simply been ordered to conduct any trials by Christmas 1678 as the King was equally cautious in balancing how he responded. He could not be seen to do nothing, but nor would he let anyone interrupt the succession. In general, he was slow to act, and did so in a limited way, issuing a proclamation for all Catholics to depart London on 30 October. Trials, however, were inevitable and over the next two years, more than twenty treason trials were held for those implicated, trials that are notable for what they reveal about the collective state of mind that existed within the English political milieu. As the plot rumbled on, Edward Coleman was tried in November; William Ireland, John Pickering and John Grove immediately after; and Sir George Wakeman in July 1679, while the Catholic Archbishop of Armagh, Oliver Plunkett, ended up a victim of Oates's accusations in 1681.

The first three of these trials were presided over by Sir William Scroggs, Lord Chief Justice of the Court of King's Bench. Scroggs represents all of the problems that befell those faced with early modern royal justice. He was appointed at the behest of his political mentor, the Earl of Danby, whose star was on the wane by the time the plot emerged. Scroggs had proved himself before he secured promotion, first to the Court of Common Pleas in 1676 and then to King's Bench in 1678. He was also an avowed royalist, having won the attention of Charles through several addresses that praised loyalty to the monarchy. When presented with Oates's testimony, he wholeheartedly believed it and wasted no time in issuing warrants for arrests, not pausing to question the evidence in the face of growing calls for justice from the public and the House of Commons. Between November 1678, when he tried William Staley, and July 1679, he sent fourteen men to their deaths for supposed involvement in the plot. In presiding over these trials in the manner that he did, at first refusing to accept any alibi or denial, as was the case for Staley or Coleman, and only later hesitating in the face of the weakness of Oates's evidence, Scroggs did much to perpetuate the tensions that existed in England. Treason trials at this time were theatre and were rarely balanced and it was the Lord Chief Justice's role, as much as the Crown's legal officers, to impress upon the members of the jury the guilt of the accused. In this he was largely successful, until Wakeman's trial.

Coleman's trial was the first time that Oates was examined publicly not by ministers or parliamentarians but by legal professionals. The charges against Coleman were unsurprising: that he had plotted to raise sedition and rebellion in England; that he had intended to depose Charles, by death if necessary, and alter the religion of England. What seemed to have annoyed the court most was that Coleman intended to do this with the help of Louis XIV. To the charges in the indictment, Coleman pleaded not guilty, but the Attorney General reminded the jury that there was no need for the court to prove all elements of the indictment, just one would do to condemn and convict. Guilty or not of the specific crimes (and there was inconsistent evidence to convict him on all the charges), Coleman was certainly guilty of the sins, so the Crown's legal officers focused their case on the contents of the letters, how they came to be written, and with whom Coleman had conspired. For this, Oates was presented as a witness, but his examination at the bar did not go smoothly and Scroggs was adamant that he wanted to clearly understand the timeline of events that Oates alleged, as well as how and why Oates had not immediately disclosed the details of what he claimed to have uncovered. But Oates's lies had become so convoluted that his answers were unsatisfactory and Scroggs was at times very impatient with him. Seeking to present a veneer of impartiality Scroggs gave Coleman sufficient opportunity to rebut Oates's claims, which he did with notable deftness. Ultimately, it was not Oates's testimony that convicted Coleman, but the letters that he had written and received. Summing up for the jury, Scroggs said: 'The things he is accused of are two sorts; the one is to subvert the Protestant religion and to introduce popery; the other was to destroy and kill the King. The evidence likewise was of two sorts; the one by letters of his own hand-writing, and the other by Witness *viva voce*. The former he seems to confess, the latter totally to deny.' The jury took little time to reach a verdict of guilty and on 28 November, Coleman was condemned to death. He pleaded to be allowed to spend time with his wife, which was granted; on 3 December 1678, he was brought to Tyburn and executed.

On 17 December the trial of William Ireland, Thomas White (or Whitbread), John Fenwick, Thomas Pickering, and John Grove commenced. Again, the court focused on the timeline. Oates had elsewhere claimed to have been at St Omer in April 1678 and therefore could not have been witness to any of the planning for the conspiracy that was allegedly taking place in London in May when the supposedly conspiratorial meeting was held at the White Horse Inn. Although this was addressed in court, it did not alter the outcome for those charged and Ireland, Grove and Pickering were executed in February 1679. The delay between their trial and execution lay with the King, who was having increasing doubts about Oates, but political necessity saw him sacrifice the men, stipulating, however, that they should be hanged until dead, thus granting a small mercy. Thomas White and John Fenwick had been returned to Newgate during the trial for lack of substantial evidence, but they were eventually tried and executed in June 1679. Despite these executions, the clamour for further investigations remained so Charles dissolved the Cavalier Parliament. He gambled that an election would return a more amenable parliament, but the opposite happened. Inevitably, the King's chief minister, the Earl of Danby, was forced to resign as those who clamoured for the exclusion of James increased. Danby was temporarily placed in the Tower of London, not under arrest, but for his own safety, while the Privy Council was remodelled with the admission of the Earl of Shaftesbury as Lord President, along with other leaders of the opposition, as Charles tried to stem the momentum that his opponents were gaining. In stacking the council with his enemies, he hoped to neutralise their attacks.

In this environment, the newly elected House of Commons, with the backing of Shaftesbury and his allies, introduced its first Exclusion bill in March 1679, which, if it had passed, would have removed James from the succession. It passed the second reading 207–128, so Charles prorogued Parliament, killing the bill. The King also took the precautionary measure of sending James into exile at Brussels on 3 March. Against this background, further treason trials of Jesuits were held in May and June, and in each case Oates's lies were not emphatically challenged by Scroggs and his fellow judges, resulting in further executions. Three men, Robert Green, Henry Berry and Lawrence Hill were also successfully prosecuted and executed for the murder of Justice Godfrey, while one further was charged with being an accessory to the murder, but his case was dismissed by the jury. Then in June, alongside the aforementioned trials of Thomas White / Whitbread and John Fenwich, William Harcourt (or Barrow), John Gavan, and Anthony Turner, all priests, were tried on treason charges. Again, Oates was caught out by his lies, but it mattered little and the men were condemned to death and executed. Justice had to be seen to be done, regardless of it being unjust to those who suffered. Meanwhile, Oates continued to revel in his position as national saviour and in April published his broadsheet, *A True Narrative of the Horrid Hellish Popish Plot*, where he lavishly described for a wide audience the threat he had imagined, which served to cause further panic. It proved particularly popular and was quickly reprinted.

Emboldened by this, and the emergence of other unscrupulous men who were keen to spread fear and gain notoriety (as well as financial profit from informing to the security services), Oates overstretched himself. He continued to insinuate that the Catholic Queen Catherine of Braganza was implicated in the plot, which was a step too far. Yet, such was the public's demand for the rooting out of Jesuits that a trial proceeded and Sir George Wakeman was brought to the King's Bench alongside three Benedictine monks in July 1679. While Catherine and Charles did not have any children (and no legitimate heir), it appears that the King was intent on defending his wife's honour, but having always maintained a scepticism about Oates, he was now alarmed. Wakeman's trial had huge implications for the state, for if he was implicated, Catherine was also guilty, even if only by association. The consequences for Charles II would have been catastrophic. Instead, we witness the first failure to prosecute a person accused of treason arising from Oates's allegations. Sir William Scroggs heard the case again, but he and Wakeman took exception to the nature of Oates's allegations that Wakeman was to receive £15,000 from the Jesuits for poisoning the King with the assistance of the three monks. The glaring inconsistencies in Oates's claims were, for the first time, comprehensively challenged by Scroggs and his fellow justices, who had joined him on the bench due to the seriousness of the case, all of whom stringently undermined Oates and Bedloe, and in turn the case against Wakeman. Wakeman himself played a prominent role in this, demanding of Oates how he came to such stories and refuting the evidence and hearsay that Oates presented. The jury requested that they be allowed to file for misprision of treason, but Scroggs refused, demanding a verdict of not guilty, which the jury supplied. Charles is reputed to have wept with relief when he heard the verdict. The trial was a turning point, but it may not have seemed so at the time. The efforts to exclude James continued into 1680, but as pressure mounted on Charles, nemesis loomed.

Wakeman's trail marked a shift from the courtroom to the public forum. While Scroggs faced an extraordinary backlash for returning a verdict of not guilty, Charles dissolved what became known as the first Exclusion Parliament on 12 July 1679. Having tried to maintain the pressure on the King, Shaftesbury announced to the privy council in March 1680 that Irish Catholics, backed by the French king, had risen, but this was outlandish and understood to be such. Yet such was the momentum of the Whigs that Shaftesbury could seemingly outflank his opponents. The same cannot be said of Scroggs, whose career never recovered and while he remained in post until 1681, he now faced the wrath of the opposition, who attacked him in the press. He defended himself, particularly in a speech from the bench in October 1679, where he was adamant that he had conducted Wakeman's trial 'without fear, favour, or reward; without the gift of one shilling'. Elections for a new parliament were held in August and September, but the King pre-emptively prorogued it before it met and continued to keep it apart until October 1680, prompting the beginning of the great Whig petitioning campaigns. These kept the pressure on the monarchy to exclude James, who having returned from Brussels was then promptly despatched to Scotland. A second Exclusion bill was introduced in November 1680, which passed the Commons but was defeated in the Lords. A rueful Commons then turned its frustrations on Scroggs, demanding his impeachment. Eight articles were prepared against him, but Charles dissolved Parliament before they could be implemented. Scroggs thus escaped a legal punishment but not a personal one, and he was dismissed from office in April 1681.

By this point, the Popish Plot hysteria had all but dimmed and the King had seen off the worst of the efforts to exclude his brother from the succession. Charles began the pursuit of his political enemies, issuing treason charges against Shaftesbury, although these were rejected by a Middlesex grand jury and Shaftesbury escaped into exile to the Netherlands, where he died in 1683. This did not mean that there were no more victims of Oates's lies. Peter Talbot, Archbishop of Dublin, had been arrested in October 1678 and imprisoned in Dublin Castle because, according to Oates, Talbot was the figurehead to a rising in Ireland with

French support. Oates repeated the lies at Coleman's trial, preying on the fears that Ireland would be used as a backdoor to England by the French. Talbot never left Dublin Castle, dying in prison in 1680, where he had been held next to Oliver Plunkett, Archbishop of Armagh. Both men were Jesuits, had been educated in Rome during the 1640s and 1650s, were urbane and metropolitan in outlook, but equally zealous to re-establish the Catholic Church in Ireland after it had been decimated in the 1650s. Plunkett, however, met significant resistance as he sought to impose episcopal discipline on a country that was overwhelmingly Catholic but often resistant to outside influence. By 1678, significant reforms had been implemented and structure had been imposed on the Irish Church, facilitated by sympathetic, or at least sanguine governors, who tacitly tolerated Plunkett's efforts. But Shaftesbury used the English fear of Irish rebelliousness to his advantage. Plunkett had gone into hiding at the emergence of the Popish Plot in 1678 but travelled to Dublin in 1679 and was arrested. He was brought to trial in Dundalk in 1680, but the key witness, Francis MacMoyer, an immoral and offensive man, failed to appear because he knew that his testimony was false and he himself might end up in prison. The case collapsed. Plunkett remained a prisoner but the English Privy Council under Shaftesbury's leadership was not content with this, so Plunkett was sent to London for trial, being imprisoned at Newgate. He was arraigned before the King's Bench in May 1681 and charged with conspiracy to kill the King, to raise a rebellion in Ireland and overthrow the Protestant religion there, and of bringing in the support of a foreign power, namely the French. Each of these were fictitious, but it mattered not to Lord Chief Justice Francis Pemberton, Scroggs's replacement. Plunkett was given five weeks to call witnesses, but bad weather and fear of arrest meant none of those he had assembled for his trial at Dundalk were willing to travel to London.

Plunkett's tactic was to argue that he had been tried on the same charges in Ireland and therefore could not be retried in England, but Pemberton rejected this, saying that as no verdict had been reached in Dundalk, no trial took place. This was false, but Plunkett's efforts to dispute it were overruled. Francis MacMoyer did appear this time and his evidence was of paramount importance in convicting Plunkett, but like Oates, he was a deeply disgruntled man. Plunkett had initially appointed him a curate but was forced to punish him after MacMoyer revealed himself as a drunkard and a tory sympathiser (a tory was a disparaging term for a cattle raider in Ireland). As with Oates's testimonies, MacMoyer and the other witnesses (lay and ecclesiastical) recounted how they knew intimate details of a planned invasion of Ireland by the French and how Plunkett, as primate, intended to overthrow royal government in Ireland and replace it with Catholic authorities supported by Louis XIV. Despite the litany of lies that were spoken about him, Plunkett's defence of his supposed involvement, and his character in general, was measured and exact. He tried in vain to cast doubt on the charges laid against him, in particular that he had organised an invasion force. His efforts proved fruitless and he was executed by strangulation, disembowelment and beheading on 1 July 1681, being spared none of the suffering that Charles II had granted to others.

Plunkett was by no means the last person executed on charges of treason as a result of the Popish Plot, but his was the last high-profile case. As Shaftesbury's power was broken and the King reasserted himself, further trials took place in England that prosecuted Catholics. In all, charges were laid against over forty people for involvement in the plot that Oates invented. If others, including those falsely accused of involvement in Edmund Godfrey's death, are added, we are witness to an extraordinary period in legal and political history, where the political conditions in England were at such a pitch that Oates's stories were given credence.

The law eventually caught up with Oates. While Israel Tonge and William Bedloe had died of natural causes in 1680, Oates was pursued by James, Duke of York, in 1684 on charges of perjury. His trial took place in May 1685, having been delayed by Charles II's death. He was convicted of having falsely sworn in 1678 that a 'consult' of Jesuits had gathered at the White Horse Inn on the Strand in London and that he had falsely sworn to William Ireland being present in London at the same time, when of course Ireland had travelled to Staffordshire. His sentence was imprisonment for life and he was to be pilloried annually. His prison conditions were bleak and he was regularly punished for his previous actions, being dragged around London five times per year and whipped. He was released from prison after William III ascended the throne, but he never reached the heights he had. He died in 1705 in obscurity.

Oates was a fantasist who saw himself as the saviour of his nation, and for a time he was treated as such. A base man, his behaviour was uncouth, even at times repulsive. He should have remained largely anonymous in his own time, and then been forgotten. But his actions were given momentum by circumstances, political weakness, vice, and ambition. Much of the blame for this is aimed at Shaftesbury and his allies, who saw in Oates an opportunity to weaken the King. In doing so, many men and a number of women suffered considerably at the hands of the authorities. Although the Popish Plot receded, the general attitude towards James did not. After Charles II dissolved the Exclusion Parliament, he ruled for what became the final years of his reign without recourse to a parliament. In turn, he denied his enemies an opportunity to regroup. But he died unexpectedly in February 1685 and James ascended to the throne. While the new king secured the support of the bishops of the Church of England for a time, it did not last, and James's efforts to integrate Catholics into the political establishment proved a step too far. Parliament invited his nephew and son-in-law, the Dutch Stadholder William of Orange, to overthrow the monarch and govern in his stead, while James rather meekly went into exile as support for him in England was thin. The same cannot be said of Scotland or Ireland, particularly the latter, where a vicious war was fought in James's name and the repercussions of that conflict remain to this day.

While the revolution has been described as Glorious, it was not bloodless. In James we witness the stubbornness of a man wedded to an idea, rather than a reality. His Catholicism, first secret and then overt, allowed his enemies to project the fears of an embattled England onto him. In doing so, men like Shaftesbury and Oates could achieve fame and fortune, but their actions meant that others suffered horribly, often for innocuous reasons. Oates saw an opportunity to thrive on fear. He aimed to be seen as credible, even important, but reality caught up with his fantasy. The Popish Plot was to have repercussions for decades, cementing as it did the emergence of an organised opposition to government in the Whigs, as well as the government supporters, the Tories. It is hardly believable that a man like Oates, both inconsistent and vulgar, could have been given such prominence in English society and be permitted to act as the key witness in the trials of so many. But circumstances were exploited and Oates, for a time, thrived, while others were executed.

Despite being deposed, the Jacobite threat did not immediately dissipate, and James's advocates remained a threat to the government into the eighteenth century. An attempt in 1715 to regain the thrones of England, Scotland and Ireland ended in failure as the Stuart monarchy died out and was replaced by the Hanoverians. But the Stuart threat did not diminish until 1745, when the grandson of James II, the so-called Bonnie Prince Charlie, sought to overthrow George II but his efforts were ill-fated. Nonetheless, those Jacobites who did rebel were harshly treated, suffering the full force of the Treason Act. The failure of the Jacobite rebellions coincided with the end of the perception of Catholics being a threat to the succession in Britain. Having started with the imposition of Henry VIII as Supreme Head of the Church of England, the Catholic threat, both real and perceived, was a substantial part of the English Protestant psyche for two centuries. As modern nation states began to form, and the British monarchy played a less direct role in the government of Britain, new threats emerged to the state.

Part III

TOWARDS
A MODERN
TREASON

◆

ADDRESS

TO THE

NATION,

FROM THE

LONDON CORRESPONDING SOCIETY,

ON THE SUBJECT OF A THOROUGH

PARLIAMENTARY REFORM;

Together with the RESOLUTIONS which were paſſed at a
General meeting of the SOCIETY;

———

Held on MONDAY, the 8th of JULY, 1793.

AT THE

CROWN AND ANCHOR TAVERN STRAND,

———

Printed by Order of the SOCIETY, and diſtributed [Gratis.]

In Mr Gleſon's 26 July 93 25 July 1793

Address to the Nation on 'the calamitous situation of our country', published in July 1793 by the London Corresponding Society, and calling for parliamentary reform and universal suffrage. 20,000 copies were printed. (TS 24/3/5)

Eleven

NEWFANGLED TREASONS, 1794

*But now all is to be changed ... Kings will be tyrants from
policy when subjects are rebels from principle*
EDMUND BURKE, *REFLECTIONS ON THE REVOLUTION
IN FRANCE*, 1790, PP. 114–16

In December 1792 Charles Craufurd, the commander of a detachment of 2nd Dragoon Guards billeted across the south west of England, staged spectacles of hate. In each of the towns where his men were quartered, an effigy was led through the town in front of numerous crowds, mounted on an ass and led by a hangman. Shown 'every possible mark of indignity', the effigy was then burned amidst repeated exclamations of 'God Save the King', and 'constant cheering and huzzahring [*sic*]'. The dummy was dressed up as Thomas Paine, the radical writer, whom many considered a traitor.

The French Revolution of 1789 reverberated globally, not least in Britain. Its ideas of equal rights and representation found willing ears across the Channel, where just 4 per cent of the population were unevenly able to elect members of Parliament. Paine, whose *Common Sense* had been so central to the intellectual culture of the American Revolution, published his two-part *Rights of Man* in 1792, defending the French revolutionaries and attacking Britain's constitutional settlement – he became the foremost voice of the French in the English-speaking world.

Rights of Man was written as a riposte to the work of another former supporter of the Americans, Edmund Burke MP. In 1790, Burke had published his *Reflections on the Revolution in France*. Burke claimed that the revolution would collapse into violent anarchy, and that the British constitution was the ultimate safeguard of liberty and happiness. The Treasury Solicitor obtained a copy of Paine's work, underlining the most dangerous passages.

Paine and Burke were the pre-eminent voices of two factions of popular politics that were invigorated by the Revolution: loyalism, against it; and radicalism, sympathetic and aiming at parliamentary and wider reform in Britain.

Parliamentary reform was not a new idea in Britain. It had been spoken about since the 'Glorious Revolution' of 1688, but previously it had typically been led by the already enfranchised upper and middle classes. What was novel about the explosion of reformist political societies, associations and unions established in the 1790s was the presence of groups led by the working classes.

One such group, the London Corresponding Society (LCS), held its first meeting in late January 1792 (subscription just 1 penny). The inaugural meeting had just nine attendees. A fortnight later there were twenty-four. By May there were enough for the LCS to divide into nine 'divisions', reporting to a general committee. Radicalism, sympathetic to the French Revolution and intent on fundamentally changing Britain, was an existential threat to the ruling class.

The Home Office's correspondence from late 1792 is awash with alarmist reports of radical activity. Paine's works were being distributed cheaply, even for free, sometimes to troops. A radical dinner proposed toasts to the 'Abolition of Feudal Tyranny', and the 'Virtues of Revolutions'. The radical Society for Constitutional Information (SCI) were (falsely) rumoured to be stockpiling muskets for a French invasion. The Home Office also received specimens of pamphlets attacking Paine. Loyalism was as strong, if not stronger, than radicalism in many communities, as Craufurd's popular spectacles showed.

To try to quell the radical press the government issued a Royal Proclamation on 22 May 1792 against 'wicked and seditious Writings ... endeavouring to vilify and bring into Contempt' the constitution. Magistrates and loyal subjects were charged with seeking out the authors and printers of such material. Paine was implicitly the target.

So it was that on 18 December 1792 Thomas Paine was tried *in absentia* for seditious libel. Sedition was the close, but less serious, cousin of treason. Paine was in France at the time, a member of the new National Convention. The Attorney General, Sir Archibald Macdonald, said his book had made 'the lower orders of society disaffected to Government'.

Paine was defended by the talented barrister, Thomas Erskine, who used his opening speech to defend the freedom of the press. Such was the public vilification of Paine, however, that the jury informed the prosecution there was no need for a reply, and immediately declared him guilty. Erskine had warned that a conviction would 'stamp and brand ... with the mark and reproach of disaffection' anyone who supported Paine's doctrines. This was the intent. The ideas of organisations like the LCS were in effect declared unlawful.

The May 1792 proclamation against seditious writings had spoken of 'Riots and Tumults', but these were not in themselves something the government was overly bothered by. Rioting was commonplace – but rioting animated by a political purpose – parliamentary reform – was dangerous. Political networks and organisations like the LCS, carrying a 'latent threat of mass political violence', were the enemy.

Developing networks was one of the LCS's main purposes. Its secretary, Thomas Hardy, was highly politically sociable. He had been inspired to form the LCS by the intellectual culture of the American Revolution (he owned many pamphlets from that time). Among his personal correspondence in 1792, we find a letter from Gustavus Vassa (Olaudah Equiano), the prominent, formerly enslaved abolitionist writer, a friend of Hardy. Hardy's 'loving wife, Til death', Lydia, convalescing in Chesham, writes to him too, blending matters domestic (reminding him to pay the rent and close the windows) with those political, asking after the anti-slavery movement.

The LCS's activities reflect a desire to exercise political pressure in the manner of the abolitionists – they held meetings and dinners, established democratic bodies to debate matters and pass resolutions, organised petitions for parliamentary reform, and as their name suggested, corresponded with like-minded organisations.

On 2 April 1792 the LCS, by then swelling in numbers (by the end of the year, it would have some 650 paid-up members attending its meetings) published its first Address, a public statement of its principles and intent. Liberty was a man's birthright, the Address stated; without a vote he was not free.

The Address situated the LCS as part of a network of similar organisations, and made resolutions regarding Britain's democratic deficit: the link between unequal representation and corruption, high taxes and oppression – universal male suffrage was offered as the cure to this. However, its authors also expressed their desire not to resort to force, expressing an '*Abhorrence* of Tumult and Violence'. They sent their resolutions to branches of the SCI.

The LCS attempted to forge links with France, too, offering the country's new National Convention their 'inviolable Friendship' in September 1792, and railing against the 'all-consuming Aristocracy'. The LCS's Address was endorsed by four other societies, with another eleven sending follow-up addresses. It marked Hardy's group as a leader among the radical movements of the time. The Convention itself soon issued an Edict of Fraternity, encouraging similar groups around the world.

The radicals aped the political culture of their French cousins – they called one another 'citizen'. France was at war with much of Europe at the time but Britain was technically neutral. This changed in 1793 – Louis XVI was executed in January, France declared war on Britain on 1 February. In the summer the so-called 'Reign of Terror' began as the Jacobin Government attempted to safeguard the Republic, something that British loyalists saw as a vindication of Burke's predictions.

British radicals were suddenly the supporters of an enemy state. Prime Minister William Pitt embarked on what some characterised as his own Terror against domestic foes. However, if the radicals were disquieted by events in France, that did not dampen their efforts at home.

In early 1793 they launched a mass petition to support the motion of parliamentary reform Charles Grey, was to introduce to the Commons. Grey, later the 2nd Earl Grey was a prominent Whig politician, and longtime supporter of parliamentary reform, prominent in the aristocratic reformist Society of the Friends of the People. He would go on to lead the Whig government of 1830–4, which passed the Great Reform Act and abolished slavery in the British Empire. By 22 April the petition had 2,000 signatures. The LCS ordered 200 large posters and 1,000 small bills be printed advertising it for signature. But Grey's motion was heavily defeated. *The Times* remarked that, looking at France, they could not support 'admitting all the *rag-tag* and *bob-tail* to the right of Voting at Elections'.

Rebuffed, the LCS published another Address to the Nation on 'the calamitous situation of our country', in July 1793. They bemoaned the costs of war, encouraged political education, and demanded universal suffrage and annual parliaments. They printed 20,000 copies, producing a petition to the King on similar grounds in September.

In October a mass meeting was staged in Shoreditch, with a crowd of more than 1,000. They elected delegates to a convention of radicals in Edinburgh. Closely watched, magistrates arrested their host, Thomas Breillat, who had lent the LCS a field he owned for the meeting, for sedition as soon as they dispersed.

The Edinburgh Convention of 1793 (one had been held the year before) sat twice, first between 29 October and 6 November. The LCS delegates, Joseph Gerrald and Maurice Margarot, arrived on 7 November, and the convention resumed sitting on 19 November.

The Convention's proceedings were typical of reforming societies. They set out orders for their sessions, discussed universal suffrage and how to obtain it, as well as how to disseminate the results of their discussions and foster political education. To the authorities, however, the very name 'convention' was provocative, recalling the French Republic's legislature. Margarot, claiming to represent 13,000 Londoners, proposed a convention in England. Fearing suppression, on 4 December he also proposed a secret committee, to facilitate subsequent confidential meetings. The next day he, Gerrald and the convention's secretary, William Skirving, were arrested for sedition. They were convicted and sentenced to fourteen years' transportation, a harsh sentence.

Yet the LCS were not to be cowed. On 20 January 1794 they published another Address to the People. They claimed the 'critical moment' had arrived. The prosecutions in Scotland proved the liberties enshrined in Magna Carta and the Bill of Rights had been undermined – 'We must now chuse at once either liberty or slavery.' The meeting that drew up the address, attended by more than 300 members, resolved to organise another convention in England. Spies reported insurrection had been discussed. On 27 January, the LCS published an Address to the other 'Patriotic Societies of Great Britain', again calling for a convention and bemoaning '*an inquisitorial system* of SPIES and INFORMERS, and *formal processes of* PERSECUTION FOR OPINION'.

They issued another circular to radical societies at the beginning of March. 'Britons must either assert with zeal and firmness their claims to liberty ... or yield without resistance to the chains that ministerial usurpation is forging for them,' they cautioned. They proposed a convention and asked for a response. Hardy personally wrote to the SCI on 27 March suggesting a '*Speedy Convention*', and met with them to discuss it further on 4 April. By 14 April, spies informed the government that the SCI and LCS were to form a union; the more bourgeois Society of the Friends of the People. What was more, there were reports of radicals being involved in 'Exercise Societies', training in 'military movements' (with mop handles in one case) behind closed doors.

At around 6 a.m. on 12 May 1794, Hardy was awoken by an 'uncommonly loud knocking'. King's Messengers and a Home Office official were at the door of his house in Piccadilly, London, with a warrant for his arrest under suspicion of high treason. Lydia, six months pregnant, had to remain in bed in a state of undress as the King's Messengers, 'ransacked trunks, boxes, drawers, and desk'. They seized Hardy's LCS papers (wrapped in four silk handkerchiefs) and a 'corn sack' (an obsolete measurement, roughly 109 litres in volume) of political pamphlets. His shoemaker's shop was searched too. Hardy was taken to a King's Messenger's house initially, and on 29 May he was imprisoned at the Tower.

The day after Hardy's arrest the LCS convened an emergency committee. John Thelwall, a prominent poet and radical, read out legal commentaries on treason, deriding Hardy's arrest. They passed resolutions concerning his innocence and vowed to continue their work, departing the meeting to communicate them to the LSC's divisions. Thelwall himself was arrested on suspicion of treason as he left.

There were further arrests in Scotland in the days after Hardy's. David Watt was a bankrupt wine merchant. He had also been active in the Edinburgh convention, but had previously been an ineffective government informer. Searching his house on behalf of creditors, officers discovered a stash of pike heads. Watt, it seemed, was planning a rebellion to seize banks and post offices and establish a provisional government in Scotland. The plan appears to have existed mostly in his mind, although a goldsmith, David Downie, was implicated. Charged with treason in May 1793, they were found guilty in September. Watt was executed, Downie transported. Watt was an untrustworthy fantasist and double agent, but he was also a radical, and could therefore be used by the authorities to implicitly accuse others of harbouring treasonable schemes.

Armed with the papers of the LCS and SCI seized in the arrests of Hardy and others, the House of Commons quickly convened a Committee of Secrecy, to examine the papers and determine the evidence for a conspiracy, and formulate a likely solution. The Committee presented its report in just four days, on 16 May, and another followed soon after.

The Committee's two reports itemised the history of the SCI and LCS, using their own papers. They documented their promotion of Paine's works, their 'panegyric' addresses to the French, and their adoption of Jacobin forms and language. Their attempts to establish 'a general correspondence and concert among the other seditious Societies' in London and beyond, and creation of 'exercise societies like the Lambeth Loyal Association', as well as reports of Sheffield radicals procuring arms, featured too. Much was made of Watt's conspiracy (only just discovered and not yet tried), his connection with the convention, and therefore with men like Hardy.

It was 'impossible', the Committee's first report concluded, not to see in light of all these things that Hardy's proposed General Convention was intended, possibly by force of arms, to 'supersede' Parliament as the representative body of the people – 'a Traitorous Conspiracy for the Subversion of the established Laws and Constitution'.

The second report made much of the links between the English radicals and Watt's role in the Edinburgh convention, by extension implicating them in his (only just discovered) plot. Paine's *Rights of Man*, adjudged by law to be seditious, was quoted extensively – its promotion by the radicals seemingly showing the treasonous motives which animated the plot to overthrow the government. Altogether, the committee said, the evidence they had collected proved the existence of a concerted plan for 'sudden violence' in the style of French revolutionaries to realise the reformers' dangerous doctrines.

The reports were a tapestry of conjecture and hyperbole, a series of events, words and people, sometimes only vaguely connected, pulled and stretched into the shape of bona-fide conspiracy. But they served their purpose. Parliament quickly legislated to suspend habeas corpus, the right not to be arrested without charge enshrined in Magna Carta, for suspected traitors. This came into force on 23 May, and would last until 1 February 1795. It allowed the government to arrest reformers up and down the country with little pretext, seizing their papers. Regardless of whether any of the subsequent arrests – and there were many – resulted in conviction, this allowed the state to imprison radical leaders at a crucial time, and prejudge their criminal intent in Parliament and the press.

Throughout summer there were arrests, seizures, examinations. Thomas Spence,* a bookseller and member of the LCS and the Lambeth Loyal Association, published an account of his interrogation by the Privy Council. He accused them of trying to 'pick up a little from every one you examine with a view to make up something like a plan, for the purpose of alarming the nation', and claimed that a government minister had said he was correct.

The LCS continued to meet and publish spiritedly, despite the arrests, defending their principles' legality in spite of their leaders' detainment, and raising funds to provide for Lydia Hardy and other dependants. But with Britain at war with France, and the Reign of Terror at its height, the government's report of the supposed conspiracy fed into a hysterical Francophobia. In the hot days of 1794's summer, this mad blood stirred into a storm of violence and, for Hardy, tragedy.

On the 'Glorious First of June' 1794, Admiral Lord Richard Howe's fleet won a decisive victory in the Atlantic against the French. News reached London some ten days later. There were days of widespread festivities, including 'illuminations' in which building were lit up with lanterns and projections in celebration. But there was an ugly side. Businesses in the City which did not illuminate their facades were attacked by a loyalist 'mob', who also targeted the homes throughout the city of those perceived to be pro-French, including Hardy's house in Piccadilly.

Hardy was in the Tower, but a heavily pregnant Lydia remained at the property as the mob began banging the windows and attempting to force entry. She had to escape via a small window, but 'being very large at the waist', she got stuck and was bruised being dragged through.

---

* Spence (1750–1814) was an unusual and visionary political theorist. An autodidact, he advocated the common ownership of all land, gender equality and total democracy. His admirers would go on to found the Spencean Society of Philanthropists after his death. But while Spence predominantly advocated peaceful reforms, the Spenceans would go on to be the principal instigators of the Spa Fields and Cato Street Conspiracies in the 1810s and 1820s (see Chapter 12).

She died in childbirth on 27 August. Hardy believed that the events of 12 June contributed to her death. She left a last, unfinished letter telling her husband, 'You are never out of my thoughts, sleeping or waking.'

The government spent the summer framing the charges against Hardy and the other LCS men in their custody. It was a difficult task – the 1352 Act was conceived as a remedy to dynastic struggle, open rebellion, assassination, not nebulous political network and a few pike heads in Edinburgh. Future Prime Minister Spencer Perceval** (at the time a government prosecutor) noted that the task was complicated by the 'caution' radicals showed in keeping their actions within the bounds of misdemeanours like sedition, 'and out of the reach of a heavier charge'.

Nevertheless, an indictment was presented to a grand jury for proving on 10 September 1794. James Eyre, the Lord Chief Justice, explained why Hardy and his co-defendants were treasonous. 'Compassing' the King's death did not necessitate a design to kill him, Eyre said, for the Crown was the 'common centre' of the realm, 'all traitorous attempts upon any part of it are instantly communicated to that centre'. The convention would have 'usurped' Parliament, possibly by force, to achieve its ends. Such a course inevitably led to the monarch's death, and was treason.

The grand jury proved the indictment against Hardy and eleven others: John Horne Tooke, John Thelwall, John Bonney, Thomas Holcroft, Stewart Kyd, Jeremiah Joyce, Thomas Wardle, John Richter, Matthew Moore, Richard Hodgson, and John Baxter. They were indicted for conspiring, compassing, imagining and intending to, 'excite Insurrection Rebellion and War against the King, and to subvert and alter the Legislature and Government and to depose the King ... and to put him to Death'.

** Perceval would go on to be Prime Minister between 1809 and 1812. His term was characterised by problems abroad and at home, not least radicalism and the crisis of George III's madness, leading to the Regency of the Prince of Wales in 1811. On 11 May 1812 he was shot dead in the lobby of the House of Commons by John Bellingham, a merchant. It was initially feared the killing was politically motivated, but Bellingham was acting alone, motivated by a grievance over his belief he had been wrongly arrested in Russia. It is notable that Bellingham was tried (and executed) for murder, not treason.

This was followed by nine 'overt acts' which proved the defendants' treasonable intentions. These included: conspiring to secure a convention to subvert Parliament, publishing and distributing writings encouraging delegates to the convention, and to incite the public to 'aid & assist' their subversion; procuring arms with the intention of levying war to deny the King the 'exercise of his Royal Power', and also publishing writings to inspire this. The men pleaded not guilty. Hardy's trial was first, on 28 October. Security around the Old Bailey was tight, as there were fears of disturbance by radicals.

Opening the prosecution, Sir John Scott, the Attorney General, made the government's case clear – the arrest and prosecution of radicals was necessary to prevent a revolution in Britain. Treason could be an offence against either the monarch's person, or his government, and this was the latter. The conspiracy's aim was to subvert Parliament, and this would have necessarily led to the King's imprisonment, which was held to be the same as his death under the Treason Act. He told the jury that underneath the radicals' 'handsome language', there was a 'hidden intent destructive of truth and justice ... subversive to the liberties of this country'.

Then came their extensive evidence – the public and private papers and correspondence of the LCS and other organisations were read, seemingly endlessly. Witnesses were called, including George Lynman, an active LCS delegate who also happened to be a government spy. Criminal trials in the eighteenth century rarely lasted more than a day but by half past midnight, the Crown had only just begun. Hasty arrangements were made to sequester the exhausted jury.

Much was made of the Edinburgh Convention, and Watt's treason. Since Hardy had sent Gerrard and Margarot there as the LCS's delegates, he was therefore a conspirator in their sedition, and Watt's treason, all stemming from the convention. Thomas Erskine, now Hardy's barrister, intervened, outraged that the Crown claimed that a man could be held accountable for another's 'wicked intention'. The Crown said it showed his tacit approval of their actions. They began reading the convention's papers at length.

The prosecution lasted for days. The same passages from *Rights of Man* that the Treasury Solicitor had underlined in preparation for Paine's 1792 seditious libel prosecution were read out, and many more sections besides. Erskine mischievously requested for Paine's preface to be read by the Crown, only to be told that it would, just after the dedication.

Much was made of the disconnected attempts to secure weapons – Watt's grandiose imaginings and the mop-handle drilling of some London radicals. Particular attention was paid to Henry Redhead Yorke, a mixed-race reformer born in Barbuda, who was prominent among Sheffield radicals. William Camage, another reformer, was called to testify that Yorke had told him that they should procure arms for defence. Yorke and Hardy had corresponded, so the Crown offered this as proof of Hardy's involvement in an armed conspiracy. However, Erskine used his cross-examination to clarify that the weapons were intended for self-defence against angry loyalists, and were never intended to wage war against Parliament.

All this voluminous evidence, the prosecution claimed, proved a conspiracy to subvert Parliament and overthrow the King. The defendants may not have said 'no King, no Parliament', the Solicitor General stated, but that was their obvious intention. Hardy may not have committed some of the overt acts, but he was plainly a conspirator, and thus implicated by the acts of others.

Erskine was ill and was provided an adjournment when the prosecution rested, partly to allow him to look at the seized papers used as evidence, before he opened the defence at 9 a.m. on Saturday 1 November (the Crown had only concluded at 2 a.m. that morning). He had told the court that he was not just fighting for Hardy's life, but for the liberty of all Britons in the face of unjust prosecution. His speech, when it came, was a comprehensive deconstruction of the prosecution's case.

Hardy, Erskine said, was being subjected to 'tyrannical laws, more tyrannically executed'; a case predicated on 'speculations concerning consequences, when the law commands us to look only to intentions'.

Trying to organise a convention, publishing pamphlets, even procuring arms for self-defence – these did not constitute treason. Whatever Hardy may have had to do with sending delegates to Edinburgh, whatever they had done there, was immaterial unless the prosecution could prove that the whole was animated by a 'wicked contemplation to destroy the natural life and person of the King', even obliquely. Erskine stated that the prosecution could not do so. 'Which of us all would be safe, standing at the bar of God or man', he asked, 'taking upon him the crimes or rashnesses of others?'

The Crown had invoked the history of prosecutions for treason to show Hardy's actions as an evolution of those of former traitors, but Erskine cautioned the jury against following the examples of 'state trials in bad times' – after all, if the government were so convinced of Hardy's guilt, why not simply attaint him? And he railed against the evidence of spies like Lynman. How could you trust a man who was both 'faithful to serve, and faithful to betray! correct to record for the business of the society, and correct to dissolve and punish it'? You could not.

Erskine promised to show by evidence that 'the views of the Societies were what I have alleged them to be; that whatever irregularities or indiscretions they might have committed, their purposes were honest; and that Mr Hardy's, above all other men, can be established to have been so.' There was no proof Hardy had procured arms, and no connection between him and Watt's conspiracy.

Erskine's speech was apparently met with an 'irrepressible acclamation' in the court, spreading to Hardy's supporters outside. This was trial as spectacle, a battle between the two predominant popular movements of the age. The defence proceeded to present their evidence and witnesses, all further demolishing the Crown's inferences of Hardy's true intentions.

The trial lasted nine days. The jury retired on 5 November, Gunpowder Treason Day, a fateful date for accused traitors. After three hours the jury returned a verdict of not guilty – the foreman fainted from exhaustion. Hardy, Erskine and others' coaches had their horses unharnessed, and were drawn by their jubilant supporters through London. The acquittals, or the dropping of charges as the government realised their case was hopeless, of the others indicted followed.

Yet the government were not deterred by the acquittals in their pursuit of radicalism. The next session of Parliament began on 30 December 1794 – opposition MPs used the opportunity to propose the reinstatement of habeas corpus, the acquittals having proved that no conspiracy existed. One, Joseph Jekyll, demanded an enquiry on 'the subject of new-fangled treasons, introduced by Ministry, in direct and unconstitutional contraction to the statute of Edward the Third'.

The Prime Minister made an astonishing reply. Although acquitted of 'formal or technical treason', the radicals bore 'moral guilt ... as destructive to the State as any treason'. Moreover, they were also guilty in the court of public opinion, and if the law at present was not sufficient to punish them, he would have new laws made.

Meanwhile, the country experienced a wave of disaffection: in August 1794, London had seen the 'Crimping Riots', protests against the military's 'press gang' of forcible enlistment of men; 1795's poor harvest caused the 'Revolt of the Housewives', a series of food riots in which women took a prominent role; and George III's carriage was stoned at the opening of Parliament on 29 October 1795. An LCS open-air meeting in Islington had, with more than 40,000 attendees, immediately preceded this on 26 October, the crowd being regaled with speeches, resolutions and addresses attacking the government's conduct and calling for parliamentary and constitutional reform. Meanwhile, LCS members were arrested in the 'Pop-Gun Plot', a seemingly fictional scheme to assassinate George III with a poisoned dart (the alleged plotters, four members of the LCS, were acquitted through lack of evidence in 1796).

On 4 November a Royal Proclamation was issued, directly linking the LCS meeting and their 'seditions' with the stoning of the King's carriage. The government used the stoning, the meeting, the Pop-Gun Plot and the widespread disaffection as a *casus belli* to amend the law and deal with radicalism. The result was the 'Two Acts': the Seditious Meetings Act 1795, which made public meetings of more than fifty people illegal without a magistrate's approval; and a new Treason Act, to codify the 'new-fangled treasons'.

The latter act widened the definition of compassing the King's death, made it an offence to 'levy war' to force the monarch to change his 'counsels and measures', and to engage in the intimidation or 'overawing' of Parliament. Publishing was explicitly described as an overt act, the printed word suddenly had parity with a pike head under the law of treason. Inciting hatred against the royal family or government was made a lesser treason, punishable by transportation. Despite protest, both Acts of Parliament received Royal Assent and became law on 18 December 1795.

The LCS was not named in these acts, but its members were clearly targets. They passed a new constitution so as to avoid meetings of more than fifty people, but repression combined with internecine squabbling to send the society's membership and influence into decline. Four years later, after rebellion in Ireland and naval mutinies at home, the LCS and other radical associations and corresponding societies were explicitly banned by the Unlawful Societies Act 1799.

The radicals might have won in court, but the government carried the day. Pitt had been right about their being found guilty by the public. Loyalism, strengthened by wartime patriotism, viewed them as agents of the French. Paine remained a folk villain for decades. Parliamentary reform seemed more distant in 1800 than it had a decade ago – the Solicitor General told the Commons it was 'inconsistent with order and the true administration of justice and the laws'. Now the government was armed with a new conception of treason to prosecute its more radical promoters.

The 1795 Act was an attempt to reimagine treason for the modern age, as a primarily political crime. Initially a temporary measure, it was made permanent in 1817. Its clauses concerning levying war to compel a change in measures by seemingly innocent acts of publishing or uttering words and forming societies, and its broadening of the of the monarch's deposition to include not just the actual dethroning of the King but any threat, material or immaterial, to any part of the constitution, became mainstays in indictments against radicals in the ensuing century.

Yet treason still remained an anachronistic and difficult crime to prosecute. The 1795 Act merely codified actions that the Crown had argued were treasonous anyway, its foundation and language were still born of the exigencies of the fourteenth century, not the eighteenth and nineteenth.

The law of treason drew power from its historicity, but that also limited its expansion. The way judges and barristers discussed its lineage made clear it was as essential to the British constitution as Magna Carta and the Bill of Rights. Its misuse was popularly considered tyrannical, hence Erskine's remarks about attainder. In his defence of the LCS radicals, Erskine had quoted Burke's remarks that the British constitution was globally pre-eminent in its safeguarding of personal liberty. Such an argument was central to loyalism and to the government against radicalism. To amend the law of treason substantially, then, would be to undermine this argument and the constitution itself, something judges, parliamentarians and jurors would not readily stand for.

Now all was changed. Treason was no longer a blunt instrument of the Crown's power – it was a crime, tried under due process with evidence, advocates and jurors, all complicating assured conviction. But it was still the ultimate sanction against men and their ideas – and those of radicalism, although, diminished, had not gone away.

By the KING.

A PROCLAMATION.

GEORGE R.

WHEREAS divers wicked and seditious Writings have been printed, published, and industriously dispersed, tending to excite Tumult and Disorder by endeavouring to raise groundless Jealousies and Discontents in the Minds of Our faithful and loving Subjects, respecting the Laws, and happy Constitution of Government, Civil and Religious, established in this Kingdom, and endeavouring to vilify and bring into Contempt the wise and wholesome Provisions made at the Time of the glorious Revolution, and since strengthened and confirmed by subsequent Laws, for the Preservation and Security of the Rights and Liberties of Our faithful and loving Subjects: And Whereas divers Writings have also been printed, published, and industriously dispersed, recommending the said wicked and seditious Publications to the Attention of all Our faithful and loving Subjects: And Whereas We have also Reason to believe that Correspondences have been entered into with sundry Persons in Foreign Parts, with a View to forward the criminal and wicked Purposes above-mentioned: And Whereas the Wealth, Happiness, and Prosperity of this Kingdom do, under Divine Providence, chiefly depend upon a due Submission to the Laws, a just Confidence in the Integrity and Wisdom of Parliament, and a ... nuance ... that zealous Attachment to the Government and ... of the Kingdom, which ... Minds of the People thereof: And Whereas ... is nothing ... so earnestly desire, as to secure the Public ... and Prosperity, and to preserve to all Our loving Subjects the full Enjoyment of their Rights and Liberties, both Re... and Civil: We therefore being resolved, as far as in Us lies, to repress the wicked and seditious Practices aforesaid, and to deter all Persons from following so pernicious an Example, have thought fit, by the Advice of Our Privy Council, to issue this Our Royal Proclamation, solemnly warning all Our loving Subjects, as they tender their own Happiness, and that of their Posterity, to guard against all such Attempts which aim at the Subversion of all regular Government within this Kingdom, and which are inconsistent with the Peace and Order of Society; and earnestly exhorting them at all Times, and to the utmost of their Power, to avoid and discourage all Proceedings tending to produce Riots and Tumults: And We do strictly charge and command all Our Magistrates in and throughout Our Kingdom of *Great Britain*, that they do make diligent Enquiry in order to discover the Authors and Printers of such wicked and seditious Writings as aforesaid; and all others who shall disperse the same: And We do further charge and command all Our Sheriffs, Justices of the Peace, Chief Magistrates in Our Cities, Boroughs, and Corporations, and all other Our Officers and Magistrates throughout Our Kingdom of *Great Britain*, that they do, in their several and respective Stations, take the most immediate and effectual Care to suppress and prevent all Riots, Tumults, and other ... which may be attempted to be raised or made by any Person or Persons, which, on whatever Pretext they may be ... not only contrary to Law, but dangerous to the most important Interests of this Kingdom; And We do further ... and command all and every Our Magistrates aforesaid, that they do, from Time to Time, transmit to One of Our Principal Secretaries of State, due and full Information of such Persons as shall be found offending as aforesaid, ... y Degree aiding or abetting therein; it being Our Determination, for the Preservation of the Peace and Happiness of ... faithful and loving Subjects, to carry the Laws vigorously into Execution against such Offenders as aforesaid.

Given at Our Court at the *Queen's House*, the Twenty-first Day of *May*, One thousand seven hundred and ninety-two, in the Thirty-second Year of Our Reign.

God save the King.

LONDON:
Printed by CHARLES EYRE and ANDREW STRAHAN, Printers to the King's most Excellent Majesty. 1792.

A Royal Proclamation issued by George III on 21 May 1792 against 'Seditious Writings ... tending to excite Tumult and Disorder'. The Proclamation was clearly aimed at Thomas Paine's *The Rights of Man*, although it is not named. (TS 24/1/1)

Fire Ball _ 20

Take 2 oz Rosin
2 oz Muttonsuit
2 oz Horse Turpentine
melt together and
when beginning to cool
add 2 oz powder'd salt
petre _ make it into
a ball _ with a fusee
fixed in from the centre
composed of brown paper
smeared over with the
above ingredients
without the salt petre
rolled up & firmly
fixed into the ball

A recipe for 'Fireballs', rudimentary incendiary grenades apparently planned to be used by the Cato Street Conspirators in 1820. This was almost certainly acquired by the government via one of their informers amongst the conspirators. (HO 44/4)

Twelve

A MALIGNANT SPIRIT,
1815–48

If one spark of honour, if one spark of independence still
glimmered in the breast of Englishmen they would have rose
to a man – Insurrection became a public duty.
ARTHUR THISTLEWOOD, 1820

O n 11 April 1817 Samuel Bamford wrote a letter to his wife, Jemima,
asking for a change of trousers, a hat and 'a white handkerchief
&c.... I wish to be decent' to be sent to him. This Lancashire reformer was
in Cold Bath Fields prison, London, held on suspicion of high treason.
The Home Office stopped his letter, like it did many of those sent by
proponents of parliamentary reform.

In 1817 England was in acute economic distress – the end of the Napoleonic
War, 1816's terrible harvest and the Corn Laws, which put a premium on
imported wheat to protect Britain's landowners, all contributed. Riots were
common, but Prime Minister Lord Liverpool's government was far more
scared of radical reformers making use of the general distress to further
their political cause. This they considered treason.

On 24 February of that year, Lord Sidmouth, the Home Secretary,
rose to speak in the House of Lords. There was, he said, a 'malignant
spirit' in the country that had existed since the French Revolution, but
was now taking advantage of 'the reduced and burthened state of the
country' and applying them to its 'own desperate purposes'. To deal with
this, he proposed three pieces of legislation, which were quickly passed

into law by Parliament. The Habeas Corpus Suspension Act temporarily rescinded the ancient right not to be arrested or imprisoned without charge; the Seditious Meetings Act banned meetings of more than fifty people without permission from the authorities, with the death penalty if the assembly did not disperse. The third made permanent the provisions of the 1795 Treason Act, passed in the wake of the acquittals of the members of the London Corresponding Society, just as the first two measures had temporarily been on the statute books during their suppression. The Prime Minister assured peers the danger now was even greater than in the 1790s. There was some dissent (Thomas Erskine, who had been created Baron Erskine in 1806, voted against), but the bill passed easily.

Bamford and other prominent reformers were arrested soon after. Realising that he might soon be charged with treason (he never was), Bamford, suddenly terrified, 'beheld the sort of death that was preparing for me'.

Sidmouth, and Parliament's Committee of Secrecy on radicalism, identified two main threats to the government – one active across the country, the Hampden Clubs, and one local to London, centred around the Spa Fields riots.

Hampden Clubs took their name from a Parliamentarian in the Civil War. The first was formed in London in 1811. Like the corresponding societies, they and similar groups linked working- and middle-class reformers; and like them, they professed the peaceful tactics of petitioning, pamphleteering, and meetings. But mass political action carried a latent threat of violence in the state's eyes. Delegates from clubs across the country met in London in January 1817 and resolved in favour of universal male suffrage without a property qualification. Sidmouth concluded that the clubs 'had parliamentary reform in their mouths, but rebellion and revolution in their hearts'.

Spa Fields was an open common in Clerkenwell, London (it is now a small park). Meetings were organised there by the Spenceans, ultra-left radicals inspired by the writings of the late Thomas Spence who advocated universal suffrage and the common ownership of all land, 'the PEOPLE'S FARM'. The Spenceans decided to call a meeting on Spa Fields for 'Distressed Manufacturers, Mariners, Artisans And others', in order to consider petitioning the Prince Regent and Parliament for measures to relieve 'the misery which now overwhelms them'. They invited a number of popular radical speakers, among them Henry 'Orator' Hunt, a middle-class radical known for his dramatic speeches.

The first meeting took place on 15 November 1816. A large crowd assembled on Spa Fields to hear Hunt and petition the Prince Regent and Parliament. The Spenceans adjourned the meeting until 2 December, stating that 'The Nation's wrongs must be redressed'. This second meeting, however, dissolved into a riot – flags, cockades and weapons were distributed (and nearby gunsmiths were broken into) and while many stayed to listen to Hunt, groups broke off in different directions. Some headed to the Tower of London, where allegedly they appealed to the soldiers to open the gates and join them, offering 100 guineas and double pay for life as an inducement. Troops were deployed and fire was exchanged, but eventually the riot was ended. It seemed that the government had been forewarned.

In the aftermath of the riots some of the leading Spenceans – John Hooper, James Watson the elder and his son (also called James), Thomas Preston and Arthur Thistlewood – were arrested. The younger Watson escaped to America. The other four were brought to trial for high treason in the Court of King's Bench, Westminster, on 9 June 1817. James Watson the elder was tried first.

Such was the interest in the trials that *The Times* printed the indictments in their entirety. There were four counts. First, compassing and imagining the King's death, with some fourteen 'overt acts' attached to it: the accused had conspired, by force of arms, to subvert the constitution and government (which was, in effect, to compass the King's death), seize the Bank of England and the Tower of London, recruit soldiers to their cause or otherwise burn their barracks, and unveiled banners in a warlike manner.

The third count was one of 'levying war' for the same purpose and with the same overt acts. The second and fourth counts were repetitions of the first and third, but framed under the 1795 Treason Act – compassing and imagining the King's *deposition* rather than his death; levying war to compel the King 'to change his measures ... and counsels'.

The Attorney General, Sir Samuel Shepherd, prosecuting, opened Watson's trial, making clear that if he were found guilty then his fellow defendants would follow, 'the act of one is the act of all'. Petitioning had been a mere fictitious aim of the meeting, he said; their real aim had been to collect together 'a multitude armed against the authority of the King'.

The Crown's star witness was one John Castle. Castle had met Watson in October 1816, and alleged that the radical had immediately inducted him into the Spenceans and spoken incessantly of revolution. Castle was to have been a 'general' in the insurrection.

Castle's evidence painted the Spenceans as actively planning a coup – recruiting workers, drawing up plans to blockade the Bank of England and London Bridge, neutralising barracks. They were to set up a 'Committee of Public Safety' as a provisional government.

So far, so damning. But the Spenceans, like Hardy et al. in 1794, were blessed with a capable defence barrister, Charles Wetherell, whose cross-examination of Castle proved that he was not all he seemed.

Wetherell's deconstruction of Castle's testimony was masterful. Castle had been arrested, then his treason charges dropped, but he was still living in a prison, except that he admitted he was allowed out to procure and induce prosecution witnesses. Not only that, he had twice previously been indicted for capital offences, but had turned Crown's witness and seen his co-defendants hanged or transported. He had lived in a brothel and had many 'wives', one of whom had been despatched quietly to Yorkshire with government funds lest she be called as a witness.

And Castle was seemingly one of the most vociferous revolutionaries of the Spa Fields conspirators. He brought pike heads to Spa Fields, he seemingly exaggerated or invented the support of London's workers, he had outraged Henry 'Orator' Hunt by toasting the King's death at a dinner. His testimony was inconsistent. When Wetherell asked him about government cannons being brought up the Thames, he suddenly remembered that the Spenceans planned for a citizen's navy.

In his closing statement, Wetherell waxed historical on treason's history to show that this charge was the most 'absurd and futile' in its annals. All the 'overt' treasonable acts, 'independently of the mere riots, were proved by Castle only', a government provocateur. The accused men might be guilty of riot, but not of treason.

After nine days, on 17 June, the jury reached a verdict in just two hours. Watson was found not guilty. A crowd received him with 'tumultuous congratulations'. The charges against Preston, Hooper and Thistlewood were dropped. Thistlewood was subsequently gaoled for a year after challenging Lord Sidmouth to a duel over his arrest. We will meet him again.

The presence of government agents in radical movements was not unusual. The Home Office and magistrates around the country maintained a domestic 'secret service' of informers, funded by a blank Treasury cheque. The Seditious Meetings Act made them all the more vital, as reformers went underground. Castle prompted questions in Parliament, the Prime Minister admitting that sometimes spies 'go farther than they ought'. On the night of 9 June 1817 (the first day of Watson's trial), however, near the Derbyshire village of Pentrich, the Home Office's spy system was to gain even more infamy.

In the Home Office's records from this period we find collections of radical pamphlets found on prisoners, including one John Latchford. In Latchford's possession was 'Address to the People', an influential 1816 tract by northern radical Joseph Mitchell. Mitchell spoke of poverty being a symptom of Britain's *political* disease', and its cure, 'RADICAL REFORM IN THE REPRESENTATION OF THIS COUNTY'.

Mitchell was nowhere near Pentrich on 9 June – he had been arrested in May. But in April 1817 he had toured the disaffected areas of the North and Midlands accompanied by a man called William Oliver, whom he had recently met. 'Oliver the Spy', as he became known, was a Home Office agent, reporting back to the Home Office throughout.

Oliver reported on Mitchell's work in London to gain support for a Northern Rising, and then his tour to Birmingham, Liverpool, Manchester, Huddersfield and other principal towns. Oliver's two accounts of his journeys (which continued alone after Mitchell's arrest) survive in the records of the Home Office. He found that the radicals were meeting in secret for fear of being arrested on suspicion of treason, with Bamford disconsolate about success after his arrest earlier in the year. They discussed the arrests of the Spenceans, and radical literature, particularly William Cobbett's.

Oliver also claimed to have attended many conventions of delegates from across the North and Midlands to discuss the plan for the coming insurrection, including one on 5 May 1817 where, as he informed the Home Office, he learned the numbers of men to be sent to the rebellion from each of the delegates' areas. Birmingham and its surrounds were apparently to provide 150,000 men, Derby and Nottinghamshire 30,000. Altogether, delegates pledged an army of 216,000 men. Oliver told his masters that they planned to secure 'all the arms, ammunition and divest all the magistrates of their power' in their areas, then gather around the River Trent and make for London en masse.

He further claimed that the rebels' aim was the 'Destruction' of the present government. They would 'invite all classes to join the patriotic standard', assure the soldiers that they owed no loyalty to the King or his 'corrupt ministers', and establish a provisional government.

What actually happened in the Derbyshire countryside late on a rainy night in June was rather different. About fifty men assembled near the village of South Wingfield at about 10 p.m., mostly textile artisans, many related to each other. They stopped at houses, trying to gain more guns and men. A shot was fired, killing a servant called Robert Walters. Now a hundred-strong they headed to an ironworks, intent on seizing ammunition. Twelve volunteer constables saw them off. Disconsolate and soaked, they stopped at a number of public houses.

The authorities knew something was afoot, hence the guard at the ironworks. The magistrates and soldiers of Derby had been up all night in anticipation of a 'simultaneous rising'. Lancelot Rolleston, a Nottingham magistrate, rode out in the early hours of 10 June and found the rebels. He returned with about twenty dragoons. The insurgents fled: 'twenty eight Men were taken, with about Fifty Pikes and Twenty or Thirty stand of Arms [a complete set of weapons for a man, in this instance most likely a gun of some kind]'. A total of eighty-nine arrests were made in the coming days.

John Cope was one of those men, released after he gave information about what had happened. Seven months previously, while drinking in a pub, he had been invited to join a Hampden Club. Cope duly joined and heard that they 'did not intend to rob and murder but to petition parliament in a constitutional manner'. He signed petitions but was soon told of a plan for 'general insurrection'. On 5 June he attended a meeting at Pentrich, where 'a Nottingham man' explained the plan of attack for the revolution.

Cope heard nothing more until the early hours of 10 June, when 'the mob armed with guns, pikes and many swords' arrived at his home. They believed themselves a vanguard in the larger rebellion, 'one large army with the [River] Trent in their front and the Derbyshire Hills in their Rear'. Each was promised beef, rum and £100. A mounted rebel galloped up to the party and told them Nottingham had already fallen, the soldiers were on their side. All public property was to be seized, 'the National Debt extinguished and no taxes', and a new currency minted. It seems also that the declaration of a republic was planned. None of this was true.

The 'Nottingham man' who was commander-in-chief was identified as Jeremiah Brandreth ('a well-known character'), also fingered for the shooting of Walters. William Turner and Isaac Ludlam Senior were also identified as ringleaders, and George Weightman was the man who had brought the erroneous news of Nottingham's capitulation. The Derby authorities initially planned for indictments for murder and conspiracy to be brought. The government, however, convened a special assizes at Derby to try thirty-five rebels for treason.

The indictment had three counts: levying war to subvert and destroy the government, compassing and imagining the King's deposition, and levying war to compel a change in the King's measures and counsels. The men pleaded not guilty. Brandreth was tried first, on 16 October.

Sir Samuel Shepherd, the Attorney General, opened the prosecution for his second treason trial in less than six months with the now customary disquisition on the historical and legal precedents of treason in general and levying war in particular, so as to make this ancient crime clear to the jurors and convince them of Brandreth's guilt. He said they needed no uniforms or battle-standards to levy war; 'attempting by force and arms to effect a general purpose' was enough. The degree of success or otherwise mattered not a bit, whether they had consumed the country in 'flagrant war' or been scattered by twenty dragoons, they had assembled 'with treasonable purpose' and were guilty.

The Crown then called many witnesses who, to support the prosecution's case, testified to both Brandreth's treasonable words and his overt acts. His defence did not try to defend his 'outrages' on the night of the Rising, but claimed there was not enough evidence to elevate his offences from those against the person or public (murder, riot), to that against the state – treason. Only one witness was called for Brandreth, testifying to his poverty.

Brandreth's counsel concluded his defence by blaming reformist literature and economic deprivation for radicalising the Pentrich men. He then recalled the last conviction for levying war, in the 1745 Jacobite Rebellion, when Derby had been the southernmost point of the rebels' invasion of England. He asked the jury, did they want theirs to be the only county where such treason had occurred in the last one hundred years?

The jurors were apparently sanguine about such a prospect, returning a guilty verdict the next day, 18 October 1817, after just twenty minutes. Brandreth's usually 'ferocious' countenance became paler. He was offered a pipe, a restorative drink and a large packet of sandwiches, then taken back to gaol.

Despite their counsel now arguing that Brandreth was the real traitor and a manipulator, William Turner, Isaac Ludlam and George Weightman were similarly convicted. The nineteen other defendants changed their pleas to guilty, having been told that this would save them from the gallows. Weightman also received clemency and was transported for life.

Brandreth, Turner and Ludlam were sentenced to be hanged, drawn and quartered, although the Treason Act of 1814 (which 'modernised' the brutal ancient punishment) and 'mercy' from the Prince Regent meant that on 7 November they were only drawn over a hurdle, hanged, then beheaded. Asked if he had any last words, William Turner said, 'This is the work of Government and Oliver.'

Oliver had been the trial's ghost at the feast. He was not called as a witness (the government had learnt their lesson), but his name was on everyone's lips. The *Leeds Mercury* had been reporting on the actions of Oliver – a 'prototype Lucifer' – prior to Pentrich, claiming he was a government provocateur and the author of the rebellion, always heard talking of revolution. Graffiti was seen in Derby reading, 'Jurymen, remember Oliver'.

Oliver's conduct led to questions in Parliament about Sidmouth's 'creatures'. Privately, the Home Secretary was disquieted by how industriously Oliver had sought to sow the seeds of rebellion. The reformers and their allies in the press made hay – they painted a picture of naive, impoverished workers led to ruin on government orders.

The truth is probably more nuanced. With the benefit of the Home Office's archive from the period there is little evidence to suggest orders to entrap reformers, but intelligence privileges results, and there is little doubt that Oliver and Castle provoked and invented to help procure the realisation of the plots and justify their employment.

To portray the Spenceans and Pentrich men as innocents guided to their doom, though, is a disservice to them. The government's refusal to countenance measures to relieve the poverty of workers, or give them political voice, and their restriction of even their limited civil rights, no doubt drove many to the belief that physical force was their only route to redress.

However, for all their grandiose claims of multitudinous armies and provisional governments, the reality – a riot, a gang of roving, rain-soaked artisans who fled at the sight of a soldier – belies the government's insistence that this was an attempt to 'levy war', no matter how they contorted the loose, medieval definition of the phrase. In London the government had failed, in Derby they succeeded – Brandreth was worm's meat, his cause was tainted. The causes of disaffection remained, though; if ministers truly knew the state of the country, Bamford told Sidmouth, 'they would be surprized from the distress of the people, that it was not a scene of bloodshed'.

The sensational trials in 1817, restrictions on political activity, and improved harvests meant that the drive for reform abated for a short while. However, a 'sunset clause' in the Seditious Meetings Act of 1817 meant that public meetings became easier to hold in July 1818. The constitutionalist reformers, who sought to use the crowd as merely a threat as opposed to a weapon, were in the driving seat.

In 1819 the constitutionalist campaign reached a bloody, tragic apotheosis in Manchester. Despite being the engine of the Industrial Revolution, Manchester elected no MPs in the unreformed parliament. It became a vibrant centre of political and labour activism. The working and middle classes united, and Female Reform Societies emerged, perhaps the first instances of self-organised women's mass political activity in Britain. That summer, Henry 'Orator' Hunt was to speak at a great meeting on the city's St Peter's Field.

Hunt wanted the meeting to be the largest ever held, and to prevent the authorities from exciting 'any act of violence' (his post was being intercepted by the Home Office). In preparation, groups of Lancashire reformers drilled in the hills, ready to maintain order on the day. The authorities, however, saw an army preparing, and

'Principles and Doctrine of Sedition and Infidelity' abounding. Henry Hobhouse, the Home Office's permanent undersecretary, remarked that the matter could only end in bloodshed, 'by the Law or the sword'.

The meeting took place on 16 August 1819. It was a tragedy. Some 60,000 people attended, peacefully. But the Manchester magistrates sent volunteer and regular cavalry, swords drawn, into the crowd to arrest Hunt and others. Panic and terror seized the crowd and the troops set about a bloody project. In what came to be called the 'Peterloo Massacre', 650 people were injured and 17 killed, including a child.

'Peterloo' was a scandal and, even more so than the case of William Oliver, a public-relations disaster for the government. Widespread meetings were called in support of the victims, criticism of the government was extensive among the public and the press, with even *The Times* joining the chorus of condemnation.

Sidmouth was undeterred. Hunt and others were arrested on suspicion of treason (for want of evidence they were gaoled for seditious conspiracy); and the government passed the notorious 'Six Acts' – prohibiting drilling, tightening the content and taxation of radical publications and renewing the terms of the Seditious Meetings Act.

The reform movement was traumatised – a campaign of illegal public meetings was mooted, but Hunt and the constitutionalists demurred. Efforts were instead put into innovative commemoration – no law could prevent reformers 'from *dining* together', noted William Cobbett.

Before the restrictions on meetings came into force, however, Arthur Thistlewood, just out of gaol himself, organised a grand reception parade for Hunt in London. Hunt made speeches cautioning peace, although Thistlewood and others seemed keen to incite a riot. But attendances dropped and insurrection seemed unlikely; the repressive measures were effective. Undeterred, the Spenceans sank into the underground of clandestine meetings and schemes.

On 23 February 1820, the Spenceans' plot exploded. Thistlewood and his company were rushed by Bow Street Runners (London's proto-police) in their hideout, a small loft on Cato Street, off the Edgware Road.

They had been about to go to the house of the Lord President of the Privy Council, Lord Harrowby, where the Cabinet were apparently having dinner, to assassinate all of them. Thereafter, the Spencean playbook of Spa Fields would follow: fires across the capital; the capture or collaboration of the troops; coordinated risings across the country; a revolutionary government.

The dinner was a fiction, the government pre-warned. The plotters, well-armed for their endeavours, fought back against the Runners. Thistlewood stabbed one, Richard Smithers, killing him, before making his escape. He was soon arrested, and he and twelve others were indicted for high treason. At least one of their number was a spy.

George Edwards had been working for the Bow Street Runners since 1818, his reports carrying his codename, 'W---r'. By the winter of 1819 he had become a confidant of Thistlewood, all the while submitting voluminous, closely written reports on thin strips of paper to his employers.

According to Edwards, in November and December 1819, the Spenceans were becoming restive. Thistlewood believed there would be risings in the North and Scotland. William Davidson, the mixed-race illegitimate son of a Jamaican slave owner (Edwards gave him the sobriquet 'Black Davidson') was counselling immediate action.

Desperate to do *something*, the assassination plot landed in their lap in December. A carpenter they knew spoke of Cabinet dinners, which would give the Spenceans a 'favourable opportunity'. This seemingly took precedence over their other schemes, for they found their meetings poorly attended, and condemned the constitutionalist strategy that aimed to wait and 'drink water for 2 or 3 years'. They began amassing an arsenal – pikes, guns, grenades and rudimentary 'fire balls'. They also began running low on cash, with Davidson procuring money from a vagrants' charity to take a blunderbuss out of pawn.

Unfortunately, the parliamentary recess over December, and the mourning period for George III (who died in January 1820), meant that there was no Cabinet dinner for some weeks. The plotters contemplated individual assassinations, but squabbled over their effectiveness.

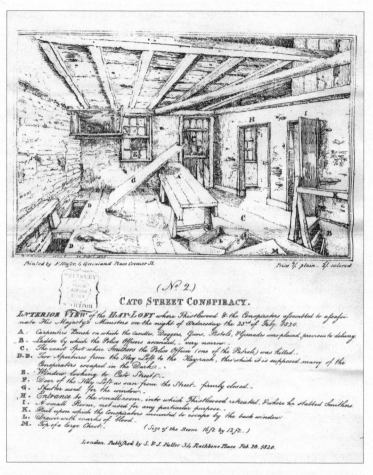

Printed diagram showing the hay loft on Cato Street in which the conspirators were raided by the Bow Street Runners. Part of the Treasury Solicitor's papers on the case, this was actually a mass produced print, showing the public notoriety the conspiracy immediately gained. (*TS 11/202*)

Suddenly, though, a notice appeared in the obscure daily newspaper *New Times* (published in London 1818–30) on 22 February, announcing a Cabinet dinner the next evening at Harrowby's house. The notice had been placed by the government in that paper alone, and Edwards 'just happened' to notice it.

Thistlewood ordered them to action. The plan was as follows: gaining entry under the ruse of delivering a despatch box or letter, they would pacify the servants. Then, on bursting into the room where the Cabinet was assembled, they were to evoke the memory of Peterloo and finally, on the command of 'Citizens ... do your duty!', murder the ministers. But it was they who had been tricked, and a warrant for their arrest was issued that day.

That evening, a band of twelve Bow Street Runners, led by James Ellis, raided the Spencean hideout on Cato Street. They were meant to be assisted by a party of soldiers, but these had assembled in the wrong place and only came when they heard shots. Ellis afterwards described what happened. The Runners entered the ground-floor stables and found Davidson, armed, on guard. He was arrested and they went upstairs, Richard Smithers the second man up. Thistlewood adopted a 'fencing attitude', Smithers rushed at him as Ellis raised his pistol to shoot Thistlewood down. Too late, Thistlewood stabbed Smithers, who shouted, 'Oh my God', then shortly afterwards died. Ellis's shots missed and the Spenceans tried to escape. Davidson briefly got away, but was recaptured.

Thistlewood, Davidson and eleven other men were charged with treason. The result was not a foregone conclusion, for treason was difficult to convict. The Derby authorities had initially thought to charge the Pentrich men for conspiracy to murder Robert Walters, the servant who was shot dead. Similarly, charges framed around the killing of Smithers were considered for the Spenceans, but the Cabinet decided on treason, because it would be, Henry Hobhouse noted in his diary, 'highly expedient to develop to the public ... evidence of the treasonable conspiracy'.

The men were indicted on four counts of treason: conspiring to depose the King, conspiring the death of the King, conspiring to levy war for the purpose of compelling the King to change his measures and counsel, and levying war against the King. As with the Spa Fields and Pentrich trials, these counts were drawn from both the 1795 Treason Act (1st and 3rd) and the 1352 original (2nd and 4th). On Saturday 15 April the suspects were arraigned (Thistlewood and others were also indicted for Smithers's murder and malicious shooting, but not tried on these charges at the same time) and severally pleaded not guilty. The trials commenced on 17 April, with Thistlewood the first at the bar.

The prosecution's case made much use of former members of the conspiracy. Thomas Hiden had apparently found Lord Harrowby in Hyde Park and let him know the plans. Thomas Dwyer had gone to the Home Office to confess. John Monument and Robert Adams had turned Crown's witness after arrest. Edwards was not called, for the same reason Oliver had not been in 1817. In court, Adams outlined the conspiracy as related above, but claimed he had always been reluctant. The defence said he was only interested in saving his own neck. Monument said much the same, but claimed that Thistlewood had told him, after arrest, to blame everything on Edwards.

The defence called the daughter of one of the conspirators, who said Edwards had been active, bringing arms to her father's house, even on the day after the arrests. The editor and court writer of the *New Times* testified that the notice of the dinner had been placed unusually. Lord Harrowby did not exactly deny that the dinner was a hoax, but he did admit the government were aware of a plot.

John Aldophus, defending Thistlewood, made his closing arguments on 19 April, his client looking 'pale and haggard'. He did not deny Thistlewood's overt acts, the meditation of assassinating ministers, but he called into question the idea of a treasonable purpose. The claims of nationwide insurrection and revolutionary governments were fanciful, he averred, even if Thistlewood had spoken them – and the only testimony to that came from his erstwhile friends, now keen to save their lives – the idea that he would overthrow the government with fewer than thirty men was so ridiculous as not to be taken seriously. The men had plotted to kill Privy Councillors, and while that was a crime (the Treason Act makes provisions for the murder of ministers, but it seemingly these have to be successful), it was not treason; the King's throne or life were not threatened, no war was levied. Aldophus cautioned the jury that convicting Thistlewood would expand the definition of treason in such a way as to threaten the liberty of all. Thistlewood attempted to call witnesses to discredit his betrayers, but the judge said the time for evidence was over as Adolphus had finished his arguments.

Thistlewood was found guilty by the jury on the third and fourth counts of levying war under both the 1352 and 1795 Treason Acts. Henry Hobhouse called this a 'capricious' verdict, and lamented the reluctance of juries to convict people of compassing the monarch's death or deposition unless he was physically threatened.

James Ings was tried next, his trial nearly a carbon copy of Thistlewood's, and he was found similarly guilty. William Davidson and Richard Tidd, whose daughter was a defence witness, came next. More details emerged of the conduct of Edwards and Adams. Adams said that Edwards was forever whispering conspiracies into Thistlewood's ear, while a friend of the conspirators said the two men had come to his house drunk and laughed that they were going to kill the Cabinet, and 'will have blood and wine for supper'.

Davidson, testifying in his own defence, claimed he was entrapped by Edwards. He was looking for work, and the spy had said he could get him some, and find a buyer for his recently pawned blunderbuss. He also offered the fact that, as a black man in Regency London, he was often mistaken for other black men, as further proof of his innocence. He asked the jury, why would he be so foolish as to join 'a few weak men' in this madcap scheme? It only worked in part. He and Tidd were convicted of only the third count, levying war to compel the King to change his measures. The other defendants immediately changed their pleas to guilty, again to avoid the noose, just as the Pentrich men had after the initial convictions.

The men were sentenced on 28 April. Thistlewood, Ings, Davidson, Tidd and Brunt were to be drawn on a hurdle, hanged, then beheaded. All but one of the others were transported for life, the last being imprisoned.

Before they were executed the men were given a chance to explain themselves, and plead for mercy. Thistlewood, realising the futility of such an exercise, instead gave an incendiary oration.

He cried a mistrial, for if he had been able to give the evidence which he had, late in his trial, obtained to the character of those who informed on him, the latter's testimony would have been discarded. Edwards, he said, was 'ever at invention ... ever the most active', in treasonous plots. He should not have trusted a man who never had 'money to pay for a pint of beer', but always cash for arms. He then turned on the judiciary – 'implacable enemies' of the people – and the government. 'The assassination of a Tyrant has always been deemed a meritorious action', he said – as the judge said such talk could not be allowed – Peterloo had made 'Insurrection ... a public duty'.

The conspirators were executed outside Newgate Gaol on 1 May 1820. The Privy Council feared a rescue attempt as the men mounted the gallows, but none materialised. There were few shouts of support, just a display of squeamishness as the heads were removed. The bodies were ordered to be buried in the prison, with quicklime poured on them, to avoid the machinations of martyrdom or anatomists.

Cato Street was another nail in the coffin of parliamentary reform, although Thistlewood's claimed rising in Scotland, the 'Radical War', did take place in April 1820, and there is some evidence for collaboration between Scotland and London. Some 60,000 workers rose up in strikes and protest, and once again provisional governments were mentioned. But troops brutally suppressed the Rising, and treason convictions, executions and transportation followed.

The Spenceans' families, meanwhile, were left to pick up the pieces. Susan Thistlewood, Sarah Davidson and other female relatives of the conspirators petitioned the King to 'alleviate [their] acute sufferings' by granting them return of the 'mutilated remains' of their men. They also attempted to have Edwards indicted for treason, as the real author of the plot. But they were left with nothing but grief. Reform had again burned brightly, then burned out.

Lord Grey's Whig government was formed in 1830, after decades of Tory rule. This combined with riots, economic distress, and the spectre of the second French Revolution to put parliamentary reform in prospect. The 1832 Great Reform Act was the result, but while this greatly expanded the vote, still only about 3 per cent of the population were enfranchised. Working-class men and their allies renewed their campaign for universal suffrage.

Chartism, which emerged in 1838, became the largest mass working-class political movement of the nineteenth century. It took its name from the People's Charter, a blueprint of 'six points' for reform: a vote for every man aged twenty-one or over; a secret ballot; an end to the property qualification; the payment of MPs (who at that time were not salaried); constituencies of equal size; and annual parliaments to ensure accountability.

Chartism's tactics built on what had come before – mass petitions and 'monster meetings'. Its newspapers were widely circulated, with a larger readership than *The Times*, it had a network of some four hundred local groups by 1839, who organised industrially and fought the New Poor Law and other issues. They were all, of course, kept under continuous surveillance by the Home Office.

Like the radicals of the Regency era, the Chartists were also ostensibly divided in the way they approached achieving their aims. The 'moral force' camp advocated petitioning and campaigns palatable to the middle classes. The 'physical force' faction contemplated strikes, riots, revolution. Yet they were not diametrically opposed; for there was nuance, shades of grey. Just as a Henry Hunt, preacher of peace, had admired and worked with Thistlewood, there was crossover between the two factions. A third approach has been proposed by historians: 'intimidation' – mass mobilisation as an implicit threat of political violence, should accommodation not be made (which was also perhaps closer to Hunt's modus operandi).

An example of the latter approach can be seen in a poster advertising a Chartist meeting 'on the Sands' at Carlisle on 21 May 1839. Professing non-violence, it requests that attendees come without any 'offensive weapon'. However, the wording of the poster concludes in a threatening tone, stating that it is hoped that the town's employers will allow their workers to attend, *so that any unpleasant collision between them may be avoided* (original's italics). The threat is implicit, but it stops short of incitement.

Dr John Taylor was the speaker at this meeting, which was attended by some 8,000 people. Taylor was a wealthy surgeon, famed Chartist, and leading advocate of physical force. Chartism presented its first great petition to Parliament (1,280,000 signatures long, quickly rejected) in 1839, and held a national convention. A general strike was to follow, but disorganisation and disagreement meant that only a few disconnected protests actually took place. Taylor, furious, began planning for a coordinated rising across the north and west of Britain. One of the men he seems to have conspired with was John Frost, the delegate for Newport in South Wales.

Frost had been a Newport councillor, mayor and magistrate. He was also a longstanding reformer. Initially a 'moral force' advocate, a government campaign of arrests against the Chartists, including the orator Henry Vincent in nearby Monmouth, radicalised him. On 4 November 1839, Frost led the Newport Rising.

Reports of increasingly inflammatory public remarks by Chartists and the open distribution of arms meant the Welsh authorities were fearful of something happening. In May 1839 Newport's Mayor, Thomas Phillips, appointed 500 special constables. Monmouth's Mayor requested that guns and swords be sent for his constables, fearing that the Chartists would attempt to break Vincent out of gaol. Residents of nearby Pontypool warned of an impending 'outbreak' by their district's 4,000 Chartists, but things did not come to a head in Newport until early November.

Phillips feared that Bonfire Night 1839 – 'always a scene of much riot and confusion in Newport' – would be when the Chartists struck. He called some of his special constables and a detachment of the 45th Regiment to readiness. But on the morning of Sunday 3 November, men were fleeing Chartists, who were compelling them to join their ranks. Phillips marshalled all 500 special constables and made the Westgate Hotel in Newport his head quarters. It was pouring with rain. His scouts took prisoners, some of whom were kept at the Westgate.

Job Tovey was a collier and paid-up Chartist from Blackwood, some 13 miles from Newport. He later gave a statement to the Crown as to how the events of 4 November came about (he does not seem to have been called at Frost's trial). Tovey had first heard Frost speak at a meeting in May 1839, where he entreated his audience to use 'all their endeavours' to realise the Charter, but went no further. By early October, however, Frost told another meeting that they were to form in 'companies' of ten men for a coordinated rising with Chartists in the North and Scotland, and 'by that means they would have a Charter Parliament'.

On 1 November delegates from Chartist lodges in Monmouthshire gathered in Blackwood. Frost asked Tovey if he might stay at his house afterwards. While staying with the Toveys, Frost apparently explained his plan. On Sunday 3 November Chartists would gather at Blackwood and elsewhere, arriving at Newport at 3 a.m. With the element of surprise they would give three terrifying cheers and thereby force the mayor and soldiers to surrender. The town's mail coach would be stopped, its failure to arrive in Birmingham being the signal for other risings to begin. And so the Charter would be achieved. He apparently talked of beheading 'tyrants' at dinner that evening (although Tovey's wife, Susanna, did not recollect this remark in her own deposition). Tovey left with Frost that night for the rain-soaked march to Newport; he recounted how Frost ordered pikemen and musketeers forward at different points.

As the rain lashed down, things fell apart. The men from Pontypool were delayed. The 9,000 Chartists arrived in Newport at 9 a.m., not the dead of night. They marched to the Westgate, to confront Phillips and free their friends. Thirty troops had by this time been stationed there in a 'public room' with its internal window shutters closed.

Phillips watched the Chartists, 'marching abreast in regular order armed with muskets, pikes, spears', wheel round the Westgate to its front door, where they forced entry.

Returning to the troops, Phillips and their commander threw open the shutters. The mayor was immediately struck by a slingshot and bullets to his arm and hip. He retreated to a pantry to be bandaged. The soldiers opened fire through the windows at the mob, and into the passageway where they were breaking in, 'so fast that they was knocked down as fast as they approached', one of the troops said.

The Newport Rising was the most lethal civil disturbance in modern British history. Fifty were wounded, and at least twenty-two Chartists died, the youngest of whom was eighteen-year-old George Shell, who was shot as he tried to confront Phillips.

Retribution followed for the Chartists. Many were charged with conspiring to riot. John Frost, William Jones and Zephaniah Williams, considered the three commanders, and ten other men were soon committed for high treason by the magistrates. Again, as in the case of the Pentrich Rising and the Cato Street plot, the question arose of whether treason was the right offence to prosecute. The Attorney and Solicitor Generals' legal opinions were sought – Frost and others could easily be convicted of aiding and abetting Phillips's wounding under the 1837 Offences Against the Person Act, a capital offence. That did not, however, carry the same awful portent as treason.

John Campbell, the Attorney General, opened the Crown's case against John Frost on New Year's Day, 1840. Frost and his co-defendants were indicted on four counts of high treason, by now familiar to readers: two counts of levying war with a litany of overt acts attached to these, one of compassing and imagining to depose the Queen, and finally one of levying war to compel the Queen to change her measures and counsels. Again, these were a mixture of crimes from the 1352 and 1795 Treason Acts. The same, occasionally somewhat farcical, courtroom drama of the Crown attempting to explain how a medieval crime was applicable to modern rebels played out, while the defence claimed that these crimes were free of the crucial treasonable objects.

The Attorney General, as was customary, waxed historical. Edward III's codification of treason had rescued the country from 'miserable servitude', and the Yorkists, Jacobites and London Corresponding Society were in turn discussed. He assured the jury that there was no concealed government agent provocateur, as there had been before, and contended that Frost and his comrades' purpose was not private revenge or industrial dispute but an 'armed force seeking to supersede the law and to gain some public object ... Charter law universally and instantly established' by Newport and the chain of English risings it was apparently to trigger. Witnesses were produced by the Crown, members of the mob, local residents and soldiers to attribute to Frost and the others the kind of statements Job Tovey had claimed to have heard.

The defendants were represented by Sir Frederick Pollock, a Tory lawyer who had been Attorney General in Sir Robert Peel's short-lived minority government (December 1834–April 1835). Despite this, Pollock was a relative newcomer to criminal proceedings and had never been involved in a case of treason. Yet he made a good go of it. He had buried himself in Acts of Parliament and original historical documents to inform his argument, and found the Crown's case a weak one of 'scattered fragments'. The witnesses' testimony (some thirty-nine were called) delivered the only evidence of Frost making a definitive declaration of treasonable intents or objects, and he believed them unreliable. He talked of processions of tens of thousands of men to present petitions, and riots around the passage of the Great Reform Act that were not considered treasonable, and asked why they were not. Arms were not necessary under the Treason Acts for the levying of war. He said the Chartists were not aware of the troops' presence, and fled as soon as they started firing – Frost and his comrades' intent was not revolution, but the liberation of the Westgate's prisoners, and then of Vincent and others in Monmouth Gaol. Of many crimes they might be guilty, but there was no evidence that their 'overt acts' were unified by a treasonable object.

The jury were not convinced. After seven days they retired for twenty-five minutes before returning a guilty verdict. Williams and Jones were found similarly guilty in the days that followed. The other ten men, seeing the game was up, changed their pleas to guilty.

But in all cases of conviction the jury also made a request for mercy for the men. This was partly because the proper forms of a treason trial, particularly the delivery of a list of witnesses to the defence, had not been observed, and while the court had not agreed to Pollock's suggestion that this warranted a mistrial, it was still a concern. In addition, the convicted men were not the drunken artisans of Pentrich, or Thistlewood's hardened revolutionaries, but men of standing in their community, driven from moral to physical force by the arrest of their friends and the dismissal of their campaigns.

Treason is political theatre. Traditionally, it had a gruesome final act, complete with a chorus of revulsion, opprobrium and occasionally solidarity: the execution of the ringleaders. Thanks to the witness-list controversy, however, and a petition signed by some 200,000 people (even the Lord Chief Justice, who had presided over the trial, became involved), Frost, Jones and Williams did not go to the gallows, but to Australia, transported for life.

The Newport trials did not mark Chartism's end, and neither was it the end of the 'physical force' Chartists. However, whereas the 'moral force' faction, under the leadership of Fergus O'Connor, proprietor of the Chartist *Northern Star* newspaper, gained ascendancy. Another national petition, signed by three and a half million, was presented to and rejected by Parliament in May 1842. Throughout the economically depressed 'Hungry Forties', Chartism became the dominant political movement among the industrial working classes as a wave of strikes and riots rocked the country. Despite arresting leaders like O'Connor, the government could not make serious charges like sedition and treason stick easily.

The year 1848 was the 'Springtime of the Peoples', as first France, then much of Europe erupted into revolution. Meanwhile, the Chartist national convention and executive were organising a third petition. The campaign culminated in a meeting on Kennington Common in South London on

10 April. The idea was that the 'monster meeting' would march across the Thames to present the petition, carrying some five million signatures to Parliament (some three million of these would later be ruled inadmissible by the authorities). But the state, fearing insurrection, revived an early modern law restricting the number of people who could present such an address, and recruited some 100,000 special constables.

O'Connor backed down, leaving the peaceful meeting of some 50,000 behind to go to Westminster without the crowd, the petition carried in three coaches due to its size. But 'physical force' Chartists were outraged by what they saw as capitulation, and promised a wave of unrest. The government meanwhile stirred into legislative action. With a revolutionary spectre haunting Europe, Chartist support for and cooperation with Irish nationalists, and 'capricious' juries, increasingly squeamish about sending men to the gallows for political crimes, Lord John Russell's Whig government decided a new Treason Act was necessary.

The Treason Felony Act 1848, which came into law on 22 April that year, was a different beast from the 1795 Act. It created a new offence, treason felony, which carried a punishment not of death but of transportation or imprisonment. Under section 3 of the Act, it became treason felony to compass and imagine depriving the monarch of her crown, levy war against her, compel her to change her measures or counsels; 'intimidate or overawe' Parliament, or 'move or stir' foreigners to invade the United Kingdom or its empire. It was also explicit in saying that these compassings and imaginings could be proved by overt acts including printing, writing or 'open and advised speaking' at a public meeting. It also did away with the need for Felony Treason indictments to carry by now near impossible to convict charges from the 1352 Act. The new law made clear that it did not 'lessen the force' of the original Treason Act, and allowed for felons convicted under it to be tried for Treason proper later on.

In the Commons, the Prime Minister explained that 'as new modes of overturning the Government of the country are resorted to ... the Legislature [must] be prepared to meet the various evils which arise.' O'Connor (the only Chartist MP) told the House that the Bill was 'a violation of the constitution'. It passed with an overwhelming majority and became law. Public professions of republicanism and constitutional change were now explicitly criminalised, and by a law far better suited to the modern courtroom than the 1352 or 1795 acts anachronistic clauses.

The new law's first victim was John Mitchel, an Irish newspaper editor convicted in Dublin for publishing articles supporting armed resistance to British rule. But in Britain, one of its first victim was a London Chartist, William Cuffey.

Sixty years old, balding, four-foot-eleven with a deformed spine and shin bones, Cuffey was mixed race, descended from enslaved people. A tailor, in the 1830s he became a trade union organiser, then a leading 'physical force' Chartist. After Kennington Common, London 'physical force' Chartists staged demonstrations and riots across the summer of 1848. Rumours of revolutionary plots abounded. Cuffey was arrested for his involvement in one such alleged scheme, the Orange Tree Plot, named after the public house that many of conspirators were arrested at in a raid on 15 August 1848. Cuffey was arrested at his home in Soho the following day.

Cuffey was indicted under two counts of Felony Treason, along with two others, William Lacey and Thomas Fay (although the Treasury Solicitor's draft shows that many other men were initially to be included in their trial). The first charge was compassing and imagining to levy war against the Queen, the second conspiring to depose her via this insurrection. There were four overt acts in the indictment: conspiring for the purpose of levying war, purchasing and procuring arms, conspiring to burn police and railway stations in London, and being members of 'secret and dangerous' clubs communicating clandestinely to organise an insurrection.

The prosecution claimed that Cuffey and his co-defendants had formed a secret 'Ulterior Committee' which had procured weapons and secretly organised for a coordinated rising of 5,000 armed Chartists on the night the Orange Tree was raided. They were allegedly planning to burn London down and either establish a republic or force Parliament to grant the Charter by setting off a wave of risings in Britain and Ireland – the judge informed the jury that if the accused had intended for Parliament to be compelled, or for rioting to break out in Ireland, they were guilty; Felony Treason was less ambiguous than its venerable medieval cousin, apparently.

The defence made clear that this law and its interpretation had the appearance of a show trial (the judge disagreed). The prosecution witnesses were almost all either police officers (who had indeed found a quantity of weapons) or police informers. One, Thomas Powell, was shown by the defence to have been an agitator, often vociferously calling for Chartism to turn violent at meetings. Powell at least had the decency to admit, in his occasionally inconsistent testimony, that he was a spy. However, he claimed to have not done it for the money but 'for the good of my country' to show Chartism for what it was.

On 30 September Cuffey, Lacey and Fay were all found guilty. Cuffey rose to protest an unfair trial under a 'disgraceful' law, but did not express any surprise – he had always expected his career to end this way. He would face punishment not in fear or anger but pitying the government for their actions. The men were, like the Newport rebels, sentenced to transportation to Australia. Chartism declined rapidly, it had not achieved its aims, but it had changed Britain.

What had also changed was the way 'political' traitors were treated – for the Newport men and Cuffey and his alleged conspirators did not face a life of bonded labour on the other side of the world.

Cuffey, like the others, received a ticket of leave, effectively a probation, immediately on his arrival in Tasmania. He was pardoned some three years later. Frost, Jones and Williams's supporters continued to petition for their pardon and release. They were pardoned in 1854. George Weightman and other Pentrich rebels were pardoned in 1834 after a campaign of petitioning.

How can a traitor be pardoned, someone deemed, legally, to have, at 'the instigation of the devil' turned against not only their monarch, but their god? It is, conversely, for the same reason that in this period the

R. White ad vivum   delin et Sculp:

TITUS OATES.
Anagramma
TESTIS OVAT.

This is the true Originall taken from the Life,
done for HEN: BROME and RIC: CHISWELL. All others are Counterfeit.

Portrait of Titus Oates by Robert White, 1679. © Chronicle / Alamy Stock Photo

Left: A satirical print of Edmund Burke, author of *Reflections on the Revolution in France*. Burke is shown kneeling in reverence before a vision of the late Queen of France, Marie Antoinette. By Frederick George Byron (uncle of the famous poet), 1790.

Right: An engraving of Thomas Hardy, Secretary of the London Corresponding Society, in the dock while on trial for treason in 1794.

Left: Samuel Bamford, radical reformer, writer and poet, c.1860. Bamford was arrested on suspicion of treason in 1817 but was released. © *FLHC14 / Alamy Stock Photo*

Below right: Handbill advertising the Spencean Society of Philanthropists, c. 1816. Thomas Spence (1750–1814) was a radical who advocated the common ownership of land and direct democracy in Britain. After his death, Arthur Thistlewood and others formed this society, which would go on to be involved in the Spa Fields Riots and the Cato Street Conspiracy.

© *The National Archives* (HO 40 / 9, folio 76)

Below: Print depicting the Bow Street Runners' raid on the Cato Street conspirators' hideout, 23 February 1820. At centre, Arthur Thistlewood is depicted stabbing the Runner Richard Smithers.

© *Pictorial Press Ltd / Alamy Stock Photo*

Engraved for the New Lady's Magazine.
Published by Alex.r Hogg at the Kings Arms N.o 16 Paternoster Row, Sep 30 1786.

M.rs MARGARET NICHOLSON,
who attempted to Stab the King of Great Britain
Aug.t 2.1786 and being judged Insane was sent to Bedlam
Aug.t 9.1786, where it is supposed she will remain for life.

Left: An engraving of Margaret Nicholson c.1786, who attempted to stab George III and was subsequently declared insane. © *Chronicle / Alamy Stock Photo*

James Hadfield !!!
Who made an Attempt on the Life of his Majesty
at Drury Lane Theatre on Thursday May 15.th 1800

Right: Depiction of James Hadfield, who tried to assassinate George III in 1800. Hadfield was tried for treason but acquitted on the grounds that he was insane. The government passed the Criminal Lunatics Act 1800 in response.

© *Zuri Swimmer / Alamy Stock Photo*

A stylised representation of Edward Oxford's attempt to shoot Queen Victoria, 10 June 1840. Oxford was declared insane at his trial and remanded to Bethlem, before emigrating to Australia. The artist was J. R. Jobbins, 1840. © *Heritage Image Partnership Ltd / Alamy Stock Photo*

Left: Copy of the United States Declaration of Independence, which denounced King George III as a tyrant.

© *The National Archives* (EXT 9/1)

Below: 'A representation of the figures exhibited and paraded through the streets of Philadelphia', 30 September 1780, being the first time an effigy of the traitor Benedict Arnold was burnt.

© *Bridgeman Images*

Nº 2

Return of the Killed and wounded of the Troops at the Attack on the 8th Inst. April 12th 95.

Killed

	Lt Coll	Major	Capt	Subn	Staff	Serj.	Drum.	Rank & File
9th Regt.	"	"	1	"	"	1	"	4
25th Regt.	"	"	"	"	"	"	"	"
29th Regt.	"	"	"	1	"	"	"	9
58th Regt.	"	"	"	"	"	"	"	"
68 Regt.	"	"	"	"	"	1	1	2
St Georges Militia	"	"	"	"	"	"	"	1
Total killed	"	"	1	1	"	2	1	16

Capt. Stopford 9 Regt.
Ens. Baillie 29 do. killed

Wounded

	Lt Coll	Major	Capt	Subn	Staff	Serj.	Drum.	Rank & File
9th Regt.	"	"	"	"	"	2	"	8
25th Regt.	"	"	"	"	"	"	1	10
29th Regt.	"	"	"	"	"	1	1	8
58 Regt.	"	"	"	1	"	3	"	7
68 Regt.	"	"	"	"	"	"	"	8
St Georges Militia	"	"	"	"	"	"	"	2
Total wounded	"	"	"	1	"	6	2	43

Lt Power wounded 58th Regt.

(signed) J. A Campbell
Lieut. Coll.
Commg the Troops.

A return of killed and wounded British troops during an early engagement of Fédon's Rebellion, 12 April 1795. © *The National Archives* (CO 101/34 folio 68)

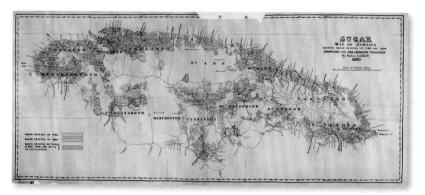

Above: An 1890 map of Jamaica, showing sugar estates that were in cultivation in 1790 (red), those in cultivation in 1890 (blue), and those continuously in cultivation during those hundred years (purple, unfortunately this colour has faded). This map shows the decline of the Jamaican sugar economy in the nineteenth century, due to economic and agricultural reasons. © *The National Archives* (CO 700/JAMAICA37)

Left: An engraved likeness of Samuel Sharpe, the leader of the Jamaican slave rebellion of 1832, as it appears on the Jamaican $50 banknote. Sharpe was conferred the Jamaican government's Order of National Hero, one of only seven recipients.

© *Janusz Pieńkowski / Alamy Stock Photo*

Left: Photograph of Patrick Pearse, the man who read the proclamation of the Irish republic at the start of the Easter Rising in Dublin in 1916.

Below: Irish Citizen Army soldiers (pre Easter Rising).

Crown pursued tricky treason trials, even though insurgents and reformers might be convicted of all manner of offences, more straightforward but still capital. Treason was a 'stain ... of the blackest and the deepest dye', remarked Pollock at Frost's trial. This was its appeal to the government as they battled parliamentary reform movements, for a conviction for treason tarred not only the guilty parties but their whole political creed in a way that no conviction for riot, murder or wounding could. By the time they were pardoned their factions and their threats were spent. The mark of treachery was no longer required to ward off the threat to Crown and state. Treason indictments were more a product of political calculation than jurisprudence.

Universal male suffrage was not realised until 1918, the same year in which some women received the vote, in a great part because of campaigns, moral and physical in force, for women's suffrage. But no suffragette was ever prosecuted for treason, despite committing many overt acts to try to effect constitutional change. But parliamentary reform, while not necessarily the early-twentieth-century governments' priority, was no longer the existential threat it had been in the six decades after the French Revolution. The indelible stain of treason was not needed.

In 2001 the *Guardian* newspaper made a legal challenge against the Treason Felony Act, claiming its effective criminalisation of republicanism would have a 'chilling effect' on newspapers like itself, and was therefore in breach of the Human Rights Act 1998. The House of Lords dismissed the case as 'unnecessary' – Felony Treason was 'a relic of a bygone age and does not fit into the fabric of our modern legal system'.

Old Bailey
10 July 1840

My dear sir,

The Jury went out at
20^m. p. 5 and returned at 15^m p.
6 and pronounced this verdict
" We find the prisoner guilty
" Of discharging the contents of
" two pistols at the Queen but
" whether they were loaded with
" bullet we have not satisfactory evidence
" sufficient to prove he being at the time labouring
" under a state of mind —

After some discussion they
were directed to retire and reconsider

Note to government reporting on the verdict (insanity) in Edward Oxford's trial for shooting at Queen Victoria, 10 July 1840. (TS 11/10)

Thirteen

INJURE OR ALARM HER MAJESTY, 1786–1848

On 15 May 1800 James Hadfield went to theatre. Having heard that the King would be attending the Theatre Royal, Drury Lane, that evening, he had decided to go along too. He had borrowed the three shillings and sixpence needed for admission to the theatre's pit and, after dining at home and going for a walk 'to consider himself', proceeded to the playhouse.

Hadfield would have known its environs well; the second of his 'two wives', a sex worker who went by the name Yonge, operated in the area. He took his seat before the monarch arrived. Sitting next to him waiting for the show begin was John Holroyd. Holroyd, a plumber, noticed nothing unusual about his neighbour – he did not say anything and appeared not in the slightest agitated.

George III arrived, accompanied by his son, the Duke of York, and proceeded to the Royal Box. He stood before the crowd as the National Anthem was played. Holroyd noticed movement. As 'God Save the King' was sung, James Hadfield stood up on the bench and aimed a pistol at the monarch. Holroyd and others went to restrain him, but he managed to get a shot off, before being tackled and bundled into the orchestra pit.

Hadfield's shot missed. The King and his son came to see the would-be assailant where he was detained in the theatre's musicians' room, where Hadfield apparently told them, 'This is not the worst of it.'

As the British state developed after the settlements of the Restoration and the 'Glorious Revolution', its power was increasingly articulated by, and lay with, not the monarch (who nonetheless remained the constitutional centre), but with ministers, exercising many of the Crown's prerogative powers, and with Parliament legislating on its behalf. The result was that after the Stuart claimants to the throne had expired, treason was, as we have seen, directed not at the King's person but at the executive and legislature, since overcoming these would be the route to change in the realm. Jurisprudence around treason developed to account for this, as had been noted at the 1794 trial of Thomas Hardy when jurors were told that, because the Crown was the centre of the British state, any attempt to destroy or supplant one of its constituent parts was communicated to that centre, in effect bringing about the King's death.

Yet although they waned, direct attempts on the King or Queen's person did not cease in the Georgian and Victorian periods. However, bar some notable exceptions, such as the 1794 Pop-Gun and 1887 Jubilee plots, both most likely fabrications born of political or personal animosities, the direct attempts on the monarch's life in the 'modern' period took on a different character – mental distress, media spectacle and public notoriety all figure heavily.

And just as the threats posed by Catholicism, Jacobites, and Jacobins had led to a modification of treason laws to codify and deal with them, these rather different treasons led to new legislation.

Hadfield was examined before the Privy Council at 10 p.m. on the night of his attempted assassination. He informed them that 'he fired the pistol not to hurt his Majesty's person, but that it might be thought so, and he might be killed.' His death was necessary, divinely decreed, 'he knows when he is at an end, the World is to be at an end – he was told it by him that made him.' It became clear that Hadfield was consumed by delusion; he was not sane. Nonetheless, he would soon be tried for treason.

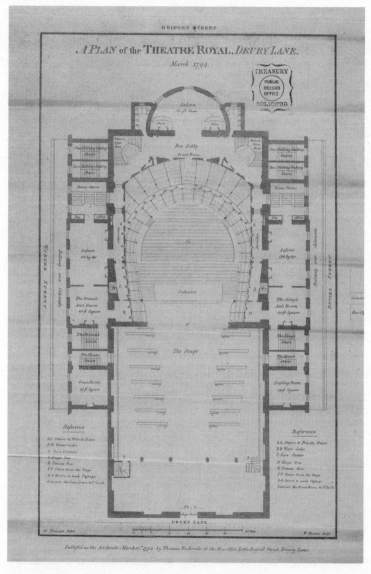

A plan of the Theatre Royal, Drury Lane (dated 1794) where James Hadfield fired at George III. The plan shows the position of the King's Box, the pit where Hadfield sat, and the orchestra pit where he was bundled into by the crowd. (*TS 11/223/937*)

Hadfield's was not the first such case. Margaret Nicholson was a casually employed seamstress whose acquaintances had remarked on her odd habits. In July 1786 Nicholson had sent a petition to the Privy Council, full of disconnected statements about pretenders to the Crown. On 2 August she waited patiently in the crowd outside London's St James's Palace for George III's carriage to arrive from Windsor.

The King arrived and Nicholson went towards him brandishing a blank piece of paper, pretending it was a petition to him (petitioning the Crown was an ancient right, and it was not unusual at the time to do it directly). However, this was a ruse – she took out a small knife and made to stab the monarch. Her attempts were clumsy and unsuccessful, and she was overpowered and might have been killed by the incensed crowd if George III had not cried out, 'The poor creature is mad; do not hurt her, she has not hurt me.'

Nicholson was imprisoned and brought before the Privy Council in the ensuing days. Her testimony is inconsistent, rambling to the point that she herself could not fully explain herself. Nicholson was unmarried and childless, seemingly a virgin, but her actions seem to have hinged around her claim that she had carried, or was carrying, royal children – she referred to this as the 'Mystery'.

She claimed to have 'a Right in Blood and understanding to have the Crown of England by marriage ... her care was to bring up the two Infants one for the Reason and the other for the Crown,' but these phantom children could only be directed and understood by the Mystery. The children were yet without a father – she would 'bring [them] up' by marrying the Prince of Wales. She asked for all of this to be communicated to the King, and for his mercy.

Nicholson was also interviewed by John Monro, a doctor at the Bethlem Hospital, one of the oldest institutions in Britain specialising in the treatment of mentally ill patients. Monro told the Privy Council he 'never in his life had seen a Person more disordered'. Nicholson seemed to understand her actions, but not that they were a crime. She talked incessantly 'upon the subject of her right to the Crown and the mystery', and fell into sudden, violent fits of laughter. He had, he said, never seen 'a clearer case of insanity'.

The King intervened to save her life again. Under George's influence, she was not charged with treason. The *London Gazette* soon published a statement, accompanied by copies of addresses of thanks from around the country that the King had survived, that the Privy Council were unanimously of the opinion that 'she was and is insane'.

Nicholson lived out her days in Bethlem, where she apparently troubled the hospital's staff little. A casebook from 1816 noted that she was profoundly deaf (she had told the Privy Council she was 'not very quick of hearing'), 'and apparently very destitute of all the powers of the mind', but otherwise neat, quiet and civil. She died in Bethlem in 1828, aged about seventy-eight.

In 1790 John Frith threw a stone at George III's carriage as he proceeded to the state opening of Parliament. Frith too was a man with a history of unusual actions and statements, religious mania, and paranoid delusions concerning what the Crown owed him. Unlike Nicholson, he was brought to trial for his treason, although he denied wanting to harm the King. He was tried at the Old Bailey on 17 April 1790, where the jury told the judge that 'we are all of the opinion that the prisoner is quite insane.' Frith objected, demanding to see a physician, and claiming to be perfectly in his senses. However, he was subsequently remanded by the judge, sent to Bethlem, and latterly given over to the care of his friends.

Placing Nicholson and Frith in Bethlem or in the care of the community spoke to a contemporary ambiguity in the treatment and internment of mentally ill people dangerous to themselves or others. To be found not guilty by reason of insanity, as they were, was to be acquitted, and therefore set at liberty. Obviously, this could not stand, considering their deeds. So compromises were made – they were in effect made state prisoners, committed not by a magistrate but directly by the Privy Council using the Crown's prerogative powers, as people suspected of political treason were. They were sent to Bethlem under the same powers, or by a subsequent civil order, but the legality of such indefinite detention was shaky. It would be tested, and transformed, by Hadfield's case.

The story of Hadfield's life was a sad one. He had been a solider in the British Army and sustained multiple head wounds during the 1794 Battle of Tourcoing in northern France, an engagement against the French Republic. He was initially left for dead, then imprisoned by the French, who he said had flogged him and manacled him. Recounting his mistreatment before the Privy Council, Hadfield said he 'did not feel it ... his blood and bones [had] been let loose'. Returning to Britain, he showed signs of a total 'derangement'. His behaviour was noted as strange and occasionally violent by those who knew him. His wife at one point had to apply to the parish authorities for a straitjacket to restrain him. In his interviews, Hadfield reiterated again and again that he meant no harm to the King or anybody else; he had only pretended to aim at George, so that 'somebody would do for' him and bring about the death Hadfield desired for himself, by means other than suicide. Witnesses on the night, however, gave statements to the contrary, that Hadfield had seemed carefully and deliberately to aim at the King.

He was charged with high treason, one count of compassing and imagining the King's death, evidenced by overt acts detailing his premeditated assassination attempt in the theatre. His trial opened at the Court of King's Bench on 26 June 1800, with the Lord Chief Justice presiding. Hadfield was represented by Thomas Erskine, who had secured the acquittals of the members of the London Corresponding Society who had been tried for treason in 1794.

Erskine faced two challenges. Firstly, on the face of it Hadfield had committed treason. It seemed that he had been drawn into millenarian religious beliefs by Bannister Truelock, a shoemaker and religious fanatic who prophesised the Second Coming. Truelock had convinced Hadfield that if he were to die at the state's hands, punished as a traitor, he would bring about the return of the Messiah. Hadfield told the Privy Council that his dying for his crime would bring the apocalypse stating that, 'when he is at an end, the World is to be at an end'. So there had been a conspiracy with treasonable intent, which had been accompanied by overt acts to attempt to carry it out.

Secondly, despite Hadfield's clearly distressed mind, it was questionable whether he would be considered insane before the law, which set the test as someone being completely senseless and unable to consider the consequences of an act. Hadfield's own testimony belied this – however bizarre his reasoning, he had gone into the theatre calmly cognisant of what he had to do.

When the trial began, Erskine again proved his reputation as one of England's greatest and most significant advocates. Prior to the hearing he successfully requested that doctors specialising in mental illness interview Hadfield, so that he could use their expert testimony to support his argument for the defendant's insanity. He called witnesses, those who knew Hadfield and his habits, not just to testify to his odd behaviour and the dreadful effects of his injury, imprisonment and torture in France, but also to his loyalty to Britain and King George III. Erskine asserted in court that Hadfield's clear delusions, although 'unaccompanied by frenzy or raving madness', were still clearly evidence of his insanity. The judge made clear that the trial was moving towards an acquittal on those grounds.

The Crown prepared – their papers show that they consulted volumes of the *State Trials* for precedents such as Frith's, and also cases like that of Robert Nalcot, acquitted of murder in 1790 on grounds of insanity, but subsequently remanded and incarcerated due to the danger he posed at large.

The papers show their working in a draft of the order, with crossings-out, made by the Lord Chief Justice after the not guilty verdict. Hadfield's freedom, it decreed, was not consistent with the safety of the King or his subjects, due to his 'frequent fits of insanity', and he therefore could not be at liberty. Like Frith and Nicholson before him, he was destined to spend the rest of his life in Bethlem, where he died in 1841, aged sixty-nine or seventy. But his case, and the ambiguity of how to deal with it if he was acquitted, had a wider impact. Erskine's successful defence of the

London Corresponding Society radicals in 1794 had led to the refinement and tightening of treason law the following year. Now, his defence of Hadfield also changed the law.

Parliament initially attached terms to the 1800 Treason Act, which amended the way trials were conducted, to deal with cases where the defendant was found to be insane. But this was hived off into a separate piece of legislation, the Criminal Lunatics Act 1800. This provided that people charged with treason, murder and other serious crimes, if declared by the jury to be insane, were to be kept in 'strict custody ... until His Majesty's pleasure shall be known'. It was effectively a sentence of indefinite detention. The act would not be repealed until 1981.

Queen Victoria came to the throne in 1837, and in the course of her long reign faced at least seven attempts on her person and life. Again, these were often grounded in her would-be assailants' paranoia and delusions, and led to Parliament creating new treason laws to meet their threat.

On 3 June 1840 J. P. Rhoades boarded a coach from London to Chichester. The service was to stop at Epsom Racecourse along the way, the destination of one of his fellow passengers, a young man who throughout his journey conducted a one-sided conversation with the coach's guard. The man spoke of his habit of practising shooting with a rifle, then said something which shocked Rhoades: 'If the Queen was to die, there would be some fun for those of us fellows who have nothing to do.' The guard asked him how so, only to be told that if Victoria were to die then 'old Ernest' – Victoria's uncle, Ernest Augustus, King of Hanover, an unpopular figure in Britain – would, 'come over, and there would be a fine shindy [quarrel or fight] in the country then, and we should soon find something to do'.

Rhoades was disturbed but did not report the man's words to anyone. However, ten days later, he wrote to the Home Office about it. He had realised, reading the newspaper, that the man he was on the coach with was eighteen-year-old Edward Oxford, who had tried to shoot the Queen.

On 10 June 1840 at about 4 p.m., Queen Victoria and her husband,

Prince Albert, were riding in an open carriage down Constitution Hill, near Buckingham Palace, a regular occurrence. Oxford was waiting. Seeing them, he fired at them twice with two pistols, missing both times. He was restrained but seemed happy to admit what he had done and quite calm.

Oxford was arrested by the Metropolitan Police, then handed over to the Privy Council for examination. His statement to them was brief – he pointed out that witnesses to his deed did not agree on whether he shot with his left or right hand first, and how far away he was. He mentioned that after he fired his first pistol it seemed that Albert had stood up to confront him 'and sat down again, as if he thought better of it'. He would say no more.

He was charged with treason, for compassing and imagining Victoria's death by attempting to 'maliciously shoot' her. The Queen's journal recorded that Oxford had 'not appeared to be in the least mad; and was very impudent & flippant during the examination'.

But enquiries into Oxford's family and childhood revealed a more complicated picture. He had been born in Birmingham in 1822, although his parents moved to London soon afterwards. His father was possibly insane – he had apparently coerced Oxford's mother into marriage, and had at times threatened to kill her and himself, although it was possible that his heavy drinking, rather than mental illness, was the cause of this; he died in 1829. Oxford's own history, too, spoke of a disturbed mind. Accounts of his time at school and as an apprentice revealed 'extraordinary' conduct – he was at times cruel to other children, but then also capable of acts of great generosity. A 'singular boy ... mischievous and unmanageable', he was often observed laughing, but also nearly crying, seemingly at nothing. His former employer said he was 'hardly right'.

Oxford was tried at the Old Bailey on 6 July 1840. Like Hadfield's, his defence was not based on disproving his treasonable actions, but proving his insanity, inherited from his father, or otherwise. Again, the Crown consulted precedent in cases of treason and insanity, anticipating the defence's course. The Treasury Solicitor's papers for the case contain a note sent to the prosecution as the verdict was received – Oxford was found not guilty on grounds of insanity. In line with the Criminal Lunatics Act he was detained – first at Bethlem, then at Broadmoor in Berkshire, a purpose-built asylum for 'criminal lunatics', opened in 1863. Latterly, based on his good behaviour, he was allowed at liberty on condition that he left Britain. He lived out his days in Australia, where he died in 1900, aged seventy-eight.

Similar attempts on the Queen's life followed this first one. John Francis tried to shoot Victoria twice in 1842, successfully absconding but returning to attempt to shoot her again the next day, when he was arrested. Convicted of treason, he had his death sentence commuted to transportation, reflecting the bizarre and bungled nature of his crime and the increasing reluctance to carry out capital sentences. John William Bean tried the same year, but with a pistol loaded with paper and tobacco. He desired to be imprisoned in Bethlem or transported, possibly partly inspired by Oxford. He was imprisoned for a short time.

These all led to legislative changes. The 1842 Treason Act was specifically for 'the further Security and Protection of Her Majesty's Person'. It regulated the trials of those who made direct attempts against the sovereign, and also explicitly codified the punishment for treason involving the discharge of firearms 'with Intent to injure or alarm Her Majesty', setting the penalty at transportation or imprisonment. It made clear, however, that it did not set out to alter the punishments set for high treason and misprision of treason. However, the reluctance to impose such terrible sentences as required by treason on deluded individuals and political actors led to the passage of the 1848 Treason Felony Act, which allowed for those convicted to be sentenced to transportation or imprisonment rather than the gallows. Once again, treason's history was one of reaction to the changes in society.

Part IV

TREASON
OVERSEAS

.

BY THE KING

A PROCLAMATION,

For fuppreffing Rebellion and Sedition.

GEORGE R.

WHEREAS many of our Subjects in divers Parts of our Colonies and Plantations in *North-America*, milled by dangerous and ill-defigning Men, and forgetting the Allegiance which they owe to the Power that has protected and fuftained them, after various difor-derly Acts committed in Difturbance of the publick Peace, to the Obftruction of lawful Commerce, and to the Oppreffion of our loyal Subjects carrying on the fame, have at length proceeded to an open and avowed Rebellion, by arraying themfelves in hoftile Manner to withftand the Execution of the Law, and traitoroufly preparing, ordering, and levying War againft Us; AND WHEREAS there is Reafon to apprehend that fuch Rebellion hath been much promoted and encouraged by the traitorous Correfpondence, Counfels and Comfort of divers wicked and defperate Perfons within this Realm: To THE END THEREFORE that none of our Subjects may neglect or violate their Duty through Igno-rance thereof, or through any Doubt of the Protection which the Law will afford to their Loyalty and Zeal; We have thought fit, by and with the Advice of our Privy Council, to iffue this our Royal Proclamation, hereby declaring that not only all our Officers civil and military are obliged to exert their utmoft Endeavours to fupprefs fuch Rebellion, and to bring the Traitors to Juftice; but that all our Subjects of this Realm and the Dominions thereunto belonging are bound by Law to be aiding and affifting in the Suppreffion of fuch Rebellion, and to difclofe and make known all traitorous Confpiracies and Attempts againft Us, Our Crown and Dignity; And we do accordingly ftrictly charge and command all our Officers as well civil as military, and all other our obedient and loyal Subjects to ufe their utmoft Endeavours to withftand and fupprefs fuch Rebellion, and to difclofe and make known all Treafons and traitorous Confpiracies which they fhall know to be againft Us, Our Crown and Dignity; and for that Purpofe, that they tranfmit to one of our principal Secretaries of State, or other proper Officer, due and full Information of all Perfons who fhall be found carrying on Correfpondence with, or in any Manner or Degree aiding or abetting the Perfons now in open Arms and Rebellion againft our Government within any of our Colonies and Plantations in *North-America*, in order to bring to condign Punifhment the Authors, Perpetrators, and Abettors of fuch traitorous Defigns.

GIVEN at our Court at St. James's, the twenty-third Day of August, *One Thoufand Seven Hundred and Seventy-five, in the fifteenth Year of our Reign.*

A Royal Proclamation for 'Suppressing Rebellion and Sedition', issued by George III on 23 August 1775, denouncing the American rebels as traitors and encouraging his loyal subjects in the colonies to bring these people to justice. (CO 5/993)

Fourteen

TREASON IN AMERICA, 1672–1794

O n 4 July 1776, the thirteen colonies of British North America declared themselves independent from British rule. To the British Crown, up until that point they had been treasonous subjects, levying war against the King in his dominions; George III had issued a proclamation in August 1775 decrying the rebels as such. To the founding fathers of the United States, they were rejecting the tyranny of an unjust king, just as the High Court of Justice in England had done when they tried (and executed) Charles I over a century earlier.

When the 1352 Statute of Treasons was first enacted, the definition of a treasonous act was relatively straightforward, limited to crimes against the king's person or his ability to rule within his kingdom. By the eighteenth century, although the 1352 Act continued to be the foundation of treason law, the world was much changed. Events in the sixteenth and seventeenth centuries had seen treason shift from crimes against the person of the king or queen to crimes against the state. England (and later Britain) had amassed a global empire, which raised questions about the applicability of treason in these colonial states. The American Revolution, and the final decades of British colonial rule in that region, brought into focus the challenges of applying treason laws overseas.

As colonies, the British North American territories had their own laws against rebellion, sedition, and traitorous acts, similar to the terms of the 1352 Treason Act, although these crimes were not specifically defined as treason. Listed among the capital offences in a 1672 book of laws for the jurisdiction of Connecticut was the crime of conspiring or attempting 'any invasion, insurrection, or public rebellion against this colony', or attempting to subvert the 'frame of government fundamentally established by his majesty's gracious charter' by betraying the same into the hands of any foreign power.

Thirty years later, Connecticut's 1702 book of acts included an Act Against High Treason, virtually identical in wording to the 1352 English Treason Act:

> Be it enacted by the Governor, Council and Representatives in General Court assembled, and it is hereby enacted and ordained by the authority of the same; that if any person or persons, shall compass or imagine the death of our sovereign lord the King, or of our lady the Queen, or of the heir apparent to the Crown; or if any person shall levy war against our lord the King, or be adherent to the King's enemies, giving them aid ... [then they] shall be deemed, declared, and adjudged, to be traitors, and shall suffer pains of death, and also lose and forfeit as in cases of High Treason.
>
> ACTS AND LAWS OF HIS MAJESTY'S COLONY OF CONNECTICUT IN NEW ENGLAND, 1702. CO 5/537

In colonial America, treason was still predominantly a crime against the monarch. It was also influenced by political events and upheavals in England. After 1664, when English forces took control of the Dutch colony New Netherland – which included the areas now known as New York, New Jersey, Delaware, and Connecticut – Charles II gave the territory to his brother James, Duke of York. James succeeded his brother in 1685 and established the Dominion of New England the following year; the new king appointed governors to attempt to centralise control of the region. This was a deeply unpopular move in the North American colonies because it revoked several of their colonial charters.

When James II was replaced by William of Orange during the Glorious Revolution of 1688, years of pent-up resentment against James and his governors sparked uprisings and rebellions in the American colonies. In 1689, a popular uprising took place in Boston against the rule of Sir Edmund Andros, the Governor of the Dominion of New England. Andros had been appointed by James II, who had been deposed as king, so the rebels saw an opportunity to remove Crown officials in Boston, the capital of the dominion.

Andros was overthrown and the New England colonies made moves to restore the governmental structures that they had enjoyed before James II had annulled their charters. An early sign that the North American colonies – though loyal to the English Crown – expected a certain degree of self-governance, and would vehemently defend their liberties (as they saw them) against tyranny and bad government.

New York, too, experienced rebellion in the aftermath of the Glorious Revolution. Francis Nicholson, lieutenant governor of the dominion, had learnt of the Boston revolt and the usurpation of James II and attempted to keep the news quiet, for fear that similar uprisings would occur in New York. Nicholson was also under pressure to improve New York's defences; France had declared war on England, which renewed the threat of attacks on New York's northern borders with what is now Canada, much of which had been colonised by the French. Nicholson made himself even more unpopular by attempting to impose import duties to pay for improved defences, and by making enemies of the town militia.

Events came to a head in May 1689, when the militia called on Jacob Leisler, a German-born merchant and captain of the militia, to seize control of Fort James, at the southern end of Manhattan Island. He did so, issuing a declaration that they would hold the fort until a properly accredited governor – appointed by the new monarchs, William III and Mary II – arrived. Nicholson left for England, and Leisler then attempted to consolidate power in the province. The council in the province did not recognise Leisler's authority, and a proclamation sent by William and Mary gave the council permission to continue operating while Nicholson was absent. However, Leisler marched on the customs house with a troop of militia, effectively driving out the council and giving him control. Delegates from the local area then accepted Leisler as the province's leader, until further orders were received from William and Mary.

Even so, Leisler had not been granted any official commission from the King and Queen to govern the area. In fact, he had usurped and driven out the most recent Crown appointments; although they had been appointed by a now-deposed monarch, they were the closest legitimate rulers of the province. The longer Leisler governed without a royal commission, the greater risk he ran of falling foul of treason.

In December 1689, Leisler received a letter from William and Mary addressed to Nicholson or, in his absence, to whomsoever would preserve the peace and administer the laws in New York. Leisler claimed this legitimised his position, and began to rule as 'lieutenant governor'. He maintained control of the region throughout 1690.

However, late in 1690 William III finally commissioned a new governor for New York, Henry Sloughter. Sloughter's lieutenant governor, Richard Ingoldesby, arrived first in January 1691, but since he did not hold official documents of his (or Sloughter's) commission, Leisler refused to yield power. From January to March 1691, Ingoldesby and Leisler fought in minor skirmishes for control of Fort James. Leisler still controlled the local militia and so was able to resist Ingoldesby. When Sloughter arrived in New York in March, still Leisler refused immediately to acknowledge the former's commission from the King. When Leisler did eventually surrender, Sloughter had him arrested on charges of treason.

It was Leisler's militant resistance to Ingoldesby that brought his crimes within the scope of treason. In denying the authority of a Crown-appointed official, and, worse still, in rejecting this authority with a military force, Leisler – it could be argued – had levied war against the Crown. He was sentenced to death and executed on 16 May 1691.

In the fallout of Leisler's Rebellion, a provincial act was passed in

New York that provided that any person who disturbed the peace of government, by force of arms or otherwise, would be deemed a traitor. But Leisler had many sympathisers. He had been motivated to act against James II and his governors; in that respect, he shared a common aim of William and Mary.

In 1702, another treason trial occurred in New York that centred on the 1691 provincial treason act, although it also cited interpretations of English treason legislation. The man on trial, Colonel Nicholas Bayard, had actually been involved with the trial and subsequent execution of Leisler, and had sponsored the 1691 New York treason law.

Bayard's alleged crime was drawing up and distributing petitions to the Crown, the House of Commons, and Lord Cornbury (the incoming governor), accusing Lieutenant Governor Nanfan and other members of the ruling committees in New York of bribery and oppression. Bayard was accused of persuading people to sign these petitions in the town's coffeehouse. His warrant charged him with disturbing the peace, 'by force of arms or other ways', technically a treasonable offence according to the 1691 act; his accusers argued that in conspiring to draw in soldiers and others to sign scandalous libels, he was undermining the authority of the monarch's elected government in New York.

This case for high treason was a weak one, however. When the offending petition was sent to New York's Attorney General Samuel Broughton for his opinion, he responded that there was nothing illegal in the document. Regardless of this, Nanfan and some of his council members issued an arrest warrant. Keen to expedite the trial process, they convened a special court of oyer and terminer rather than wait until the next appointed session of the province's Supreme Court.

Broughton refused to prosecute, as he'd already asserted that there was nothing criminal in the petition. Instead, Thomas Weaver, temporarily appointed Solicitor General, presided and proceeded to trial. Bayard pleaded not guilty to the treason charge, and complained of the partisan composition of the bench; all three of the judges sat on the governor's council, and had signed the warrant for his arrest. The prosecution easily established that papers had been signed at the coffeehouse, but proving that Bayard was responsible for soliciting signatures, or that these papers contained treasonous material, was another matter entirely.

By the time Bayard's defence was allowed to the stand, it was clear that the 1681 New York Treason Act was being misused and misinterpreted to satisfy a personal grudge. As such, Bayard's attorney, James Emott, issued a lengthy submission to the court, considering the place of the English law of treason in the colonies. The key argument for the defence was that even if these acts were proved, they were not treasonable. Aggrieved subjects always had the right to petition the king, without fear of committing treason. Emott argued that the 1691 New York law on which Bayard's indictment rested contravened English common law governing cases of treason, citing the English jurist Sir Edward Coke's interpretations of the treason law in his legal treatise, *Institutes of the Lawes of England*. This work remains relevant in the US today, and has been cited in over seventy cases decided by the Supreme Court of the United States.

However, William Atwood, Chief Justice of the New York Supreme Court, ignored much of this defence plea, asking (after several days' deliberation) that the jurors base their judgement only on the facts of the case (i.e., was Bayard involved in the production of the pamphlets?) rather than whether these acts constituted treason. Since this was much easier to prove, Bayard was found guilty of producing the petitions and soliciting signatures. Atwood then sentenced Bayard to be hanged, drawn, and quartered, as was customary for convicted traitors.

Despite this wilful misconstruing of treason law, Bayard's enemies did not succeed in having him executed. He was granted a stay of execution until the Crown could confirm they were happy with the verdict. When Lord Cornbury, the new governor, arrived in New York, he reversed Bayard's attainder and suspended Atwood from office.

As part of the British Empire, the North American provinces demonstrated a strong desire and ability to self-govern, while at the same time respecting the Crown and being vigilant of threats to it. Their treason acts were based on English common law and protected the monarch's interests from would-be traitors and usurpers. As the eighteenth century progressed, however, ideological differences between Americans and the British Government concerning sovereignty and – by extension – treason, put the North American states on the path to independence.

By the 1760s, Britain had emerged as the dominant force in the eastern half of North America. The Treaty of Paris of 1763 removed France – Britain's main rival on the continent up to that point – from North America. However, these new territories required defending. Historically, the British Government and the Crown turned to taxing the locals to raise money for defence. This was one of the core causes of Charles I's unpopularity, who sought to find ways to raise money without the need to refer to Parliament. In the case of North America, the British Government concluded that as these territories were in North America, the other British provinces in America should help meet the cost of defending them. The first of several Acts of Parliament aimed at increasing revenue from Americans was the 1764 Sugar Act. This updated the 1733 Molasses Act, enforcing the collection of duties on certain products, including sugar. The wording of the bill made it clear that this was a revenue-raising act. Though the act was not popular in the colonies – it arrived during a period of economic depression – its unpopularity was for economic reasons, rather than ideological ones about unlawful taxation of the provinces.

The same could not be said for the Duties in American Colonies Act – widely known as the Stamp Act – enacted a year later in 1765. This imposed a direct tax on almost every form of paper used in the colonies. Legal documents, bonds, deeds, newspapers, even playing cards, were all required to be produced on a particular stamped paper produced in London, carrying an embossed revenue stamp. Again, the British Government claimed that this act was to repay the expenses of the Seven Years' War – known as the French and Indian War in America – which had ended in 1763, and to raise revenue to defend the British territories in America from future invasion.

This was the first time the home government had levied a direct tax on this scale in the colonies, and it was fiercely rejected. Articles against the tax were published in American newspapers, protests occurred throughout the provinces, and American colonists threatened to boycott any imports of British goods until the act was repealed. This act was objectionable on a constitutional level. How could the British Government be justified in levying a direct tax on the American colonies, which were not represented in Parliament? The slogan 'No taxation without representation' was adopted. But the fallout from the Stamp Act went further. Colonial governments began seriously to consider the relationship between the colonies and the Crown. The seeds of American independence had been sown.

At a Continental Congress (also known as the Stamp Act Congress) held in New York in October 1765, attended by representatives from a number of the British colonies in America, these ideas started to germinate: 'It is inseparably essential to the freedom of a people, and the undoubted rights of Englishmen ... that no taxes should be imposed on them, but with their own consent, given personally, or by their representatives.' Americans were not represented in the House of Commons, and should therefore only be represented and taxed by persons, chosen by themselves, in their respective provincial legislatures.

The parliamentary position was thus: everyone within the British dominions is virtually represented by Parliament, even if they have no elected members, just as domestic subjects in Britain who did not have the vote – the majority of the population – were represented.

Sensing that they may have underestimated the opposition to the Stamp Act, Parliament summoned the Pennsylvania Assembly's London lobbyist, Benjamin Franklin, to answer the many questions they had. His answers – published shortly afterwards as a pamphlet – showed just how much damage the Stamp Act had caused to the relationship between Great Britain and its American colonies. Where once America 'submitted willingly to the government of the Crown, and paid, in all their courts, obedience to acts of parliament', now they questioned whether that obedience was misplaced. The colonists used to consider the Parliament of Great Britain 'the great bulwark and security of their liberties and privileges, and always spoke of it with the utmost respect and veneration'; now their respect for the institution was 'greatly lessened'.

Franklin reaffirmed to the House of Commons that, to the American people, the Stamp Act was an infringement of their rights. By their provincial charters, granted by the Crown, the American colonies were entitled to all the privileges and liberties of Englishmen, including the freedom from non-consensual taxation. When this was questioned, Franklin responded that 'the common rights of Englishmen, as declared by Magna Charta, and the petition of right, all justify it.'

Franklin was asked 174 questions in total, with Members of Parliament trying to find any inconsistency in his argument that would allow them to justify upholding the Stamp Act. They could not, however, and in March 1766 the Act was repealed. Despite this victory for the colonists, however, Parliament wanted to ensure that they would be able to enforce laws and taxation on the colonies in future – regardless of the opinion of the people in those provinces – and so enacted the 1766 Declaratory Act, which asserted the government's right to pass laws in the colonies 'in all cases whatsoever'. Nevertheless, the American territories celebrated. The Stamp Act was repealed and the Declaratory Act was acceptable – as long as Parliament did not enforce it.

In 1767 and 1768, Parliament once again attempted to tax the American colonies without their consent. The Townshend Duties – named after Charles Townshend, the Chancellor of the Exchequer – proposed new taxes on all lead, glass, paint, and tea imported into the colonies. Again, Americans protested; in Boston, hundreds refused to purchase any of the taxed British imports. Many of these Townshend Duties were subsequently repealed in 1770, barring the duty on tea.

Parliament's actions had prompted the American colonies to develop further their own ideas of sovereignty. In 1768, John Dickinson's *Letters from a Farmer* argued that though Parliament rightly had power over the American colonies, it only did so in the context of empire; although it could regulate commerce, it did not have the power to tax the colonists. Rights to levy tax were reserved for the national, not imperial, authority. A national sovereignty, separate to an imperial one, was articulated. As the reign of Charles I had demonstrated, ideas of split sovereignty could often lead to revolution, particularly when both sides believed themselves to be right.

By the eighteenth century, 'levying war' against the monarch, one of the key treasonable acts of the 1352 statutes could be construed not only as directly rebelling against the monarch in order to dethrone them, but also violently or forcibly rebelling against the Crown's lawful authority or endeavouring to reform the government. All laws were passed in the monarch's name; to reject any could be construed as treason. To some in Parliament, American resistance to what they viewed as lawful government could therefore constitute treason, and from the late 1760s British officials favoured the idea that colonial resistance was a treasonous act. They hoped that making an extreme example of a few rebels would bring the majority in line. They did not want to lose face in the same way that they had by backtracking over the Stamp Act.

In November 1768, George III made a speech to Parliament, alarmed by the 'acts of violence' and 'resistance to the execution of the law' that was occurring in the American colonies. The town of Boston was a particular concern, appearing 'to be in a state of disobedience to all law and government, and has proceeded to measures subversive of the constitution, and attended with circumstances that manifest a disposition to throw off their dependence on Great Britain.' The King authorised the dispatch of troops to Boston to deal with the rising lawlessness.

Parliament viewed the actions of the Boston dissidents as treasonous, and accordingly passed a resolution that would allow traitors in the American colonies to be arrested and transported to England for trial. The Governor of Massachusetts was to take the most effectual methods to investigate all treasons committed in the province and to transport all those accused of treason to England for trial. A statute made in the reign of Henry VIII – an Act for the Trial of Treasons Committed out of the King's Dominions – originally designed to bring Irish traitors to Westminster for trial, was used as legal precedent for these measures.

There were those in Parliament, however, who thought these steps foolhardy at best, and incitement to further disobedience at worst, 'more calculated to promote rather than to prevent rebellion'. In addition, when the Massachusetts General Court learnt of the proposal to remove colonists to England for trial, they complained to the King. The province had its own treason laws, based on England's, and their courts had the jurisdiction to try any of their residents; just as the residents had the right to be tried by a jury of their peers. To deny either of these was 'highly derogatory of the rights of British subjects'. As with their right to tax themselves, the American colonies also had the right to administer (the King's) justice among themselves.

For all Parliament's bluster, none of the colonists who resisted imperial authority in these years was formally charged with treason or prosecuted for it; in most cases, these rebellions did not constitute treasonable acts. Yet tensions between the American colonists and imperial officers remained strained, as Parliament continued to attempt to impose duties on the colonies. In June 1772, a group of Rhode Island colonists set fire to and destroyed HMS *Gaspee*. The customs schooner had been posted to America to help enforce the Navigation Acts, English laws that regulated trade between Britain and its overseas territories. Lieutenant William Dudingston of the *Gaspee* had made enemies of the locals by being overzealous in his searches of merchant ships for smugglers and by raiding local farms for supplies for his ship. The crew of the *Gaspee*, who had been removed from the schooner before it was destroyed, reported to Admiral John Montagu – based in Boston – who commanded British naval forces in North America. Wishing to know how to proceed, Montagu sent these reports to the Earl of Hillsborough, the Secretary of State for the Colonies, who in turn forwarded these papers to the Attorney General, Edward Thurlow, and the Solicitor General, Alexander Wedderburn, asking for their legal opinions; specifically, was the incident an act of high treason? Thurlow and Wedderburn responded that they considered the destruction of the *Gaspee* treasonous:

> [We are] of the opinion that the attack made in the manner it was upon His Majesty's Commission was an act of high treason vizt of levying war against His Majesty & that the offenders may be indicted of the high treason either here or in Rhode Island taking that assertion of the Gov'nr to be true that the ship was stationed within the body of some county in that province.
> CO 5/1284

Yet, despite this legal advice, no one was indicted for the destruction of the *Gaspee*. The King appointed five commissioners to investigate the incident, who all hailed from the colonies. Though these officials could investigate the affair and question witnesses, a trial couldn't proceed without the cooperation of the colony's law officers. Either a Rhode Island grand jury needed to hand down indictments, or the colony's attorney general had to issue the commissioners with a list of accused to stand trial. When neither of these happened, presumably because local sympathies lay with the colonists threatened with being tried for high treason, the commission gave up and the perpetrators went unpunished. Admiral Montagu lamented that 'British Acts of Parliament never go down in America unless forced by the point of a sword'.

Still, too, the debate over the proper location of sovereignty in the American colonies raged on, with neither side willing to compromise. In January 1773, Governor Thomas Hutchinson of Massachusetts gave a speech to the two houses of the Massachusetts legislature, in an attempt to persuade them that Parliament held sovereignty over the colonies. To his mind, there could not be two independent legislatures in one single state, and to declare as such would be to declare that America was as separate from Britain as England and Scotland had been before the 1707 Act of Union. The Massachusetts House of Representatives called his bluff:

> If there be no such line, the consequence is, either that the colonies
> are the vassals of parliament, or, that they are totally independent.
> As it cannot be supposed to have been the intention of the parties in
> the compact, that we should be reduced to a state of vassalage, the
> conclusion is, that it was their sense, that we were thus independent.
> THE SPEECHES OF HIS EXCELLENCY GOVERNOR HUTCHINSON, TO THE
> GENERAL ASSEMBLY OF THE MASSACHUSETTS BAY...WITH THE ANSWERS (1773)

As part of these debates, John Adams – Founding Father and later the
second President of the independent United States of America – gave
a long and detailed legal justification to Hutchinson of the colonists'
claim of independence from Parliament. The colonies still considered
themselves subjects of the King; it was only Parliament's sovereignty that
they rejected in favour of their own. This became a common theme of
the patriotic pamphlets written by Benjamin Franklin, Thomas Jefferson,
Alexander Hamilton, and Adams himself.

By the end of 1773, Governor Hutchinson had to contend with another
rejection of British parliamentary taxes on the colonies, when a group of
Boston rebels destroyed an entire shipment of tea as a protest against the
Tea Act. As with the earlier *Gaspee* incident, reports were submitted to
the Attorney General and Solicitor General. Again, they adjudged the acts
treasonous and recommended that trials be pursued, either in the colonies
or by bringing the accused over to England. And, once again, the Crown's
officers in North America found it difficult to prosecute, in the face of
underwhelming support; there was no desire among the colonists to see
those protesting against the controversial taxes punished.

With Parliament unable to prosecute individuals, the government
were forced to impose sanctions on the whole of the town and province.
In March 1774, Parliament closed the port of Boston until such time as
they paid for the tea they had destroyed the previous December. In May,
the King approved the suspension of the Massachusetts government.
This only antagonised the aggrieved colonists further. In the counties of
Massachusetts, their leaders met to discuss how best to respond to these

sanctions. The Suffolk County Resolves denounced the acts passed by the British Parliament to punish Massachusetts, dubbed the Intolerable Acts. To their mind, these actions violated the British constitution. They therefore resolved, along with the other counties in Massachusetts: to boycott British imports; to demand resignations of all those appointed to positions under the (unconstitutional) Massachusetts Government Act; not to pay any taxes until said act was repealed; to support an independent colonial government in Massachusetts until such time as the Intolerable Acts were repealed; and to encourage other colonies to follow suit and raise militia of their own people.

To make matters worse for the British government, the other American colonies had watched the imperial actions in Massachusetts with alarm, and were mobilising to respond collectively to the British government's actions. In September 1774, twelve of the thirteen British colonies that would later form the United States of America met at the First Continental Congress. They received the Suffolk Resolves, and agreed to impose an economic boycott on British trade, until such time as the Intolerable Acts were repealed. The Congress drew up a petition to the King, outlining their grievances: they wished the freedom to self-govern, as was their constitutional right; they did not, and would never, accept that they could be directly taxed by Parliament; and they thought it unlawful that the 1543 Treason Act (35 Hen VIII c 2), which allowed those suspected of treason to be sent to England for trial, was being applied in the colonies. They resolved to reconvene in May 1775 if their petition was not answered satisfactorily.

Hutchinson left for England in June 1774. His replacement, Thomas Gage, did little to ease tensions in North America. On his arrival, discovering that it was nigh on impossible to enforce Parliament's controversial acts against the colonies, Gage proceeded to accuse dissenters of treason and increase the military presence in Boston. The colonists' response to these accusations showed a hardened resolve against such sanctions; ideas of independence were now very much a reality to the oppressed American colonies:

Your excellency [Gage] is too well acquainted with the human heart, not to be sensible that it is natural for the people to be soured by oppression, and jealous for their personal security, when their exertions for the preservation of their rights are construed into treason and rebellion. Our liberties are invaded by acts of the British parliament, troops are sent to enforce those acts. They are now erecting fortification at the entrance of the town of Boston, upon completing those, the inhabitants of the town of Boston will be in the power of a soldiery, who must implicitly obey the orders of an administration who have hitherto evidenced no singular regard to the liberties of America.

Printed in the Georgia Gazette no 578, Wed 2 Nov 1774. CO 5/664

In February 1775 the King declared Massachusetts to be in rebellion, and Gage was authorised to use force to restore British rule. The battles of Lexington and Concord in April marked the beginning of armed hostilities between Britain and America. When the Continental Congress met again in May, the only 'response' to their 1774 petition had been this military show of force by the British Crown; they took this to be a declaration of war. By the end of 1775, the King had proclaimed that all Britain's North American colonies were in a state of 'open and avowed Rebellion ... arraying themselves in hostile manner to withstand the execution of the law, and traitorously preparing, ordering, and levying war against us'. In short, the American rebels were now treasonous.

At home, George III and his government were forced to take a strong stand against those speaking or writing in support of the American rebels, or criticising the imperial treatment of the colonists. London printers were brought before the Court of King's Bench to account for why they had printed works designed to 'alienate and withdraw the affection, fidelity, and allegiance of his said majesty's subjects from his said majesty'. Reports of the battles of Lexington and Concord published in London described the attacks by the British troops as inhumane, leading to the murder of the King's subjects; such dissent needed to be stamped out.

To the Americans in rebellion, they were merely defending themselves from tyranny and unjust rule. In this way the American rebels
were in the same position as the Parliamentarians who had fought
against Charles I in the 1640s. They were fighting against infringements
upon their sovereign rights. The civil wars of the 1640s had resulted in
the treason trial and execution of the King. In 1776, Americans were
coming around to the view that their true goal was to free themselves
from the shackles of imperial rule.

A key text in advancing the idea of American independence was
Thomas Paine's *Common Sense*, first published in pamphlet form in
America in January 1776. Paine argued for an independent America.
The skirmishes which had already occurred in the colonies showed
that America had the means and resources to defeat the British;
they had nothing to gain (and everything to lose) from remaining
part of the Empire. In just two months, 120,000 copies of *Common
Sense* had been sold, proclaiming the ideals of independence to the
American people.

Once the American colonies set independence as their final goal, the
language of their proclamations changed, from defending themselves
against accusations of treason to accusing those who aided and abetted
their enemies of the same. On 24 June 1776, just two weeks before it
adopted the Declaration of Independence, the Second Continental
Congress passed a resolution amending the definition of treason so that it
could be applied in defence of the American colonies:

Resolved ... that all persons, members of, or owing allegiance to
any of the United Colonies, as before described, who shall levy war
against any of the said colonies within the same, or be adherent to
the king of Great Britain, or others the enemies of the said colonies,
or any of them, within the same, giving to him or them aid and
comfort, are guilty of treason against such colony.

JOURNALS OF THE CONTINENTAL CONGRESS, P. 475

'The unanimous Declaration of the thirteen united State of America' – the Declaration of Independence – marked the culmination of the debates surrounding the sovereignty of the American colonies. In the declaration, the thirteen colonies proclaimed that they regarded themselves as

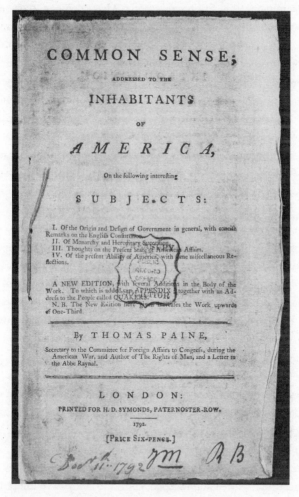

Title Page of *Common Sense* by Thomas Paine, first published in 1776, in which Paine encourages the American people to declare themselves independent from British rule. (*TS 24/3/5*)

independent sovereign states, no longer under British rule. As with Charles I's judges before them, the American colonies felt compelled to this course of action in defence of their rights against a tyrant:

> Governments are instituted among Men, deriving their just powers from the consent of the governed ... whenever any Form of Government becomes destructive of these ends, it is the Right of the People to alter or to abolish it, and to institute new Government, laying its foundation on such principles and organizing its powers in such form, as to them shall seem most likely to effect their Safety and Happiness ... The history of the present King of Great Britain is a history of repeated injuries and usurpations, all having in direct object the establishment of an absolute Tyranny over these States. To prove this, let Facts be submitted to a candid world.
> AMERICAN DECLARATION OF INDEPENDENCE

George III's refusal to allow the colonies to self-govern was a key charge, along with his support in subjecting them to jurisdictions 'foreign to our constitution'. Their complaints about parliamentary taxation had gone unresolved for years, and the attempts by the British government to try Americans in England were – they claimed – an infringement upon their rights to trial by their peers. The King's actions in taking away provincial charters, abolishing their laws, and suspending their legislatures, were not the actions of a just ruler, but a despot.

The articles most similar to the charges levied against Charles I more than a century earlier were the accusations that George III had waged war against the people of America, plundering their seas, ravaging their coasts, burning their towns, and destroying their lives. In short, the King had levied war against the colonies and incited domestic insurrections against them, undeniably treasonable acts. The declaration ends with the statement that 'as free and independent states, they have full power to levy war, conclude peace, contract alliances, establish commerce, and to do all other acts and things which independent states may of right do.'

Unsurprisingly, the British did not accept this declaration, and George III would continue to claim dominion over the United States until the 1783 Treaty of Paris ended the American Revolutionary War and acknowledged the US as independent sovereign states. Until then, the British government continued to treat the American states as rebellious colonies, attempting to impose law on the region and prosecute rebels. In 1776, Parliament passed the 'Act to empower his Majesty to secure and detain persons charged with, or suspected of, the Crime of High Treason, committed in any of his Majesty's Colonies or Plantations in America, or on the High Seas, or the Crime of Piracy'. This suspended the rights of habeas corpus to anyone suspected of treason in America, and empowered Crown officers to arrest and bring the suspects to England for trial. The Habeas Corpus Suspension Act, as it was also known, was only a temporary measure; to enforce it in perpetuity would go against the rights and liberties as enshrined in Magna Carta. However, it was extended year on year from 1776 until 1782, while Britain continued to claim dominion over the American states. In America, the British Crown still offered pardons to rebellious subjects.

All the while, the newly independent United States developed its own laws. They may have been free from British rule, but they still relied on English common law precedent to shape the legal system. The language of treason had been used to declare independence; now it needed to be used to consolidate power. Enemies of the state still existed, and therefore treason legislation was still necessary. The treason clause of the US Constitution, created in September 1787, was the only criminal law in the US founding document. The Constitution followed the pattern of treason legislation passed in colonial America – that is, adapting the 1352 Treason Act (though removing any mention of protecting the head of state):

Treason against the United States, shall consist only in levying War against them, or in adhering to their Enemies, giving them Aid and Comfort. No Person shall be convicted of Treason unless on the Testimony of two Witnesses to the same overt Act, or on Confession in open Court. The Congress shall have Power to declare the Punishment of Treason, but no Attainder of Treason shall work Corruption of Blood, or Forfeiture except during the Life of the Person attainted.

THE CONSTITUTION OF THE UNITED STATES, ARTICLE III, SECTION 3

This was a shrewd move by the authors of the Constitution. Edward III's treason statute was – by the eighteenth century – so enshrined in criminal law that its clauses were not open to interpretation; any debates over specific phrasing in the statute had been settled long before. America's treason legislation, in mirroring the wording of the 1352 Act, thus granted the new legislation a well-settled interpretation from the start.

The most famous treason against this new United States was that of Benedict Arnold, the American major general who, in 1780, during the War of Independence, defected to the British side. Arnold's name became synonymous with treachery in the United States, his betrayal seen as far worse than any treason before it. The sovereign whom Arnold betrayed was not a single person, but the whole citizenry of the United States; 'Judas sold only one Man, Arnold three Millions'. The personal betrayal was felt throughout the United States. Just a week after Arnold's betrayal was uncovered, on 30 September 1780, an effigy of the traitor was paraded through the streets of Philadelphia and burned on High Street Hill. In Benedict Arnold the Americans had found their Guy Fawkes. The general populace may not have understood the intricacies of treason in the common law, but they understood Arnold's crime.

Taxation of the populace was also still a delicate issue. In the 1790s, the Whiskey Rebellion – a protest against US legislation, the 1791 Excise Act – saw the resurgence of familiar arguments about whether such rebellions were treasonous. As with the highly contentious Stamp Act and Tea Act, the justification for the whiskey tax was to generate revenue for the war debt. Local farmers – who resisted the tax – argued that this was another example of taxation without local representation; the very charges levelled against the British Parliament after the introduction of the Stamp Act in

1765. The sometimes violent protests continued for three years. Events came to a head in 1794, when several hundred armed men in Western Pennsylvania attacked the home of a tax inspector, General John Neville, and burned it to the ground.

President George Washington asked his Attorney General, William Bradford, for legal advice regarding the protests. Bradford – like the British Attorney General before him – concluded that the protests were acts of high treason against the United States for levying war against them. Washington issued a proclamation in August 1794 calling on the insurgents to desist, and amassed a militia of 13,000 men to quell any remaining rebels. Thirty-five rebels were indicted for levying war against the United States, making this the first judicial consideration of the US Constitution's treason law. In the end, only two men – John Mitchell and Philip Vigol – were convicted of high treason; sentenced to death by hanging, they were later pardoned by President Washington.

In the first twenty years of the independent United States, treason law was used to stabilise the new nation. Rebellions were suppressed through threats of charging the perpetrators with treason, although even when individuals were convicted, the government favoured pardons over death sentences. The treachery of Benedict Arnold against the American people as a whole brought them together against traitors to the state.

The history of treason in the American colonies highlights the challenges of maintaining law when the centre of government is thousands of miles away. Like Charles I before them, the British Government underestimated the sovereign authority that the American colonial governments held, accrued (legally) through provincial charters. The United States were successful in their 'treason' of usurping the authority of George III in America; they had shown the world how to resist tyranny.

For Britain, which had many more colonies with similar ideas of personal sovereignty, the challenges of imposing law overseas were just beginning.

A map of the island of Grenada, c. 1796. Described as a 'Ceded' island, the plan is a revision of a French one of 1763, but with anglicised place names shown. (CO 700/GRENADA8)

Fifteen

DEPREDATIONS, GRENADA, 1795–6

The events of history often lead to the islands. Perhaps it would
be more accurate to say that they make use of them.

FERNAND BRAUDEL

In July 1796 Alexander Houstoun, recently arrived Governor of the British colony of Grenada, an island in the Lesser Antilles of the Caribbean Sea, wrote to his superior, the Home Secretary, the Duke of Portland, (after the loss of the American colonies, the office of Colonial Secretary was abolished, and the Home secretary became responsible for the colonies) to report on the distressed condition of the island.

Grenada had been gripped by a brutal rebellion since 2 March 1795, when a French-backed rebel force of predominantly francophone free black, white and enslaved Grenadians led by Julien Fédon launched surprise attacks on the ports of Charlotte Town and Grenville, capturing the incumbent Governor, Ninian Home, in the process. Over a year of attritional, scorched-earth warfare had followed: plantations were burned, Home and other prisoners executed, enslaved people on both sides of the dispute were massacred, civilians were murdered, people went hungry, disease and heavy storms wreaked havoc.

However, Houstoun's arrival had coincided with the arrival of one of largest armies ever sent across the Atlantic by the British, despatched to secure the island and Britain's strategic interests in the Caribbean.

Things were looking up – the 'Insurgents'' stronghold had been captured, many rebels had been killed, and others had fled into the forests. Houstoun was reasonably sanguine about the colony's return to relative 'tranquillity'.

Houstoun had a number of problems to contend with beyond the last, straggling forest rebels, 'dangerous not so much from their numbers, as from the diabolical principles of murder and devastation'. The colony was financially ruined – it had spent £234,127 18s 1d (approximately £18.5 million in today's money) on militia provisions and vessel hire during the rebellion; the sugar harvest had been destroyed; most of its livestock had been killed as famine raged, crippling the island's future economic prospects – estimates of the ultimate cost to Grenada range between £2.5 and £4.5 million, an enormous amount of money (between £197 and £355 million today).

Over 7,000 of the island's 30,000 enslaved people had been killed during the war, while many others had become 'maroons', absconding to live in the interior away from slavery. Around 1,000 of the island's 5,000 white European and free Black population had also perished. The bloodshed and destruction of 'Fédon's Rebellion' were far beyond those of any previous rebellion in the British Caribbean, perhaps only equalled anywhere in the Caribbean Sea by the slave rebellion and subsequent revolution in the French colony Saint-Domingue from 1791, which became Haiti in 1804.

Yet even with the British back in control of the island, the bloodshed in Grenada showed no sign of abating. The colonists wanted vengeance. In September 1795 the island's Legislative Assembly had passed a bill of attainder against 469 free rebels (not enslaved, as opposed to at liberty), black and white, who had, 'traitorously and in hostile manner taken up arms and levied War against His Most Gracious Majesty'.

On 27 June 1796, with about one hundred and sixty free rebels in custody or surrendered, a special court convened, presided over by prominent British slave owners, to enforce the attainder, beginning with forty-eight rebels. The trial records are not particularly engaging, because there was no proper trial, only the motions of one, since the jury were mostly concerned with determining whether the men in the dock were named in the attainder, rather than with their guilt. All were sentenced to death on 30 June and informed by the Chief Justice that only the Royal Prerogative of Mercy, exercised by the Governor, could save them. Despite this, a warrant was drawn up for the executions the very next morning, 1 July.

Houstoun felt the gap between condemnation and execution 'greatly too short', but allowed the executions of fourteen of the men to proceed, granting temporary respite to the other thirty-four. Such mercy was common in the case of death sentences for rebellions in Britain – the ringleaders would be executed, the other sentences commuted. But the members of the court were outraged by Houstoun's grant of respite. If they were 'impeded' in their execution of the law, they would rather attend to their 'private concerns', effectively saying that they would go on strike in the face of grants of mercy by the King's proxy. The island's plantocracy, exhausted by 'the Horrid Rebellion which has existed for sixteen months and is not yet quelled', were determined to exact revenge.

Britain's Empire and its slave colonies were physically separate and distant from the 'mother country', but to paint a dichotomy of 'here/there' is incorrect. They were interdependent, indivisible. Just as the British state used treason to stain indelibly its political enemies, so the owners and brutalisers of human property in the Caribbean attempted to use treason's awesome power to eradicate their enemies.

The next two chapters therefore consider two instances when colonists used rebellions as pretext to attempt to remake their islands by applying the laws of treason. First in Grenada, the long-reviled francophone population were targeted, then in Jamaica the non-conformists and the anti-slavery cause fell victim. The brutality with which the colonists wielded the crime of treason created a tension between colony and metropole – the viciousness of the former offending the sensibilities of the latter, even as they aided and abetted this conduct in order to safeguard the strategic importance of the Caribbean, and the economic value of chattel slavery, to Britain's global interests.

The conflicts of the European powers had long played out in the Caribbean Sea, its islands both tactically important and great economic engines – enslaved people flowed from the west coast of Africa to their shores; sugar, other commodities and enormous profits flowed out. France had handed Grenada to Britain at the end of the Seven Years' War, only to retake it during the American Revolution, handing it back under the terms of the 1783 Treaty of Paris. Grenada was the crown jewel of the 'Ceded Islands' won in peace treaties, and by the end of the eighteenth century was Britain's third most profitable Caribbean colony after Jamaica and Barbados.

However, although the island was part of the British Empire, it had a significant francophone population, including a sizeable number of French 'free people of colour', generally mixed race and often plantation and slave owners. Although nominally British subjects, francophones generally, and free people of colour particularly, suffered a gradual deterioration of civil, political and economic rights under British rule in the eighteenth century. Catholics were prohibited from sitting in the island's assembly unless they took an oath against transubstantiation, effectively barring them from taking seats. Free Black people meanwhile were villainised and had heavily restrictive political and economic freedoms. In the late 1770s Grenada's governor told London he saw little chance of the francophone and anglophone populations assimilating together.

The Caribbean was an important theatre in the French Revolutionary Wars. In 1794 the British invaded Guadeloupe, supporting French Royalist plantation owners rebelling against the new republic. But a French force led by Guadeloupe's governor, Victor Hugues, recaptured it. The French National Convention had decreed the 'absolute abolition of slavery', and Hugues had been sent to the Antilles to spread revolutionary doctrine and terror. He declared that Guadeloupe's enslaved were now free and led a massacre of their owners. He then began to foment rebellion on British islands and to harass British ships and commerce.

It was in this context that Julien Fédon, a mixed-race francophone plantation owner, and his co-conspirators launched their attack in early 1795. On the face of it, Fédon seems an unlikely ally of Hugues and the French Republic. He was a slave owner and indeed had, with other francophones, petitioned the Grenadian government in 1790 for their protection against the Jacobin menace. By 1795, however, he had clearly changed his mind – whether as the result of ideological conversion or naked self-interest remains unclear. Fédon directed his enslaved workers to fortify his estate, Belvedere, in Saint John Parish.

At the outbreak of the rebellion Grenada's governor was Ninian Home. He apparently did not see it coming. In November of 1794 he was more concerned with his own health and an outbreak of fever than a rising. The Duke of Portland wrote to him in May 1795 asking for news, uneasy over reports of a French invasion and subsequent 'depredations'.

Grenada is thousands of miles away from London, and the naval war being conducted in the Atlantic, as well as the ocean's weather, meant that correspondence sometimes took months to arrive. So it was that after sending his request for a report, Portland received a letter from the island dated 28 March 1795. It was from Kenneth Francis Mackenzie, the president of the island's council (and attorney general), not Home. Mackenzie reported that 'a General Insurrection of the French Free Coloured People' had begun on 2 March with coordinated attacks on the port village of Grenville Bay, where white English people had been 'massacred', and Charlottetown. Home had been captured while attempting to get back to the capital, St George's, as the rebellion began.

Mackenzie, acting Governor, had immediately placed the island under martial law and ordered Grenada's few hundred militia and regular troops to destroy the rebellion. They had failed. Attacking the enemy camp of Fédon's Belvedere estate, they found it protected not only by fortifications but captured artillery. Some 150 troops arrived from Martinique on 12 March under Brigadier-General Colin Lindsay to reinforce the British, but their attempts, on 15 March, to take Fédon's camp also failed. Several days of heavy rain followed. Lindsay committed suicide, seemingly driven to a 'temporary delirium' by fever and the weather.

Mackenzie estimated the rebels' numbers: 350 men armed with muskets, 250 with pikes, and some 4,000 enslaved 'negroes'. They were led by Fédon, but also by French officers sent by Hugues from Guadeloupe, while many of the francophone inhabitants of the colony had joined. Such was the rebels' strength, and highly defendable nature of the wooded and mountainous territory where their camp lay, that the British forces could not feasibly attack. Instead, they focused their resources on garrisoning towns, not least St George's, and mounting naval patrols to try to stop communication and supply between the rebels and their French allies. Mackenzie begged for reinforcements: 'every moment of our inactivity must increase the evil within, as the Negroes are daily joining the Insurgents and desolating the Estates; all of which have been plundered.'

Attritional warfare raged throughout 1795 – the rebels in effect controlling much of the island's interior, the British holding on to ports and towns. Mackenzie bemoaned the economic impact of the 'defensive war' pursued by Brigadier-General Oliver Nicolls, who arrived and took command in April. But the British were weakened. Despite reinforcements from other islands and the gathering of an army to be sent from Europe, they were still short of manpower, as the country waged a war across the Atlantic and Europe. What men who did arrive were inexperienced, ill-trained, had 'imperfect' discipline, were often killed or incapacitated by disease, and frequently drunk. As the rainy season and the end of active campaigning approached in May 1795, Mackenzie was concerned that the status quo would continue – the rebels could easily plunder estates, even those near British posts, and their resupply, coming from nearby Guadeloupe, would be more reliable than that of the British forces' in hurricane season. Meanwhile, French propaganda was being 'industriously distributed', contributing to the desertion to rebel ranks, or otherwise into a kind of wartime maroonage, of the island's enslaved. The colony's financial reserves were nearly exhausted, and its plantations all but ruined 'for every valuable purpose'.

Governor Home, like many of the other forty-two white British prisoners taken in the first days of the rebellion, was dead. In the days after 2 March, General Fédon (Hugues had commissioned him and other leaders as French officers) had sent the British a demand that the island be turned over to him as 'Commandant General'. If it was not, and if his encampment was attacked, he would execute his hostages. The British, obviously, refused, the island's council resolving to 'spill the last drop of our Blood rather than disgrace eternally ourselves and our Country'. They considered the threat to the hostages to be empty, and the Duke of Portland thought so too. After Lindsay's abortive attack, however, Fédon made good his threat, executing all but three of the prisoners, the survivors being shipped to Guadeloupe.

Things got worse for the British in Grenada, as troops and ships that might relieve them were diverted to other, more strategically pressing theatres, and the promised army from Britain was delayed.

The rebels made good these opportunities. In late September a French ship landed 200 troops, with arms and ammunition. 'Inspirited', (and despite the British having had some nine hours' warning of the landing), the rebels captured the important, defendable port of Charlottetown in a midnight raid. The British were now only garrisoning St George's and a few small outposts. The insurgents took to the seas too, launching armed canoes, 'prepared in the woods', and capturing a provisions-laden ship as it made its way through calms approaching St George's. Mackenzie left the island for Europe on 13 December 1795, putting his private interests and health before the fate of Grenada and its people.

He was replaced as acting Governor by Samuel Mitchell, who wrote to Portland on 22 January 1796 with news of the worsening state of the British position on the island. The port of Grenville had been attacked by the rebels for eight days, and while it had resisted, the enemy had gained a nearby harbour, and more French reinforcements were arriving. Another British ship, this time carrying munitions, was taken by armed canoes on 18 February. On 20 February the rebels attacked Grenville again, this time successfully. The insurgents now effectively controlled the island, except for St George's. On 9 March 1796 their forces began an assault on the capital.

Their dominance was short-lived, however. Across the Caribbean the tide of the war was turning against the French, and reinforcements began arriving in Grenada in the nick of time. Six hundred men arrived on 3 March, enough to help partially repel the rebels' assault, though not enough to counterattack comprehensively. More troops arrived from Barbados on 13 March, landing in Grenada's north. Nicolls launched a successful attack on the rebels' positions at Grenville and Port Royal, beginning on 22 March, routing them back to Fédon's fortified estate, although with 'considerable' losses on both sides.

Houstoun arrived with the reinforcements, taking over as Governor. Armed with fresh troops the British made headway. It seemed that the rebels' assault on St George's had been driven in part by their own desperation. Fédon and the other commanders had fallen into internecine squabbling, and their scorched-earth tactics had left their forces hungry as French resupply dwindled. And so it was that by July, with the rebels all but defeated – killed, fled, captured, surrendered or otherwise reduced to a woodland guerrilla force – the new Governor had to try to administer the peace, faced with the restive and vengeful spirt of Grenada's British plantocracy.

The bill of attainder had been passed by the island's legislative assembly in September 1795, when British prospects had been at a low ebb. It was part of series of theatrical proclamations and statements issued by the embattled colonists to project the awesome power of the mother country when her troops and ships were not forthcoming. The first of these had been the declaration of martial law, effectively bringing all white men under military discipline and directing the island's energies to defence alone. Then, on 4 March 1795, as Fédon was demanding the island be surrendered to him, Mackenzie issued a Royal Proclamation. In it he offered a general pardon to anyone involved in the insurrection if they surrendered, unless they had committed 'cruel and unmanly murders'. Those who did not give themselves up would be pursued with 'the most rigorous measures'. Mackenzie also offered a substantial reward for the capture or killing of rebels. Yet all this did little to induce rebels to give up.

The attainder also offered surrender as an escape to the over 400 people named in and therefore attainted by it. Mitchell characterised the measure as 'undoubtedly severe, but ... absolutely necessary'. In October the assembly passed another act, confiscating the estates of 'certain Traitors' and vesting them in the King, under the management of Grenadian commissioners. Yet once again this had little effect on the rebels.

Throughout its history, treason has so often been theatre, but this was treason as a kind of shadow puppetry – the colonists threw up the shapes of the great and terrible power of the King and his forces, at a time when they had no ability materially to affect the situation. It was statecraft, the sceptre and orb replaced by a carrot and stick. In his March proclamation, published in both English and French, Mackenzie had spoken of the rebels' 'savage barbarity', but stated his belief that the Rising was the work of a very few individuals, with the majority joining in a 'moment of delusion'. He was sure the latter rebels were 'interested in the welfare of a colony', and assured of its 'mild Government and Laws', would take the opportunity of the amnesty to admit their misapprehension and 'return to their duty'. Deadly consequences were promised for those who did not repent.

The colonists sought to project their vision of British rule – 'mild ... affording equal protection to every individual', willing to forgive, but unrelenting if provoked. But theirs was not the only game in town. French propaganda was flooding the British Caribbean and offering a different vision of society, a different kind of legitimacy of rule, and the prospect of brutal punishment for those perceived to commit treason against it.

On 21 February 1795, before Grenada had exploded but in keeping with his campaign of fomenting rebellion against British rule across the archipelago, Hugues and the other Republican commissioners in Guadeloupe had issued a declaration, again in French and English.

Nominally addressed to the commanders of Britain's forces in the West Indies, it was pure revolutionary propaganda, anticipating and justifying rebellions like Fédon's. It spoke of the 'infamous' barbarities committed by British soldiers and promised retribution. It extended French protection to all who declared themselves Republican, 'whatever colour he is, and in whatever Island', but stated that those who assisted the British against Republican troops or rebels were committing treason.

The message of the declaration is clear: assist the Republicans and you will receive their protection and recognition as an equal citizen, whether you be black or white, enslaved or free, French or British; show 'punic [treacherous] faith' in Britain and stand guilty of treason. 'This law which inflicts the pain of death,' the declaration asserted, 'shall here continue in full force.' Indeed, the rebels were keen to emphasise the French-backed legitimacy of their actions. Grenadians commissioned as officers wore French uniforms. Their rebellion fell into a pattern of French-backed revolts against British rule in the Caribbean, Ireland and elsewhere – these were not disorderly insurrections, but part of the wider, self-consciously liberating war of the Republic.

It was the British vision that eventually won out in Grenada, but when the colonists resumed control of the island they were not inclined to administer 'mild' government. Houstoun, writing to Portland about his 'extremely unpopular' act of leniency as the attainder trials began in late June 1796, was worried. Even if he did not give way to the demands made of him to brook no mercy for those attainted, even allowing as he thought right to make examples of some, he could not contain the islanders' 'popular spirit within the bounds of justice and propriety'.

GRENADA.

By the KING.

A PROCLAMATION.

K. F. MACKENZIE.

WHEREAS an Infurrection has broke out in this our Colony of Grenada, which has diftinguifhed itfelf in its commencement by the moft horrid acts of favage barbarity; and whereas there is ftrong reafon to believe that it has been excited by the machinations of a very few individuals joined in a moment of delufion by others of a different defcription, who are interefted in the welfare of a colony, under whofe mild Government and Laws, affording equal protection to every individual, they have long enjoyed every comfort; and who feeing how much they have been mifled, may be upon maturer confideration anxious to return to their duty : Influenced by fuch confiderations and motives of humanity, We have therefore thought fit, by and with the confent of His Honor Kenneth Francis Mackenzie Efquire, Prefident, and the Members of our Council for the faid ifland, to publifh this our Royal Proclamation, declaring a general pardon and amnefty to all perfons concerned in the faid infurrection, upon their furrendering themfelves, excepting only to thofe individuals who have committed the cruel and unmanly murders that have fo difgracefully characterized the conduct of fome of the faid infurgents ; and We do hereby farther declare, that unlefs they accept this offered clemency the moft rigorous meafures fhall be inftantly purfued againft them; and We do hereby offer a reward of Twenty Johannes's to any perfon bringing in any of the faid infurgents either dead or alive.

GIVEN at St. George's this Fourth day of March in the Year of Our Lord One thoufand feven hundred and ninety-five and in the thirty-fifth Year of Our Reign.

GOD SAVE THE KING.

By His Honor's Command,
MATHER BYLES.

A royal proclamation issued by Kenneth Francis Mackenzie, acting Governor of Grenada, on 4 March 1795, just two days after the Rebellion broke out. Mackenzie offers clemency to those rebels who immediately surrender, while promising brutal retribution to those who do not. The proclamation was also printed in French. (CO 101/34, folios 27-28)

The cruelties and devastation of the previous sixteen months had 'raised a strong spirit of resentment against the whole body of the Insurgents'. He feared that if the colonists could not bring them to the scaffold via the courts they would seek extra-judiciary redress.

The Duke of Portland and George III were furious with the colonists' conduct. Portland allowed that retaliation would happen during rebellions, but that such a 'Spirit of Revenge could have possessed itself of British Minds' astonished and disgusted him. The King's Prerogative of Mercy, his 'most precious and darling', had been attacked. However, by the time this reproach was sent from London to the island, the court was again sitting, having made their point.

In July 1797 Charles Green, Houstoun's successor, reported the continued activities of the special court dealing with rebels. Three white men and fifty-nine 'free persons of colour' had been lately convicted of high treason, all sentenced to death. The white traitors had been reprieved until the King's 'pleasure' was known, while some of the free black men had been banished from the British Empire. The execution of traitors was declining but had by no means abated after its initial flourish in July 1796 – at least seventy-seven men suffered a death sentence. Julien Fédon was not among them – he either escaped or drowned trying. In October 1796 Houstoun had reported that almost all the executions were of mixed-race men, while 400 others were transported or banished. In the British Caribbean mercy, like everything else, was racialised.

But the attainder had been effective for the colonists. When it had first been passed Mackenzie had remarked that it would affect 'an entire deliverance from all French Connexion', which the assembly believed vital for Grenada's security. Indeed, to scan the 469 names listed in the act of attainder is an education in the variety and etymology of French surnames, for few British names appear. This number represented a significant proportion of Grenada's francophone population.

Combined with those who had fled and been killed, as well as a raft of legislation the assembly passed to punish those implicitly guilty by association of kinship, not least the free mixed-race people, the attainder helped achieve the further anglicisation of Grenada's property- and slave-owning class. Their prize was a ruined island.

Houstoun reported on the work of the island's confiscation commissioners in June 1796. It seemed that 'all the French men of good properties kept themselves out of the scrape' so the number of confiscated properties was not as large as might have been hoped – those estates taken had become wild for lack of cultivation and their enslaved workers had 'suffered greatly & be greatly decreased'. An ostensibly short-term loan to the Colony of £100,000 (some £7.9 million today, an enormous amount of money at the time) from the Treasury, showed no prospect of being paid back in 1799, Green informing London that the colonists complained of ruined estates and a lack of troops.

And what of the enslaveds' role in the insurrection? The rebellion was long considered one primarily of the island's mixed-race francophone property owners, taking its name from one of them. Mackenzie initially reported it as a revolt of the 'French Free Coloured People'. But this seriously downplays the central role enslaved combatants played on both sides of the conflict, even though few contemporary sources give them a voice.

The more than 7,000 enslaved who flocked to Fédon's banner, no doubt in part because of his Republican promises of emancipation and equality, formed the bulk of his force. They influenced the way the war was prosecuted, participating in outrages like the massacre of white people in Grenville on the first night of the rebellion (led by Fédon), and engaging in the destruction of plantations and the coercion of other enslaved people to the rebels' cause. It seems that some wished to take revenge on the masters who had brutalised them. Fédon seems to have been unable to control the rebellious spirit of these men, their efforts to destroy the plantations on which they had been imprisoned contributing to the rebels' food supply difficulties.

	Present fit for duty 3 March 1795					Present fit for duty 30 April 1796			
Unit	Officers	NCOs	Privates	Total		Officers	NCOs	Privates	Total
Troop of Light Cavalry	3		30	33		3	3	24	30
St George's Regiment	25	47	223	295		10	19	148	177
St John's Regiment	1	1	12	14		4	6		10
St Patrick's Regiment	9	4	67	80		6		23	29
St Andrew's Regiment	15	8	43	66		10	2	7	19
St David's Regiment	11	2	34	47		3	2	11	16
Total	64	62	409	535		36	32	213	281

Return of strengths of Grenadian militia, 3 March 1795 and 30 April 1796. Source: despatch from Alexander Houstoun to the Duke of Portland, 3 May 1796.

However, the enslaved rebels numbered less than a third of the island's population. Many remained neutral, went into maroonage or actively supported the colonists, perhaps motivated by the British offer of amnesty, or indeed the often brutal coercion the rebels employed to bring enslaved people into their ranks. In August 1795 the increasingly desperate assembly passed legislation to establish units of Loyal Black Rangers made up of enslaved men (their owners were compensated if they were killed). The rebellion was the first time the British had made extensive use of enslaved soldiers in the Caribbean. They needed their help for, as the table above shows, the rebellion massively depleted the active strength of the island's militia. By October 1795 Mackenzie said they were greatly reduced by 'weariness and disease' (and rum, no doubt), just as the regular troops on the island were. In fact, Mackenzie revealed that by this point the defence of St George's, the capital, was mostly in the hands of enslaved men.

The divide between enslaved rebels and loyalists was not linguistic – there were francophones fighting for the British and anglophones in Fédon's camp. They seem to have treated one another appallingly when they met in battle – reports to London detailed 'ill-usage' and 'implacable revenge' committed by emancipated rebels against those enslaved who had remained loyal, and subsequently been left abandoned by British military withdrawals; the Loyal Black Rangers played an important role in hunting down formerly enslaved rebels after the revolt had ended.

Such was the scale and strategic importance of enslaved combatants in the rebellion, each side driven to either the French or the British vision of the island's future, either based on belief of calculation of success, it might be better to think of 'Fédon's' revolt as a slave rebellion against a slave counter-revolution.

In the history of treason, however, it was significant in demonstrating the way that the plantocracy of the British Caribbean, desperate to maintain their economic and racial dominance over their islands, would use the opportunities created by their distance from Britain and exigencies of crises, to use the Crown's jealously guarded power to decide who was treasonous to stamp out their enemies and safeguard their interests. As the British Parliament decreed the adoption of 'amelioration', a process in which the conditions of slavery would supposedly gradually improve before an eventual, unspecified emancipation, the conflict between the state and its colonists over who wielded this power would intensify.

A PROCLAMATION.

By His Excellency SOMERSET LOWRY, EARL OF BELMORE, Captain-General and Governor-in-Chief of this our Island of Jamaica, and other the Territories thereon depending in America, Chancellor and Vice-Admiral of the same, &c. &c.

WHEREAS it has been ascertained that certain Incendiaries have been employed to poison the minds of the Slaves in some parts of the Island, and to induce them to be guilty of acts of outrage and insubordination :—And whereas it is necessary that the **Ringleaders** of this disturbance should be brought to condign punishment, I do hereby, in his Majesty's name, offer a reward of *Three Hundred Dollars* to any person or persons who shall apprehend either of the following slaves :—

A slave calling himself COLONEL GARDINER, belonging to Greenwich Estate, Hanover.
A slave calling himself CAPTAIN DOVE, belonging to Belvidere Estate, St. James's.
A slave calling himself CAPTAIN JOHNSON, belonging to Retrieve, St. James's—and
GENERAL RULER, SAMUEL SHARP, or THARP, *alias* DADDIE RULER SHARP, or THARP, director of the whole, and styled also, Preacher to the Rebels, belonging to Craydon Estate, St. James's.

And in order to afford encouragement to such Slaves who may be disposed to assist in apprehending the aforesaid Rebels, I do hereby promise his Majesty's most gracious Pardon to any slave or slaves who may assist in such purpose, except those who have been actually guilty of setting fire to the works or houses on different Properties, or attempted the life of any peaceable inhabitant.

Given under my Hand and Seal at Arms, at St. Jago de la Vega, this third day of January, Annoque Domini, one thousand eight hundred and thirty-two, and in the second year of our reign.

BELMORE.

By His Excellency's Command,

W. BULLOCK, *Sec.*

GOD SAVE THE KING.

Proclamation issued by the Earl of Belmore, Governor of Jamaica, on 3 January 1832, during Sharpe's Rebellion. The Proclamation names 'DADDIE RULER SHARP' and others as ringleaders of the Rebellion, offering a reward for their apprehension, and a pardon to the other rebels.

Sixteen

DEVASTATION, JAMAICA, 1832

As Fédon's Rebellion came to an end in Grenada the colonial government was sent a copy of a resolution passed by the House of Commons on 6 April 1797. It addressed the conditions of enslaved people, and how these should be improved to 'obviate the Causes which have hitherto impeded' the 'natural increase' of resident populations of the enslaved in the British West Indies. This would reduce the need for the slave trade to exist, the Commons resolved, allowing eventually for its complete termination. What's more, colonial governors were to be requested to also effect the moral and religious improvement of the enslaved, and offer them protections in law. Received by the Governor, Charles Green, in July that year, he forwarded to London copies of an act of the Grenadian Assembly 'for the Better Protection and for Promoting the Natural Increase and Population of Slaves within the Island of Grenada' passed February 1798, although he lamented that 'the regulations it contains are not so full as might be wished'. Green explained that the colonists were reluctant to go further due to the damage and disruption caused by the late insurrection.

This was a familiar chorus throughout the British West Indies at the time: the movement to abolish the slave trade had been growing apace in Great Britain for over a decade, and many desired the end of the importation of enslaved African labour to the colonies, some for moral reasons, others for economic and geopolitical, and some indeed because of the belief that there was something dangerous in the character of imported Africans, and that a native enslaved population would be more docile and less likely to revolt against their masters. But emancipation was, at this point, hardly anyone's goal. Even committed abolitionists did not speak of it, believing that ending the trade would be a crucial first step to the ending of chattel slavery in a piecemeal fashion, with the moral and religious education of the enslaved needed to allow their eventual freedom. In principle, at least during the late eighteenth century – a time of great success and therefore scrutiny of sugar production by enslaved people – even planters, both absentee and resident, supported the end of the trade and the 'amelioration', as it was called, of the conditions that the enslaved lived under, although there is little evidence that such high-minded statements survived contact with the economic realpolitik and principles of white domination which persisted in the colonies. The motion of the House of Commons, and the Grenadian reaction to it, was therefore typical.

The Slave Trade was abolished in 1807 and from then on, with the economic importance, coincidentally, of Britain's Caribbean slave colonies waning, there were increased calls for the emancipation of Britain's enslaved. In 1823 the House of Commons unanimously adopted a motion which called for the increased amelioration of the conditions of the enslaved and their moral and religious instruction, 'such as may prepare them for a participation in those civil rights and privileges which are enjoyed by other classes ... with a fair and equitable consideration of the interests of private property'. While the government had backed this compromise motion by amending the original, which called slavery 'repugnant' and explicitly mentioned abolition, this was still clearly a directive from the imperial legislature that the British Empire was to eventually end slavery.

The slave owners in the Colonies, particularly those of Jamaica,

Britain's most important territory in the Caribbean, found this move disturbing, but it continued to gain support and be Government policy. But the excitement caused by these moves among both the planters and the enslaved of Jamaica, as pro- and anti-slavery campaigners propagandised and sensationalised, meant that another explosion of treason and rebellion was brewing in the Caribbean.

Slave rebellions had been common in colonies of all empires since enslavement had existed. In British colonies, not least Jamaica, the history of slave rebellions shows how the rebels were aware of political, military and cultural currents on their island, in the wider Atlantic world, and in Britain. The series of rebellions in 1760 and 1761 commonly referred to as Tacky's Revolt saw rebels take advantage of the space and comparative British weakness brought about by the Seven Years' War (1756–63), for instance. The growth of the movement for the abolition of the slave trade and slavery, as well as the British government's indication that this was its, albeit glacial and prevaricated, direction of travel, brought a further dimension to the causes of slave rebellions. In both Bussa's rebellion of 1816 (in Barbados) and the Demerara Rebellion of 1823 (Guyana), the largest slave rebellions in their respective colonies' histories, part of the motivation of the rebels was a knowledge of the British government's support for abolition, even possibly a conviction that it had actually been enacted, and a belief that resistance (usually taking the form of the withdrawal of labour and property damage before colonial reprisals brought widespread violence) would bring it about.

One thing rebellions did not lead to was treason charges for the enslaved participants. Just as in the American colonies, Caribbean colonies like Jamaica passed their own laws. They borrowed the terms of the Treason Act 1552, passed under Edward VI, which allowed for treason offences committed in the 'outward parts' of the British realm (for example, a colony) to be treated and tried as they would in England. A further Act of 1823 passed by Jamaica's Legislative Assembly clarified the form and procedure of treason prosecutions. But such laws did not apply to the island's enslaved population – they could not, as the enslaved were not subject to general laws covering the conduct of colonial subjects, but their own. This was logical: the laws of treason bound the fringes of the social contract between citizen/subject and state/crown. This would not be applicable to the enslaved, a class apart with no real legal or civil rights. Each colony passed its own codes of law for the government of its enslaved population. Parts were intended to safeguard their condition (although these provisions were often ignored by planters) but they also governed the behaviour of the enslaved and set out punishments for crimes.

So, in the Jamaican Slave Code of 1816, the punishment of death, transportation (usually to continental America, into further slavery), or any other punishment a court sees fit is set out for the wide-ranging crime of 'rebellion ... any rebellious conspiracy ... murder, felony, burglary, robbery', or indeed the crimes of setting fire 'to any houses, out-houses, negro-houses, cane-pieces, grass or corn pieces', or breaking into or stealing anything from them.

More than this, the code further clarifies that death or any other punishment considered suitable is due to any enslaved people who '*compass or imagine* the death of *any white person* [author's emphasis]'. This phrasing is directly borrowed from the 1352 Treason Act, but whereas that makes it an offence to compass or imagine the monarch's death, here it is any white person. The intention is clear: the Treason Act sets out a duty of loyalty to the monarch and the state they embody, but in Jamaica it is not the divine right of kings from which power and dominance flows, but white skin, and any attempt to subvert that dominance was worthy of the harshest punishment.

It was with the continuous fear of revolts by the enslaved, not least rumours 'as to the excitement which prevails in the minds of the slaves in some of those islands', that the Secretary of State for War and the Colonies, Frederick John Robinson, 1st Viscount Goderich (later the Earl of Ripon), sent a circular despatch to the Governors of the British West Indies in June 1831. Goderich wrote that, as these rumours had made the Cabinet 'uneasy', they had decided to take precautionary measures, and although the distance from Britain to the Caribbean meant he could offer little immediate practical assistance in the case of a revolt he enclosed a Royal Proclamation which he hoped might calm things, recalling that a previous proclamation issued in 1824 had served as 'warning the slaves of the danger they would incur by any violation of the law ... [and to] induce them to yield a cheerful obedience to the authority of their owners'.

The King's proclamation warned the enslaved that while they might have been, 'erroneously led to believe that orders had been sent out by Us for their emancipation', this was not the case. He commanded obedience to the laws of the colonies and their masters – or otherwise, through insubordination, they would excite the monarch's 'highest displeasure' and feel the full force of the law. Goderich left it up to Governors whether they thought it necessary to release such a proclamation, but asked for intelligence as to the mood of the enslaved in the colonies. He also entreated his juniors to try to dispel 'any illusions' which enslaved people or owners had regarding the government's 'real designs' or the principles that guided them. The 'ultimate extinction of slavery', by means of a 'course of progressive improvement' remained the government's 'avowed object', Goderich said, and it was for Governors to try to keep the slave owners from withholding their 'cheerful co-operation' towards this goal, and the enslaved from being 'goaded by impatience ... to seek, through any desperate and lawless enterprizes' their freedom.

Somerset Lowry-Corry, second Earl Belmore, the Governor of Jamaica, wrote back to Goderich on 20 July 1831. He said that if he'd received the proclamation a month before, he would have immediately written back, saying it was not needed. But now he was less sure, there had been cases of arson in Kingston (Jamaica's largest settlement), although he said that these were 'considered by many as insulated acts of mischief, divested of any combined purpose'. He, however, had greater concerns about rebellion and sedition brewing, although not necessarily among the enslaved.

Jamaica's slave owners had by this time, Belmore reported (and Goderich would have been aware, as the events were accounted in both the Colonial and London newspapers), been in the habit of meeting to adopt resolutions concerning what they saw as the threat to their lives and property posed by the British government's desire to emancipate the enslaved.

These meetings had taken on a character of that close cousin of treason, sedition. Over the coming months Belmore submitted copies of the resolutions passed at meetings to his masters in London. One such meeting, held by the freeholders of the Parish of Saint Thomas-in-the-East (on the south-eastern corner of the island, some sixty miles from the capital, Spanish Town, and covered with numerous plantations) on 8 August 1831, is typical of the sentiment, although perhaps slightly more explicit in its language than the resolutions of some other meetings.

The slave owners' sources of complaint were twofold. First, proposals to increase the duties charged on West Indian sugar and other products imported to England. Improvements in sugar production in other parts of the world had rendered supporting the dominance of West Indian sugar in Britain an increasing expense rather than economic benefit, which a burgeoning free trade faction in Parliament used as a cause to end the West Indies preferential treatment (they would eventually succeed with the 1846 Sugar Duties Act, which sounded the death knell of British West Indian sugar production). Second, and perhaps most importantly, proposals for the abolition of slavery.

The meeting made clear that there were no greater supporters of the amelioration of the conditions of slavery than themselves (although in fact it had taken the Jamaican Legislative Assembly eight years to legislate for it after 1823, despite requests from the British government), and that they even supported abolition (although they thought it would be 'more a curse than a blessing' to the enslaved) as long as these schemes protected their physical property and compensated them for their loss of human property, and were not incompatible with 'the maintenance of necessary authority, without which no state of society can exist'.

They made these clarifications due to the 'calumnies' circulated by their opponents (abolitionists) in England and Jamaica, a 'bigotted faction, who most basely revile and persecute us; nay, who thirst for our very blood'. These, combined with the 'indiscreet and alarming declarations made in Parliament by the present Ministers of the Crown' with regard to West Indian matters, led them to believe that such policies, if carried through, would 'deprive us of a right so essential to the protection of our lives and property'.

They went further than this: backed into a corner by their enemies, their very lives threatened, they unanimously resolved that, although there were no more loyal subjects of the King than they, threats to their lives and property by the British Government, 'whether by the sword or by a system of robbery under the name of fiscal regulations ... will be resisted by every means in our power, and to the last extremity; that if destroyed we are to be, England may have the honour and glory of the deed, but that we ourselves may stand acquitted of having been accessory to our destruction'. They further resolved that, their previous petitions having been ignored, they would form a committee with other such meetings across the island to decide what measures should be adopted and collectively petition the King.

Meetings in the parishes of Saint Mary's, Saint Ann's, Manchester, Trelawney and others, some chaired by the Parish Custos (the senior magistrate) all passed similar resolutions. Here was clear sedition – meetings passed resolutions that rejected the authority of the King's ministers, explicitly stated that they would violently resist the state if necessary, and sought to establish a sort of shadow legislative body in defiance of the powers of the Jamaican Assembly. They even, in perhaps a direct reference to the arguments of successful traitors of the American colonies in 1776, declared their belief 'that taxation, legislation and representation are inseparable' and so if they were not allowed by London to make their, and their human property's, laws, and were subjected to conditions which, they said, would threaten their lives and assets, they would, as the meeting in Saint Mary's Parish put it, not 'be bound by the duties of allegiance when the protection of their sovereign is withheld from them'.

If artisans had uttered such oaths in a committee room some four thousand miles away in London in support of universal male suffrage, then the Home Office would have quickly sought for their arrest, possibly on a charge of high treason. But these were colonial slave and property owners, the dominant faction of the island (some were members of the Island's Assembly) so Belmore merely contented himself with reporting the meetings to London and letting it be known, via his attorney general and the Custodes of the island, that while the Jamaican government supported free expression, these committees of parish delegates risked conflicting with 'those functions which reside in the House of Assembly as the constitutional organ of the public'.

It is difficult, perhaps impossible to feel great sympathy for these men, lashing out and talking of acts of armed resistance as their soil, so intensively cultivated for sugar for so many years, diminished in quality, their economic importance to Britain waned, their political representation in the British Parliament declined. The liberation of the greatly more numerous men women and children they had for so many decades brutalised, loomed. Even if the owners' lives and property weren't really threatened by emancipation, as the abolitionist MP William Wilberforce pointed out, prior to the abolition of the slave trade some of the planters had claimed such a move was impracticable and dangerous.

But despite Belmore's assurances to Goderich that he believed there was no concerted campaign of resistance by the enslaved brewing in Jamaica, he having been assured by local officials, something was afoot. And just as the Grenadian planters had sought to use treason to attempt to remake their island free of francophone influence in the fires of Fédon's Rebellion, so now would the Jamaican slave owners use another explosion of conflict to try to fight emancipation and remove the influence of their ideological enemies, Baptist and other non-conformist missionaries from the island.

Conversion to and observance of Christianity was seen as a key pillar in 'preparing' the enslaved to enjoy something approaching civil rights after emancipation. Even Charles Rose Ellis MP, an extensive slave owner and generally not a supporter of emancipation, allowed that religious instruction would allow for freed persons to live a 'civilised life' with Christian morality 'substituted for the authority of the master'.

However, in the past there had been resistance from the planters to promoting religion (and education) among the enslaved; they believed it would cause trouble, and the Church of England in places like Jamaica had not been active in the cause. It was non-conformist Protestant sects, such as Baptists, Methodists, Moravians, Quakers and others who had taken the task of missionary work, evangelism and conversion among the enslaved of the Caribbean upon themselves with energy. The Baptist Missionary Society, for instance, had, they said, begun their mission in Jamaica on invitation from a sympathetic planter in 1813. By 1832 they had seventeen missionaries, preaching at forty different stations to a collective congregation of nearly 30,000 'black and coloured people'. Indeed, one MP held in 1823 that non-conformist sects were in a large part responsible for baptising some 100,000 of the approximately 800,000 enslaved people in the British West Indies.

Although some were sympathetic, many planters viewed the work of Baptists and other missionary sects in Jamaica with at best suspicion and at worst open hostility – they were abolitionists who, 'with heaven in their eyes,' said one planter, 'but hell in their hearts, seek our destruction', not least by supplanting the authority of the enslaved peoples' owners and managers with religious leaders, some indeed drawn from the ranks of the enslaved themselves. So when, during Christmas 1831 (a key time for the sugar crop), a wave of strikes and incendiarism broke out among the enslaved of Jamaica, turning violent in some instances, the colonists once again, as they had in Grenada, sought to use the terrible laws of rebellion and treason to attack their enemies and their ideologies and remake their island without their influence.

As the end of the year approached, said Belmore, the 'apprehensions which appeared to disturb the public mind during the summer had nearly subsided' – the planters complained of poverty and their delegations continued to make statements in the same vein as before, but no rumours of widespread discontent or rebellion among the enslaved reached Belmore; 'the brink of Danger on which they stood', he commented, 'formed no part of their deliberations'.

But on the 19 December 1831 disturbances began to break out in the parishes of Saint James and Trelawney, in the north-west of the island. This was to become one of the largest slave rebellions in the history of the British Caribbean, with somewhere between 20,000 and 60,000 of Jamaica's roughly 300,000 enslaved population taking part in a wave of desertion, strike action, insurrection and eventually conflict with local militia and regular troops (as well as ultimately maroons, free black communities of the formerly enslaved and their descendants who lived in the hills and were often involved in suppressing slave rebellions).

On 22 December Colonel Lawson, commander of the Saint James militia and a magistrate, wrote to Belmore, telling him of trouble on the Salt Spring estate in that parish. The enslaved there had apparently been 'insolent' to Mr Gignon, the attorney manager. Two constables had been sent to the estate the next day to arrest the ringleaders of this incident, but they had been disarmed and their mules taken, with the enslaved there expressing 'their determination not to work after New Years Day'. Gignon requested a detachment of militia be sent to the property, but Lawson, who said he knew the enslaved well, first went with the neighbouring estate's owner to speak to them and 'prevail on the negroes to return to their Duty'. They did not comply so he sent fifty militiamen the next morning, but the estate's enslaved had 'disappeared'. Although most, save six ringleaders, returned, the magistrates of the Parish began to receive word that enslaved people on other estates were declaring that they would not work after New Year. They requested detachments of regular troops and began mobilising militia, worried about more widespread trouble.

However, they were in no way prepared for the scale or speed of rebellious actions by the enslaved. On 23 December further reports were received from Portland Parish, in the north-east of the island, requesting a warship be sent, 'on account of some unpleasant rumours which had reached them of discontent amongst the Slaves in that Quarter'. On 23 December 'a strong spirit of insubordination amongst the slaves' in Trelawney was reported – the enslaved there had burnt down the trash houses (where used sugarcanes were stored for fuel), telling the attorney they intended to burn down the rest of works. By the time the militia arrived, they had fled.

The insurrection spread and spread, like the fires its participants ignited. On 29 December Belmore received 'still more alarming accounts of the state of the Country – The work of destruction had begun and Fires had been seen both in Saint James's and Trelawney to blaze the previous night'. Other incidents, across the north of the island but particularly the north-west, began mounting up. Some of the enslaved made clear that after Christmas and in the new year they would not work, some set fire to their own and other estates. By 30 December 1831 Belmore had despatched Sir Willoughby Cotton, who had previously fought in the Indian subcontinent and the Peninsular War, along with regular troops and Royal Navy ships to Saint James's capital, Montego Bay. He called a council of war, which unanimously supported the declaration of martial law on the island. Cotton was placed in overall command, and directed first of all to surround the disaffected areas to prevent rebellion spreading to other parts of the island. Belmore, who was also dealing with epidemics of smallpox and dysentery, was first concerned with stopping the contagion of rebellion spreading on an island where the white inhabitants were outnumbered ten to one by the enslaved.

The declaration of martial law was not a light step to take, suspending as it did the civil courts and the conduct of business, with the entire non-slave male population expected to be ready to fight under the strict terms of the Articles of War. But it was the blunt, bloody tool that successive governors across the British Colonies reached for if anything more than a localised disturbance broke out. This was the 'formal militarisation of racial slaveholding', as the historian Vincent Brown said in his discussion of the 1760s rebellions – the whole of the island's free populace were directed towards keeping their neighbours in bondage by any means necessary, with courts martial meting out sentences of death to those caught with rapidity and little compunction. Along with the support of the Royal Navy's ships, their resupply, reinforcement and visual deterrent allowing the articulation of, as Brown says, 'the British Empire's component parts', the Jamaican plantocracy, committed to end a campaign of labour unrest and targeted (but not generally deadly) incendiarism by waging a brutal war against the enslaved rebels.

After Christmas 1831 the insurrection continued apace across the north of Jamaica. On 26 December it was reported that insubordination had appeared on the Salt Spring estate in Saint James. 'The negroes,' wrote the reporting officer, 'were determined to strike work at Christmas', but he also reported that 'no slaughter [was] to be committed, unless any of the rebels were killed in taking arms from the white people'. On 28 December the Custos of Trelawney informed the government that the parish was in an 'actual state of rebellion' – around nine-tenths of the enslaved population had refused to turn out for work (in one case an estate with 700 enslaved people had seen a total strike) and much of the parish had been ablaze the night before due to the activities of incendiaries. He said that the circumstances could not 'well be worse', but that as yet 'no blood had been shed'. He called for regular troops, warships and martial law, so as to put into military order planters who would otherwise be 'clamorous' to first protect their own interests – the militia were 'very weak' in the face of the scale of rebellion.

By New Year's Eve 1831 the rebellion saw its first major engagement between troops and rebels. Militia Major-General Robertson reported that in Saint Elizabeth Parish militia and regular troops had clashed around the Ginger Hill estate. The troops had arrived as, it seems, the rebels were preparing to attack the nearby Ipswich estate. The rebels were 'in great force' at Ginger Hill, they had a great quantity of arms and munitions and had also prepared 'a great quantity of meat, liquor, &c. for a feast', which Robertson saw as an indication of their confidence at success in attacking Ipswich. However, they had been surprised, with twenty killed in the fight and the rest routed into the surrounding hills and country.

On 2 January 1832, Cotton wrote from his Montego Bay headquarters to Belmore at King's House, Spanish Town. There had been further pitched battles, this time around Montpelier in Saint James'. While again, the colonial forces had repulsed an attack, they had not the strength to occupy the positions they took. Such was the scale of the rebellion that he could not protect every estate nor take the fight to the rebels 'in detail' – 10,000 troops would not be enough. Instead, he was employing his forces to try and prevent the 'horrid incendiary system ... and the spirit of rebellion from contaminating the districts now tranquill [*sic.*]'.

On 3 January 1832 reports came in from Manchioneal on the north-eastern coast of the island in Portland Parish. Whereas before there had been hints of insubordination in that quarter, Edward Panton, magistrate there, now reported that the conditions amounted, 'I may almost say, to rebellion'. Panton recounted that the workers on his own estate, despite 'every persuasion', as well as the four adjacent plantations, had refused to work. 'Every hour since,' he said, 'informs us of similar delinquency on the part of other estates; and from the manner in which the insubordination first shows itself, there can be no doubt it is an organized system.' He complained of having only about forty militia to defend the planters' interests in a parish fourteen miles in length and containing 3,000 enslaved people, and asked for regular troops. His letter finishes with an alarmed postscript: he had just receivednews 'that a number of disaffected negro men were met last evening in the immediate neighbourhood of those estates who first struck work, *armed with cutlasses*'.

Cotton wrote the same day, also detailing the organisation of the rebels. The estate burnings were seemingly executed by signals from the hills surrounding them and were not carried out by the enslaved of a plantation but by 'moveable parties' of rebels who seemed to gain the cooperation of the resident workers on arrival. Cotton said he was opening communications with the maroons, so that they might be employed in the fight and capturing rebels in the hills and forests, where the militia and regulars were not effective.

By this point Cotton's forces had taken a toll on the rebels they had met in battle; he had also set up courts martial which delivered swift executions ('as immediate example ... both politic and necessary') of captured rebels. To accompany this he had issued a proclamation to 'the Rebellious Slaves' on 2 January; it held out a pardon to all those (excepting the ringleaders) who surrendered immediately, while promising that 'all who hold out will meet with certain deaths'. He was offering substantial rewards of $300 for ringleaders. On 4 January it seemed his tactics were having an effect – despite one officer reporting seeing rebels in military garb who 'holooed War, war' at soldiers from the hills – many absent enslaved people were returning to their plantations. A ringleader had been taken, and Cotton had ordered his immediate trial and execution, claiming that 'it is the fear of punishment that alone acts upon them to come in'.

By 6 January 1832 Cotton reported that 'the neck of this widely spread and organised insurrection was broken' and that the rebels, although in many different places, were continually moving without any fixed plan. There were still clashes and some fighters were taking to the mountains, where it would be difficult to pursue them. Cotton credited the assistance of the maroons, the offer of clemency and above all 'fear' to his success. By 5 February 1832, with the insurrection all but suppressed and a majority of the enslaved who had been absent returned to their estates, Belmore proclaimed the end of martial law (in part so that attorneys, managers and overseers of estates could cease militia service and return to their plantations). By 19 March Belmore reported to Goderich that the rebellion was over.

When the Jamaican Assembly inquired into the rebellion in June that year they made accounts for the financial 'injury sustained' through fires, robberies by the enslaved, as well as calculating the cost by loss of labour during the rebellion (they did not include the loss of the enslaved killed or executed). It stood at £1,154,589 2s 1d. Added to this was £161,569 19s 9d expended in the suppression of the rebellion (the provisioning of troops and militia, payments to the maroons), bringing the total to approximately £1,316,000. This was a huge financial loss to an already economically struggling colony facing bad harvests and gradually diminishing sugar production and prices, amounting to around 19 per cent of the island's estimated gross domestic product in 1832, and precipitating an increase in tax rates by about 2 per cent to pay for it.

And questions remained – what caused the rebellion? What motivated the enslaved to rise up in the coordinated way they did, and what was their objective? And how did the island's plantocracy, once the immediate danger began diminishing in the first weeks of 1832, respond?

The testimony of one of the first white prisoners of the rebels, William Annand, the Overseer of Ginger Hill plantation, who was recovered by troops after the battle with rebels there on New Year's Eve, 1831, sheds some light on how the rebellion took shape.

Annand, who had been a (relatively well treated) prisoner of the rebels for eight days when he was found, gave a deposition as to what happened on 1 January 1832. He said that just before Christmas, another overseer had warned him that the enslaved intended to disarm the white people over the holidays, and that he should come and shelter with a greater number of people. He did not pay this much regard, nothing of his plantation's workers' conduct led him to believe it to be true – he admitted though that 'I was, however, undeceived' of this notion.

On 28 December matters came to a head. When the enslaved of Ginger Hill were asked to turn out they seemed disaffected. He asked what they wanted and William Buchanan, one of their number, 'said they had come to beg Busha [a dialect term for an overseer] for to-day, as Sunday was Christmas Day'. Annand said that he informed Buchanan that this was his intention, he just wanted the workers to turn out so he could see they were there. 'With this,' Annand said, 'they seemed dissatisfied.' He went to the house, but Buchanan followed him, laid hold of him, saying, 'Busha, you now my prisoner', and called for a number of other of the estate's workers.

Asked by Annand what was the matter, they said they had worked long enough as enslaved people and they now intended to fight for their freedom, which had long been promised. They said if he delivered up his arms and powder he could remain on the property undisturbed as long as he didn't interfere.

He tried to reason with them on the 'impropriety of such conduct' but to no avail (the testimonies from the rebellion are full of white men incredulous as to why the workers they held in bondage would not listen to them):

They said that I knew as well as themselves that Jamaica was now free, and half the estates from there to Montego-bay were burnt down the night before; that they were obliged to assist their brethren in this work of the Lord; that this was not the work of man alone, but they had assistance from God.

Annand saw that he could not persuade them otherwise so gave up his arms and powder, was told to remain in the house, or a guard might shoot him. He remained, observing arms being brought in throughout the day.

On 29 December Annand reports that he saw a 'great many strange negroes' arrive at Ginger Hill, some with guns, others armed with cutlasses and lances. The rebels had scouts all around the area and when they briefly thought Ginger Hill was to be attacked by militia, they retreated to a nearby narrow defile so as to better repel them, but the forces went elsewhere. After this, Annand became aware that the rebels intended to burn the estate down. A Ginger Hill driver (an enslaved worker who acted as a kind of gang leader on the plantation) confirmed this and said he should go and save his own life – he found Annand refuge at the house of a nearby freeman. The estate's enslaved inquired after him there, and were pleased he was out of harm's way. Ginger Hill was then put to the torch, after it had been gutted of provisions and other stores.

That evening, Annand met the man identified as the leader of the rebellion, Samuel Sharpe. Sharpe, around twenty-seven years old, was an urban enslaved person working in Montego Bay town. He was literate and ambitious, and he had found a calling in the Baptist Church, where he had become a 'Daddy' or 'Ruler' among the enslaved congregation.

Annand recounts meeting Sharpe, who seemed to command the party who came to the house. 'Brandishing their cutlasses over my head, and pointing their muskets at me, [they] made me swear that I would never stand between them and their rights.' Then Sharpe himself addressed him, saying, 'he did not wish to take away the life of any person who did not stand between him and his rights.' Sharpe reportedly said that he had recently begun to 'know much' of religion and that in consequence he knew, as Annand did, that letters had been sent from England ending slavery, but the planters of Jamaica kept him and his comrades enslaved without any authority.

'He said a great deal more,' Annand added, 'all tending to show, that, from the religious notions he had imbibed, he conceived that slaves had a right to be free.' Annand closed his statement by hinting at a wider conspiracy, suggesting that the rebellion might have been coordinated by white Baptist missionaries. During his time as a captive, Susannah Crawfurd, an enslaved woman from Ginger Hill, had told him that a free acquaintance of hers had told her that Mr Burchell, a Baptist missionary who had recently left Jamaica, had returned on 28 or 29 December, and was concealed on board a ship in Montego Bay. According to these reports, Burchell had written to his deputies (Daddies and Rulers like Sharpe) to say that he would not come ashore until 'this affair' was settled, cautioning that no blood should be shed, but however saying he would always support 'his dearly beloved children'.

Trials of rebels began in court martial as the rebellion was still taking place, then continued in the separate slave courts which administered sham justice to the enslaved, predominantly charged with the broad offence of rebellion defined in the 1816 Slave Code. Testimony collected by the Jamaican Assembly as they inquired into the rebellion, and at the trials of enslaved rebels at slave courts (including Sharpe, who was eventually captured) and trials of missionaries (at regular courts) that followed, reflected this impression of the ideology and intentions of the rebels.

The rebels, it is true, had in part been inspired and took an ideological framework from the gospel; Annand made much of the 'religious notions' Sharpe had 'imbibed … that slaves had a right to be free', and his claim that the enslaved people who detained him believed themselves to be carrying out the work of the Lord, while the condemned rebel Linton told a visiting minister that 'religion says we cannot serve two masters, but must only serve Jesus Christ'. Much was made in confessions of rebels published by the Jamaican Assembly's inquiry and in the trials of Sharpe and others identified as ringleaders of the religious connection: Thomas Dove's confession, which identified Sharpe as the leader and 'only instigator' of the revolt, claimed that Sharpe's authority was drawn from his status as a 'head leader' in the Baptist church at Montego Bay. This, combined with his literacy and intelligence meant 'the negroes considered that what Sharpe told them … must be true as it came from their church.' Statements and witnesses that emphasised Sharpe and other rebels' insistence on their acolytes swearing on the Bible to either 'sit down' from work in non-violent resistance, or drive the white people from the island (testimonies differ), were also given prominence. All this tended towards the planters' wish to put the Baptists particularly, and non-conformist missionaries in general, in the frame for the rebellion.

But this was no millenarian movement with Sharpe, the other black 'Rulers' and the white missionaries as spiritual leaders and spiritual salvation the goal – the objectives of the rebellion's leaders, Sharpe particularly – as elucidated by the confessions of prisoners and trial witnesses, were temporal and material, amounting to an immediate emancipation of the enslaved on the island and a transformation of the economic relations between those erstwhile in bondage and their white masters. The tactics were not those of prayer or martyrdom but of economic disruption, property destruction, the withholding of labour, and latterly, once they were met with resistance, guerrilla warfare.

The confession of Robert Gardner, an enslaved man from the Greenwich estate in Saint Ann's, who as a junior leader or 'colonel' in the rebellion testifies to Sharpe's materialist aims and his justifications. He reported that the plans for the rebellion, which had been spoken about casually for some time, crystallised in the run-up to Christmas. At a meeting after prayers at the Montego Bay chapel (which had capacity for over two thousand people), the various black leaders gathered and Sharpe addressed them, according to Gardner, thus:

> The thing is now determined upon, no time is to be lost; the King of England and Parliament have given Jamaica freedom, and it is held back by the whites, we must at once take it. The King sent the law since March last, and it has been withheld by whites; rise at once and take it.

Gardner's testimony is to be questioned: he was after all a prisoner and in his confession is keen to point out his reluctance to pursue Sharpe's plan, his attempts to stop burnings and his praise for the treatment given to him by his white captors. But it tallies with the other evidences given during the trials and inquiry. John Davis, in his confession, also spoke of a meeting of the Rulers at the Montego Bay chapel prior to rebellion. He reported that 'Daddy Ruler Sharp', at the suggestion that the rebellion be delayed 'very nearly knocked the man down for saying so', adding, 'if we put it off till after Christmas the white people will over-come us; let us do it now before any guards are put on, and then we will get the arms belonging to different houses and estates easily.' Edward Barret, enslaved people on the Seven Rivers estate (Saint James'), who gave evidence in Sharpe's trial, said that Sharpe had instructed him and others that they must not work until they were granted half pay by their masters. Here were men with a plan to gain emancipation and an understanding of how the island's disease, weather and economic problems, increasing pressure from Britain for emancipation, as well as the disruption to normal movements by the slaveholders due to the Christmas holidays presented them with the opportunity to seize freedom.

The testimony of the imprisoned rebel Linton (given to priests who spoke to the condemned) did not offer up much about other participants ('a great many') as he was to die anyway and was not minded to as a consequence, but gives further insight into the rebels' plans and planning. He said there had been talk among the enslaved of such a rebellion for two or three years – 'every year back at Christmas or October we were to begin, but were afraid to jump off until this year; we were very near beginning it either last March or last October.' As well as stating his religious arguments for freedom he gave an account of how the political discourse around abolition had influenced the rebels:

> We all believed this freedom business, from what we were told and from what we heard in the newspapers, that the people in England were speaking up very bold for us; we all thought the King was upon our side.

He added that Robert Gardner had gone further, saying that the King had ordered the regular troops on the island (as opposed to the militia of planters and employees) not to fight the enslaved, and was sending arms for the enslaved. This was seemingly a widespread belief, leading to calls from various militia commanders during the rebellion for small detachments of regulars to dispel the myth among the rebels.

He then hinted towards what he thought were the designs of the rebel leaders if they had been successful in driving the whites out of the colony:

> The head people among all us negroes were then to divide the estates among us, and to work them with the common negroes, who were not to get their freedom, but work as they do now. I might as well tell the truth, though they would have had bad

treatment from us; we could not treat them as white people now treat them; we would have been obliged to rule them hard to keep them down.

This perhaps speaks to an awareness of the systems of nominally free but still coercive and restrictive plantation labour put in place by Toussaint L'Ouverture of the successful Haitian Revolution in the French colony of Saint-Domingue (1791–1804) which reverberated in Jamaica, although Linton rightly identifies that very little could be worse than the condition of enslavement.

Linton closed his statement, seemingly accepting death and awaiting eternal life, by warning his interviewer that 'if the gentlemen do not keep a good look-out, the negroes will begin this business in three or four years, for they think the Lord and the King have given them the gift.'

Samuel Sharpe did not speak at his trial. After the prosecution witnesses had testified, mostly enslaved people who attested to his instigation and command of the rebellion and the armed parties that burned estates and fought the colonists, his defence offered little more than claims the witnesses were lying (the details of their testimonies are occasionally inconsistent, and many were prisoners who would do well from identifying a ringleader who swept them up). Sharpe was found guilty of being a 'principal leader' in the rebellion on 19 April 1832 by the slave court and sentenced to be taken to a place of the Governor's choosing and hanged.

An account of Sharpe's own words does however survive in a book published in 1853 by Henry Bleby, a Methodist missionary who at the time of the rebellion was residing in Lucea, Hanover Parish in the northeast of the island and one of the places the insurrection raged.

Bleby, who was a campaigner for abolition and sympathetic to the rebels (he lamented that someone as charismatic and noble as Sharpe had been 'immolated at the polluted shrine of slavery'), says he spoke to a number of imprisoned rebels in the aftermath of the rebellion, including Sharpe.

Copy Sentence

The King against Samuel Sharpe

Tried and found Guilty the 19th day of April 1832 –

Sentence. –   That the said negro Man Slave named
Samuel Sharpe be taken from hence to the place from whence he
came and from thence to the place of Execution, at such time
and place as shall be appointed by His Excellency the Governor,
and there to be hanged by the neck until he be dead—

Continued

Copy of the death sentence passed against Samuel Sharpe by a Jamaican slave court on 19 April 1832 for being the 'principle leader' of the recent slave rebellion there. The court also awarded Sharpe's owner compensation for his loss of human property.

From these testimonies, drawn by a man with a very different objective to the plantocracy's witnesses and confessors, we get a similar picture of the shape and objectives of the rebellion. Hylton, a prominent enslaved conspirator, told Bleby that Sharpe made use of Baptist prayer meetings to recruit the enslaved to his cause and spread the message of insurrection, telling one meeting that if 'black men did not stand up for themselves, and take their freedom, the whites would put them out at the muzzles of their guns, and shoot them like pigeons'. His plan was seen as dangerous but his arguments were apparently convincing. He swore recruits on the Bible to the aims of the campaign and secrecy. Sharpe and the other leaders of the rebellion were also clearly cognisant of the political circumstances they faced – Sharpe made use of the seditious resolutions of the slave owners' meetings to show they would withhold emancipation, that they had even discussed secession from the British Empire in favour of the United States to sustain slavery.

Bleby also discusses the origins of the misapprehension of some of the enslaved that legal emancipation from Britain was either imminent or already enacted – certainly the newspapers, which were circulated and read aloud among the enslaved, and Bleby maintains that Sharpe and his fellow leaders, although aware that this was not strictly the case, allowed such rumours to circulate in order to strengthen their support.

Bleby's interviews with Sharpe (while he was in prison awaiting execution) provide us with as close an account of the man's own thoughts as we might find. Sharpe told him that while he was personally well-treated by his owner (also called Samuel Sharpe), he had come to understand via the Bible that enslavement was morally repugnant and impossible and had to be ended by struggle, saying, 'I would rather die upon yonder gallows than live in slavery.' Sharpe also discussed his tactics and regrets from the rebellion. He regretted the loss of life and property caused by fighting and rebellions, indeed Hylton told Bleby that Sharpe's campaign was intended as one of '*passive resistance*, and to fight only in case the buckras [white people] used force to compel them to turn out and work as slaves'. Sharpe was apparently angry and crestfallen when he saw the first burnings – he knew then 'the *buckras* would shoot and murder the people without mercy, and have an apology for doing so' and the rebellion would fail – claiming to Bleby that he thought the relative docility of the enslaved under their owners would persist under his command but finding that, 'the spirit of revolt, once evoked, was not susceptible to control'.

Sharpe was executed at Montego Bay on 23 May 1832. There were a great many spectators come to watch him die, but he marched to gallows with 'a firm and even dignified step', wearing a new suit of white clothes that some of his owner's family, who remained fond of him, had made.

In his speech at the gallows he acknowledged, apparently, that he had transgressed the laws of God and the country and expressed regret and hopes of forgiveness from God. He also vindicated missionaries from involvement, exhorting people to follow the instructions of Christian ministers. Sharpe's owner marked this 'decrease' in his property in the slave register he was legally mandated to maintain, the court ordered he be paid £16 10s, the 'value' of the leader of the rebels.

Sharpe was the last of the 312 enslaved people executed for involvement in the rebellion, of some 626 tried. Added to this were, officially, 307 enslaved people killed during the rebellion (although the real toll is almost certainly much higher from *ad hoc* executions). Fourteen white people lost their lives.

The Jamaican colonists' bloodlust was rapacious in the rebellion's aftermath. Even though as the trials continued into 1832, Goderich requested that death be saved only for those rebels who had 'earned a peculiar notoriety by the guilt, or the audacity of their conduct', with Belmore attempting to persuade the planters on the courts' benches that he should be allowed to show mercy to the condemned (commuting their sentence to transportation on imprisonment, generally), and despite a February 1832 Royal Proclamation declaring a general amnesty if the enslaved returned, the slave owners would not listen.

Just as 'the Spirit of Revenge' with which the Grenadian colonists had in 1796 pursued the deaths of their former belligerents, to the point of refusing the Governor his prerogative of mercy, had excited the 'indignation and astonishment' of London, their Jamaican counterparts did the same.

In April 1832 Belmore informed London that the island was still trying enslaved people, despite the amnesty. He said he supported this as a way of distinguishing the 'different shades of their guilt'. He had however, been disturbed by the conduct of trials and the insubordination shown by the island's jurors against his authority as Governor. On 10 February 1832, returning to King's House from a tour of the insurrection's area, he felt 'serious alarm' that, of ten prisoners tried at the Montego Bay Slave Court, seven had been executed. He instructed the Chief Justice, Attorney General and Custodes to show leniency and humanity where they could, releasing minor offenders without trial – but found when receiving a list of prisoners for trial at slave courts on 20 March, there were still sixty-eight listed. Belmore asked that in the case of capital judgements he be sent evidence, to review cases and grant clemency in all but the most aggravated. But, in the cases of rebellion, the courts at Montego Bay (Saint James) and Lucea (Hanover) did not comply, and it seems carried out the sentences almost as soon as the prisoners were condemned.

Belmore and his masters in London lamented such proceedings – not out of human feeling for the enslaved (although there may have been a little of that, and certainly some moral indignation over quite so many executions), but because they feared it would continue to keep the rebellion, and the unhappy circumstances of bondage in the minds of the enslaved and lead to further revolts. 'It is of the utmost importance,' Viscount Goderich told the Governor, 'that the minds of the Negroes should be diverted from the dangerous recollections with which the history of the late rebellion unhappily abounds.'

But the colonists didn't just pursue their enslaved enemies. 'Free persons of colour', such as James McIntosh, Donald McIntosh and John Largie, tried 23 March 1832 for, 'endeavouring to excite and stir up ... Slaves to commit traitorous and rebellious practices ... [to] ... change in the state and condition of Slaves of this Island' – all three were convicted, with only Largie saved from death. Goderich regretted the executions, commenting that their conduct 'was not marked by any peculiar inhumanity ... [with] ... no proof of their having been leaders in the revolt'; Bleby, who interviewed the men several times, found them 'very ignorant' and concluded that they only became involved in the rebellion due to Sharpe's charisma.

However, the group they pursued most doggedly, if unsuccessfully, were the white non-conformist missionaries they saw as the source of the rebellion. The missionaries, particularly the Baptists, already hated by many of the slave owners, were quickly accorded culpability as the insurrection raged. Royal Navy Commodore Arthur Farquhar, who was involved in the revolt's suppression (and received thanks and gifts from the Jamaican Assembly for it) had a letter published in two Jamaican newspapers, *Watchman* and *Jamaica Free Press*, published 18 February 1832, in which he blamed the 'unnatural rebellion of the deluded negroes ... in a great measure' on, 'the fanatical teaching and preaching of a sect called the Baptists'.

Such was the feeling that the Hon. Henry Cox (variously a Custos of St Ann Parish, a major-general in the militia and a Member of the Assembly) wrote to the Governor's Office on 25 January 1832, calling the non-conformist 'sectaries', a 'dangerous set of people to the island', adding that they should either be expelled or interned, the latter being for their safety as he believed otherwise, 'men driven desperate ... [would] wreak their vengeance on them'. The pro-slavery *Jamaican Courant* newspaper meanwhile ominously commented in January 1832 that there were 'fine hanging-woods' for preachers in the disaffected parishes.

Thomas Burchell, a Baptist missionary who had left Jamaica and returned as the insurrection was going on, was identified as one of the principal instigators, such as by the testimony of Ginger Hill's overseer, Annand, who said that an enslaved woman told him the preacher was lying offshore, waiting for the colonists to be overthrown. Based on this, and confessions of rebels after condemnation that suggested they looked to his arrival as the time of their freedom, Sir Willoughby Cotton had him arrested and, although his papers were examined and found to be innocuous, he was confined to the ship he came on.

Burchell was released and headed ashore, but on the evening of 10 February 1832 a mob attacked and tore down the Baptist chapel in Montego Bay. Burchell, living nearby, was made aware of a threat to his life and so boarded a ship (with some difficulty), meaning to quit the island. However, an affidavit stating that he had incited the rebellion was sworn against him by one of his black congregation and he was arrested. Burchell was due to be tried for his part in the rebellion on 13 March 1832, but the indictment against him was not proved, as his accuser had admitted he had been bribed to lie about Burchell, and there was no other evidence. Once again free, Burchell was again threatened by a mob, and so he left the island, this time requiring military escort.

Another prominent missionary tried was the Reverend Henry Gottlob Pfeiffer, a Moravian missionary. On 12 January Pfeiffer pleaded not guilty at court martial. He was charged with enticing and persuading 'sundry slaves to join and engage in a traitorous and rebellious conspiracy against

His Majesty's authority'. The prosecution's witnesses were all people of colour, both free and enslaved, and generally attested, although in an inconsistent manner, that Pfeiffer had told the enslaved that they had been made free, and that they should stop work to obtain their freedom.

Sarah Wilson, one of the enslaved witnesses, who claimed to only have reluctantly struck work after seeing her fellows do so said, 'Mr Pfeiffer told me I was free and I took it.' John Sutton, a free mixed-race man, meanwhile claimed that enslaved rebels he had spoken to had said the missionary had assured them of their freedom. (Sutton was labelled by the defence as a 'bad character', and was subsequently shot for involvement in the rebellion.) The inconsistencies of the testimonies were picked apart by the defence, as well as 'respectable' white witnesses attesting to Pfeiffer's character, and he was acquitted.

Despite the acquittals of all missionaries tried for treason, incitement or other crimes associated with the rebellion, they still faced the wrath of the Jamaican mob. The attack on the Baptist chapel in Montego Bay, immediately before Burchell's first attempt at flight and subsequent arrest, was perhaps the most notorious of these (but was not by any means an isolated incident – by 10 February three chapels had already been destroyed). The Custos of the parish reported that he was perplexed as to why the 'crowd of slaves, free black and white men and sailors' were not stopped, as the chapel was adjacent to the courthouse where the constables and militia were stationed (he claimed not to have been there).

Belmore issued a proclamation condemning what Goderich, in London, termed 'disgraceful tumults', charging the custodes with bringing the perpetrators to justice. However, he noted that no prosecutions, nor information as to the culprits came from the parish officials who were at the same time pursuing anyone suspected of rebellion with a vengeful alacrity. Indeed, this might have been because the Baptist Missionary Society in London submitted evidence suggesting many of the parish's 'respectable' inhabitants, including magistrates, were involved. The Society bemoaned that the planters had fixed 'the odium of the revolt on its missionaries', imperilling lives and costing some £14,000 in damage to their properties. Goderich, furious, ordered Belmore to compensate them, and if Jamaican law did not allow this, to pass a law to facilitate it.

The slave owners had only really succeeded in wreaking revenge on the enslaved by judiciary and extra-judiciary means, but this was a Pyrrhic victory – tending only towards further exposing their brutality to an increasingly disturbed mother-country and making further revolts all the more likely. Goderich, in a despatch to Belmore of 1 March 1832, hoped that the planters and their assembly members would come to their senses, stop their reprisals and finally agree to amelioration in preparation for eventual emancipation – otherwise, he feared, the recent rebellion would be 'but the precursor of disasters still more lamentable'.

He was to be disappointed. Despite the acquittals of missionaries and the disbelief and fury of London, the Jamaican slave owners continued with the rhetoric of before the rebellion. In their report on the causes of the rebellion, produced in 1832, the Jamaican Assembly identified four principal sources, each a reprise of the themes developed prior to the Christmas outbreak. First was the 'evil excitement created in the minds of Our Slaves' by the interference of the British government and Anti-Slavery Society, subverting the Jamaican legislature. Second was the 'machinations of craft and evil-disposed' persons to use this excitement to promote the belief that the enslaved were to be free after Christmas.

Robbed by a paucity of evidence of identifying them as the provocateurs of the rebellion, they thirdly identified the Baptists, Wesleyans and Moravians missionaries' practices of appointing church officers (rulers, leaders, etc.) as a cause, claiming this practice allowed the 'less ambitious and more peaceable' enslaved to be 'made the dupes of the artful and intelligent' men selected by the preachers. Finally, they said that discussion of further amelioration and the preaching of the non-conformists, promoting 'a belief that they could not serve both a Spiritual and a Temporal Master', had given the enslaved ideas above their station and caused the revolt.

Hyperbolic as this diagnosis was, it was perhaps more accurate than most of the colonists' analysis of the rebellions caused. Certainly the enslaved were aware from newspapers and gossip of the debate around their forthcoming emancipation and these, not least their masters' increasingly hysterical resolutions and missives in the months preceding the revolt, may have convinced some that emancipation was either imminent or already legally arrived, or that it should be forced before the slave owners began the work they promised to ensure it never came. These notions seemed to have been seized upon by Sharpe and other rebel leaders in order to recruit men and women to their mass 'sit down' and subsequent incendiarism.

Their point about the evils of the non-conformist practice of appointing some enslaved members of their congregations into leadership positions allowing for men with 'violent passions and criminal intentions' to gain command over their fellow enslaved speaks to a (probably wilful and cognitively necessary) underestimation of the qualities and resilience of the people they daily brutalised. Throughout the 400 or so years that Atlantic slavery persisted, revolts had too – charismatic and ambitious people, like Sharpe, always existed among any body of enslaved, from Spartacus to Harriet Tubman and beyond.

This too was true of the Assembly's claims about the problems of instructing the enslaved in religion. It was not just the (falsely) alleged Baptist tactic of teaching that a man could only serve a spiritual master, but the whole concept of proselytism among the enslaved that was held up as a cause. The gospel was dangerous – Pfeiffer, in his defence, called a Church of England minister who testified to this fact: on Christmas Day 1831 this minister had thought to introduce into his sermon John, 8:36, 'If the son hath made you free, then you are free indeed', but had discarded this, 'from an apprehension that such an expression might be misunderstood by the slaves'.

Goderich, in response to news of the colonists' excitement about religion replied (reflecting the long-held thinking of many in this period), that the transition of enslaved populations from imported 'heathen'

African labourer to an English-speaking, Christianised, 'indigenous race' would always tend towards an incompatibility with, and eventual end of chattel slavery.

Even the colonists' claims about how churchgoing facilitated a dangerous opportunity for the enslaved to mix with those from other estates, away from their oppressors, which led to rebellions, spoke to a universal problem for would-be enslavers, not one specific to Christianity. 'I am of opinion,' slave owner Richard Barrett told the Assembly's inquiry, 'that whenever societies are permitted to form in this island, under whatever denomination they may pass, if they are composed entirely of slaves, are permitted to congregate in large masses without the admixture of those superiors whom they are in the habit of being controlled by; if they act under leaders and have passports under the name of tickets, which will carry them all over the island, that under such circumstances we may expect periodical rebellions'. He was right: spaces of discussion, socialisation and worship had long been viewed by both colonial and metropolitan governments as the potential fomenters of disobedience. But slavery was resisted by those subjected to it because it was inhuman, whatever the spatial and ideological basis of that resistance – in the 1760s passports and tickets, as well as the use of enslaved people in skilled trades, had been identified as causes of Jamaican rebellions, now it was Christianity and the abolitionist press – the urge to resist persisted.

So, what were the consequences and after-effects of this rebellion, and their attempts to use them as a pretext to blame the island's problems on their religious and political opponents – attempting to use treason to render these people and their very ideas verboten? They had failed to leverage the legal power of treason and rebellion to destroy the non-conformist 'sectarians', whom they likened to the Catholic priests punished for the Irish Rebellion of 1798. Not satisfied with this, the white inhabitants of Jamaica took to extra-judiciary measures.

In January 1832 they formed a Colonial Church Union which mounted a campaign of devastation against non-conformist missionaries and free people of colour they identified as enemies. By May 1832 they had destroyed fourteen chapels. Reprisals against missionaries did not win the Jamaicans friends in Britain. *The Times*, long a bastion of pro-slavery thought, described the Union as 'raving mad!' in their stated aim of driving all 'sectarians' from the island, ominously inviting the colonists to try it and, 'see who will first be "expelled" – the missionaries or their hateful persecutors'. Even Belmore, who had resisted at every turn pursuing his white population for sedition or attacks on missionaries and free people, was moved by the Union's activities to issue warrants for arrests, which were ignored by the island's constables.

Against the enslaved of the island they had fared better in their campaign for revenge – both judicial means and others had yielded much blood for the colonists, Belmore boasting to London that the enslaved had been shown 'their utter incapability of withstanding the constituted authorities'. But the costs of the insurrection's brutal repression, which may well have prolonged it, had been massive property damage and a handy demonstration to anti-slavery campaigners of the brutality of the slavery. The abolitionist Thomas Foxwell Buxton said he was pleased that the colonists 'had disclosed their conduct to the world', and indeed in 1833, Edward Stanley, who replaced Goderich as Colonial Secretary and oversaw the passage of the Abolition Bill, warned that the clear consequence of delaying emancipation in Jamaica was 'certain to lead to insurrection'.

The Earl of Belmore was dismissed as Governor of Jamaica in March 1832. This decision had actually been taken before news of the insurrection had reached London, Belmore's constant conciliation to the increasingly restless and seditious planters (possibly because he was keen to establish good commercial relationships with them) sealing his fate. He was outraged, using his valedictory speech to the Jamaican Assembly and subsequent publications to promote the preservation of slavery. His successor, the Earl of Musgrave, who was less sympathetic (although no radical abolitionist), was announced on 16 March 1832. His delay in arriving, and Belmore's departure, left a void in Jamaican authority, however, which the colonists filled with more vengeful reprisals.

But the tide was not in their favour. Foxwell Buxton remarked in May 1832, as the British Parliament debated the rebellion, that he was 'convinced that, from the change that had taken place in the public mind, the time was not distant – if it had not then arrived – when slavery must cease'. It seems he was right – a select committee he had chaired had brought further to light in the collective British mind the true misery of slavery; the House of Lords had broken with its long-held stance and voted in favour of emancipation; and *The Times*, *The Spectator* and other publications previously firmly supportive of the 'West India Interest' became markedly less so, if not initially full-throated abolitionists. However, by 1833, with the previous year's first election to a reformed Parliament returning a large majority for the pro-emancipation Whigs, *The Times* stated that 'the time for palliatives and half measures is now past' – abolition, though not yet a legal fact, was 'as certain as if it had already been part of history'.

After delay and prevarication on the government's part the Slavery Abolition Act 1833 declared that 'all slaves in the British Colonies [are] emancipated from the 1st August 1834'. Although this was no panacea of humanity – most of the newly freed were to be 'apprenticed' to their former master for a period of years, replacing one form of forced labour with another, and slave owners were 'compensated' to the tune of some £20,000,000 (some £1.8 billion today) – it was a major step towards ending the great evil which had persisted in the Atlantic world for centuries.

Just as the planters of Grenada had attempted to assert the dominance of anglophone slaveholders over their island in 1795 by leveraging the great and terrible power of treason to eradicate their francophone and abolitionist neighbours, so too had the Jamaican colonists attempted to use both threats of treason and its legal power to defeat their ideological enemies when the insurrection that was surely in part their making gave them the opportunity. They manifestly failed, in spite, or perhaps because of the amount of blood they spilled in the process. The success or not of Sharpe's traitorous conspiracy hangs more in the balance, though – he and his fellows did not achieve their aims, and many of them died horribly. But the conflagration that consumed Jamaica in the early days of 1832 can be seen to have hastened the ultimate end of chattel slavery on the island. Sharpe is a national hero of Jamaica, his face on a bank note; he may well have been 'immolated at the polluted shrine of slavery' but he and the other rebels helped to burn its whole edifice down.

but we do not expect that they will
spare the lives of the leaders. We
are ready to die and we shall
die cheerfully and proudly. Personally
I do not hope or even desire to live.
But I do hope and desire and believe that the lives of all our
followers will be saved, including
the lives dear to you and me (my
own excepted) and this will be
a great consolation. You must not
grieve for all this. We have preserved Ireland's honour and
our own. Our deeds of last week
are the most splendid in Ireland's history. People will say hard
things of us now, but we shall be
remembered by posterity and blessed
by unborn generations. You too will
be blessed because you are my
mother.

If you would like to see
me, I think you will be allowed to
visit me, by applying to the Headquarters
Irish Command, near the Park. I shall
hope, have another opportunity of
writing to you. Love to W.W., M.B, Miss Byrne,
Micí and to your own dear self.
P.

Letter from Patrick Pearse to his mother from Arbour Hill prison. (WO 71/135)

Seventeen

TREASON AND THE FORGING OF MODERN IRELAND, 1791–1921

> *Light as a skiff, manoeuvrable*
> *yet outmanoeuvred,*
> *I affected epaulettes and a cockade,*
> *wrote a style well-bred and impervious*
> *to the solidarity I angled for ...*
> SEAMUS HEANEY, 'WOLFE TONE'

On Easter Monday 1916, Patrick Pearse stood on the steps of the General Post Office in Dublin and proclaimed that Ireland was a republic. Pearse was a member of the Irish Republican Brotherhood, a revolutionary group that sought to overthrow British rule in Ireland. Their proclamation began by directly addressing 'Irishmen and Irishwomen: In the name of God and the dead generations from which she receives her old tradition of nationhood, Ireland, through us, summons her children to her flag and strikes for her freedom'. Justifying their use of physical force to overthrow British rule, Pearse continued:

> We declare the right of the people of Ireland to the ownership of Ireland and to the unfettered control of Irish destinies, to be sovereign and indefeasible. The long usurpation of that right by a foreign people and government has not extinguished the right,

nor can it ever be extinguished except by the destruction of the Irish people. In every generation the Irish people have asserted their right to national freedom and sovereignty; six times during the past three hundred years they have asserted it in arms. Standing on that fundamental right and again asserting it in arms in the face of the world, we hereby proclaim the Irish Republic as a Sovereign Independent State, and we pledge our lives and the lives of our comrades in arms to the cause of its freedom, of its welfare, and of its exaltation among the nations.

The rebellion, known as the Easter Rising, ended in military failure as the British forces in Ireland quashed the movement. But the trials for treason that followed fundamentally altered the politics of Ireland and led, over the coming decade, to the outbreak of a War of Independence during 1919–21, the creation of Northern Ireland and the eventual emergence of an Irish Free State in 1922. Treason played a large role in the creation of modern Ireland, and the rebels of 1916 made direct references to those who had previously tried to overthrow British rule but failed. This chapter will look at some of those failures to trace the influences of republicanism in Ireland from the late eighteenth century to the twentieth.

After the defeat of James II in 1690, Catholic Ireland succumbed to the forces of Protestantism. While Jacobitism briefly flared in 1715 and 1745, the ruling Protestant Ascendancy class was largely undisturbed in its position of dominance, controlling government and the legal system. Yet, as decades passed, Ireland's constitutional relationship with Britain became a sore that festered for Irish Protestants. While the Irish Parliament was notionally equal to its English counterpart, the realities of power lay firmly in London. From the 1740s onwards new ideas emerging in France found voice in Ireland and a movement of Irish Patriots started to demand an equal footing for the Irish Parliament. Irish merchants were repeatedly exempted from trade opportunities that emerged from the burgeoning British Empire, especially across the Atlantic as resentment in Dublin increased. Efforts at reform built momentum, especially in the 1770s, but they came to little and often devolved into rancour as sectarian divisions could not be overcome. Nonetheless, Irish Catholics began to find their voice creating a distinct identity that dispensed with loyalty to the Stuarts but demanded an equal participation in the governance of Ireland. None of this was welcome to the Protestant elites who governed the country. A form for Irish patriotism emerged that sought to remove what increasingly came to be resented as English interference in Irish matters. The government attempted to counter these movements, especially after the outbreak of the American War of Independence, and concessions were offered, notably to Catholics, but they remained piecemeal and unsatisfactory. By the 1780s, the reform movement was again gathering some momentum as a new generation of men emerged who sought not just to amend Ireland's constitutional relationship with Britain, but to actively sever ties and create a republic. The French Revolution hugely challenged the monarchy and aristocracy in Ireland, where Edmund Burke epitomised those who deemed it disastrous, and Thomas Paine its emboldened defender. The writings of both men were to prove hugely consequential as the 1790s developed and their ideas, alongside those emanating from France, were both lauded and resisted.

From 1791, the ideas of the Irish Patriots were given a distinct new voice by Theobald Wolfe Tone in his pamphlet, *An argument on behalf of the Catholics of Ireland*, where he declared that religious differences must be overcome if separation from Britain was to be achieved. Through his prose, he eased a political logjam between the competing separatist and sectarian groups in Ireland, Church of Ireland Protestants, Roman Catholics, and religious dissenters, mainly Ulster Presbyterians.

Tone was born in Dublin in 1763 and educated at Trinity College Dublin, where he read law. Although suspended for a year for his involvement in a duel, he was a prolific if unambitious student. He enrolled in the Middle Temple, London, in 1787 and was called to the Irish Bar in 1789, but he had no enthusiasm for practising law. He had married in 1785 and had to provide for his growing family, but was drawn into political affairs. His writings largely precluded him from securing a seat in the Irish Parliament but in 1790 he made acquaintance with Thomas Russell, a radical reformer. Russell aroused an interest in Tone in radical separatism from Britain, and from this, Tone published his *Argument* in 1791. This is one of the finest political polemics ever written in Ireland and it brought him to the attention of a group of Belfast radicals who espoused an anti-sectarian desire to unite and overthrow British rule in Ireland. In October 1791, Tone and Russell travelled to Belfast and were instrumental in the formation of the Society of United Irishmen, with a Dublin branch founded a month later. The following year, Tone took up a role as secretary to the Catholic Committee, which sought to secure the full franchise for Irish Catholics as well as an acceptance that Catholics could sit as MPs in the Irish House of Commons. The Catholic Committee's efforts were somewhat successful, securing a vote equal to that of landed Protestants, but the restriction on Catholic MPs sitting in Parliament remained. Tone left the Catholic Committee in 1793, just as a government crackdown on radical groups began. Responding to the outbreak of war with France, the British authorities sought to quash any groups that espoused republican ideals, and the United Irishmen were left in disarray. Tone was arrested in 1794 and could have faced charges of treason, but he made a deal with Dublin Castle, providing them with no more intelligence than they already had, in return for which Tone's punishment was not a trial but exile instead.

He travelled to America in 1794 but was left disenchanted after George Washington refused to support the French in their fight with the British. Tone was deeply cynical at what he perceived as the mercantilist priorities of American politicians and secretly sought passage to France in 1796 to secure the support of the Directorate in raising an army to invade Ireland. Although he was well received, and created a brigadier general (*général de brigade*) in the French army, French support for an invasion of Ireland was slow to materialise. He struck up a friendship with General Lazare Hoche, who was advocated for an Irish invasion force, and in December 1796, a French fleet sailed from Brest with a force of over fifty vessels and

14,500 men, but it failed to make landfall at Bantry Bay, County Cork due to severe storms, and the fleet was forced back to France. Tone licked his wounds and eventually persuaded Napoleon Bonaparte, the new leader of France, to sponsor an invasion, which arrived in Ireland in 1797, but no general rising took place. Napoleon can hardly be said to have given his full support to an invasion of Ireland as his priorities were focused on the Mediterranean, which eventually became a source of deep frustration among the United Irishmen. Throughout 1798, sectarian tensions had been rising and by summer a rising erupted across Ireland. Known as the 1798 Rebellion, it caused horrific suffering on all sides, and over 20,000 people are believed to have died in the fighting and the vicious reprisals that were imposed across the country. An extraordinary series of treason trials were held in Ireland, with separatists severely punished for their political and physical resistance to Britain.

The Rising caught Tone off guard but he was able to secure a force to sail for Ireland in September 1798. British spies, however, were operating in France and knew of the fleet's departure from Brest, ensuring that London was well warned. They even knew that Lough Swilly, County Donegal was the fleet's likely destination. Despite it sailing far out into the Atlantic to avoid detection, it was spotted and pursued before a series of battles ensued, and the French were forced to capitulate. Tone had fought bravely but upon landfall he was immediately recognised and arrested. He thought of himself as an officer in the French army and expected to be treated as such, but the British only saw him as a traitor. Tone's demeanour served to anger his captors and unlike other French officers who were transferred to Britain, he was imprisoned as a criminal in Derry. Despite his protests, the British were adamant: 'Theobald Wolfe Tone is known only to his Excellency as a traitor, who sought to return to Ireland in order to attempt by armed force what he failed to achieve by intrigue, who has never ceased to promote rebellion and discord, and who at last is about to receive the punishment due to the crimes he has been guilty of committing against his King and country.'

Brought to Dublin in chains, Tone nonetheless remained composed, despite the shock at his treatment. His trial by court martial was held at the Royal Barracks in Dublin and began on Saturday 10 November, overseen by a judge advocate and seven officers. Tone provocatively wore his French officer's uniform: 'a large and fiercely cocked hat, with a broad gold lace, and tricoloured cockade, a blue uniform coat, with gold embroidered collar, and two large gold epaulets, blue pantaloons with gold laced garters at the knees, and short boots bound at the tops with gold lace'. Despite his demeanour and dress, the court immediately sought to establish that Tone was not a French citizen but 'a natural born subject of our lord the king'. Continuing, Major-General Loftus, the judge advocate, charged Tone with:

> having traitorously entered into the service of the French republic, at open war with his majesty, and being taken [arrested] in the fact, bearing arms against his king and country, and assuming a command in an enemy's army approaching the shore of his native land for the purpose of invasion, and acting in open resistance to his majesty's forces, with several other charges of a treasonable nature.

Tone did not deny the charges, but was displeased at being called a traitor, believing as he did that he was engaged in an honourable war. But given the terrible suffering that had taken place in Ireland throughout 1798, it is hard to understand how he could have thought he would not be treated as a traitor. The court demanded that he enter a plea, but Tone instead asked if he could address the court. Tone's oration has become one of the foundational speeches of modern Ireland, addressing as it did what he saw as the plight facing the country. It is both pugnacious and downbeat, justifying his life's endeavours but also recognising that he had failed. No definitive version exists but a copy was made and sent to Whitehall and now survives in the Home Office papers on Ireland from the time. It is marked as not being for circulation.

It is understood that Tone was pleased to be tried by court martial rather than in the common law courts, believing as he did that he was at war. Consequently he was respectful to the court, accepted full responsibility for his actions and declared:

> It is not my intention to give the Court any trouble; I admit the charge against me to the fullest extent; what I have done I have done, and I am prepared to stand the consequences.

Acknowledging that he had sacrificed everything for his cause, including his life, as well as his family's future, he nonetheless continued:

> Whatever I have said, written or thought on the subject of Ireland I now reiterate: looking upon the connexion with England to have been her bane I have endeavoured by every means in my power to break that connexion.

The copy of Tone's speech reflects how the court interrupted him for the first time, warning him that if he continued in this manner he was likely to act in his own prejudice. One of the judges also worried that he was intentionally addressing the court in such a way so as to create propaganda. Accepting that he would strike out the opening section, Tone continued:

> I have laboured in consequence to create a people in Ireland by raising three Millions of my countrymen to the rank of Citizens. I have laboured to abolish the infernal spirit of religious persecution by uniting the Catholics & Dissenters.

He then sought to justify his recourse to France, believing as he did that because the resources to defeat the British were not available within Ireland, he went elsewhere in search of them. Somewhat outlandishly, he then attempted to distance himself from the sectarian violence that had broken out across Ireland since 1795, arguing that as he had been abroad, he was not guilty of incitement. Tone had an ability to compartmentalise his own actions from that of their consequences and in this he was illusionary. While he had not physically led the 1798 Rebellion, he was a figurehead for it. His speech then concluded by noting that he had failed in his life endeavours:

> I will not detain you longer; in this world success is everything; I have attempted to follow the same line in which Washington succeeded and Kościuszko failed; I have attempted to establish the independence of my country; I have failed in the attempt; my life is in consequence forfeit and I submit; the Court will do their duty and I shall endeavour to do mine.
>
> THE COPY OF TONE'S SPEECH, WITH THE FIRST SECTION STRUCK OUT, CAN BE FOUND AT TNA, HO 100/79, FF. 96-97

Tone's final request was to be given a soldier's death by firing squad, but this was ultimately denied to him. The following day, Sunday, having refused to take any visitors to say his final goodbyes for fear he would lose his composure, he learned that he was to be publicly hanged on Monday 12 November at Newgate in Dublin, although the usual subsequent beheading was remitted.

The next and last events in Tone's life remain controversial to this day. Having written his final letters, including a deeply moving one to his wife Matilda, Tone slit his own throat. This has been denied by generations of Irish nationalists who have been unable to accept he would take this course of action, and it has been alleged that a botched murder attempt took place in his cell. He was found at 4 a.m. in a pool of his own blood, having failed to die of his wounds. Tone lasted a further week before dying, but there should be no doubt that he meant to take his own life. That he initially failed to do so does not diminish the intent, which was in accord with the principles he had adopted while in French service and there are multiple other examples of officers and politicians committing suicide rather than face what they believed to be a dishonourable death.

Theobald Wolfe Tone died on 19 November 1798 and his remains were buried at the family plot in Bodenstown, County Kildare, a place that would eventually become a shrine to Irish republicans. Tone's death also allowed the government to save face. On the morning of 12 November, his family and friends lodged a complaint at the Court of King's Bench when it opened, asking that the common law courts hear Tone's case rather than a military court. This was accepted but the court officials were not allowed access to the barracks where Tone was being held. A stand-off was only averted by news of Tone's injuries. The army had tried Tone, but it should have handed him over to the civil authorities. Its failure to do so meant he was deprived due process, although it's unlikely the outcome would have been any different, especially with Tone not contesting the charges. Nonetheless, London was of the opinion that the Irish administration had a lucky escape. The same mistake was not made when the United Irishmen revived the revolutionary spirit in 1803.

The most immediate and ultimately longest-lasting consequence of the events of 1798 was the dissolution of the Irish Parliament and the full integration of Ireland within the newly created United Kingdom of Great Britain and Ireland. It was intended that this would placate Protestants who felt London unduly interfered in Irish matters, while also defending them from Catholic insurgency. But the creation of the United Kingdom only served to inspire dissidents who continue to seek the creation of an Irish republic. Although largely in disarray in Ireland, the United Irishmen once again turned to France for support, although after Tone's death, they were split between seeking self-determination without French support or attempting to reignite French interest. One man emerged from the failures of 1798 with a renewed belief in the need to pursue self-determination without France. His name was Robert Emmet.

Like Tone, Emmet was from middle-class Protestant Dublin. He attended Trinity College Dublin and read law, but his real interest seems to have been debate. Despite the restrictions that had been placed on the debating societies, through Emmet's leadership, they managed to introduce deeply contentious topics inspired by the American and French revolutions, and for this Emmet was expelled. He then poured his energies into supporting the United Irishmen. After their failure to separate Ireland from Britain, he was part of the leadership group that undertook a review of why the 1798 Rebellion had failed. Their findings dwelt foremost on a lack of security around that rebellion's plans, believing that they had been heavily infiltrated by spies. The lesson was clear: any subsequent efforts must only be made known to the smallest possible group of insurgents. Emmet travelled to France in 1800 seeking French support, but he became bitterly disenchanted by their lack of interest in Ireland and now sought to launch an insurgency independent of any outside assistance.

Returning to Ireland at Christmas 1802, by March the following year Emmet had devised plans for a general rising across Ireland. Emmet's innovation was to devise a plan that was to take Dublin Castle completely by surprise, but the secrecy with which he prepared to proclaim Ireland a republic also sowed the seeds of its demise. While taking extreme precautions to ensure that the intelligence services in Dublin knew nothing of the plan, Emmet also failed to generate enough support from across Ireland to ensure a general uprising. Everyone outside his close circle was taken by surprise. His plans soon fell into disarray after an explosion at a depot alerted the authorities to a potential plot. He decided to proceed nonetheless, but only hundreds not thousands of insurgents took up arms. It quickly descended into farce, especially as Emmet read to those who had assembled a proclamation for a republic, which was sneered at. Eventually Emmet and his comrades went into hiding but he was arrested in August 1803. Emmet was cross-examined and inadvertently disclosed that he was in a secret relationship with Sarah Curran, whom he adored. This disclosure also saw his trial delayed as he had initially secured John Curran, Sarah's father, as his defence barrister. John Curran was the leading defender of the United Irishmen but on learning that Emmet was in a relationship with his daughter, he refused to represent Emmet at trial being furious that his family (and his reputation) had been dragged into the botched revolt. Emmet was similarly distressed, but because he thought he had imperilled Sarah as the authorities had discovered their correspondence on Emmet's person when he was arrested. Emmet's interrogators, however, misinterpreted the correspondence and thought they were coded letters when in fact they were love letters.

Emmet's was not the only treason trial for insurrection in Dublin in 1803 but it has cast the longest shadow. He was arraigned to Green Street courthouse for trial by special commission on 7 September but his need to reassemble a defence team delayed proceedings, and his trial did not commence until 19 September. He was charged with treason with intent to kill the King and overthrow British rule in Ireland. The alleged overt acts were his meeting with fellow conspirators on 23 July at a house on Thomas Street in Dublin with the intention to levy war against the Crown. To do so, the court further alleged, he had prepared a manifesto that declared a Provisional Government of Ireland with the intention of handing Ireland to France. Emmet pleaded Not Guilty but refused to offer any defence of his actions. The Attorney General, Standish O'Grady, led the counsel for the Crown and his opening remarks painted a bleak picture for Emmet. He insisted that Emmet had contravened the Treason Act of 25 Edward III (1352) by compassing and imagining the death of the King, forming an alliance with the King's enemies, and attempting to levy war. O'Grady also made clear for the jury that while other insurrectionists had been tried by special commission that year, Emmet was the ringleader:

> We have now brought to the bar of justice, not a person who has been seduced by others, but a gentleman to whom the rebellion may be traced, as the origin, the life and the soul of it.

Emmet's attitude frustrated the court, but he was adamant that he was to take full responsibility for the aborted rising. Witnesses were called, all of whom corroborated the charges, and the jury did not even need to retire before a verdict of guilt was pronounced.

What happened next is one of the most important moments in Irish history. Robert Emmet's speech from the dock, unlike Tone's, was intended as an address not to the court but to the world and is now regarded as one of the finest of its kind. Emmet was deeply affronted that he had been accused of acting as an agent of France and his speech was partly an attempt at rebutting this allegation. The second purpose was an opportunity to explain his actions and to plead that while his rebellion had been an almost complete failure, the idea behind it was not. In both cases he was successful.

On the charge that he intended to establish Ireland as a French protectorate he said:

On the contrary, it is evident from the introductory paragraph of the address of the provisional government of Ireland that every hazard attending an independent effort was deemed preferable to the more fatal task of introducing a French army into the country. For what?

Acknowledging that the United Irishmen did have agents in France (including his brother), but not for the purpose alleged, Emmet then continued: 'If the French come as a foreign enemy, oh my countrymen, meet them on the shore with a torch in one hand – and a sword in the other – receive them with all the destruction of war. Immolate them in their boats, before our native soil shall be polluted by a foreign foe.' Emmet continued in this vein, disparaging the court for insinuating that he was in league with the French. 'Our object,' he argued, 'was to effect the separation from England.'

The presiding judge, Lord Norbury, then interrupted Emmet, warning him that he was making 'an avowal of dreadful treason'. Conscious that he was further implicating himself, Emmet responded: 'What I have spoken was not intended for your lordships, whose situation I commiserate rather than envy'. Instead he argued, it was for his countrymen:

When my spirit shall have joined those band of martyred heroes who have shed their blood on the scaffold and in the field in defence of their country, this is my hope, that my memory and name serve to animate those who survive me.

Despite the loftiness of Emmet's words, he and Norbury exchanged barbs about proper conduct in court, Emmet then issued his closing statement:

> My lords, you are impatient for the sacrifice ... Be yet patient! I have but a few words to say: my ministry is now ended. I am going to my cold and silent grave; my lamp of life is nearly extinguished. I have parted with everything that is dear to me in this life for my country's cause, and abandoned another idol I adored in my heart, the object of my affections. My race is run. The grave opens to receive me, and I sink into its bosom. I am ready to die. I have not been allowed to vindicate my character. I have but one request to ask at my departure from this world: it is the charity of its silence. Let no man write my epitaph; for as no man knows my motives dares now to vindicate them, let not prejudice or ignorance asperse them. Let them rest in obscurity and peace: my memory be left in oblivion and my tomb remain unsubscribed, until other times and other men can do justice to my character. When my country takes her place among the nations of the earth, then, and not till then, let my epitaph be written. I have done.

Emmet was hanged and beheaded the next day on Thomas Street, Dublin, where he grew up. Maintaining his composure until the end, he impressed his most potent enemies and changed the minds of many who were only vaguely sympathetic to his goals before July 1803.

Emmet also bequeathed another legacy to Irish republicans. In his proclamation he had rejected the idea of relying on a foreign power, in this case, France, to achieve independence. His own movement, shambolic as it was, had advocated for the creation of an independent republic that was not reliant on any other power. Although he was ridiculed in court for giving his life for such a cause, his proclamation and final oration, alongside Tone's attempts at achieving separation from Britain, became the core of an increasingly violent republicanism as the nineteenth century progressed. The Young Irelanders of the 1840s tried to emulate them, as did Thomas Davis. From the 1850s, the Irish Republican Brotherhood, known as the Fenians, sought to overthrow the government in Dublin. After Charles Stuart Parnell and the Home Rule movement failed to achieve any sort of self-government in the 1880s, nationalism in Ireland was rudderless.

The first decade of the twentieth century saw the energies of Irish MPs at Westminster try to revive the Home Rule movement, and like Parnell before him, John Redmond, the leader of the Irish Party, held the balance of power in the House of Commons. The outbreak of the First World War intervened and prevented the introduction of a Home Rule bill, but its passage through Parliament in London was hugely resisted by entrenched interests in Ireland, especially in Ulster. The Irish Party rallied to the war cause in the hope that it would ensure the swift revival of the Home Rule bill after the war, but it was in this febrile environment that a group of men and women aspired to revive the efforts of Tone and Emmet and seek independence for Ireland. Although it did not enjoy significant support, the Irish Republican Brotherhood plotted and sought to strike while Britain was distracted by the war, hoping to draw support from the Irish Volunteers, a group who opposed Irish participation in the war. The militants who planned the Rising also drew on the support of the Irish Citizen Army, led by James Connolly, alongside the women's organisation, Cumann na mBan, who organised with the goal of pursuing Irish liberty. Together, they numbered about 1,500 fighters during Easter week of 1916.

The Rising was to commence on Easter Sunday, 23 April, but a failure to land German guns on Good Friday caused commanders to seek to postpone the Rising. Patrick Pearse, chosen as president of the republic, disagreed and the rebels mobilised on Easter Monday among much confusion. Questions of flawed military planning remain to this day as several key buildings in Dublin were not taken, especially those with large caches of weapons, meaning that the positions the rebels did take were largely defended with rifles. In response, the

British forces declared martial law, first in Dublin and then extended it across Ireland before flooding troops into Dublin, securing many of the key areas, including the information exchanges (telephone and telegram centres). The rebels also failed to control the ports surrounding Dublin, meaning that the British were able to rapidly land troops and heavy weaponry in Ireland. Fighting largely focused on Dublin city-centre locations, including around the General Post Office (GPO), Mount Street Bridge and North King Street, where severe casualties, including civilian, were inflicted. By Friday, the British shelling of the GPO became so heavy that the rebels were forced to abandon it in order to avoid further loss of civilian life. By Saturday, Pearse gave the order to surrender. Four hundred and eighty-five people died during the fighting, including over 250 civilians.

The 1916 Proclamation was largely written by Pearse, who drew most on the influence of Tone and Emmet, having emerged as a militant republican slowly and by stages. He was heavily influenced by, and subsequently influential within, the Gaelic Revival movement, which drew on Irish culture and history and sought to advance the revival of the Irish language. Like Tone and Emmet, he read law, but it was language, and then education that preoccupied him. He sought to break from the Anglocentric educational system in Ireland and established a pupil-focused bilingual school in Dublin in 1908. He had been supportive of the Home Rule Bill of 1912 but such was the strength of resistance to it in Ulster, he began to drift towards militant groups. His opinions appear to have hardened by 1913 and the influence that Tone had on his ideals became clear. In an oration at Tone's grave at Bodenstown, Pearse declared:

> We have come here not merely to salute this noble dust and to pay our homage to the noble spirit of Tone. We have come to renew our adhesion to the faith of Tone; to express once more our full acceptance of the gospel of Irish Nationalism which he was the first to formulate in worthy terms, giving clear definition and plenary meaning to all that had been thought and taught before him by

Irish-speaking and English-speaking men.

The following year, addressing a meeting in New York that commemorated Robert Emmet, Pearse declared:

> Patriotism is in large part a memory of heroic dead men and a striving to accomplish some task left unfinished by them. Had they not gone before, made their attempts and suffered the sorrow of their failures, we should long ago have lost the tradition of faith and service, having no memory in the heart nor any unaccomplished dream.

By this stage he had joined the Irish Republican Brotherhood and the hardening of his outlook reflected his involvement in the planning for a Rising and the drafting of the proclamation. He was elected president of the Irish republic and it was his role to proclaim it from the steps of the GPO on Easter Monday.

Pearse and the other rebels were not offered terms upon surrender on Saturday 30 April. Instead, the army rounded up, largely indiscriminately, anyone whom they believed to be involved or sympathetic to the rising. In total, 3,430 men and 79 women were arrested in the following days as a tussle began between the civil and military authorities over how the government should proceed against the rebels. General John Maxwell was appointed Commander in Chief in Ireland on Easter Sunday 1916 and quickly travelled to Dublin. Although he had little to do with the initial repression of the rising, his legacy in meting out justice has cast a long shadow over Ireland. Whether his direct course of action would have differed from that of anyone else appointed to suppress the rebellion is debatable, but the outcome was not. Maxwell immediately clashed with the Irish law officers, who cast doubt on the legality of trying the rebels by court martial. Maxwell disagreed and sought to expedite trials by the military courts. Thereafter, any sympathy the general population may have had for the government was spurned as public opinion quickly shifted from anger at the rebels to support, even adulation.

Maxwell was not wholly to blame. The Home Office was indecisive on how to proceed. The Defence of the Realm Act (1914) introduced at the start of the war had not anticipated open rebellion. The options considered under it revolved around treating the prisoners as enemy aliens and transporting them to prison camps in Britain and trying them in civil court. But this would still have required evidence to be gathered in Ireland. The prisoners could not be held indefinitely in England and there was a fear that they would start to apply to British courts for writs of habeas corpus. Yet, there was a clear reluctance to allow civil trials to take place in Ireland as this would allow prisoners to publicly declare their motives and defend their actions. The solution was for court martials to proceed in Ireland while prisoners were to be transferred to Britain.

But by the time this decision had been made in London, Maxwell had already commenced the court martials. Prime Minister Asquith issued orders that only ringleaders were to be tried by court martial, but no clear definition of what constituted a ringleader was provided. By contrast, Downing Street was unequivocal that under no circumstances were any women to be executed. Maxwell, however, was intent on creating examples of those captured in Dublin city centre. On 2 May, three of the signatories of the proclamation, Patrick Pearse, Tom Clarke, and Thomas MacDonagh, were charged with taking 'part in an armed Rebellion and in the waging of War against His Majesty the King, such act being of such a nature as is calculated to be prejudicial to the Defence of the Realm and being done with the intention and for the purpose of assisting the enemy'. The three men were condemned to death by firing squad and executed at dawn on 3 May at Kilmainham Gaol.

On 4 May, Ned Daly, Willie Pearse, Joseph Mary Plunkett and Michael O'Hanrahan were similarly tried and convicted. Only Plunkett was a signatory of the proclamation and the evidence against the rest was circumstantial. On 5 May, John McBride was tried and executed while Eamonn Ceannt, Seán Heuston, Con Colbert, Michael Mallin and Thomas Kent were all executed by 9 May. The last two ringleaders, James Connolly

Patrick Pearse's court martial record. (WO 71/135)

and Sean MacDiarmada, were tried on 9 May and executed the following day. Connolly's execution was to inspire a new generation of rebels: he had been injured during the fighting and was unable to stand so he was shot seated in a chair. The civil authorities in London were keenly aware that punishments must look just and Maxwell was warned to avoid 'anything which might give rise to a charge of hasty procedure or want of due care and deliberation in confirming sentences.' The opposite prevailed.

In the end, 90 death sentences were handed down by court martial and all but the 15 men named above were commuted. In one sense, this was notionally lenient. But the fact that the trials were held in secret, and despatched with such speed, caused shock not just to the government in Dublin, especially the Irish law officers, but also to politicians in London. In total, 3,430 men and 79 women were arrested in the weeks after the Rising was suppressed. Of the women, the most notorious was Countess Constance Markievicz. Born Constance Gore-Booth, she was descended from a seventeenth-century planter family and was raised in considerable comfort. Studying art in Paris, she met her husband, Count Casimir Dunin-Markievicz, a Pole also studying there. They married in London in 1900 and thereafter established themselves as the centre of the Irish cultural scene. The marriage did not last and they separated amicably in 1909 as Markievicz became increasingly involved in republican and socialist politics. She joined the Irish Citizens Army and Inghinidhe na hÉireann (daughters of Ireland) and then Cumann na mBan. Fiercely opposed to Irish involvement in the World War, she was active during the Rising, serving as second-in-command to a troop of Irish Citizen Army combatants, but after a week of increasingly intense fighting, she surrendered. Maxwell had intended that she be dealt with like her male counterparts, but he was overruled by London. Asquith was adamant on this point.

Considerable attention was paid to Markievicz's fate. To get around the charges laid against the men, an alternative charge was lain against her: that she 'Did attempt to cause disaffection among the civilian population of His Majesty'. While found not guilty of rebellion, she was guilty of the latter. Sentenced to death by firing squad, it was then immediately commuted 'solely and only on account of her sex'. Instead she was given a life sentence, transferred to prison in Britain but released in June 1917 as part of a general amnesty. Markievicz went on to become the first woman elected to Westminster parliament, although like all Sinn Féin MPs, she did not take her seat. Instead she became minister for labour in the first Irish Dáil (parliament) before partaking in the Irish War of Independence, 1919–21. She was re-arrested multiple times and a life on the run eventually caught up with her and she died in 1927. In the official record of her 1916 trial, she is reputed to have commented, 'I went out to fight for Ireland and it doesn't matter what happens to me. I did what I thought was right and I stand by it.' A much later private memoir by William Wylie, the prosecutor for the army, recounts that she broke down and threw herself at the mercy of the court. Whatever version is true, and both may be apocryphal, Markievicz played a hugely important role in the direction of Irish politics in the early twentieth century.

The trials of the 1916 rebels were a defining moment in Irish history. Before the Rising, the rebels had little support, but the manner of the secret courts martial, and the prompt executions thereafter, saw public support quickly shift to the insurgents in Ireland. The opposite, of course, happened in England, as the British authorities were severely distracted by the conflict on the Western front in the summer of 1916. Circumstances in Britain demanded justice for those who conspired with Germany and there was some sympathy for this view in Ireland. But the trials changed everything, and a unity of purpose emerged among those who continued to seek separation from Britain. By 1919 war had broken out in Ireland that was on scale that dwarfed that of the 1916 Rising. Ending at a stalemate in 1921, a truce was called and negotiations on Ireland's fate took place between October and December 1921. The Anglo-Irish treaty that emerged saw the state of Northern Ireland remain part of the United Kingdom, while the rest of Ireland was given partial independence. Eventually, not by the gun but by political means, the Irish Free State first left the Commonwealth and eventually declared itself a republic in

1948. This is what Pearse had hoped for when he surrendered, supposedly commenting that he was proud of his accomplishments, believing as he did that other generations would follow his lead.

Many of the ideals of the 1916 proclamation were never achieved, especially surrounding gender and religious equality. An independent Ireland eventually emerged, but the words spoken at treason trials had inspired multiple generations and it is clear why governments, especially in the twentieth century, and during periods of total war, chose to avoid public trials in civil courts. While Theobald Wolfe Tone had intended his oration to be for the court, having spent a life publishing his opinions, Robert Emmet saw his trial as an opportunity to speak to the world. Infused with Enlightenment ideals and the hope of self-determination, they went on to inspire generations. Perhaps the most-repeated quote in Irish history is a fitting way to represent how Tone's words, rather than his actions, influenced generations of Irishmen:

> To subvert the tyranny of our execrable government, to break the connection with England, the never failing source of all our political evils, to assist the independence of my country – these were my objects. To unite the whole people of Ireland, to abolish the memory of all past distinctions, and to substitute the common name of Irishmen, in the place of the denominations of Protestant, Catholic and Dissenter – these were my means.

Form (D). Renewal of Passport.

1663

Ex 2
A

NOTES (See Regulations overleaf).

1. The fee for renewal is 2s. for each year from date of expiry (Regulation 2).

2. Passports which have been in existence for 10 years, or which contain no further space for visas, are not renewable (Regulation 3).

3. If the passport is to be endorsed for additional countries, a form of application [Form F] is also required. Fee 2s. (Regulation 7).

(a) Christian Names and Surname in full, in block capitals.

(b) Insert number of years (not exceeding five) for which it is desired the Passport shall be renewed (see Regulations 2 and 3 overleaf).

(c) Insert exact national status, e.g., "British Subject by Birth" or "British Subject by Naturalisation," "British Protected Person," &c., as the case may be. In the case of "British Subjects by Naturalisation" see Regulation 4 overleaf.

(d) Name and Qualification of person verifying the Declaration (see Regulation 4 (a) overleaf), viz. :—

Mayor, Magistrate, Provost, Justice of the Peace, Barrister-at-Law, Solicitor, Notary Public, Physician, Surgeon, Minister of Religion, &c.

Recommendations from members or officials of Banking Firms should bear the printed stamp of the Bank here below.

I, the Undersigned, (a)......WILLIAM JOYCE......

at present residing at........*3.* ONSLOW GARDENS S.W. 7

hereby make application for the renewal of British Passport No..*125243*

issued to me at *Passport Office London* on the *6 July 1933*
Diplomatic issue

for a further period of (b)..*1.* years.

I declare that I am a (c)....*British Subject by birth*....

and I have not lost that national status, and that the whole of the particulars given by me in respect of this application are true.

I further declare that I have no other Passport in my possession.

Signature of applicant......*W Joyce*......

Space to be left blank for use at the Passport Office.

Date *24/12/38*

And I, the Undersigned, (d).....*St Clair*...... Manager

of...... THE NATIONAL BANK LIMITED ...... hereby declare that,
BLESSINGTON ST, DUBLIN.
to the best of my personal knowledge and belief, the above declaration of

the said ~~Mr.~~ Mr~~s~~ ~~Miss~~ *William Joyce*

is true, and that I can from my personal knowledge of ~~him~~ ~~her~~ vouch ~~him~~ ~~her~~
as a fit and proper person to hold a Passport.

Date **26 SEP 1938**

Signed...... *St Clair*......

Galway
24 Oct 06

1 periods
1. 7. 39

Dioc 26. 9. 38

IMPORTANT.—Applicants, and persons recommending them, are warned that should any of the statements contained in their respective declarations prove to be untrue, they will render themselves liable to prosecution.

CAUTION.—The attention of persons who are asked to sign this declaration is specially called to the fact that it can only be signed from personal knowledge of the applicant and not from information obtained from other persons.

Passport application made by William Joyce in 1938, in which he falsely claims he is a British Subject. His fraudulent use of a British passport was used to demonstrate Joyce owed loyalty to George VI, and could therefore commit treason. (HO 45/24405, part 6)

CONCLUSION

For myself, I always feel anxiety in a court of justice when there
is any possibility of the introduction of political passion. Justice is
ever in jeopardy when passion is aroused.
LORD CHIEF JUSTICE READING WHEN SUMMING UP
ROGER CASEMENT'S TRIAL, 1916

While it may have been altered, tweaked and amended, the core of the Treason Act of 1352 remains in force today, and yet no individual or group has been tried under the legislation since the immediate aftermath of the Second World War. Elements of the law remain clear and obvious – an attempt to assassinate the monarch would undoubtedly be considered treason – but other clauses are more tenuous in modern society.

Treason was always theatre, the court a stage where a traitor's character and beliefs were denigrated and corrupted; the scaffold or execution ground another. But the advent of the rule of modern law meant that the state had increasing difficulty, throughout the nineteenth and twentieth centuries, in keeping the players on the stage to script. The Treason Acts of 1695 and 1800 had merged its form of trial with that of other serious offences like murder. Evidence and witnesses were scrutinised by capable defence barristers keen to win the fame that securing an acquittal would bestow. In 1820 Home Office official Henry Hobhouse complained of the 'capricious' verdicts of modern juries. Securing a conviction under the clauses of the 1352 Act had become much more difficult – jurors did not see its relevance to modern society, and were less inclined to take instruction from the judges. Where Guy Fawkes and Benedict Arnold had kept the ideas of treason in the public consciousness, the actual definition of treason as a legal offence was being lost. Treason was an anachronism, and to bring a case was increasingly risky, conviction was not assured.

The peril for the government of launching and losing a trial in the twentieth century is clear and exemplified by the trial of Roger Casement. Having been knighted for his humanitarian efforts while working for the Foreign Office, Casement then took up the cause of 'physical force' nationalism in Ireland with the intention of forcing the separation of Ireland from the United Kingdom. To arm the Irish Volunteers, he led the Howth Gun Running in 1913 to illegally import weapons into Ireland, some of which were used in the 1916 Rising. He then travelled to America, but the outbreak of war interrupted his plans to raise funds in support of an Irish Republic. Consequently, he travelled to Germany in 1914 with the intention of creating a brigade of captured Irish POWs to fight against the British in Ireland. His efforts were in vain, but his intention was not. Nonetheless, in 1916 the Germans transported him to Ireland, where he was captured on landing and quickly brought to London. He was then charged with treason under the 1352 Act and was tried in a civil court. The case against him relied on the interpretation of his actions as having sought to support the King's enemies 'elsewhere than in the King's realm'.

Casement was punished for neither obeying the letter nor the spirit of the law. He did not deny the treason charges brought against him, but he had not committed treason on British soil. Yet, he was undoubtedly guilty of crimes against the British state. He chose not to contest the treason charges, although there were grounds to do so. Instead, Casement argued that he should be tried in Ireland, where he would receive a fairer trial, but this was rejected and he was convicted of treason. He immediately sought an appeal. The court would have had to take a very narrow definition of treason to acquit Casement and the circumstances and politics of the time would not have permitted this outcome. Thus the court was faced with a political as well as a legal challenge. Significant time was spent during the appeal proceedings debating whether treason committed outside the realm constituted a crime under the 1352 definition, and the prosecution team visited the Public Record Office (as The National Archives was then known) to consult the original parliament and statute rolls in an attempt to clarify the matter by checking for medieval punctuation marks. Ultimately, Casement's appeal failed and he was hanged on 3 August 1916.

Casement's trial proved that bringing a treason charge in a civil court during wartime was a risk. The exigencies of the two total wars Britain was involved in during the first half of the twentieth century brought the process of establishing domestic treachery under the brutal and summary provisions of martial law, something which had generally only been used in Ireland since the sixteenth century and the colonies since the end of the eighteenth century. Emergency powers allowed the government quickly and straightforwardly to establish and punish a whole raft of offences, including ones relating to a form of treason.

In the First World War, the 1914 and 1915 Defence of the Realm Acts allowed court martials to impose the death penalty on anyone found to be breaching its regulations with the intention of assisting the enemy. Some ten people were executed during the course of the war for such crimes, all foreign nationals. In 1940 as the Second World War intensified, Winston Churchill's war ministry passed the Treachery Act. It explicitly made sabotage and espionage treachery, removed treason's questions of allegiance to the King (to deal with foreign agents), and made it an offence to aid the enemy in any way. The penalty was death. Introducing the Bill to the Commons, Sir John Anderson, the Home Secretary, explained why it was necessary: 'The Treason Acts are antiquated, excessively cumbrous and invested with a dignity and ceremonial that seems to us wholly inappropriate to the sort of case with which we are dealing here.' Sixteen people were executed for treachery. It was suspended in 1946.

The Treachery Act provided a straightforward way to deal with enemy agents in wartime. Treason remained cumbrous, ceremonial, and fraught with the dangers of acquittal. Discussing how to deal with Nazi war criminals, including Hitler, when the war finished, Churchill told his Cabinet he thought any trial would be a 'farce', 'all sorts of complications ensue as soon as you admit a fair trial'. To proceed with a trial would be the 'worst of both worlds', the Cabinet agreed – Hitler and his henchmen would have an opportunity to speak, present themselves as martyrs, and the foregone conclusion might bring the judicial process into contempt. If there had to be a formal conviction, as the Americans and Russians believed, Churchill suggested an act of attainder be passed to deal with them.

The risks of testing a treason charge in a courtroom were further proved in the case of William Joyce, the last person to be executed for treason in the United Kingdom. Joyce was an avowed, committed fascist. Shortly before war broke out in 1939, he and his wife Margaret fled Britain for Germany rather than be interned as Nazi sympathisers. He became a German citizen in 1940. He found work as a Nazi radio propagandist, his broadcasts to Britain extolling the virtues of the Nazis and urging surrender. He was nicknamed 'Lord Haw-Haw'.

Joyce was captured on 28 May 1945. In a wood on the German-Danish border he encountered some intelligence soldiers gathering firewood. His appearance was dishevelled but he tried to help them, speaking to them at first in French, then in English. One of the men recognised Joyce's voice from radio broadcasts and accused him of being Haw-Haw. Joyce reached for his pocket to retrieve a false passport, but he was shot in the buttocks by the soldiers, who thought he was going for a gun. Searching him, they found another passport, in the name of William Joyce. Three days later, Joyce made a statement from his hospital bed explaining his actions. He remained convinced that National Socialism was the only thing that could save Britain and its empire, and that malign Jewish influence had caused Britain to go to war against Germany. Realising his ideas would be forbidden in wartime, he had fled to Germany to promote, he said, 'Anglo-German' understanding. Joyce acknowledged that he had been 'denounced as a traitor', but claimed he had engaged in no 'underhand or deceitful act against Britain'. He was also keen to emphasise that he had become, and was, a German citizen.

This fact of Joyce's citizenship, and therefore to whom he owed loyalty, became a key problem for the Crown. On Monday 17 September 1945 he pleaded not guilty to a charge of high treason at the Old Bailey. He was indicted on three counts, all of adhering to the enemy, by variously broadcasting propaganda and obtaining German citizenship when Britain was at war with the nation. The indictment's third count was careful to avoid the problem of German citizenship by specifying only Joyce's broadcasts before he obtained it as treason.

But there was another question – did Joyce ever owe loyalty to George VI? Joyce's father, Michael, was born in Ireland but became an American citizen in 1894, and it was likely that legally William was too, having been born in Brooklyn, New York, in 1906 before the Joyce family returned to Ireland in 1909. William had held a British passport but it seems this was obtained fraudulently. The Crown knew that his defence would make much of this fact, and discussed whether the obtaining of a passport, whether falsely or not, was enough to prove he owed loyalty to the King, and could therefore commit treason. In the event, the judge directed the jury to acquit Joyce on the first two counts, but ruled that Joyce, having held a British passport, did owe loyalty to the King in the period specified by the third count. They found him guilty.

Joyce was sentenced to death, but the argument around his passport was shaky. He appealed, the government were genuinely worried he might succeed as an acquittal would have been disastrous. But he failed. Joyce was hanged on 3 January 1946. His trial had been a close-run thing, proving a treason charge was a dangerous thing to embark on, with such high stakes always at play. He remains the last person tried for and convicted of high treason to this day.

The trial of Lord Haw-Haw demonstrated the risks of using treason in a modern state. There were too many variables – of shifting allegiance, of defining the sovereign – to form a comprehensive case against traitors. As such, new acts were introduced, which were less broad in scope but could be applied to the traitors of the age.

In 1955, as the Cambridge Spies were exposed as traitors working for the Soviet Union, foreign secretary Howard Macmillan likened Britain to the era of the traitor-spies of Elizabeth I. Where once there were Catholic insurgents, now there were communist. Yet, the Cambridge Spies were never tried for treason. Instead, new laws such as the Official Secrets Act or terrorism laws were favoured, as they were more relevant to the crimes being committed, and had a greater chance of securing a prosecution.

Why then does the 1352 Statute remain on the statute books? Britain is not above repealing statutes that no longer apply. The Treason Act of 1352, however, though it may not be used as the legal basis for treason trials any longer, still holds a huge emotional, historical, and legal weight. Like Magna Carta and the Bill of Rights, it has entered the pantheon of talismanic documents which define the unwritten British constitution. It persists as a reminder that there have always been laws to protect the sovereign and the state.

Throughout English history, when the definition of treason has been drastically expanded beyond the bounds of the 1352 Act, the potential dangers of tyranny have emerged. Under Richard II's 'Revenge Parliament' and throughout the reign of Henry VIII, new treasons emerged at moments when the power of the Crown was strong, and could force through new legislation. In both instances, broad swathes of repeal were required at the start of the following reign. In the years of religious reversal, which took place under Edward VI, Mary and Elizabeth, treason legislation likewise needed to revert to the strict confines of 1352. At moments of Crown weakness, treason could also expand through the machinations of royal favourites, factions and aspiring or ambitious nobles, as the lines between the state and the subject blurred once more. When treason becomes too broad, it loses its purpose, becoming instead sheer brutality in the punishment of criminals, a police or military state rather than a specific and limited crime in which all parties knew where they stood.

When we set out to tell the story of treason we assumed it would be a legal history with cases chosen as examples. In this we were wrong. What we ended up charting was a constitutional history of England and its possessions through the prism of treason. Many of the trials that we have included in this book were epoch-defining. We also realised, that by examining them over a longer duration, the extent to which the royal justices and the Crown's legal officials used them as precedent and referenced back to previous decisions on multiple occasions, and the original act continued to carry weight for centuries. But we have only scratched the surface of how charges of treason were used to ensure control was maintained and the 'King's Peace' was not disturbed. Pre-modern monarchs used treason convictions as weapons to ward off challenges to their rule and legitimacy. In the modern times, treason has been used less, but to be a traitor is still universally understood.

To raise a crime to treason, one must have treasonous intent – to 'compass and imagine' the monarch's death. These terms are archaic, but speak to what treason is in essence – an imaginative, generative act. Eleanor of Cobham was accused and Elizabeth Barton was executed attempting to predict when the King would die, imagining his demise. The Pentrich and Cato Street plotters saw their crimes raised above murder and riot to treason because their actions were said to be aimed at overthrowing the government, however serious or realistic that intent was. The Irish and American rebels conceived of an escape from British rule. All treasons are an exercise in the counterfactual, imagining a new, changed state.

It is a creative act for the state, too. They used treason to mark people and ideas that were incompatible with the constitution and dangerous to the body politic. Traitors said this 'is what could be', their pursuers used treason to say 'this is what is'.

The modern-day limitations of the 1352 Treason Act are uncertain. The Act has not has not been tested in a court of law since the years immediately following the Second World War. However, if treason does anything, it sets the extremes of the relationship between state and citizen, and is its ultimate sanction. This is perhaps why despite legislation clarifying exactly the meaning and bearing of the original Anglo-Norman French text for contemporary jurors, treason has never been fundamentally amended or redrafted – to do so would be to fundamentally transform the constitution, the pact of subjecthood and rule within it, and rob treason of its historical and legal weight.

Treason's constitutional status is proved by the way other nations' written constitutions have borrowed it. It is the only crime defined in the United States Constitution, arguably the statement of principles of Britain's most successful traitors. Supreme Court Justice Joseph Story commented that the Americans had 'adopted the very words of the Statute of Treason of Edward the Third', assured of its 'well-settled' interpretations. It was frequently the earliest defined offence of a nascent state, and near universally carried their heaviest penalty. England is the 'mother of parliaments', the Westminster model spreading around the world via its empire. It is also the mother of treasons.

NOTES ON THE SOURCES

The following notes are not meant to be definitive but instead are intended to give the reader options if they wish to engage further with any of the stories within this book in more detail, be that at the archives or in secondary publications. The notes are not exhaustive but instead are intended to illustrate the materials used to write this book.

The authors have been conscious throughout the writing of this book that they are white men, who have been privileged enough not to suffer any of the persecutions, mistreatments and (often deadly) interactions with criminal-justice systems described throughout this work. They have attempted to treat subjects, whether traitor, victim, or agent of the state with compassion and humanity, allowing them and the records they inhabit to speak with their own voices, conscious with the benefit of hindsight of the injustices of the past.

In particular, Chapters Fifteen and Sixteen deal with the experiences and mistreatment of black people in the British Caribbean, particularly the enslaved. The choice of language, outside of quotations from historic sources, has been shaped by guidance produced by scholars of colour, not least the community-sourced guide by P. Gabrielle Foreman et al., 'Writing about Slavery/Teaching About Slavery: This Might Help'. Undoubtedly, though, mistakes remain. Some of the quotations concerning enslaved people from documents and other older sources contain offensive, racist language. These have been kept in, necessary to show the racialised and racist nature of Britain's empire, and to demonstrate the attitudes of slave owners, politicians, even avowed abolitionists.

PART I: DEFINING TREASON

The authoritative academic work on medieval treason remains the writing of J. G. Bellamy, primarily *The Law of Treason in England in the Later Middle Ages* (Cambridge, 1970), which draws on a wide variety of archival sources, legal treatises and chronicle accounts. This book, and the footnotes cited within, should be the first port of call for the reader interested in taking a deeper dive into the legal and political development of treason in the Middle Ages. The archival sources for studying a history of treason are wide ranging. For much of the pre-modern period, the main record collections held by The National Archives are the records of Parliament and the central law courts, primarily the Court of King's Bench. These include the Parliament Rolls (series C 65), which for the medieval period (here covering the period 1275–1504) have been edited with an extensive commentary in *Parliament Rolls of Medieval England (PROME)*, ed. Chris Given-Wilson, Paul Brand, Seymour Phillips, Mark Ormrod, Geoffrey Martin, Anne Curry and Rosemary Horrox (Woodbridge, 2005), available through *British History Online* http://www.british-history.ac.uk/no-series/parliament-rolls-medieval. These are supplemented by records of parliamentary process in the records of the Chancery and Exchequer (C 49 and E 175) and the series of parliamentary petitions in SC 8. For the period up to 1469 noteworthy final acts of parliament, including the 1352 Treason Act, were also enrolled on the Statute Rolls (C 74), which are reproduced and translated (alongside later acts of parliament) in *Statutes of the Realm* (London, 1810–28) (*SotR*). Given the centrality of Parliament's role in the history of treason, we have utilised the authoritative series of biographies published by the History of Parliament, an ongoing project to produce biographies for all historical members of the Commons and Lords. Details of their various publications can be found at https://www.historyofparliamentonline.org/. These supplement the exhaustive series of biographies of leading figures by the *Oxford Dictionary of National Biography* (*ODNB*), available online at https://www.oxforddnb.com/.

The records of the Court of King's Bench consist primarily of the plea rolls (KB 27), where pleadings, indictments and court process were recorded. The reader interested in treason will normally be concerned with the 'Rex' section of the rolls (*rex* being the Latin for 'king') which contain instances where the Crown had a direct interest in a case. These are indexed in series KB 29, with supplementary material also found in the court's own process files, with Crown writs found in KB 37 and additional content among the 'Recorda' files in KB 145.

More broadly, the administrative mechanics of government that regulated everyday life, including the issuing of commissions of inquiry, Crown orders, proclamations, grants and directives are found among the records of the Crown's writing office, the Chancery. Letters patent (often grants of land, titles or other similar gifts) are found in the Patent Rolls (series C 66) and calendared in *Calendars of Patent Rolls* (HMSO, 1891–1986), while letters close (often orders, directives or proclamations) can be found on the Close Rolls (series C 54) and calendared in *Calendars of Close Rolls* (HMSO, 1900–63). The National Archives' series of online research guides provides extensive detail on the content of these records, and the many other medieval sources in the collections at Kew.

ONE EARLY TREASONS AND THE TREASON ACT 1352

For the earliest legal understandings of treason in England, F. Pollock and F. W. Maitland's *The History of English Law before the time of Edward I* (Cambridge, 1895) remains an authoritative work.

An excellent biography of Edward I can be found in Michael Prestwich, *Edward I* (London, 1991; Yale English Monarchs series) which provides valuable background detail for the conflicts which led Edward to pursue new, dramatic, state trials and treason charges against the Scots and the Welsh. *Edward I* is part of the Yale English Monarchs series published by Yale University Press. This series contains useful biographies of many of the medieval and early modern kings and queens discussed in this book. For the legal background to the wars of Edward I see: M. Strickland, 'A Law of Arms or a Law of Treason? Conduct of War in Edward I's Campaigns in Scotland, 1296–1307', *Violence in Medieval Society*, ed. Richard W. Kaeuper (Woodbridge, 2000), and M. H. Keen, 'Treason Trials under the Law of Arms', *Transactions of the Royal Historical Society*, xii (1962). Much of the detail for the first state trials comes from narrative sources, including *Annales Monastici*, ed. H. R. Luard (Royal Society, 1864–9), which describes the details of the punishment suffered by Daffyd ap Gruffydd. The charges laid against William Wallace can be found in *Chronicles of the Reigns of Edward I and Edward II*, ed. W. Stubbs (London, 1882–3). *Documents and Records Illustrating the History of Scotland*, ed. F. Palgrave (London, 1837) also provides useful context for the Scottish wars. The payments made for Wallace's execution at Smithfield, in which it was claimed he sought to be called 'King of the Scots', can be found in E 372/150.

J. R. S. Phillips's *Edward II* (Yale English Monarchs, London, 2010) provides a detailed examination of the troubled king's life and reign. The principal chronicle accounts for the events of Edward II's reign include F. W. D. Brie (ed.), *The Brut* (1908); *Vita Edwardi Secundi*, ed. N. Denhold-Young (London, 1957), as well as the more recent edition of the *Vita* by W. R. Childs (Oxford, 2005); *Chronicles of the Reigns of Edward I and Edward II*; and J. Froissart, *Chronicles*, ed. T. Johnes (London, 1862), which includes the famous illumination depicting the younger Despenser's execution. For the Ordinances of 1311 the primary examination remains M. Prestwich, 'The Ordinances of 1311 and the Politics of the Early Fourteenth Century', *Politics and Crisis in Fourteenth-Century England*, ed. J. Taylor and W. R. Childs (Gloucester, 1990). An English translation of the Ordinances can be found in *English Historical Documents: King John–Henry VI*, ed. P. Chaplais (Oxford, 1971), while the original Anglo-Norman text can be found in *SotR* i, 157–67 and in PROME. For Edward and the Despensers see M. Lawrence, 'Rise of a Royal Favourite', *The Reign of Edward II*, ed. G. Dodd and A. Musson (Woodbridge, 2006); N. Fryde, *The Tyranny and Fall of Edward II, 1321–1326* (Cambridge, 1979); J. C. Davies, 'The Despenser War in Glamorgan', *Transactions of the Royal Historical Society*, ix (1915); and G. A. Holmes 'Judgement on the Younger Despenser', *English Historical Review*, lxx (1955), among others. The younger Despenser's letter to the sheriff of Glamorgan, in which he claimed that the King treated him better than any other, is now found among the artificial Victorian series of 'Special Collections' at The National Archives: SC 1/49/143. The collected essays in *The Reign of Edward II*, ed. Dodd and Musson, also form a valuable new consideration of Edward's reign. For Lancaster and the role of the Steward, see L. W. Vernon Harcourt, *His Grace the Steward and the Trial of Peers* (London, 1907).

NOTES ON THE SOURCES

The political and legal background to the passing of the Treason Act in 1352 has been much debated. The best analysis can be found in Bellamy and the *PROME* entry for the parliament of January 1352, alongside I. D. Thornley, 'The Act of Treasons of 1352', *History*, vi (1921) and M. V. Clarke, *Fourteenth Century Studies*, ed. L. S. Sutherlands and M. McKisack (Oxford, 1937). Works by the lawyers of the sixteenth and seventeenth centuries who devoted much energy to the analysis of the 1352 Act include Sir Edward Coke's *Institutes of the Lawes of England*, first published between 1628 and 1644 (part three of the *Institutes* addresses the definition of high treason), and Hale's *Historia Placitorum Coronae: the History of the Pleas of the Crown*, ed. Sollom Emlyn (London, 1778). For the gaps in the definition of treason in 1352, see S. Rezneck, 'The Early History of the Parliamentary Declaration of Treason', *English Historical Review*, xlii (1927). For the political background, W. Mark Ormrod's excellent *Edward III* (Yale English Monarchs, London), remains the standard biographical work. The enrolled act can be found on the Parliament Rolls held at The National Archives (C 65).

TWO FACTIONALISM AND TYRANNY, 1381–99

For Richard II and his reign, see Nigel Saul, *Richard II* (Yale English Monarchs, London, 1997), while narrative accounts which particularly focus on the reign include: *Historia Vitae et Regni Ricardi Secundi*, ed. T. Hearne (Oxford, 1729); and *Anonimalle Chronicle*, ed. V. H. Galbraith (Manchester, 1926). Given Parliament's fundamental role at the heart of the crises of Richard's reign, *PROME* remains a vital resource for understanding the back-and-forth of the Appellant controversy. See also: Charles Ross, 'Forfeiture for Treason in the Reign of Richard II', *English Historical Review*, lxxi (1956); M. V. Clark, 'Forfeitures and Treason in 1388', *Transactions of the Royal Historical Society*, xiv (1931); S. B. Chrimes, 'Richard II's Questions to the Judges, 1387', *Law Quarterly Review*, lxxii (1956); T. F. T. Plucknett, 'State Trials under Richard II', *Transactions of the Royal Historical Society*, ii (1952); A. Rogers, 'Parliamentary Appeals of Treason in the Reign of Richard II', *American Journal of Legal History*, viii (1964); J. S. Roskell, *The Impeachment of Michael de la Pole, Earl of Suffolk, in 1386* (Manchester, 1984); Chris Given-Wilson, *The Royal Household and the King's Affinity* (London, 1986); A. Tuck, *Richard II and the Nobility* (London, 1985); C. M. Barron, 'The Tyranny of Richard II', *Bulletin of the Institute of Historical Research*, xli (1968).

Richard II's deposition has naturally attracted a wealth of attention. Some of the key works include: B. Wilkinson, 'The Deposition of Richard II and the Accession of Henry IV', *English Historical Review*, liv (1939); C. M. Barron, 'The Deposition of Richard II', *Politics and Crisis in Fourteenth-Century England*, ed. J. Taylor and W. Childs (Gloucester, 1990); M. V. Clarke and V. H. Galbraith, 'The Deposition of Richard II', *Bulletin of the John Rylands Library*, xiv (1930). For the events of the 'Great Revolt' of 1381, the records of the King's Bench (KB 9, KB 27, and KB 145) form the key sources. The People of 1381 project has brought together numerous resources and can be found at https://www.1381.online/.

THREE TREASONOUS WORDS AND TREASONOUS WOMEN, 1402–42

Biographical context for the reigns of Henry IV and Henry V can be found in Chris Given-Wilson, *Henry IV* (Yale, 2016) and Christopher Allmand, *Henry V* (Yale, 1992). The question of whether a distinct legal definition of treason by words developed in the fifteenth century has been much debated. Bellamy provides an overview of the key arguments, notably those of Thornley and Rezneck: I. D. Thornley, 'Treason by Words in the Fifteenth Century', *English Historical Review*, xxxii, (1917) and S. Rezneck, 'Constructive Treason by Words in the Fifteenth Century', *American Historical Review*, xxxiii (1927–8). The most recent examination of the trial of John Wyghtlok and those charged with treasonous words can be found in E. Amanda McVitty, *Treason and Masculinity in Medieval England: Gender, Law and Political Culture* (Woodbridge, 2020). McVitty's excellent study is the first to examine medieval treason in a gendered context, and also includes a fascinating examination of the treason trials of Richard II's reign. Much of the information for the trials themselves comes from the Indictments (KB 9) and plea rolls (KB 27) of the King's Bench.

The main account of the trial of Eleanor Cobham remains Ralph A. Griffiths, 'The Trial of Eleanor Cobham: An Episode in the Fall of Duke Humphrey of Gloucester', *Bulletin of the John Rylands Library*, li (1969), which examines the legal proceedings found in the indictments at The National Archives: KB 9/72/1-6, 9, 11, 14. The English chronicles that recounted Eleanor's story include: *The Brut*; J. S. Davies (ed.), *An English Chronicle from 1377 to 1461* (1856); N. H. Nicolas and E. Tyrrell (eds.), *A Chronicle of London* (1827); J. G. Nicholas (ed.), *Chronicle of the Grey Friars of London* (1852); and R. Flenley (ed.), *Six Town Chronicles* (1911). Supplementary discussion of the royal precedents for treasonous royal women can be found in A. R. Myers, 'The captivity of a royal witch: the household accounts of Queen Joan of Navarre, 1419–21', *Bulletin of the John Rylands Library* xxiv (1940), while a discussion of the Witch of Eye can be found in Jessica Freeman, 'Sorcery at court and manor: Margery Jourdemayne, the witch of Eye next Westminster', *Journal of Medieval History*, xxx (2004). For the 'Lament of the Duchess of Gloucester', see Thomas

Wright (ed.), *Political Poems and Songs relating to English History, composed during the period from the accession of Edward III to that of Richard III* (London 1861).

FOUR THE WARS OF THE ROSES, 1450–85

The period of civil war known as the Wars of the Roses has produced a great number of publications on both the micro and the macro levels. Biographies of the primary figures and the wider events of the conflict include: the Yale English Monarchs volumes Bertram Wolffe, *Henry VI* (London, 2001), Charles Ross, *Edward IV* (London, 1997) and *Richard III* (London, 2011), and S. B. Chrimes, *Henry VII* (London, 1999); Ralph Griffiths, *The Reign of King Henry VI* (Stroud, 2004); Hannes Kleineke, *Edward IV* (Abingdon, 2008); Cora L. Scofield, *The Life and Reign of Edward the Fourth* (Oxford, 2016); Michael Hicks, *False, Fleeting, Perjur'd Clarence* (Bangor, 1992); Michael Hicks, *Richard III: The Self-Made King* (Yale, 2021); Rosemary Horrox, *Richard III: A Study in Service* (Cambridge, 1991); Peter Hammond, *Richard III and the Bosworth Campaign* (Barnsley, 2014); and Thomas Penn, *The Winter King: The Dawn of Tudor England* (London, 2011).

For the Wars of the Roses more generally, Christine Carpenter, *The Wars of the Roses* (Cambridge, 1997), A. J. Pollard, *The Wars of the Roses* (2013) and Michael Hicks, *The Wars of the Roses* (Yale, 2012) remain core studies of the period. Thomas Penn's *The Brothers York: A Royal Tragedy* (London, 2019) provides an interesting examination of the relationship between Edward IV, the Duke of Clarence and the future Richard III. For an overview of the process of attainder and its management, see J. R. Lander, 'Attainder and Forfeiture, 1453 to 1509', *The Historical Journal*, iv (1961) and James Ross ,'The Treatment of Traitors' Children and Edward IV's Clemency in the 1460s', *The Fifteenth Century XIV: Essays Presented to Michael Hicks* (Woodbridge, 2015), among others. The main sources for the numerous attainders enacted against individuals during this period are the Parliament Rolls (C 65) which have been published and extensively analysed in *PROME*. Petitions for the reversal of attainders can be found in The National Archives' series of parliamentary petitions (SC 8), while copies and drafts of individual acts can be found among the records of council and parliament proceedings collected in the Chancery and Exchequer records (C 49 and E 175). The investigations and trial proceedings relating to the retainers of George, Duke of Clarence (KB 8/1) would later form the first records in the series known as the *Baga de Secretis* (KB 8), the official records of many of the most important 'state trials', mainly for treason, held between 1477 and 1813. This may have been in response to the trial of Edward, Earl of Warwick (Clarence's son) in 1499, when the files were deemed to be so sensitive that they were removed to a secret cupboard at Westminster. The 'Bag of Secrets' was kept in a special closet (which is not now known to exist), access to which was controlled by three keys. One was held by the Chief Justice of King's Bench (informally known as the Lord Chief Justice), the others by the Attorney General and the Master of the Crown Office. See also 'The Baga de Secretis', *English Historical Review*, xxiii (1908).

Other contemporary sources for the period consulted in the chapter include: *Letters and Papers of the Fifteenth Century*, ed. Norman Davis, Richard Beadle and Colin Richmond (3 vols, EETS, Special Series, xx–xxii, 2004, 2005); *The Crowland Chronicle Continuations, 1459–1486*, ed. Nicholas Pronay, John Cox (London, 1986), and the older translation, *Ingulph's chronicle of the abbey of Croyland with the continuations by Peter of Blois and anonymous writers*, trans. H. T. Riley (London, 1854), available online at archive.org; the *Great Chronicle of London*, ed. A. H. Thomas and I. D. Thornley (London, 1938); and *The Plumpton Letters and Papers*, ed. J Kirby, Camden Society fifth series, 8 (1996).

FIVE NEW TUDOR TREASONS, 1509–58

For the development of treason in the Tudor period, John Bellamy's *The Tudor Law of Treason* (London, 1976) remains the best overview of the whole period. For the Reformation period specifically, see Geoffrey Elton's *Policy and Police* (1985). I. D. Thornley's 'The Treason Legislation of Henry VIII (1531–1534)', *Transactions of the Royal Historical Society*, xi (1917), provides an interesting examination of treason legislation at a key moment in the Crown's expansion of the definition of treason. Numerous biographies and examinations of Henry VIII are available, including J. J. Scarisbrick's contribution to the Yale English Monarchs series: *Henry VIII* (London, 1997). As in the medieval period, the Parliament Rolls (C 65) and records of the King's Bench remain vital sources in understanding the development of treason legislation. Documents concerning the downfall of these Tudor traitors are calendared in *Letters and Papers of Henry VIII*, which link to documents collected in the State Papers in The National Archives, the British Library, and elsewhere, while acts of attainder, suppression, and supremacy are recorded on the Parliament Rolls in C 65 and printed in *SotR*. From 1497, the Parliament Rolls in C 65 are supplemented by original acts of parliament, held at the Parliamentary Archives. Many of the most important treason trials of the period are found in the 'Baga de Secretis' (KB 8), with lesser cases on the plea rolls of the Court of King's Bench (KB 27).

NOTES ON THE SOURCES

The events of 'Evil May Day' will form the basis of a forthcoming work by Shannon McSheffrey examining the riot in minute detail. A summary of the key points can be found at https://legalhistorymiscellany.com/2017/04/30/evil-may-day-1517/ and in Martin Holmes, 'Evil May Day, 1517: The Story of a Riot', *History Today*, xv (1965). The two primary chronicle accounts of the riot are Edward Hall, *Hall's Chronicle*, ed. Henry Ellis (London, 1809), and Raphael Holinshed, *Chronicles of England, Scotland, and Ireland* (London, 1577). The sole legal record of the charges brought against the rioters comes from the indictment of Richard Marten, enrolled in the records of the King's Bench when he was pardoned some years later: KB 9/478, rot. 8; KB 27/1032, rex rot. 8. His pardon can be found in C 66/633, m. 9. Details of the Crown's response, including copies of the writs and orders issued by the Crown, and details of several executions, were recorded in a Crown precedent book (C 193/142). The rioters were charged under 2 Hen. V, stat. 1, c. 6, printed in *SotR*. Context for Chief Justice Fyneux's attempts to link the riot of 1517 with a previous riot deemed to have been treasonous can be found in Paul Cavill, 'The Problem of Labour and the Parliament of 1495', *The Fifteenth Century V*, ed. Linda Clark (Woodbridge, 2005).

Given the dramatic nature of Richard Roose's punishment, and the involvement of several key figures connected with Katherine of Aragon (such as Fisher and potentially the Boleyn family) around the period of the divorce crisis, his story appears frequently as a sidenote in Tudor historiography. The two key articles that cover the legislative mechanisms employed by Henry's agents, particularly concerning the move from felony to treason, are: Krista Kesselring, 'A Draft of the 1531 Acte for Poysoning', *English Historical Review*, cxvi (2001), and William R. Stacey, 'Richard Roose and the use of Parliamentary Attainder in the Reign of Henry VIII', *The Historical Journal*, xxix (1986). The text of the finalised act can be found in *SotR*, and is recorded on the parliament roll C 65/139, while the draft act can be found among the artificial class of Parliament and Council Proceedings preserved among the records of the Exchequer (E 175), as E 175/6/12.

Anne Boleyn's trial records are held in KB 8/9 and the trial of her alleged lovers are in KB 8/8. A sixteenth-century account of the trial is published in Charles Wriothesley's *Chronicle of England During the Reigns of the Tudors* ('Wriothesley's Chronicle'), ed. W. Douglas-Hamilton, 2 vols, Camden Society (1875). The reactions of the judges in attendance to the judgement made by the Duke of Norfolk is noted in another contemporary account, the law reports of Sir John Spelman, published as *The Reports of Sir John Spelman*, I, ed. Sir John Baker (Selden Society, 1977). The King's decision for Anne to be executed by beheading, rather than burning, is recorded in a Chancery precedent book, C 193/3 fo 80. The best account of Anne Boleyn's life, for its use of original documentary evidence, remains Eric Ives's *The Life and Death of Anne Boleyn* (Oxford, 2004). George Bernard's *The King's Reformation* (Yale, 2007) provides a similarly excellent account of this tumultuous period using original documentary evidence. Thomas More's treason records are in KB 8/7. These are supplemented by more detailed accounts of the trial, published in the first volume of William Cobbett, *Complete Collection of State Trials and Proceedings for High Treason and Other Crimes and Misdemeanors from the Earliest Period [1163] to the Present Time [1820]* (34 volumes; London, 1809–28. Hereafter *State Trials*).

PART II: FROM CROWN TO STATE

SIX THE CATHOLIC TREASONS AGAINST ELIZABETH I, 1558–1603

The most notorious plots against Elizabeth I are detailed in the treason indictments against those involved, held at The National Archives in series KB 8. For instance, the key aims of the Ridolfi Plot are described in KB 8/42, being the treason records of Thomas, fourth Duke of Norfolk. Supplementing these original legal records are letters and correspondences, both of the plotters themselves and those trying to thwart them. Most of these are collected among the State Papers at The National Archives and calendared in the *Calendars of State Papers Domestic* and – for those plots that were initiated abroad – the *Calendars of State Papers Foreign*.

The State Papers also provide us with details of responses to rebellions. A draft for the pardon of the rebels involved in the Northern Rebellion is contained in SP 12/66, for example. The best account of the rebellion, drawing on surviving documentary evidence, is Krista Kesselring's *The Northern Rebellion of 1569* (London, 2007).

It was illegal to own or distribute copies of *Regnans in Excelsis*, the excommunication of Elizabeth I, in England, and so surviving copies are rare. However, the British Library holds a printed copy (British Library, 18.e.2.[114*]). A translated edition of the excommunication is contained in *Recusancy and Conformity in Early Modern England*, ed. Ginerva Crosignani et al. (Toronto, 2010).

Trials not recorded in KB 8 are described in the first volume of Cobbett's *State Trials* (which includes trials up to 1600). The court that condemned Mary Queen of Scots was set up specially to try the disgraced Queen, and so records relating to her trial are not found in the King's Bench collections, but instead are spread across the State

Papers and private collections at The National Archives, the British Library, and elsewhere. The best account bringing together this documentary evidence is John Guy's 'My heart is my own': The Life of Mary Queen of Scots (London, 2004).

Statutes enacted by Elizabeth and her government to hinder attempts on her life are recorded on the Parliament Rolls in C 65, arranged chronologically. Original acts are held at the Parliamentary Archives.

An early account of Elizabeth's reign, William Camden's Annales rerum Anglicarum et Hibernicarum regnante Elizabetha, first published in English in 1630, provides us with anecdotes not otherwise recorded, such as Elizabeth's speech to Parliament in 1586 remarking 'in trust I have found treason', or concerning the Queen's leniency towards the Babington conspirators after the brutal execution of Babington the previous day.

For an overview of the religious debates and tensions which contributed to the many plots against Elizabeth during her reign (and during the sixteenth century in general) see the work of Diarmaid MacCulloch, particularly Reformation: Europe's House Divided (London, 2004) and his collected essays on the Reformation, All Things Made New (London, 2016).

SEVEN THE GUNPOWDER TREASON, 1605

The story of the Gunpowder Treason is recounted in several original documents. The trial records of Guy Fawkes and his co-conspirators, in KB 8/59, detail how the plotters assembled and planned to blow up the Houses of Parliament. This legal record is supported by the confessions and statements of the plotters and those that knew them. The records of this investigation, starting with the Monteagle Letter that alerted the authorities to the plot, are collected in a special volume of the State Papers at The National Archives, SP 14/216. This volume contains the confessions of Guy Fawkes and all the other conspirators, plus letters recounting the hunt for Catesby and the other key players. The Calendar of State Papers provides an entry point for these records, including material from the main State Papers Domestic and Foreign collections, such as responses to the plot from foreign ambassadors.

The trial concerning Henry Oven was heard in the Court of Star Chamber, and therefore the records relating to this case are in STAC 8/5/16. Other cases concerning the fallout from the Gunpowder Plot can be found in STAC 8/227/37, STAC 8/184/33, STAC 8/18/1, and STAC 8/202/3.

James I's speech to Parliament in 1606 after the plot was foiled was published as a pamphlet, 'A True and Perfect Relation of the whole proceedings against the late most barbarous Traitors'. The trials of the plotters, plus Henry Garnet, are described in detail in State Trials, vol. 2.

The act of attainder against the plotters, and the act establishing 5 November as a public holiday, are both recorded on the parliament roll for 3 Jas I (March 1605–March 1606), C 65/182.

A consideration as to why the Gunpowder Treason has been remembered, when other attempted treasons have not, was published in History Today in November 2021: 'Why Has the Gunpowder Plot Been Remembered for Centuries'.

EIGHT KILLING THE KING, 1625–49

The proceedings of Charles I's trial are recorded in a manuscript journal, written shortly after the event, held at The National Archives in SP 16/517. Though this is the earliest such journal, other early copies of the trial proceedings survive at the UK Parliamentary Archives, Beinecke Library, Yale, and the British Library. The best account of the creation of these journals is Edward Vallance's 'The manuscript journals of the trial of Charles I', Historical Research, Vol. 94, Issue 264 (May 2021).

Sir Edward Coke's Institutes of the Lawes of England provides contemporary context for the understanding of treason in Charles I's reign. The development of treason during Charles I's reign is described in detail in D. Alan Orr's Treason and the State (Cambridge, 2002), which also includes case studies of the treason trials of Laud and Strafford. Again, State Trials provides descriptions of these treason trials. The trial of Strafford was published as a pamphlet, 'The Tryal of Thomas Earl of Strafford, Lord Lieutenant of Ireland', one of the earliest trials to be published in such a way. The protestation of William Prynne against executing Charles I was also printed as a pamphlet, 'A Briefe Memento ... Touching the present Intentions and Proceedings to Depose and Execute Charles Stewart, their lawfull King' (1649).

For the various acts and ordinances passed by Parliament during the period of civil wars and the interregnum, see Acts and Ordinances of the Interregnum, 1642–1660, ed. C. H. Firth and R. S. Rait (HMSO, 1911). Statutes of the Realm and C 65 provide the acts and ordinances passed for the remainder of Charles's reign.

Much has been written about Charles's reign and his subsequent trial and execution. For this chapter, the author relied upon the magisterial The Personal Rule of Charles I by Kevin Sharpe (Yale, 1996) for the lead up to the civil wars. For an excellent narrative of these events, see Austin Woolrich's Britain in Revolution, 1625–1660 (Oxford, 2002).

NOTES ON THE SOURCES

Finally, Clive Holmes's *Why was Charles I Executed?* (London, 2007) is an excellent book that provides much-needed clarity on a tumultuous period of British history.

NINE RESTORATION AND REVENGE, 1660–7

Charles II's restoration in 1660 saw the return of a functioning government and with it a massive increase in bureaucratic output. As a result, there is considerable archival material to draw upon related to his restoration and the pursuit of the regicides, spread across governmental and parliamentary records.

The main archival sources for this chapter are the State Papers (SP 29) for Charles II's reign, used in tandem with King's Bench records (KB 8/64) for the regicide trials, while the trial records of Henry Vane the Younger and John Lambert are found in the plea rolls (KB 27). This reflects the executive and judicial branches of government, which contain important but often overlooked parts of the story: warrants for arrests, executive correspondence and judicial rulings. The third branch of government reflected in the sources is parliamentary, and the published *Journals of the Houses of Commons* and *Journals of the House of Lords*, and the *Statutes of the Realm* can be consulted on British History Online. With these, we can trace debates in Parliament and the development of legislation and study the printed copies of the acts. The government's handwritten clerical copies of the legislation are available in C 65. The records of the Court of King's Bench provide detail about process, charges, and events at each stage of a trial, but tend to be perfunctory, so to fill in the story it is essential to read (and disbelieve) the contemporary printed reports of trials, some of which are polemical but nonetheless add detail and colour that the official accounts do not. Samuel Pepys's diaries provide the thoughts and responses of a sympathetic royalist and can be found online in authoritative editions.

Modern histories of the regicide trials are relatively sparse and tend to be included as part of larger narratives of the period. Howard Nenner's article on the regicides that appears in the *Oxford Dictionary of National Biography* is very useful and the author borrowed his line that the regicides were loosely damned for their actions but were condemned legally for treason. Tim Harris's *Restoration* (London, 2005) is the most accessible book on Charles II's reign. The author also wishes to express his thanks to the History of Parliament Trust, which provided him with an advance copy of David Aston's biography of Henry Vane the Younger. Historians eagerly await the Trust's forthcoming *History of the House of Commons, 1640–1660*, which is to be published in 2023.

Two excellent biographies of Charles II, Ronald Hutton's (Oxford, 1989) and John Miller's (London, 1991) analyse his motivations as a king and politician. Hutton's is more focused on the narrative and should be read in tandem with his study, *The Restoration: A Political and Religious History of England and Wales, 1658–1667* (Oxford, 1993) while Miller's is more reflective of the king's personality. They are complementary but help the reader to understand the larger political world of the late 1650 to the1660s.

Several works have also appeared on the hunt for those regicides who initially escaped the law. Swashbuckling histories written in grant-application prose often do little to add to the general picture, although Robert Harris's fictionalised account, *Act of Oblivion*, is a great page-turner.

TEN POPISH PLOT, 1678–81

The Popish Plot created havoc in political circles in England and Ireland, which generated a substantial amount of archival material. It also had several phases. For the first, which lasted from September 1678–April 1679, the core sources are within the State Papers, where Oates's allegations were recorded, most likely by the Secretary of State's staff. Many of the same men also acted as clerks for the Privy Council and from these we can chart the early stages of the government's response. PC 2/66 is the Privy Council Register that covers the emergence of the allegations, but another remarkable volume, PC 6/14 appears to be the clerk of the council's notebook as he tried to keep track of who was summoned for interview, arrested, or to be brought to trial, and reveals the extent of the government's knee-jerk response. Unlike the Regicides' trials, where a special commission was established, the Popish Plot trials were held (in the main) at King's Bench in Westminster Hall and the records are found within the large, bound volumes known as the plea rolls (KB 27) and associated papers (KB 29 Controlment and Recorda rolls). When it eventually emerged into the public realm in April 1679, a torrent of printed pamphlets followed and these add to the sense of hysteria that had gripped England. Like other chapters, the relevant volumes of *State Trials* were similarly used to create a narrative.

As the trials continued without any sense of abatement in the hysteria, the argument largely moved between the courtroom and Parliament, and the journals of the Houses of Lords and Commons allow the reader to follow the heated stand-off that ensued between Shaftesbury and the court party, Whigs and Tories respectively. John Kenyon's *The Popish Plot* (London, 1972) remains the predominant study. Despite being published for a mass audience, it did not shirk from recounting in detail the events as they unfolded. Few others have focused on the

Popish Plot since, such is the shadow that Kenyon's work casts. Tim Harris's two-volume study of Charles II's and James II's reigns, *Restoration* (2005) and *Revolution* (2006), both published by Penguin, are among the best modern guides to the period 1660–1700. Vincent Slater's book, *Hoax* (Yale, 2022), appeared too late for inclusion in this study, but we were pleased to see we had approached the Plot in a similar manner. Alan Marshall has written the definitive study of domestic security, *Intelligence and Espionage in the Reign of Charles II* (Cambridge, 1994), but he also tackled the unexplained murder of Justice Godfrey in a very accessible but balanced way in *The Strange Death of Edmund Godfrey: Plots and Politics in Restoration London* (London, 1999). Oates and Tonge remain without modern biographical studies, despite their influence on later British and Irish history but entries on them can be found within the *Oxford Dictionary of National Biography*.

PART III: TOWARDS A MODERN TREASON

ELEVEN NEWFANGLED TREASONS, 1794

Central to the Crown's evidence in Thomas Hardy's trial, the writing of Parliament's Committee of Secrecy's reports, and the writing of this chapter, are the papers of the London Corresponding Society and other radical organisations seized when Hardy and others were arrested. Used as evidence when formulating the prosecution of Hardy and others, many of the societies' papers and the personal papers of their members are now found in the records of the Treasury Solicitor held at The National Archives. The records TS 11/951-966, for instance, contain pamphlets and addresses, minutes and spy reports on meetings and all manner of other papers created by or reporting on the LCS and other radical organisations. The record series TS 24 (Miscellaneous Papers on Sedition Cases) also contains many seized pamphlets and other publications, including the government's copies of Paine's *The Rights of Man*, in which seditious passages have been underlined. Other papers from the LCS are now found in the British Library's additional manuscript collection. The author is indebted to Mary Thale's *Selections from the papers of the London Corresponding Society, 1792–1799* (Cambridge, 1983) for her work locating, transcribing and contextualising many of the key documents relating to the London Corresponding Society within The National Archives, British Library and elsewhere.

These papers are complemented by the many, often alarmist, reports of radical activity and loyalist reaction in the Home Office series HO 42 (Domestic Correspondence, George III, 1782–1820) a vast collection of correspondence on all aspects of domestic government in the late eighteenth and early nineteenth centuries, which are an essential source to any student of popular politics in the period.

Parliamentary Papers, including the reports of the Committee of Secrecy (both published by J. Debrett, London, 1794), and the *Parliamentary Register* covering the period, were the source of accounts of the proceedings and speeches in Parliament. Joseph Gurney's vaguely stenographic account of *The Trial of Thomas Hardy for High Treason* (London, 1794, 2 vols), as well as other published transcripts of the trial, were the main source for the account of the prosecution's case, while James L. High's two-volume accounts of the *Speeches of Lord Erskine, while at the Bar* (Chicago, 1876) provided transcripts of Thomas Erskine's speeches at both Paine's and Hardy's trials, supplementing the official records of the Court of the King's Bench in The National Archives (KB 33/6/1) and newspaper reports of various political persuasions. Partisan accounts by radicals, such as Thomas Spence's *The Examination of Thomas Spence* (London, 1794), and Thomas Hardy's *Memoir* (London, 1832) were also used.

Secondary sources consulted included the excellent *Oxford Dictionary of National Biography* entries for many of the key characters. Clive Emsley's article, 'Repression, "Terror" and the Rule of Law in England during the Decade of the French Revolution' (*English Historical Review*, 1985), and Frederick Brunswick's, 'The Language of High Treason' (*Huntington Library Quarterly*, 2000) provide excellent overviews of the tactics employed by the state against the radicals, and their language and forms, respectively. Meanwhile, Katrina Navickas's *Protest and the Politics of Space and Place, 1789–1848* (Manchester, 2017) provides an excellent overview of how the 'associational cultures' of the late eighteenth century and first half of the nineteenth, both radical and loyalist, were constructed and operated.

TWELVE A MALIGNANT SPIRIT, 1815–48

As the anecdote about Samuel Bamford writing in vain for a change of clothes suggests, the Home Office papers are a key source for this chapter. The Crown had prerogative powers, delegated to the Home Secretary, to seize the mail of people suspected of crimes. These powers were much used against the reformers of the first half of the nineteenth century, which makes the Home Office archive a treasure trove of radical and loyalist correspondence, publications and ephemera. Thomas Erskine makes another of his frequent appearances in this chapter, voting against Sidmouth's suspension of habeas corpus in 1817. He had been made Baron Erskine in 1806, when he was appointed Lord Chancellor in Lord Grenville's short-lived 'Ministry of All Talents'; by all accounts he was not as good a parliamentarian as he was a lawyer.

Particularly of use in this chapter were the Home Office's 'Disturbances Correspondence', a discrete series of records relating to radicalism, riots, sedition and treasonous activities hived off from the general run of 'Domestic' unsorted correspondence, initially comprised of material prepared by Sidmouth's Home Office for a House of Lords Committee of Secrecy prior to the 1817 suspension of habeas corpus. HO 40/3–HO 40/10 are the sources for many of the records relating to Hampden Clubs and the Pentrich Rising, including Joseph Mitchell's 'Address to the People', and copies of William Oliver's account of his journey in HO 40/9. Papers in HO 44, a series of 'domestic' correspondence seemingly organised by the Home Office on thematic grounds, contain the 'Thistlewood Papers', which have been drawn on for the parts of the chapter relating to the Spa Fields Riots and Cato Street Conspiracy. The Disturbances Correspondence pieces HO 40/45 and HO 40/47 were used to source material relating to Chartist risings in Newport and elsewhere in 1839. The domestic correspondence in HO 42, previously used in Chapter Eleven, supplemented this material, as did the Home Office disturbances (HO 41) and private and secret (HO 79) 'entry books' (which record copies of outgoing letters). Alongside this, material created by the Home Office in its capacity as the administrator of the criminal justice system, including criminal registers in HO 26 and HO 27, judges' reports on criminals in HO 47, and petitions for clemency in the series HO 17 and HO 18 (which contains the many petitions submitted for and by Frost, Williams and Jones), have been used to track the sentences and respite of various offenders, as well as material from the Tasmanian Archives in the case of William Cuffey.

The papers of the Treasury Solicitor held at The National Archives (in TS 11/197-208) are a rich source of documents relating to the activities of the Spenceans. TS 11/497 contains papers relating to the Newport trial; and TS 11/140 contains papers relating to Cuffey's prosecution.

The trial of the Pentrich Rebels is held in the records of the Court of the King's Bench, supplemented by newspaper reports and William Brodie Gurney's transcripts of Brandreth's and others' trials (London, 1817). *The Times*'s account was the primary source for the proceedings of the James Watson the Elder's trial after Spa Fields, while the Cato Street Conspirators were tried at the Old Bailey, so benefit from having a transcription of proceedings available on the excellent, free-to-use website 'Old Bailey Online' (reference: t18200416-1), as does Cuffey's (t18480918-2181). Joseph Gurney's *The Trial of John Frost* (London, 1840) was used to supplement the Treasury Solicitor's papers in the Newport case. Hansard's accounts of parliamentary proceedings were also utilised.

Contemporary, partisan accounts supplemented these records, not least Samuel Bamford's *An Account of the Arrest and Imprisonment of Samuel Bamford* (Manchester, 1817) and his later, expansive memoir of the period, *Passages in the Life of a Radical* (initially published in parts 1840–4, collected together by T. Fisher Unwin, London, 1882), as well as various writings by William Cobbett. *The Diary of Henry Hobhouse (1820–1827)* (London, 1947) provides a fascinating account of the period written by a government insider.

Many secondary sources were used. The author is particularly grateful to his friend and former colleague Nathan Bend, whose unpublished PhD thesis 'The Home Office and Public Disturbance, c. 1800–32' (University of Hertfordshire, 2018) is perhaps the best study of just *how* the Home Office attempted to deal with the threat of radicalism in the three decades preceding the passage of the Great Reform Act. Katrina Navickas's *Protest and the Politics of Space and Place* (2016, see above), A. F. Fremantle's *English Historical Review* article 'The Truth About Oliver the Spy' (1932), Richard Gaunt's articles on the Pentrich Rising and the Cato Street Conspiracy (2018 and 2019), Ernest Llewellyn Woodward's *The Age of Reform* (Oxford, 1962); David Johnson's *Regency Revolution: The Case of Arthur Thistlewood* (Compton Russell, 1974), and Jacqueline Riding's (London, 2018) and Robert Poole's (Oxford, 2006) works on the Peterloo Massacre, alongside *Oxford Dictionary of National Biography* entries for many of the characters involved and many other sources, all contributed to this chapter. The late Malcolm Chases's *Chartism: A New History* (Manchester, 2007) is the authoritative account of the Chartist movement, while the idea of the tactic of 'intimidation' as a halfway house between 'moral' and 'physical' force Chartism is taken from an article by Thomas Milton Kennitz (*Albion*, 1973). E. P. Thompson's magisterial *The Making of the English Working Class* (London, 1963 and many subsequent editions) remains the essential text for the study of the lives, labours, politics and culture of English working people in the late eighteenth and early nineteenth centuries.

THIRTEEN INJURE OR ALARM HER MAJESTY, 1786–1848

The details of James Hadfield's sorry case have been sourced from various records at The National Archives. The King's Bench records in KB 33/8/3 include drafts of his indictment, accounts of his interview by the Privy Council and others, depositions from witnesses, and precedents of previous insanity cases such as John Frith's and Robert

Nalcot's (whose trials are transcribed on Old Bailey Online), lists of witnesses and schedules of the trial. The papers of the Treasury Solicitor relating to the case, in TS 11/223/937/1-2 contain briefs for the prosecution and defence, allowing us to see how Thomas Erskine planned Hadfield's defence case. This was supplemented by Joel Peter Eigen's excellent entry on Hadfield in the *Oxford Dictionary of National Biography* (2004).

Eigen is also the author of a similarly useful *ODNB* entry (also 2004) of George III's other erstwhile assassin, Margaret Nicholson. Her depositions and other papers relating to her case can be found in The National Archives in the Privy Council record PC 1/17/8. Accounts of her attempt and the acclamation of her insanity were published in the *London Gazette*, while records of her time in Bethlem are in the casebooks held by the Bethlem Museum of the Mind Archives.

Records of Edward Oxford's case can be found in the Home Office correspondence within HO 44/36, with the papers of his trial, including examinations, case papers and briefs, while accounts of the trial's proceedings are in the Treasury Solicitor's records in TS 11/10.

PART IV: TREASON OVERSEAS

FOURTEEN TREASON IN AMERICA, 1672–1794

Most material at The National Archives relating to America under British rule is kept in the Colonial Office papers, series CO 5. A copy of the 1702 Act Book of Connecticut's laws is held there (CO 5/537), as are records relating to the trials of Leisler and Bayard. The correspondences between British governors in America and the Attorney General and Solicitor General are also held in CO 5.

A copy of the Treaty of Paris, which removed France from North America, is held at The National Archives in the State Papers collections, SP 108/123.

The British Acts which caused so much unrest and strife in the American colonies, such as the Stamp Act and Townshend Duties, are recorded in the Parliament Rolls in C 65 (and supplemented by original acts held in the UK Parliamentary Archives).

Many of the discussions concerning the legality of taxation in America were printed in pamphlets and in newspapers. These included Thomas Whately's 'The Regulations Lately Made concerning the Colonies and the Taxes Imposed on Them' (1765) and 'The Examination of Doctor Benjamin Franklin, before an August Assembly, relating to the Repeal of the Stamp Act'. A number of speeches and debates from the British Parliament are published in, *Proceedings and Debates of the British Parliaments Respecting North America*, ed by R. C. Simmons and P. D. G. Thomas (1982–4).

The debate by Governor Hutchinson with the Massachusetts House of Representatives was also published as a pamphlet, 'The Speeches of his Excellency Governor Hutchinson to the General Assembly' (1773). The debates between Hutchinson's replacement, Thomas Gage, and the American colonists were printed in newspapers, such as the Americans' response to Gage accusing them of treason, printed in the *Georgia Gazette*, no. 578, 2 November 1774.

The Proclamation of Rebellion issued by George III in 1775 is printed in *Royal Proclamations Relating to America, 1603–1783*, ed. C. S. Brigham (1911). A number of contemporary copies of the proclamation survive, for example in CO 5/993.

Prosecutions against British printers supporting the American rebels are contained in the records of the Court of King's Bench. Copies of indictments, plus the offending material, are held in KB 33/5/8.

The National Archives of the United Kingdom hold several copies of the original printed US Declaration of Independence (the so-called Dunlap print, named after their printer John Dunlap). These copies are in CO 5/1353/1, and EXT 9/1, 26, 76, and 93.

Benedict Arnold's treason against the United States was recorded in pamphlet form, in such works as 'A representation of the figures exhibited and paraded through the streets of Philadelphia, on Saturday, the 30th of September, 1780' (which depicts the effigy of Arnold). Benjamin Franklin's comment that 'Judas sold only one Man, Arnold three Millions' is from a letter he sent to the Marquis de LaFayette on 14 May 1781, printed in *The Papers of Benjamin Franklin*, vol. 35, ed. Barbara B. Oberg (Yale, 1999).

A good overview of the ideas of treason circulating in America at this time is Peter Rushton and Gwenda Morgan, *Treason and Rebellion in the British Atlantic, 1685–1800* (London, 2020).

FIFTEEN DEPREDATIONS, GRENADA, 1795–6

It is perhaps worth noting here that the French Republic's promises to emancipate enslaved people often did not survive contact with reality, remaining as high-minded rhetoric, or offering some kind of partially remunerated but

NOTES ON THE SOURCES

still bonded labour at best, despite legal abolition. Napoleon formally reintroduced slavery in French sugar-growing colonies in 1802.

Fernand Braudel, most famous as a historian of the Mediterranean as opposed to the Caribbean, may seem an odd choice for this chapter's epigraph, but his *The Mediterranean and the Mediterranean World in the Age of Philip II* contains a succinct and moving description of the 'tragedy of sugarcane' cultivation, and how it had immiserated the soil and peoples of European and then Caribbean islands successively, generalising the use of enslaved labour, all in the quest for profit.

The correspondence in the records of the Colonial Office held at The National Archives (despite the Colonial Office not existing at the time of the rebellion, the records were inherited by them) form the core primary source for this chapter. The series CO 101 contains 'original correspondence' for Grenada, despatches and other letters from the island, as well draft replies and memos from the Duke of Portland and others. The pieces CO 101/34 and CO 101/35 cover the bulk of the rebellion and its aftermath and were used extensively. The series CO 103 contains (mostly manuscript) copies of acts passed by the Grenadian Legislative Assembly, and copies of the Act of Attainder and Confiscation Act passed by the assembly can be found in CO 103/9. The British Library's Endangered Archives Programme, meanwhile, has digitised and partially transcribed the records of Grenada's Court of Oyer and Terminer for Trial of Attainted Traitors record book (reference: EAP295/2/6/1); the originals remain in the Grenadian National Archives.

Many contemporary, highly partisan accounts of the rebellion were produced, usually by British plantation owners. Some examples include those by Thomas Turner Wise (1795), Gordon. A. Turnbull (1796), Henry Thornhill (1798), and John Hay (1823).

Despite its size and significance, the Grenadian Rebellion has received only occasional historical attention. Among these the author made particular use of Timothy Ashby's fantastically detailed two-part article giving a factual account of the military operations conducted by the British (*Journal of the Society for Army Historical Research*, 1984 and 1985), Edward L. Cox's article 'Fedon's Rebellion 1795–96: Causes and Consequences' (*The Journal of Negro History*, 1982); highlighted the influence of longstanding anglophone and francophone tensions on the outbreak of the rebellion, as well as its place in the series of revolts that formed the 'Age of Revolution' from 1789–1848. Latterly, Kit Candlin's article, 'The role of the enslaved in the "Fédon Rebellion" of 1795' (*Slavery & Abolition*, 2018) focused on the significance of enslaved people to the rebellion. C. L. R. James's classic *The Black Jacobins* (first published London, 1938) although about the Haitian Revolution, shaped the author's thinking about the effects of the French Revolution in the Caribbean and among enslaved people within it. The rebellion, and Fédon's memory, remain significant to Grenada's public consciousness, not least in the light of the 1979 Grenadian Revolution. Fédon's estate is today a tourist attraction, albeit one that is difficult to get to, although probably less dangerous for visitors than it was in 1795.

SIXTEEN DEVASTATION, JAMAICA, 1832

This chapter contains mentions of estate 'attorneys' and 'managers' which may be confusing for readers. They were not lawyers. Attorneys managed the plantations and business interests of owners not resident in Jamaica, managers ran the day-to-day business of estates. The roles were sometimes combined.

The National Archives, by dint of holding the correspondence between Jamaica's governors and their superiors in London, remains perhaps the richest source in the world for the study of Sharpe's Rebellion. The Colonial Office series CO 137 contains Jamaica's original correspondence, and the pieces CO 137/181 and CO 137/182, containing correspondence and reports from the Rebellion, and CO 137/185, containing accounts of slave court trials, were the main primary sources for this chapter.

The records of the Slavery Compensation Commission, who administered the massive payment to former slave owners, are a rich source of slave registers, including the one marking Sharpe's 'decrease'. They have been used extensively by University College London's Legacies of British Slave Ownership project, whose entries, along with *Oxford Dictionary of National Biography* articles, supplemented the portraits of many of the planters mentioned in this chapter. The record series CO 139 contains acts of the Jamaican Assembly, and piece CO 139/62 includes a copy of the Jamaican Slave Code of 1816. Slave codes were instrumental in the construction of modern ideas of race, racial difference and racism, which allowed the ideological and legal consistency of chattel slavery in the Caribbean. The first English code, passed by the Assembly of Barbados in 1661, created a legal delineation between 'Africans' and 'Christians'; by 1681 the Jamaican Assembly, faced with Quakers converting enslaved people on the island to Christianity, borrowed the Barbadian code, but substituted 'white' for 'Christian', a significant event in the establishment of whiteness as a naturally dominant feature.

Henry Bleby's *Death struggles of slavery* (London, 1853) is a fascinating account of the rebellion, a defence of missionaries and a condemnation of the brutality of the Jamaican property-owning classes, despite his clear disapproval of Sharpe's and others' rebellious conduct. Hansard – the official report of all UK Parliamentary debates (available online at https://hansard.parliament.uk/) – and the *Journal of the House of Commons* were the sources of parliamentary quotes, while *The Times* remains the authoritative voice of Britain's establishment.

Some key secondary sources that informed this chapter were Eric Williams's *Capitalism and Slavery* (1944, and subsequent editions) and Catherine Hall's *Civilising Subjects* (Chicago, 2002), which have been a great influence on the way the author conceives the relationship between metropole and colony, and the British Empire's attitude towards slavery as sugar colonies declined economically. Vincent Brown's excellent *Tacky's Revolt* (Cambridge, MA, 2020) is illuminating not only in its discussion of Jamaican revolts in the 1760s, but also in the way slave rebellions must be seen in the context of the wider Atlantic world, and those writing their histories must seek to uncover the agency of their participants, as hard as the records collected by their oppressors might make this. Beyond this, Mary Turner's *Slaves and Missionaries* (Kingston, Jamaica, 1998), Mary Reckford's article 'The Jamaica Slave Rebellion of 1831' (*Past & Present*, 40, no. 1, 1968), and Michael Taylor's *The Interest* (London, 2020) were particularly utilised.

SEVENTEEN TREASON AND THE FORGING OF MODERN IRELAND, 1791–1921

Revolutionary Ireland had been extensively studied long before the Decade of Centenaries sparked widespread public interest in Ireland in the years 1913–22, but it has resulted in the release of a large number of publications re-examining the events and personalities that sought (or resisted) an independent Ireland. The Decade of Centenaries also highlighted the importance of returning to the archival record. There are extensive relevant archival sources at The National Archives, especially political and military, most of which are well catalogued and readily findable in the online catalogue. The War Office records hold voluminous papers on the Easter Rising and its aftermath and it is primarily from this department that the chapter was drawn, especially material relating to the courts martial. The Cabinet Office papers, alongside Prime Ministers' papers are essential reading to understand the British responses to the outbreaks of violence. Pearse's speeches both at Tone's grave and in New York are available online via the Corpus of Electronic Texts Editions, compiled by University College Cork.

For Theobald Wolfe Tone and Robert Emmet, the Home Office Ireland papers held by The National Archives (HO 100) are key archival sources as they detail the interaction between London and Dublin. Crucially, they also include clerical copies of their speeches during their trials which subsequently made their way into print, but via bastardised and embellished versions, which reinforces the importance of the contemporary copy, especially for Tone, who appears to have left no notes. HO 100 also serves another unintended function as it contains copies of their final letters which act as an emotional counterpoint to their public displays while on trial.

Readers who wish to understand modern Ireland better may find the following useful. Paul Bew's *Ireland. The Politics of Enmity, 1789–2006* (Oxford, 2007) is a stimulating if controversial work. The *Atlas of the Irish Revolution* (Cork, 2017) is a reflection of the range of scholarly research undertaken into the period. The *Cambridge History of Ireland*, vol. 4 (Cambridge, 2018) examines not just the political but the wider social, cultural and economic circumstances that shaped the period. Charles Townshend's books, *Easter 1916: The Irish Rebellion* (London, 2005) and *The Republic: the fight for Irish Independence* (London, 2013), both published by Penguin, provide an excellent overview of events. For those interested in the individuals who were executed for treason in 1916, the *16 Lives* series published by O'Brien Press, Dublin, tells the story of each man. Whitehall's and Westminster's responses to the events in Ireland between 1916 and 1922 are judiciously analysed in Ronan Fanning's *Fatal Path: British Government and the Irish Revolution* (London, 2013).

For the period 1790–1803, Marian Elliott's study, *Theobald Wolfe Tone* (Liverpool, 2012) remains the benchmark biography, while Patrick Geoghegan's book, *Robert Emmet: A Life* (Dublin, 2002) continues to illuminate. Geoghegan has also produced what is likely to be the definitive version of Emmet's Speech from the Dock, from which the author has quoted liberally. The *Cambridge History of Ireland*, vol. 3 (Cambridge, 2018) contextualises the whole period while Thomas Pakenham's *The Year of Liberty: The Great Irish Rebellion of 1798* (London, 2000) is erudite and accessible. For those wishing to understand more of how the events of 1798 and 1803 influenced generations of republicans in Ireland, Guy Beiner's books, *Forgetful Remembrance* (Oxford, 2020) and *Remembering the Year of the French: Irish Folk History and Social Memory* (Wisconsin, 2007) are remarkably insightful. In the same vein, Marianne Elliott's *Robert Emmet: The making of a legend* (London, 2004) traces the influence of Emmet's actions during the nineteenth century.

Special mention should also be given to the *Dictionary of Irish Biography*, published online by the Royal Irish Academy, which provides superb historical analysis in a freely accessible resource.

ACKNOWLEDGEMENTS

This book is very much a product of The National Archives. It has been a challenge, but also an immense privilege to use its unparalleled collections to chart this history of treason. The book would not have been possible without the broad knowledge of the vast collections that we have had to acquire to advise researchers. This has allowed us to flit more easily between records – political, legal, administrative – scattered across dozens of discrete, idiosyncratic series. Without the support of our colleagues Perri Blakelock, Hannah Fleming, Juliette Johnstone, and Steve Burgess we would not have begun conceiving the exhibition that led to this volume. Thanks must go, too, to our colleague Ela Kaczmarska, who saw the potential of our research and found us a publisher; to the Image Library team who digitised documents for inclusion in this book; and to Toby Buchan, Ellie Carr and all the other staff at John Blake Publishing for getting our words off the screen and on to paper. We must also thank our managers, Sean Cunningham and Juliette Desplat, for their support as we tried to balance writing a book with our jobs, and to our department's rota team who carved us time away from our public research advice services to read and write.

This book was written to an extremely tight deadline, alongside the demands of full-time jobs and small children. The greatest thanks, therefore, must go to our wives – Sophie, Alice, Emily, and Úna-Frances – who supported us, and indeed often endured us, throughout, as well as listening to us bang on about treason.

INDEX

INDEX

INDEX

INDEX

INDEX

INDEX

compassing a monarch's deposition 252, 256,
262–3, 264, 269, 272, 273
Treason Act (1800) 284, 383
Treason Act (1814) 257
Treason Act (1842) 286
Treason Act (1848) 272–3

treason, charges of 140
18th and 19th century radical movements 236–7,
240–4, 249, 260, 261–5, 266
Anne Boleyn 111–15
Arthur Poole 125–6
Babington Plot 137
Benedict Arnold 308
Bye Plot 146–7
Cato Street Plot 262–5, 389
Colonel Nicholas Bayard 293–4
common law 162, 170, 175
Commonwealth Acts of treason 178–9
the Despensers 26
Dr Roger Lopez 141
Duke of Clarence 83–6
Earl of Essex 143
Earl of Strafford 169–72
early notions of 9–10
Easter Rising 362, 376–7, 379–80, 381
Edward Coleman 213–14, 216, 218, 219, 224
under Edward I 11–17
Edward Oxford 285–6
Edward Squyer 141–2
Edward VI's amendments 118–19, 120
Elizabeth Barton 'the Holy Maid' 110, 388
Evil May Day prisoners 99–103
Felony Treason Act (1848) 272, 273–4, 275
Francis Throckmorton 135
Grenada 312–13, 319–20, 322, 325, 358
the Gunpowder Plot (1605) 145, 149–56, 161
under Henry VIII 93–4
and heresy 62, 63, 67, 70–1, 83
high treason 9–10, 16, 29–30, 67, 83–4, 99, 106–8,
114, 117, 118, 156, 161, 169, 173, 175, 179,
237, 249, 251, 260, 269, 282, 290, 293
Jacob Leisler 291–2
Jacobites 227
Jamaica 329–30, 352–3, 356, 358
James Hadfield 277, 279, 282
John Francis 286
John Frith 281
John Mitchel 273
King Charles I 161, 173, 174–8, 179
King Henry VII 87–8
King Richard II and Lords Appellant 40–54

King Richard III 86, 88–90
King Richard II's 'Questions' 40–1, 45–6, 48
Lady Jane Grey 119
legislation against the Pope 129–30
Main Plot 147
Mary, Queen of Scots 137–40
Merciless Parliament 42–8, 49, 50
misprision of treason 32, 111, 115, 154–6
and necromancy and sorcery 64, 65–72, 81
Newport Uprising 269–71
North American Colonies 298–304, 309
Northern Rebellion (1569) 127
Orange Tree Plot 273–4
overt acts 241, 242, 245, 251–2, 256, 263, 269,
270, 272, 273, 275, 282, 283, 371
Patrick O'Cullun 140
Patrixbourne rising (1496) 100
Pentrich Uprising (1817) 256–7, 389
Perkin Warbeck conspiracy 91
petty treason 32, 67, 107, 108
Piers Gaveston 20–1
poisoning 106–9
Popish Plot 213–14, 216, 218–21, 222–5
under Queen Elizabeth I 104–5
Radical War (1820) 265
regicides and exceptions to the King's pardon
187–9, 191–8, 199–205
Regnans in Excelsis 128–9
Revenge Parliament 49–55
Robert Emmet 370–3
Roger Casement 384–5
Roger Mortimer 28
Roman legal traditions 9, 18
the Somervilles and the Ardens 134–5
Spa Field riots 251–3
Theobald Wolfe Tone 365–9
Thomas Hardy 237
Thomas Howard, Duke of Norfolk 131–4, 139
treason by written and spoken word 60, 63, 74,
82, 111, 116, 118–19, 128–9, 197–8, 245
use of King's Record 12, 14, 15–16, 17, 23–4, 29
Valentine Thomas 142
William Cuffey 273–4
William Joyce 386–7
William Laud, Archbishop of Canterbury 172–4
William Staley 207–8
see also under Treason Acts
Treason Felony Act (1848) 272, 275, 286
Treaty of London (1604) 147
Treaty of Paris (1763) 295
Treaty of Paris (1783) 307, 314
Tresham, Francis 148, 154

417